Imagining Economics *Other*wise

Is it possible to be 'irrational' without being 'uneconomic'? What is the link between 'Value' and 'values'? What do economists do when they 'explain'? We live in times when the economic logic has become unquestionable and all-powerful so that our quotidian economic experiences are defined by their scientific construal. This book is the result of a multifaceted investigation into the nature of knowledge produced by economics, and the construction of the category that is termed 'economic' with its implied exclusions. It is an attempt to *think economics Otherwise*, that is, a questioning of economics as if difference mattered.

Nitasha Kaul re-examines certain understood ways of thinking about economics as a discipline, especially in relation to questions of identity and difference. This book explores the notion that economics is not a timeless, universal, objective science but a changing response to the problems of knowledge and administration. The epistemological inheritance of economics is 'rooted' in the enlightenment, and it also inherits the liberal paradoxes of that age. Kaul argues that the juxtaposition of identity with economic (culture/economy) is essential, and can only be achieved by critiquing establishment economists' discourse on identity, and taking feminist poststructural and postcolonial work seriously. The author challenges the assumption that there is a simple linkage between the category economic, the entity economy and the study of economics. She envisions an economics in the plural: contextual, social, political – econo-mixes.

This book brings together some of the most urgent topics of the day – the power of economics as a discipline, the questions of difference and the politics of identity, and feminist perspectives on this. It will be particularly relevant to heterodox economists, feminist theorists, postcolonial studies scholars, social and cultural theorists, philosophers and history of ideas or intellectual history of thought scholars.

Nitasha Kaul has a doctorate in economics and philosophy. A lecturer in economics until 2006, she is currently an independent scholar and writer. Her research and publications engage with social, cultural, feminist, poststructural and postcolonial theories, in addition to critical political economy.

Routledge Frontiers of Political Economy

1 **Equilibrium Versus Understanding**
Towards the rehumanization of economics within social theory
Mark Addleson

2 **Evolution, Order and Complexity**
Edited by Elias L. Khalil and Kenneth E. Boulding

3 **Interactions in Political Economy**
Malvern after ten years
Edited by Steven Pressman

4 **The End of Economics**
Michael Perelman

5 **Probability in Economics**
Omar F. Hamouda and Robin Rowley

6 **Capital Controversy, Post Keynesian Economics and the History of Economics**
Essays in honour of Geoff Harcourt, volume one
Edited by Philip Arestis, Gabriel Palma and Malcolm Sawyer

7 **Markets, Unemployment and Economic Policy**
Essays in honour of Geoff Harcourt, volume two
Edited by Philip Arestis, Gabriel Palma and Malcolm Sawyer

8 **Social Economy**
The logic of capitalist development
Clark Everling

9 **New Keynesian Economics/ Post Keynesian Alternatives**
Edited by Roy J. Rotheim

10 **The Representative Agent in Macroeconomics**
James E. Hartley

11 **Borderlands of Economics**
Essays in honour of Daniel R. Fusfeld
Edited by Nahid Aslanbeigui and Young Back Choi

12 **Value, Distribution and Capital**
Essays in honour of Pierangelo Garegnani
Edited by Gary Mongiovi and Fabio Petri

13 The Economics of Science
Methodology and epistemology as if economics really mattered
James R. Wible

14 Competitiveness, Localised Learning and Regional Development
Specialisation and prosperity in small open economies
Peter Maskell, Heikki Eskelinen, Ingjaldur Hannibalsson, Anders Malmberg and Eirik Vatne

15 Labour Market Theory
A constructive reassessment
Ben J. Fine

16 Women and European Employment
Jill Rubery, Mark Smith, Colette Fagan, Damian Grimshaw

17 Explorations in Economic Methodology
From Lakatos to empirical philosophy of science
Roger Backhouse

18 Subjectivity in Political Economy
Essays on wanting and choosing
David P. Levine

19 The Political Economy of Middle East Peace
The impact of competing trade agendas
Edited by J.W. Wright, Jnr

20 The Active Consumer
Novelty and surprise in consumer choice
Edited by Marina Bianchi

21 Subjectivism and Economic Analysis
Essays in Memory of Ludwig Lachmann
Edited by Roger Koppl and Gary Mongiovi

22 Themes in Post-Keynesian Economics
Essays in honour of Geoff Harcourt, volume three
Edited by Claudio Sardoni and Peter Kriesler

23 The Dynamics of Technological Knowledge
Cristiano Antonelli

24 The Political Economy of Diet, Health and Food Policy
Ben J. Fine

25 The End of Finance
Capital market inflation, financial derivatives and pension fund capitalism
Jan Toporowski

26 Political Economy and the New Capitalism
Edited by Jan Toporowski

27 Growth Theory
A philosophical perspective
Patricia Northover

28 The Political Economy of the Small Firm
Edited by Charlie Dannreuther

29 Hahn and Economic Methodology
Edited by Thomas Boylan and Paschal F. O'Gorman

30 Gender, Growth and Trade
The miracle economies of the postwar years
David Kucera

31 Normative Political Economy
Subjective freedom, the market and the State
David levine

32 Economist with a Public Purpose
Essays in honour of John Kenneth Galbraith
Edited by Michael Keaney

33 Involuntary Unemployment
The elusive quest for a theory
Michel De Vroey

34 The Fundamental Institutions of Capitalism
Ernesto Screpanti

35 Transcending Transaction
The search for self-generating markets
Alan Shipman

36 Power in Business and the State
An historical analysis of its concentration
Frank Bealey

37 Editing Economics
Essays in honour of Mark Perlman
Hank Lim, Ungsuh K. Park and Geoff Harcourt

38 Money, Macroeconomics and Keynes
Essays in honour of Victoria Chick, volume 1
Philip Arestis, Meghnad Desai and Sheila Dow

39 Methodology, Microeconomics and Keynes
Essays in honour of Victoria Chick, volume two
Philip Arestis, Meghnad Desai and Sheila Dow

40 Market Drive and Governance
Reexamining the rules for economic and commercial contest
Ralf Boscheck

41 The Value of Marx
Political economy for contemporary capitalism
Alfredo Saad-Filho

42 Issues in Positive Political Economy
S. Mansoob Murshed

43 The Enigma of Globalisation
A journey to a new stage of capitalism
Robert Went

44 The Market
Equilibrium, stability, mythology
S.N. Afriat

45 The Political Economy of Rule Evasion and Policy Reform
Jim Leitzel

46 Unpaid Work and the Economy
Edited by Antonella Picchio

47 Distributional Justice
Theory and measurement
Hilde Bojer

48 Cognitive Developments in Economics
Edited by Salvatore Rizzello

49 Social Foundations of Markets, Money and Credit
Costas Lapavitsas

50 Rethinking Capitalist Development
Essays on the economics of Josef Steindl
Edited by Tracy Mott and Nina Shapiro

51 An Evolutionary Approach to Social Welfare
Christian Sartorius

52 Kalecki's Economics Today
Edited by Zdzislaw L. Sadowski and Adam Szeworski

53 Fiscal Policy from Reagan to Blair
The left veers right
Ravi K. Roy and Arthur T. Denzau

54 The Cognitive Mechanics of Economic Development and Institutional Change
Bertin Martens

55 Individualism and the Social Order
The social element in liberal thought
Charles R. McCann Jnr.

56 Affirmative Action in the United States and India
A comparative perspective
Thomas E. Weisskopf

57 Global Political Economy and the Wealth of Nations
Performance, institutions, problems and policies
Edited by Phillip Anthony O'Hara

58 Structural Economics
Thijs ten Raa

59 Macroeconomic Theory and Economic Policy
Essays in honour of Jean-Paul Fitoussi
Edited by K. Vela Velupillai

60 The Struggle Over Work
The 'end of work' and employment alternatives in post-industrial societies
Shaun Wilson

61 The Political Economy of Global Sporting Organisations
John Forster and Nigel Pope

62 The Flawed Foundations of General Equilibrium Theory
Critical essays on economic theory
Frank Ackerman and Alejandro Nadal

63 Uncertainty in Economic Theory
Essays in honor of David Schmeidler's 65th birthday
Edited by Itzhak Gilboa

64 The New Institutional Economics of Corruption
Edited by Johann Graf Lambsdorff, Markus Taube and Matthias Schramm

65 The Price Index and its Extension
A chapter in economic measurement
S.N. Afriat

66 **Reduction, Rationality and Game Theory in Marxian Economics**
Bruce Philp

67 **Culture and Politics in Economic Development**
Volker Bornschier

68 **Modern Applications of Austrian Thought**
Edited by Jürgen G. Backhaus

69 **Ordinary Choices**
Individuals, incommensurability, and democracy
Robert Urquhart

70 **Labour Theory of Value**
Peter C. Dooley

71 **Capitalism**
Victor D. Lippit

72 **Macroeconomic Foundations of Macroeconomics**
Alvaro Cencini

73 **Marx for the 21st Century**
Edited by Hiroshi Uchida

74 **Growth and Development in the Global Political Economy**
Social structures of accumulation and modes of regulation
Phillip Anthony O'Hara

75 **The New Economy and Macroeconomic Stability**
A neo-modern perspective drawing on the complexity approach and Keynesian economics
Teodoro Dario Togati

76 **The Future of Social Security Policy**
Women, work and a citizens basic income
Ailsa McKay

77 **Clinton and Blair**
The political economy of the third way
Flavio Romano

78 **Marxian Reproduction Schema**
Money and aggregate demand in a capitalist economy
A.B. Trigg

79 **The Core Theory in Economics**
Problems and solutions
Lester G. Telser

80 **Economics, Ethics and the Market**
Introduction and applications
Johan J. Graafland

81 **Social Costs and Public Action in Modern Capitalism**
Essays inspired by Karl William Kapp's theory of social costs
Edited by Wolfram Elsner, Pietro Frigato and Paolo Ramazzotti

82 **Globalization and the Myths of Free Trade**
History, theory and empirical evidence
Edited by Anwar Shaikh

83 **Equilibrium in Economics: Scope and Limits**
Edited by Valeria Mosini

84 Globalization
State of the art and perspectives
Edited by Stefan A. Schirm

85 Neoliberalism
National and regional experiments with global ideas
Edited by Ravi K. Roy, Arthur T. Denzau, Thomas D. Willett

86 Post-Keynesian Macroeconomics Economics
Essays in honour of Ingrid Rima
Edited by Mathew Forstater, Gary Mongiovi and Steven Pressman

87 Consumer Capitalism
Anastasios S. Korkotsides

88 Remapping Gender in the New Global Order
Edited Marjorie Griffin Cohen and Janine Brodie

89 Hayek and Natural Law
Eric Angner

90 Race and Economic Opportunity in the Twenty-First Century
Edited by Marlene Kim

91 Renaissance in Behavioural Economics
Harvey Leibenstein's impact on contemporary economic analysis
Edited by Roger Frantz

92 Human Ecology Economics
A new framework for global sustainability
Edited by Roy E. Allen

93 Imagining Economics *Other*wise
Encounters with identity/difference
Nitasha Kaul

Imagining Economics *Other*wise

Encounters with identity/difference

Nitasha Kaul

Routledge
Taylor & Francis Group
LONDON AND NEW YORK

First published 2008
by Routledge
2 Park Square, Milton Park, Abingdon, Oxon OX14 4RN

Simultaneously published in the USA and Canada
by Routledge
270 Madison Ave, New York, NY 10016

Routledge is an imprint of the Taylor & Francis Group, an informa business

Typeset in Times New Roman by
Newgen Imaging Systems (P) Ltd, Chennai, India
Printed and bound in Great Britain by
Biddles Ltd, King's Lynn

British Library Cataloguing in Publication Data
A catalogue record for this book is available
from the British Library

Library of Congress Cataloging in Publication Data
A catalog record for this book has been requested

ISBN10: 0–415–38397–8 (hbk)
ISBN10: 0–203–93457–1 (ebk)

ISBN13: 978–0–415–38397–4 (hbk)
ISBN13: 978–0–203–93457–9 (ebk)

To all those who struggle for life and justice, and to the hope that we will always be able to imagine beyond the possible

Contents

Acknowledgements

In this task of reconstruction and gluing of memory, I wish to recall with immense gratitude those who made this endeavour possible. I can only inadequately thank a few of those many people I have met and shared ideas with over the course of the last years, but wish to acknowledge all such interactions at work, conferences, travel, in the course of research and teaching, online.

My first thanks are due to Kathleen Lennon who was incredibly supportive, understanding, stimulating and encouraging. The philosophy department at the University of Hull nurtured me even as I taught in the economics department. I also wish to thank Paul Gilbert for his insightful feedback on my work, Menekshe Uzbay for her inspiring conversations and Stella Gonzalez Arnal for sharing references.

Routledge as a publisher is important in enabling the circulation of much new and challenging work in economics. Robert Langham and Terry Clague at Routledge deserve a special mention for being encouraging and patient with the gestation of this book. I wish to acknowledge that parts of Chapters 1 and 7 of this book draw upon 'Writing economic theory an*Other* way' (pages 183–200, chapter 8) published in *Postcolonialism Meets Economics* edited by Eiman O. Zein-Elabdin and S. Charusheela, Routledge, 2004 and 'The anxious identities we inhabit: post'isms and economic understandings' (pages 194–210, chapter 13) published in *Toward a Feminist Philosophy of Economics* edited by Drucilla K. Barker and Edith Kuiper, Routledge, 2003. I am thankful to Rob Langham and the editors of these volumes. Sarah Hastings at Routledge UK and staff at Newgen India have been an excellent help and resource in the production and processing stage of the manuscript.

In my attempts to escape the confines of disciplinarity in order to ask new and different questions, I made connections with numerous scholars at the fringes of many institutionally defined areas of inquiry: cultural studies, history, international relations, literary studies, philosophy, political science, psychology, sociology, gender studies, and of course, economics. Several organisations and conferences became life-support systems – IAFFE (International Association for Feminist Economics) among them. I am grateful to many feminist scholars – Drucilla Barker, Suzanne Bergeron, S. Charusheela, Colin Danby, Ulla Grapard, Sandra Harding, Gillian Hewitson, Jane Humphries, Tony Lawson, Deirdre

McCloskey, Aine Ni Léime, Marilyn Powers, Ingrid Robeyns, Diana Strassmann, Tiina Vainio, Eiman Zein-Elabdin – for a mix of their work, encouragement, conversations, and friendships. I first met Drue, Ulla and Gill at a literature and economics panel at Yale; interesting scholars and fun people, they have been a joy to be friends with over the years. Numerous other IAFFE members have contributed to conversations both online and at conferences which I have gained from. The very different research works of Jack Amariglio, Rajani Kanth and Philip Mirowski have been pathbreaking. Heterodox economics organisations such as the AHE (Association for Heterodox Economics) provided an invaluable forum for intellectual exchange. Andy Denis, Sheila Dow, Steve Fleetwood, Mathew Forstater, Edward Fullbrook, Susan Himmelweit, Serap Kayatekin, Frederic Lee, Tony Lawson, Andrew Mearman and Judith Mehta deserve a special thanks for their constant efforts over the years to keep (heterodox) economics alive. Tony, especially, is a wonderful scholar to know – he challenges, supports, and inspires matchlessly.

A.J.C. Bose has been an extraordinary mentor and economics teacher from my days at Delhi University, and Alberto Ferrari, in turn, was an extraordinary economics student at Hull. Anil Nauriya has been a stimulating scholar and correspondent.

I wish to express my gratitude to Jonathan Atkins, Elizabeth Chilvers, Richard Green, Chris Knight, Anna Maffioletti, Susan Palfreman, Steve Trotter, and Michael Turner in the economics department at the University of Hull. Richard was the ideal head of school and a role model for young academics. Jon and Anna were encouraging and supportive, Liz and Chris always there with practical help and advice. Emma Coyne in the disability support office at the University of Hull was amazingly understanding. Staff at the University's Brynmor Jones Library were very co-operative; Hayley Moss went out of her way to resolve last-minute long-distance bibliographic queries. I owe Phil Borrill and Anil Kumar for their support work.

Sir Philip Reckitt Educational Trust, The Royal Economic Society, Cambridge Commonwealth Trust/Rajiv Gandhi Foundation, University of the West of England have all awarded grants in support of my research. Sir Philip Reckitt Educational Trust, in particular, was there during the early days when I needed conference funding most.

I wish to thank my grandfather B. L. Kaul for always being there for me. M. K. Kaul is no more. It is impossible for him to read this book. But he remains with me as the immortals do. I became me through him. I addressed my first questions to him, and I still haven't stopped asking.

Dibyesh Anand is my generous, spirited, loving, intellectual fellow traveller. We have shared dreams and time. This book is his as much as mine.

A final word about the book – it was originally completed in 2002 and was written up entirely with the aid of voice recognition software due to a disabling condition I then suffered from. I thought and spoke the book out loud into a machine at a desk behind paper-pasted windows in the summer sun. It was written as speech, inscribed first in sound. So, it is peculiar. Speaking complex ideas into a machine perhaps makes the idiom mannered, the exposition visual. There are many footnotes that proudly proclaim their just rights, rebelling from the servile bottoms of the page, insisting on making connexions that require an undisciplined imagination. Indulge them if you can. The computer sometimes erroneously placed similar-sounding words in the text when it misheard me (which was easy given that the software was trained on Received Standard English pronunciation, and I was not). In subsequent work on the text, I typed myself and corrected any such errors, but wish to apologise in case one may still be found. Having said that, the machine never suggested I write econo-mix for economics! The responsibility for that literal and figurative transposition, as for the rest of the content in the book, is entirely mine to own.

Part 1

Looking back, looking ahead

1 The anatomy of a discipline

> Does writing mean deliberating upon and concentrating one's energies on a single theme from beginning to end? Does a 'monograph' foreclose the possibility of writing on multiple themes, and employing multiple modes of writing such as the usual prose of the essay style, the narratives, poems, fragments, etc? How does the monograph respond itself to the 'exigency of writing' or the surging forth of all that is suppressed (repressed) under an assumed, full-rounded subjectivity, either of the Cartesian kind or of the mediatized kind in our own times?
>
> (Manjali 2001: 117)

> Monsters cannot be announced. One cannot say: 'here are our monsters,' without immediately turning the monsters into pets.
>
> (Derrida 1989: 80)

1.1 Introduction

The first thing to point out about this text is that it is not simply inter- or multi-disciplinary, but, to an extent, it can be called anti-disciplinary. The disciplinary divides in the form familiar to us today have not existed forever, but it is still striking to see the difficulty of complicating the boundaries which often act as borders, with much border patrolling. This border patrolling is especially significant in a social science like economics, but in a more general sense, disciplinarity serves an important function in the modernist specialisation, taxonomisation and professionalisation of knowledge. It allows compartmentalised knowing to be tailored to the specific needs of administration. This is not in itself problematic as long as the contingent and arbitrary nature of the compartmentalisation is constantly foregrounded. However, this often tends not to be the case, and the service of knowledge to the purposes of administration implies that one is looking for answers, the simpler the better. This preference for simple answers is not always admitted, and the result is – a disciplinary thrust to produce simple answers to complex questions, which is at the same time validated as possibly the only way of generating knowledge. This is only too visible especially in social sciences like economics, which have a long tradition of being twinned to the concerns of power and administration in society.

Against this background, this book does not squarely locate itself in a pre-given field which can be understood as 'economics'. Rather, it constantly seeks to question and challenge how we come to see something as belonging to economics, how this has been constructed as seemingly invariant but actually varies over time and across place, how a belief in the invariance of what economics is in relation to a wider terrain of knowledge actually serves to depoliticise the economic context, and how this seemingly invariant depoliticised economic context is rendered substantively unengageable by any means other than those recognised as legitimate and valid by those who have a monopoly on favourably defining the economic context.

Questioning the economic context is therefore an important part of my motivation for this work. But, I also believe that this is not simply a necessary but an urgent task, since, increasingly at various levels of social discourse (from popular culture to academics)[1] the appeal to the economic context is seen as beyond question. It is not surprising to find the opposing parties to any debate (for instance, citizenship, 'free' trade, aid/debt, asylum) appealing to the 'economic' case for their argument. This is not accompanied by any argument as to either how what is seen as being 'economic' is itself constructed, so that this construction is open to challenge, or, if the economic might not be the case-clinching magic word, so that there might be the possibility of something as being desirable even if it is not economic.

Thus, the economic context is not something that should be settled too soon. Some time ago, the media reported the following statement, '[w]ith parties on both left and right debating a new political climate, former Labour cabinet minister Peter Mandelson has also said that in purely economic terms "we are all Thatcherite now" ' ('Right and Left Blaze Thatcherite Trail' 2002). The link between the popular perception that the markets have won, the appeal to the economic as something which is final, and the role of economics in depoliticising the economic context deserves serious attention. A social science like economics – which is organised around dealing with manufactured abstractions such as the market or the economy, which are the basis for modelling the interactions of generic individuals – is consciously patterned after universalistic aspirations of extracting scientific facts from messy sociality. And this depoliticised economic context latches on to the privilege that is accorded to scientistic patterning, and appears to be unassailable.

I am therefore starting from the position of trying to question the presupposed universality of economic knowledge, and trying to ex-pose it as contingent not

1 I should point out that I am not arguing for a separation between the various levels of social discourse, and neither do I believe such a separation to be tenable. In fact, in the third part of this book, I challenge precisely the separation between the economic and cultural which is available to us in relation to separating the so-called 'levels of discourse' in society. For an interesting piece of work which challenges the representations of the marketplace in popular culture and relates them to academic discourse, see Sudan (1999).

only methodologically and epistemologically, but also argue that its creation and perpetuation is more generally ideological and interested. Any story of interested particulars passing off for disinterested universals draws attention therefore to both the structuring of knowledge in terms of an inadequately conceived relation between the part and the whole, and to the submerging of difference in such a venture. The first inaugurates the question of the *dynamics of theory*, and the second points to the *Others of knowledge*. These will accordingly be my threads of concentration in the present undertaking. What is at stake here is not only a critique of economics, but a wider multi-layered interrogation of modernist knowledge in general.

Given the anti-disciplinary nature of this text, I wish to dive straight at the heart of a crucial matter and discuss the way theory is written in economics and simultaneously trace some of its pedagogical implications. This is followed by a preliminary posing of the question 'what is at stake?' in conducting an undisciplined interrogation of the discourse of economics. This helps to situate my own endeavour that is spelt out in an overview of the chapters. Finally, there is a brief signposting of my own motivations in undertaking this work. At this point, I should just like to blend into the text for flavour the following words of Spivak (1999: xiii), 'I am not erudite enough to be interdisciplinary, but I can break rules.'

1.2 The writing of theory in economics

> A network of sociopolitical relationships and intellectual assumptions creates an invisible system of acceptance and rejection, discourse and silence, ascendancy and subjugation, within and around disciplines. Implicit cultural presuppositions work with the personal idiosyncrasies of intellectual authorities to keep certain issues from placing high on research agendas. Critics have to learn how to notice their absence. . . . A discipline defines itself both by what it excludes (repulses) and by what it includes. But the self-definition process removes what is excluded (repulsed) from view, so that it is not straightforwardly available for assessment, criticism, and analysis.
>
> (Code 1991: 25–26)

> The world has been remade in the economist's image. The ascendancy of economic theory has not made the world a better place. Instead, it has made an already troubled society worse; more unequal, more unstable, and less 'efficient'. Why has economics persisted with a theory which has been comprehensively shown to be unsound? Why, despite the destructive impact of economic policies, does economics continue to be the toolkit which politicians and bureaucrats apply to almost all social and economic issues? The answer lies in the way economics is taught in the world's universities.
>
> (Keen 2001: xiii–xiv)

Let me set the scene with examples of the existing practice of writing economic theory which will provide a useful handle to appreciate the need for change. Allen (2000), in her attempts to predict the future of microeconomic theory, illustrates some typical disciplinary attitudes.[2] To begin with, she wishes 'to avoid attempting to define economic theory – perhaps it's like pornography, in that you know it when you see it' (143). Not only is economics best defined as 'what economists do', with Allen's remarks it seems economic theory is also tautologically 'what economic theorists do'.

In March 1999, the *Journal of Economic Literature* published an article titled 'The Young Person's Guide to Writing Economic Theory' (Thomson 1999: 157–183). The reason I introduce this article here is the extremely good illustration it provides of what economists mean by 'theory' and how it should be 'done'. It is also significant that the article appears in a key journal which serves as a place for defining what economics literature is all about. In addition, the mock humorous tone of the article contains a nudge and a wink at the peculiarities of writing economics. It aims to allay anxieties for those who haven't figured out how to get 'inside' this high discourse, but in the process, it also exposes the numerous implicit value judgements that guide theorising. Let me now discuss this text and interrogate what it takes for granted.

The article provides 'recommendations for *writing economic theory*' (157, emphasis added) to an intended audience of young economists. But this is immediately followed up with the statement that, 'this essay is *mainly concerned* in its

2 In as much as the question of economic theory is a question of method, the situation is not very different in macroeconomics. As an illustration, consider Lucas Jr. (2000), who provides a model of growth for the twenty-first century which begins with a world of many countries with equal populations at some initial date prior to the onset of the Industrial Revolution. They all have the same constant income level. He writes (160):

> Now imagine all of these economies lined up in a row, each behind the kind of mechanical starting gate used at the race track. In the race to industrialise… the gates do not open all at once… at any date t a few of the gates that have not yet opened are selected by some random device. When the bell rings, these gates open and some of the economies that had been stagnant are released and begin to grow. The rest must wait their chances at the next date, $t+1$.

He admits that 'there is not much economics in the model', but later follows this up with (166, emphasis original):

> But for all these deficiencies, it is undeniably an *economic* model: no one but a theoretical economist would have written it down. It is not a theory formed by statistical methods from the Penn World Table or any other single data set. Despite its obvious limitations, the model has nontrivial implications about the behaviour of the world economy over the next century. It predicts that sooner or later everyone will join the Industrial Revolution, that all economies will grow at the rate common to the wealthiest economies, and that percentage differences in income levels will disappear (which is to say, return to their preindustrial levels).

However, his conjecture is that 'these predictions are *not due to* the mechanical character of *the model*', but that (166, emphases added), the 'central presumption of the general equilibrium models that are in wide use in macroeconomics today is that *people are pretty much alike, that the differences in their behavior are due mainly to differences in the resources that history has placed at their disposal*'. For someone who both agrees and disagrees with Lucas, see Solow (2000).

details *with formal models*' and 'does not cover the writing up of empirical work' (ibid., emphases added). Here, economic theory is seen as the ability to create and present a mathematical model. The author goes on to state that since most work anyway begins with the introduction and analysis of a model, the recommendations can be seen as quite wide-ranging. The principles of good writing – simplicity, clarity, unity – are stated at the outset as universal.[3]

In a good piece of work done by a young economist, the reader 'should be able to easily spot the main results, figure out most of the notation and locate the crucial definitions needed to understand the statement of each theorem' (158). It is a serious business to train and expect such theorisation as valid economics, as legitimate social science. Let me give you a few more examples from the text. When advising young theorists to 'choose notation that is easily recognisable', Thomson says the following (160, emphases added)

> The best notation is notation that can be guessed. When you see a man walking down the street with a baguette under his arm and a beret on his head, you do not need to be told he is a Frenchman. *You know he is*. You can *immediately and legitimately* invest him with *all the attributes* of Frenchness, and this greatly facilitates the way you think and talk about him. You can guess his children's names – Renée or Edmond – and chuckle at his supposed admiration for Jerry Lewis.

And he continues '[s]imilarly, if Z designates a set, call its members *z* and *z*', perhaps *x*, *y*, and *z*, but certainly not *b*, or *ℓ*.' Here, despite the self-ironic chuckle implied in the example, the point is a wink and a nod aimed at those who laugh precisely because they are 'in' on the discourse, and have accepted the discourse's parameters. Maybe the actual logic of parallel here is not from stereotyping Frenchness to symbols, but it is the acceptability and intelligibility of stereotyping people that allows comprehending the thread of his comparison when he gets to mathematical notation. The parameter contained in the joke is that of essentialism. Contained in the jokes about the choice of notation, abbreviations, assumptions, and the naming of agents, is, effectively, the fairly serious matter of theorisation as a process that begins with formalisation, moves on to universalisation, and, when confronted with difference, resorts to stereotyping.

But then again, attempts to characterise human behaviour and interactions in terms of 'ideal objects' will not proceed unless one is firmly grounded within an

3 As an antidote, consider the following (Butler 1999: xix, emphases added):

> The demand for lucidity forgets the ruses that motor the ostensibly 'clear' view. Avital Ronell recalls the moment in which Nixon looked into the eyes of the nation and said, 'let me make one thing perfectly clear' and then proceeded to lie. *What travels under the sign of 'clarity'*, and what would be the price of failing to deploy a certain critical suspicion when the arrival of lucidity is announced? *Who devises the protocols of 'clarity' and whose interests do they serve*? What is foreclosed by the insistence on parochial standards of transparency as requisite for all communication? *What does 'transparency' keep obscure*?

abstract essentialist individual version of identity where everyone is basically the same. This takes us to the enlightenment interest in the 'general man', the average being who can be represented systematically, without any interference of the theorist, in the practice of positivist and potentially universal modernist disciplinary knowledge.

So that, we have this instruction, 'Call your *generic* individual *i*, *his* [*sic*] preference relation R_i, his utility function u_i, and his endowment vector ω_i. The production set is *Y*. Prices are *p*, quantities *q*' (160–161, emphases added). The underlying faith in the usefulness of axiomatisation is directly correlated with a desire for objective, general, and pure universal knowledge in symbolic terms which can be manipulated to handle particular contextual complications. This ostensibly 'higher' form of knowing is seen to be achieved when the 'self' is erased from the discourse, leaving the distilled essence of the generalised abstract individual *i*. Witness Litt's remarks on the desirability of such knowing (1957: 141, emphases added)

> It is the science of objects which cannot be found readymade, and subsequently understood through the working of human reason, but which are themselves created by an independent act of reason. ... In order to create this world of conceptual objects, it is essential that the thinking being must raise itself onto the level of *'pure' and entirely general thinking*. This means, in effect, that all considerations which restrict the thinking individual to *his* [*sic*] *particular context in time and space* and which distinguish him in a qualitative sense from other individual beings *must be eliminated* in this sphere of thought. In this sense, the elevation of one's thinking faculty to the sphere of mathematical ideas implies an *act of self-elimination; of the conquest of one's own personality*.

Accordingly, the view is that scientificity about the discourse on the social demands the sacrifice of one's self, seen as the situatedness of one's context. The best knowledge is that which is universally applicable, but what passes for universal knowledge is actually profoundly parochial and provincial (see especially Chapter 3). Moreover, this view of knowledge is intimately tied to the tensions in enlightenment epistemology, and the role for theory envisaged following on from such a view of knowledge is equally problematic.

It is clear from Thomson's advice throughout the piece that writing economic theory is the same thing as presenting a well-written formal model. And, even then, we are warned '[d]o *not* populate your paper with individuals, agents, persons, consumers, and players. *One species is enough*. Universal quantifications can be written as "for all", "for any", and "for every"' (168, emphases added). One is enough in the hall of many mirrors.

Further, this pretence to scientificity does not prevent the theorist from carving out ideological niches under the guise of non-interfering abstract representation. For instance, Thomson at several places draws the distinction between what terms mean in ordinary language, and what sense they have in 'our dialect' (or 'economese', as he puts it on p. 168). Why should we use the adjective 'fair' to designate allocations that are both 'equitable *and* efficient,' he asks (169, emphasis original). After all, in common language, fairness does not have efficiency connotations, so '[r]efer to "equitable *and* efficient allocations"' he advises (ibid.). However, it could be argued that one is being ideological in delineating 'efficiency' itself as something which does not have to be 'fair', just as much as one is ideological when one argues for the undesirability of characterising a trade-off between equity and efficiency. But, in scientific posturing, efficiency is supposedly a positive realm, while being 'fair' or equitable is a normative issue (for a sociological critique, see Beckert 2002). Barker (1995: 26) reviews the historical development of the concept of economic efficiency, especially of Pareto optimality as a scientific criterion of economic welfare, as 'a response to the methodological tensions between the clearly political nature of economics and the scientific aspirations of economists'. Her opening quote from John Hicks illustrates this well (ibid., emphasis added):

> The investigator himself decides what he thinks to be good for society, and praises or condemns the system he is studying by that test. This is the method which is rightly condemned as unscientific. It is the way of the prophet and the social reformer, *not of the economist.*

As Barker points out, the propositions of economic science, were – in the eyes of its important precursors such as Lionel Robbins – composed of postulates which are neither empirical generalisations nor mere tautologies, rather they are universal truths known through introspection.[4] Thomson's suggestions are in keeping with such a spirit of supposed scientificity which sees fairness as a normative term that needs replacing with a combination of the normative 'equitable' plus the positive 'efficient'. None of this draws attention to the interestedly constructed and value-laden nature of the concept of 'efficiency' itself which is regularly used in media representations of the appeals to a so-called universal and uninterrogable 'economic logic'.[5] The idea seems to be that there is no arguing with 'economic science', and yet, when we interrogate what this characterisation of economic science takes for granted in terms of what counts as desirable knowledge and how it is to be represented theoretically, we begin to see that economic science does not represent the economic realm scientifically, but is a politically motivated belief in the desirability of general, universal, and axiomatic

4 Thus, for Robbins, '[w]hy the human animal attaches particular values in this sense to particular things is a question we will not discuss' (in Barker 1995: 32). I agree with Barker when she follows it up thus, '[w]hy not, one might ask? Because to discuss these issues would place them in historical and cultural context and thus detract from what Robbins saw as their universal nature' (ibid.).

5 For example, when a firm makes thousands of workers redundant in the name of 'efficiency', mainstream media frames this as the 'inevitable' outcome of an 'inexorable economic logic'. But while all the sides in any argument are busy appealing to the 'economic' considerations, there is no ground left to challenge the primacy of the appeal to the economic, or to point out that there is no objective consensus on what can be seen as being economic, since it is always 'values' that are fixed in 'Value' (see Chapter 6).

representations as science, and this 'science', when it is yoked with an *a priori* fixing of particular values as the general value in the 'economic', passes for a social science. The writing of such social science will then inevitably require the shelter of appeals to 'axiomatic rigour' in order to establish its scientific (and thus disinterested, but actually ideologically conservative and *status quo*-ist) credentials.

Writing in 'economese' also means writing in (good, standard) English. Thomson has the following to say (1999: 170, emphasis original): '*Get a good dictionary, and, if English is not your first language, ask for assistance.* To weed out from your text gallicisms, nipponisms, sinicisms, and so on, get the help of a native gardener.' Indeed, English as a language and Mathematics as its partner have a long history together, and Thomson further urges striking the optimal balance in the writing of proofs (ibid.: 170, emphasis original):

> *The optimal ratio of mathematics to English in a proof varies* from reader to reader. . . . A proof written entirely in English is often not precise enough and is too long; a proof written entirely in mathematics is impossible to understand, unless you are a digital computer of course. Modern estimation techniques have shown that the optimal ratio of mathematics to English in a proof lies in the interval (52%, 63.5%).

This is followed by an example of a proof that is 'just right' (171): 'Proof: this follows from the inclusion $\varphi \subseteq P$, Part (i) Proposition 1, and Lemma 1 applied to φ. QED.' Writes Thomson, 'It is indeed pleasantly short and clean. Wouldn't you like to know what theorem it proves?' Well, wouldn't you?

The writing of economic theory on these terms is not so much a theorising of the 'economic' in its content and evaluations, but rather a second order *a priori* formalised exercise where the method serves as a grid onto which any content can be mapped. Following on from this, the comprehension of subjectivity implied by such analysis is notoriously impoverished. The 'subject' of analysis is a 'universal' figure whose identity is not a function of its situatedness. An example of the extent to which naming is seen as being unrelated to the content of theorisation is as follows. Giving advice on the attribution of gender identity to the 'agents', Thomson writes (ibid.: 180–181),

> Choose the sex of your agents once and for all. Flip a coin. If it is a boy, rejoice! If it is a girl, rejoice![6] And don't subject them to sex change operations from paragraph to paragraph. . . . Two-person games are great for sexual equality. Make one player male and the other female. . . . It will also save you from the awkward 'he or she,' 'him or her,' 'his or her'! Alternatively, you may be able to refer to your agents in the plural, or choose one of them to be a firm, and refer to it as 'it'.

6 It is indeed a strange coincidence that, in the light of what he says, Thomson comes up with the widely preferred side of the tossed coin – the generic individual in the article is always referred to as a 'he'!

Like everything else, identity is also simply an uncomplicated choice.[7] Regardless of the scenario one is 'theorising', the agents remain abstract neutral essences who can be invested with any kind of identity.

The point finally is this. The writing of much economic theory is seen as the construction of formal models, which are legitimate because they are seen as attempts to generate knowledge of a general and universal kind which is unembodied and unembedded in any specific context. The appeal to the signifier 'science' performs the important function of stabilising the writing of such economic theory. And yet, this supposed generality and universality is actually a cover for uncritically invoking concepts such as the individual, firms, efficiency, scarcity, production and consumption, and so on, as universal constructs available to be studied by the universal method of the economic model. That mathematics is crucial to maintaining this facade of axiomatic rigour is obvious from the parallel Thomson draws at the very end of his piece. There, he writes that, as he started circulating his paper, 'several readers gave [him] references to similar pedagogical essays written by mathematicians' (182). He then approvingly quotes several such manuals for mathematicians, and concludes thus, '[a]n example of a beautifully written text is the monograph by Debreu (1959)'.

This apotheosis of good economic theorising refers to Monograph 17 of the Cowles Foundation for Research in Economics at Yale University by economist/mathematician Debreu, titled *Theory of Value: An Axiomatic Analysis Of Economic Equilibrium*. In the preface to this, Debreu states (1959: viii, emphasis added),

> *[t]he theory of value is treated here with the standards of rigor of the contemporary formalist school of mathematics.* The effort towards rigor substitutes correct reasonings and results for incorrect ones, but it offers other rewards too. ... Allegiance to rigor dictates the axiomatic form of the analysis where the theory, in the strict sense, is logically entirely disconnected from its interpretations.

If Robbins believed '[w]hy the human animal attaches particular values in this sense to particular things is a question we will not discuss' (see footnote 4), Debreu's theory of 'value' does not even have a sub-section on the term. The opening chapter is titled 'mathematics', and subsequent ones – commodities and prices, producers, consumers, equilibrium, optimum, and uncertainty.

Similarly, *the 'economic' in Thomson's guide is an absence*; what matters is the narrow method. Thomson is not unique in this interpretation of what we mean by economic theory, for the mainstream profession stands by him. It is a science

7 This sanguine approach to identity as an untroubling category is questionable. For instance, Bertrand and Mullainathan (2004) conduct an experimental investigation into the differential treatment by race in the US labour market; they find that White names receive 50 per cent more callbacks from employers than African-American names, and this does not vary with occupation, industry, or employer size, persisting even when African Americans have higher skills or credentials.

(never mind all the numerous arguments to the contrary) like physics, like mathematics (see Mirowski 1989, 1991a).

This focus on formalisation as the core of economic theory leaves unchallenged the underlying issues of universalism and modernist stereotypy that form the operational basis of the mainstream economic method. And it is not only formalism which requires that identity be a matter of universal essences. The particularities of inalienably situated historical contexts within which the 'economic' is experienced are simplified into the general and universal denominations. For instance, McCloskey, a theorist associated with recognising the limits of formalism and arguing for an acknowledgement of the way in which economics as a discipline is discursively constructed, is at the same time unwilling to contest the discourse of growth as an economic phenomenon unencumbered by questions of history, agency, and identity. She argues (2000: 33) that 'the problems of poor countries have little to do with the experience of imperialism', saying,

> It seems strange to go on blaming imperialism for the woes of a Third World whose growth rate has accelerated steadily in the past fifty years. India, the most confidently anti-imperialist and anti capitalist former colony, has had the lowest growth rate in Asia – mainly, I would say, not because it was once Victoria's jewel, but because it has followed Harold Laski's policies of keeping the market out. ... You could only recently buy American breakfast cereal in India. The former colonies that have embraced capitalism – [...] – have done well. You can buy anything in Hong Kong. Even parts of Africa seem to be emerging from their self-inflicted wounds since independence. ... [t]he impact of imperialism on the imperial powers has been trivial.

McCloskey slips into making a particular comprehension of the empirical into 'the' empirical – giving a status of Fact to that (i.e. to growth) which is theoretically constituted as a 'fact'. Growth is not a neutral phenomenon – leaving aside the thorny issues of trade, income-distribution and the environment, the process of growth has often meant the imposition of 'European ideas, values and institutions – largely wrecked [these] cultural systems, undermining [African] ways of life and subsistence' (Pfaff 2001). Further, how did we get to this place where we can unquestioningly designate, for everyone to understand, the 'Third World' and the 'poor nations'? As Shapiro writes, we need to practise insurrectional textuality, 'to use a particular grammar that helps to historicise phenomena that are ordinarily accepted as unproblematic. ... shift from atemporal noun like criminal to one conveying temporality like "criminalisation"' (1989a: 71). For, 'to textualise a domain of analysis is to recognise that "any reality" is mediated by a mode of representation and that representations are not a description of a world of facticity' (1989b: 13–14). The nations are impoverished and were colonised rather than poor former colonies – if only they would 'grow'!

It is important to note that the 'scientific status' of economics as a discipline (that which *disciplines* knowledge claims) is cemented by its unprecedented homage at the altar of mathematics in the twentieth century. The epistemic violence of modernist universalism can be seen in the primacy of numbers within the conception of what 'counts' – either as theory (in formalist methods) or as evidence (as with the McCloskean use of growth as empirical 'fact' that settles all questions). Poovey (1998) describes how numbers have a history of being seen as pre- and yet non-interpretive, and the crucial role that they have played in the construction of what she calls the 'modern fact'. Kanth (1997a: 4), in his critique of the eurocentrism of economics, writes 'mathematics, in effect, serves the same ideological function, in economics, that masses in Latin served the priesthood of the Church' – namely, to provide a misleading semblance of dignity to an otherwise 'self-referential language game with zero representational efficacy'. This is paralleled by a yearning for 'objectivity' within modernism.[8] General and universal knowledge is best explored in symbols that exclude the complexity and ambiguity of human contexts.

From a mainstream perspective, 'the seemingly endless disputes on the role of mathematics in economics have largely ceased'[9] and this 'hard-won silence' needs to be zealously guarded against the danger posed by 'younger members of our profession' who are guilty of 'backtracking from rigor in their work' (Allen 2000: 144). Allen attributes this 'alarming trend' to the publish or perish pressures in the academia, so that new entrants are tempted to be sloppy (strictly speaking, any article without a formal model is probably sloppy for her).[10] Any work that

8 In addition, the role of mathematics is especially important to unpack from its connections as a partner to Occidental science (compass-globe-map quests). Mathematics and science are seen as primarily European ventures (notwithstanding Aryabhatta, Bhaskaracharya, Hypatia, Susruta, Charak, and so on). On the non-European traditions, see Joseph (2000); Bishop (1995). See also Ethnomathematics Digital Library (n.d.).

9 The ceasing of these disputes may have been a function of conversation-stopping responses that obtain from the mainstream. An example is Samuelson's response to the excesses of mathematics in economics. Rather than engaging with the idea that certain things may not lend themselves to axiomatisations, or that the adoption of mathematics in economics was an interested political and sociological endeavour (see chapter two), Samuelson seems to take for granted that those who raise these objections do so because they are not capable of understanding mathematics, and will eventually end up with an inferiority complex: 'Moreover, without mathematics you run grave psychological risks. As you grow older, you are sure to resent the method increasingly. Either you will get an inferiority complex and retire from the field of theory or you will get an inferiority complex and become aggressive about your dislike of it' (1952: 65). Later on, in chapter six, it will be interesting to see that the reply of a political economist to a dissenter in 1826 was no less vitriolic.

10 But what about the sloppiness of allegiance to rigour, and empirical deception? Colander (2000: 127) mentions two cases. First, '[t]he editors of the *Journal of Money, Banking and Credit* found that even when they had requested the data from authors . . . they could not replicate the results of the studies (Dewald *et al.*, 1986).' Second, 'McCloskey and Ziliak (1996) found that statistical inference was incorrectly used in a large majority of articles in the *American Economic Review*, the premier research journal.' And as for axiomatic rigour, consider Samuelson (1952: 64), 'The convenience of mathematical symbolism for handling certain deductive inferences is, I think, indisputable. It is going too far to say that mathematicians never make mistakes. Like everybody else, they can pull some awful boners.' But, of course, 'it is surprising how rare pure mistakes in logic are. . . . I think it is one of the advantages of the mathematical medium . . . – that we are forced to lay our cards on the table so that all can see our premises' (ibid.).

does not conform to the orthodoxy becomes a worthy candidate for rejection. Allen writes (ibid.: 145, emphases added),

> Yet another *disturbing* trend in economic theory is that many researchers are choosing to step back from *genuine theory*. ... economics would be better served if theorists would *more often deliberately move in the direction of abstraction and generality*, which is where theory can most effectively contribute to *economic science*. ... until recently, I had *not* found interactions with most other social scientists to be particularly fruitful.

For a lot of economists, the irony of not being able to conclusively demonstrate what economic theory is or does (see Allen's remarks at the start of this section, 'perhaps it's like pornography, in that you know it when you see it'), while at the same time arguing for more abstraction and generality for genuine theory, does not register. The reason Allen changed her mind about interdisciplinarity is again something she has in common with the disciplinary consensus[11] – in addition to the fundamental tools from mathematics and statistics, the allure of fields such as finance, operations research and computer science, biology and engineering ('more precisely, cognitive neuroscience – the link is the relation between biological bases of behaviour and rational choice') proves to be too much. In the current climate of hyperenthusiasm about 'new' issues of information and technology, Allen further sees the potential to revise the economic treatment of technology (which for the most part still follows Debreu, 1959; see earlier), and in addressing this topic she sees 'vast potential for economists to learn from engineers' (149).[12]

Why should a young economist (or any economist for that matter) participate in this prescriptive and problematic manner of theorising? In his conclusion, Thomson promises success for someone following all of his recommendations for writing standard economic theory: '... not only will you be pleased with yourself, your seminar audiences enlightened, your classmates impressed, your parents proud of you, and you will land a job in a top-five department, but most importantly,

11 Interdisciplinarity is welcome in some directions but not others. See Nelson (1995: 134), who addresses disciplinary values which are linked to the idea that 'a "hard" economics is clearly preferable to a "soft" economics'. An interesting discussion in Nelson (ibid.: 136–137) is as follows. For a Becker (who has argued that the model of individual choice in markets is the distinguishing characteristic of economics) or a Lucas (who has stated that the assumptions of rational choice modelling provide 'the only "engine of truth" we have in economics'), even the models of Akerlof and Yellen (who borrow from psychology) 'fail to qualify, being too "soft" or "too messy", or perhaps "too sociological"'. Other models of human behaviour that Nelson mentions as not meeting the mainstream 'standards of rigor' are by economists such as Folbre, Sen, Frank (see ibid.: 137).

12 *Plus ça change, plus c'est la meme chosé* (the more things change, the more they remain the same). See chapter two for the discussion of a nineteenth-century tussle between the rival ideals of 'rigor' and 'practicality' as the basis for economic theory – the mathematician economists versus the engineer economists.

your adviser will be happy' (1999: 182). He may be overstating the case, but the picture is no doubt a rosy one, for the mainstream disciplinary consensus is firmly on his side, and this is especially the case when it comes to jobs in most departments.[13] Not only is this the way to write good economic theory (to 'do' formal models), in fact, there is no other way of 'doing' economic theory!

But what are the consequences of this kind of conformity? Professionally, it results in the marginalisation of heterodox economists who adhere to alternative approaches; their work is ghettoised and deemed ideological or non-rigorous. Intellectually, it results in the stifling of discussion between the mainstream and alternatives, and the insistence upon mainstream methods may mean important issues are not addressed for want of the right techniques. Pedagogically, it results in the homosocial perpetuation of a certain kind of economist mirroring the dominant social characteristics (masterful white male), who, even when aware of the excessive and detrimental focus on technique at the expense of a genuine knowledge of the economy, still cannot resist the disciplinary stranglehold which apportions success only to the fastidious followers.

As Fine (1999) points out, the many weaknesses of mainstream economics – strict adherence to a particular form of methodological individualism, admission of empirical evidence as neutral and external data, the unacceptably crude status of falsifiability, focus on the behavioural assumption of utility maximisation to the exclusion of all other motives – do not make a difference to its status. This apparent anomaly is unsurprising if we consider the following (405, emphases added):

> Heterodox economists who are prepared to say this are increasingly thin on the ground and risk professional suicide to the extent that their scholarship seeks alternatives. ... mainstream economics ... is currently characterized by a *lack of dialogue* with alternative approaches as never before. These are dismissed by the mainstream as *woolly or non-rigorous* if they do not draw heavily upon mathematical modelling and/or statistical estimation. Indeed, a key feature of economics as a discipline at the moment is that it has become systematically more entrenched in its *intolerance of alternative approaches*. This is true of *analytical substance as well as in professional practice*. It is extremely difficult for any heterodox economist to survive, and even harder for a new generation to emerge through academic appointments, teaching and research.[[14]]

13 A cursory glance at the curricula of any economics programme or at the research area requirements in economics job advertisements would confirm this assertion. Weintraub posed an interesting question to Dow in a review; the exchange is recalled in Dow (1995: 719) – 'Mainstream theory is not the only option facing economists. So: [Weintraub asks] "Why are there, in the United States, at least 98% Mainstream and 2% of all other kinds of economists?" '.

14 At this point, Fine mentions the impact of the Research Assessment Exercise (RAE) in the United Kingdom on the discipline of economics. He cites Lee and Harley (1998) to suggest that 'non-mainstream economics could be eliminated from British economics departments within ten years!' (1999: 405, 420).

Dasgupta (1998: ii) somewhat regretfully attends to the critics, saying thus: 'My fellow economists choose simply to ignore these writings. Understandably, they think they have better things to do. Some have told me I waste my time worrying about such attacks.' He writes (21–24, emphasis original):

> It is the fate of some disciplines to begin as a fit subject for educated gentlemen to advert upon, and to become technical, to the displeasure of educated gentlemen. . . . That a problem area is *important* has never been a clinching argument for rushing to work on it. Wisely, I think, contemporary economists study an important problem only when they think there is a chance that it will yield fruit. . . . [he gives the example that until recently economists hadn't theorised inequality because] . . . there were no promising analytical leads on the matter. . . . Economics is a quantitative subject [he adds that policy makers do not want expert advisors for philosophical discourse] . . . So mathematical modeling is essential and is here to stay. . . . in order to make progress, we have to simplify in suitable ways.

Equally interesting is the making of the young economist who writes economic theory along the lines suggested by Thomson. In their survey of graduate students at six top ranking graduate economics programmes,[15] Colander and Klamer (1987) find that the 'typical graduate student in economics at these selected institutions is a 26-year-old, middle-class, nonreligious white male who is involved in a long-term relationship'.[16] Contrast this with a discussion thread on the history of economic thought (HES) email forum, where an acknowledgement that 'most economics education is chalk and talk by white, male, middle-aged profs' (Caldwell 2002), drew a response that went as follows (Anderson, 2002):

> I think the frustration that some are experiencing with the method or style in which economics is taught has really more to do with the intransigence by which political correctness was greeted by the econ departments. While the other social sciences ran with open arms to unquestionably embrace every and all new demands made, economics resisted. And, because economics is really a much older and more sophisticated subject than many outside the field realize, it will continue to frustrate those with the 'new' agenda.

15 The six universities are: University of Chicago, Columbia University, Harvard University, Massachusetts Institute of Technology, Stanford University, and Yale University.

16 In their sample, 18.9 per cent were female, one was Hispanic, and none Black. This is not exceptional in economics. For an oral history compilation of a sample of 11 women economists in the United States who obtained their PhDs between 1950 and 1975 (the percentage of women doctorates in economics in the United States continued to fall through most of this period, while those in other disciplines rose – from 1950 until the late 1960s it remained below 5 per cent), see Olson and Emami (2002) and Kaul (2003b). For a detailed discussion of why there are so few women visual artists, mathematicians, scientists, musicians, see Piirto (2000). For a recent evaluation of how women economists in the United States have not advanced as readily as their male peers (despite their share of PhDs having risen to about 27 per cent in 1999), see Miller (2002).

The counter-question to this went, 'perhaps it is that "non-economic" theories are so much more older and more sophisticated than economists realize? It may be that in this day and age, economics is much too important a subject to be left to the economists' (Pack 2002).[17] This exchange illustrates that not much has changed since Colander and Klamer wrote about the making of an economist in 1987.[18]

Therein, they find that the students felt – graduate school gave them little opportunity for interdisciplinary discussions; knowledge of the economy and knowledge of economic literature do not make an economist successful (being smart in the sense of being good at problem-solving was seen as being 'very important' by 65 per cent, excellence in mathematics by 57 per cent, knowledge of economic literature by 10 per cent, having a thorough knowledge of the economy by 3 per cent); a strong sense that economics was a game, and the facade, not the depth of knowledge, was important (ibid.: 98–100). Further, the authors found clear evidence of the existence of a 'Chicago school' with belief in the distinction between positive and normative economics, relevance of neoclassical economics, a significantly higher degree of confidence in the market, support for rational expectations hypothesis, relatively less interest in the assumptions of price rigidity, imperfect competition and cost mark-up pricing, and finally, relatively less tension between their course work and policy interests. Colander and Klamer summarise (109–110), 'What students believe leads to success in graduate school is definitely techniques; success has little to do with understanding the economy, nor does it have much to do with economic literature.'

As I will go on to explore in this book, there is many a disjuncture between economics, economy and the economic. Perhaps the most important consequence of writing economic theory the way it is written by the disciplinary consensus in economics is the possibility of pretending that 'economic' concerns are somehow separate and separable from those of a political, cultural, social, moral, ethical, and ecological nature, and can be addressed 'scientifically' within economics.[19] This does not allow any serious questioning of the economic logic to be taken with sincerity. In its many forms, the continued prevalence of economics as a social science derives and provides nourishment to neoliberal practice, neoclassical theory, and social Darwinist metaphysics.[20]

17 This seems to be a sentiment on the rise – Keen's text *Debunking economics* (2001) begins and ends with the same note: *economics is too important to leave to the economists*. For an optimistic assessment of strategy and tactics in the pedagogy of economics, see Thompson (1999).

18 In fact, a follow-up study of a subset of the earlier survey respondents yields that the profession has become more conservative with continuing neoclassical dominance and no indications of reform. See Colander 2003.

19 An example of this practice can be seen in the following. A query on the HES list (http://www.eh.net), regarding the response of economists to inequality, was answered with a slightly puzzled response about why inequality *per se* would be a concern economically? (Gunning 2002). Someone else pointed out that Pareto was an economist who strongly thought that inequality was something natural and therefore policy can do nothing for reducing it (Bruni 2002).

20 In view of this, Gare (2002) discusses the need to overcome the hegemony of economics in order to establish a human ecological basis for the formulation and implementation of reoriented public policy.

1.3 The overview

Economics as a discipline resists definition.[21] Such indeterminacy regarding the exact nature of practice probably lent credence to the statement 'economics is what economists do'.[22] There are numerous different ways of 'doing' economics resting on different conceptualisations of the phenomena worth investigation and the attributes of the agents involved. The practice followed by the bulk of the discipline is conventionally termed mainstream economics.[23] Mainstream economics encompasses pure general equilibrium theory, neoclassical economics, new classical economics, and game theory (Dow 1995: 717–719). Implicit in these different strands is mathematical formalism and determinism. It is important to note that while there have been many histories of economics, and many ways of writing those histories, yet, there are not enough histories of contemporary mainstream economics around.[24] One reason for the lack of enough work tracing the consolidation of mainstream economics, especially after the transition from Political Economy to Economics (Mirowski 1989; Perelman 1996: 14–16), may have to do with its 'scientific' status. After all, it is ideologies that are historically situated, not universal methods. It is only to be expected that a dominant scientific discourse wishes its own history away and strives to be seen as a positivist, scientific (formalised and mathematical) rational, obvious method untainted by ideology and unlocated in its historical moment.[25]

The economic 'subject' (subject of economic thought) of this unlocated analysis is a self-transparent unembodied and unembedded amoral utility maximiser propped up by Cartesian dualisms and interested narratives of Enlightenment reason. The 'method' of accessing valid disciplinary (and disciplined) economic narratives of this subject is characterised by methodological individualism, individual rationality, mathematical formalism, heroic role of assumptions in a theory, deductive nomological explanation, operation of an

21 However, this is not to say that economics has not been defined. It has had many avatars, from the study of material prosperity to the study of choice under scarcity.

22 This remark is widely attributed to Viner. See Reder (1999: 3) – though he footnotes that there is no particular citation that can be offered for this quote.

23 Although there are folk narratives about the dissenting nature of economists ('in a room with six economists, there are seven opinions'), it should come as no surprise to those on the margins of the discipline that there is *actually* significant agreement among the mainstream (for instance, see Perelman 1996: 22–29).

24 Indeed, we need to ask the question of the relations between economics as a geo-historically situated discipline and the widespread belief in an 'economic logic' which appears to be universal. How was it that the 'economic' became universal and disciplined so that to defy the 'economic logic' you had to be a child, a lunatic, or a primitive non-European? How do we justify the triumphalist convictions of science (and social science) which lead one to think that 'history happened in order to produce my kind' (as Spivak so aptly put it when writing 'Other things are never equal', 2000: 43). These are some of the questions addressed in the later chapters of this book.

25 As an aside, be invited to think in the manner of Nietzsche: 'only that which has never had a history can be "defined"' (see Dillon 2000: 1).

extremum principle, and so on (see Addleson 1995; Arrow 1994; Chick 1998; Dow 1998; Kurien 1996; Schoemaker 1991; Weintraub 1998).

The closing decades of the twentieth century saw a fault-line appear across numerous academic (hyper-specialised, compartmentalised and professionalised) disciplines, due to hermeneutically inspired critical interventions from feminist, poststructuralist, and postcolonial theory.[26] The effect of these interventions was to pull apart the ground from under positivist anchors in the certainty of unmediated access to knowledge of an external reality. In economics, this has added to critiques of the mainstream for its exclusion of gender, race, class, environmental, and ethical issues. However, critiques of economics as a 'social science' have largely functioned within the theoretical confines set by modernism and therefore have rarely come to terms with the need for writing economics in radically different ways.

Not only are there many critics of economics, there are also many ways of critiquing economics. For instance, mainstream economics has a distinguished history of debates that have questioned either the content of the basic assumptions required for setting up an economic model or the general construction of the model itself for its implied framework. Here, the motivation is to extend or reform the existing approach. Notable examples of such critiques from within include behavioural economics and experimental economics. In response to the many problems of economics, one route has been to reconsider the notion of the economy and its functioning, focussing on its inherent embeddedness, especially in gender or ecological terms. Feminist economists have been at the forefront of raising these questions (e.g., Ferber and Nelson 1993, 2003; Folbre 1994; Strassmann 1994; Gibson-Graham 1996). Another critique of the mainstream consensus examines the ideological status of economics and its everyday significance of power and practice, such as in the policy arena (Galbraith 1970; Nelson 1991; Dowd 2000; Stiglitz 2002). Discussions of economic methodology and philosophy, while often conservative (see Blaug 1988) and limited in their reliance upon philosophy of science (see Beed 1991, 2000; Hausman 1992),[27]

26 See Bleicher (1980) for a comprehensive account of hermeneutics (defined loosely as 'the theory or philosophy of the interpretation of meaning'). Broadly, this is a strand of thought concerned with meaning and interpretation of human expression in its linguisticality. This is important because of the acknowledgment that the linguisticality of human expression carries meaning which needs to be interpreted via the subjectivity of the knower. This necessarily brings into the equation of knowledge the consideration of subjectivity as 'lived experience' drawing upon 'historical consciousness'.

27 Hausman conceives of economic methodology as philosophy of science, especially physics, and the role of philosophy of economics as having to 'trim, revise, and even invent philosophical categories and theses in trying to make sense of economic theory' (1992: 228). However, in order to do this, the philosopher of economics must 'make use of the most plausible among current philosophical views of the sciences, as ill-founded and wrong-headed as they may be. *There is no alternative.*' (ibid., emphasis added). Further, in showing that the state and development of economics manifests imperfect rationality, the philosopher of economics must employ the standard of scientific rationality, which 'comes, as it must, from existing philosophy of science,

sometimes function as critiques (Samuels 1990; Sassower 1985; McCloskey 1986, 1994; Henry 1990; Lavoie 1991; Samuels 1991; Boland 1992, 1997; Rosenberg 1992; Backhouse 1994; Boylan and O'Gorman 1995; Salanti and Screpanti 1997; Morgan and Morrison 1999; Blaug 2001; Wade Hands 2001; Barker and Kuiper 2003). A longstanding and somewhat disparate body of critique is comprised of texts which argue the overall insufficiency of the contemporary mainstream economic paradigm (Wotton 1938; Ward 1972; Wolff and Resnick 1987; Ormerod 1994; Kurien 1996; Perelman 1996; Kanth 1997; Lawson 1997; Lydall 1998; Reder 1999; Stretton 1999; Keen 2001; Lawson 2003; Fullbrook 2003, 2004). Many of these constantly repeat that 'there are alternatives' (see Foldvary 1996). Far fewer have been the critical attempts, especially by the postmodern and postcolonial economists, to self-consciously challenge the modernist aspect of mainstream economics (Ruccio 1991; Samuels 1991; Garnett 1999; Cullenberg, Amariglio, and Ruccio 2001; Kaul 2003a, 2004a; Ruccio and Amariglio 2003; Zein-Elabdin and Charusheela 2004; Kanth 2005). Such work draws attention to the possibility of letting the central themes and concerns of postmodern and postcolonial thought interpellate the discourse of economics to highlight the connection between conceptualisations of what we mean by 'economic theory' and how it draws nourishment from, and is linked to, modernism in all its hues.

To take stock of the discussion so far, it is clear that there is widespread realisation of the shortcomings of mainstream economics. Relentless and varied critiques have been levelled at the mainstream, and alternatives proposed in the manner of pluralism or heterodox lines of enquiry. At the same time, as the section on the writing of economic theory demonstrates, in practical terms, mainstream economic theory continues to flourish. This anomalous gap between the sheer amount and substance of critique and the success of mainstream economics points at no easy answers. The emperor has no clothes, the crowds are denouncing the nudity, and yet nothing happens to change the ruler or the ruling class. An old Chinese poem describes how, despite the season of spring having gone, the flowers are still there, the mountains have colour, the water nearby does not sound, and the birds are not frightened of the people. All this happens because the scene is actually a painted picture and is not real! In the case of economics, the situation is no less complicated. The painted picture still needs to be

as inadequate as it may be' (ibid.). According to him, 'philosophy is to economic methodology as science is to engineering or as economics and ethics are to public policy ... philosophers of economics are philosophers of science who recognise that they had better know quite a lot about some specific science – in this case economics ... methodologists, while concerned with the same data, are more interested in contributing to the acquisition of economic knowledge' (234–235). The problem with Hausman's characterisation is that it does not question the construction of either philosophy or economics, simply taking philosophy as a variable that can enrich economics. Note also the irony in the way the 'philosophy' of science passes into the 'methodology of a *social* science' like economics, which patterns itself after the 'sciences' in its choice of method and history (on this latter, see Mirowski 1989, 1991a).

recognised for what it is! Instead of endlessly worrying at the failure of the birds to be frightened or questioning why or how the flowers are still there when spring is gone, we need to see that the edifice of modern economics is a construction, a special highlight in the modernist architecture of the world, a life-lie (*lebensluge*) for many. In other words, this means interrogating how the underlying conceptions of knowledge in economics came into being historically. If economics as we find it is the answer, what are the questions? What was best excluded by defining explanation in economics in a way that permitted abstraction and generalisation to be seen as the norm? Importantly, *what kind of a modernist knowledge is economics*? In this text, I seek to ask these questions, without reverence for disciplinary boundaries or established modes of enquiry. Having cleared the ground in this chapter, I will begin the next by designating the enterprise of economics as an ideologically, historically, geographically, temporally situated construction which is deeply imbricated in its epistemological inheritance from the European enlightenment.

What is at stake in this present text is not a retail critique of the ways in which economics is a flawed and imperfect science or a social science in need of improvement; it is rather a wholesale examination of the peculiar status of economics as a privileged modernist knowledge which derives its legitimacy from generalisations about human behaviour rooted in a sameness that constantly elides difference. This change of emphasis already means looking at history, theory, method, ideology, power, reason, all together. It is an involved 'improper' analysis that is, perforce, messy. Why not pursue the standard of 'proper' critique, then? Because, as we have seen from the discussions earlier, those critiques that take economics at face-value are dealt with by the response that can be summarised in the words of the RUN DMC song 'It's Like That And That's The Way It Is'. Unpack this phrase, and the following fall out. Most economic theory is written this way. Criticism of the way things are done must stem from an ignorant envy at the use of mathematics. Symbols cannot tell lies; they are visible, transparent, replicable, universal. You ask, what about the critiques that underline the ideological nature of economic policy in practice and the way economic 'science' props that up? Well, that's muddy policy for you; no pure science out there. Why not focus on the normative questions? Not our job; we trade in facts. Okay, what about the huge body of very sensible critiques that just cannot be proved wrong? Oh, that! It's just the beauty of dissent in action, a lively, healthy debate in the discipline; isn't that what everyone wants? Sure, what about teaching some of this dissent then, promoting some of it, even? Come on, don't be silly, we are not Gods; we have to keep being where we are. Each to our own place, it's common sense; you chose to be marginalised, you could have played the game we do. Too bad for you that you couldn't. Now, don't give us all a bad PR. End of story. The critique in this present work is different. Let me outline the contours.

The main concern here is the relation between the issues of knowledge and those of society, and the importance of difference in writing the economic. This book is an unintended consequence of my training in economics and, accordingly, it reveals a desire to come to terms with the limitations of economics by articulating them. Perhaps, disciplinary under erasure (the word 'disciplinary' written with a line through it) is more appropriate for it than anti-disciplinary, because it simultaneously draws attention to both the need and the inadequacy of the designation. The book straddles the conventional disciplinary terrains of economics and philosophy. It deals with the 'subject-world of economic epistemology', which is meant to connote both theories of knowledge underlying economics as a subject of investigation, and also the notions of 'subject' and 'world' that hold together the dominant account of knowledge in social sciences of the economic. The re-imagining of 'theory' is to draw attention to the possibility of putting into question the consensus on what we do when we theorise in economics. Similarly, the question of difference is about pointing out how modernist knowledge has always functioned by designating its Others, and the implications of this submerging of difference which becomes apparent in the inability to think of identity and the economic as terms together.

In Chapter 2, I examine how economic knowledge came to be associated with contemporary axiomatic theories and deductive nomological accounts of explanation. I discuss the many ways in which economics as a body of knowledge bears the imprints of its intellectual heritage in the tussles over science and power. In fact, the rise of economics as a discipline cannot be understood in isolation from the rise of disciplinarity and scientism itself. The structuring of knowledge in economics is an outcome of the inherent tensions in enlightenment epistemology. In modernist social science, theories are seen as a means of providing explanation of a pre-existing reality. But, far from being a timeless and universal construct, explanation is a historical and contingent political exercise which fixes the role of theory and the position of the theorist in economics in line with a wider discursive fixing of objectivity and representation in knowledge.

Chapter 3 is motivated by the limitations of undertaking an epistemological interrogation of economics as a body of knowledge which does not afford the going beyond into the questions of difference. In this sense, Chapter 2 was a vital exhaustion of the line of inquiry that remains within the ambit of considering economics as a science. As a result, Chapter 3 raises the wider questions of how the modernist rendition of knowledge relies upon an elision of difference and desires the separation of the domains of the economic, political, moral, social, ethical, and so on. At the heart of this lies a particular version of subjectivity which is itself narrowly obtained but unjustifiably universalised. Looking at the way in which ideas such as Reason and history were reconciled in influential accounts such as the Hegelian dialectic, we find that they too fixed their Others. These Others of modernist renditions of knowledge in general were also the Others of the discourse of economics as it was beginning to take shape. The Other only functioned as a limit-phenomenon and a serious intervention of difference into economic knowledge would require us to think new taxonomies of critique.

Chapters 4, 5, and 6 take on the task of one such critical exploration: that of juxtaposing questions of identity with those of the economic. In Chapter 4, I discuss the problematics of identity in economics and more generally. A critique of the abstract individual model of identity underlying economics leads to an evaluation of the wider ways in which theorists have attempted to reconcile the diversity of subjects with the desire for systematic knowledge. The eventual limitations of standpoint theory and its political correlate of identity politics are discussed, and 'politics of identity' is put forward as a way of rethinking difference in relation to knowledge. Politics of identity is a method of interrogating any coherence, whether conceptual or experiential, for the way in which it fixes difference as its Other. Rather than take identity as the starting point for thinking about difference, politics of identity requires an interrogation of texts for their construction of identity categorisations in ways that are linked to power and privilege. Chapter 5 turns to an in-depth critical assessment of the two relatively rare instances where influential economists have explicitly spoken of identity (Akerlof and Kranton, Sen). Chapter 6 moves forward by differentiating two ways of thinking about identity: the concentric view, which is based upon the self; and the translational view, which arises from an encountering of difference that takes on a complexity which is not open to easy spatio-temporal determination or assimilation. While the concentric view can give rise to 'benevolent' projects of cosmopolitan liberal humanism, taking the example of Nussbaum, this is critiqued. Instead, a translational politics of identity is proposed as a way of 'thinking out' the relation between subjects and knowledge. The ethics of translation is what makes it possible to see what is at stake in the constructions of identity that we then want to deconstruct. Surveying the separation of identity and the economic, we find that this is also the separation of culture and economy, and addressing this involves attending to the slippage between economics, economy, and the economic; rethinking the fixing of values in rational economic Value (so that *one cannot be irrational without also being uneconomic*).

The concluding chapter examines how writing economic theory an*Other* way will also be a rewriting of the conditions of theory itself. The role of economic theories as textual productions is highlighted, and its consequences in terms of the function of critique and the theory-praxis problematique is analysed. The complexities of emancipation and epistemology are invoked, and the relation between travel and theory is outlined. Finally, I stress the need for moving beyond a modernist conceptualisation of knowledge by questioning the dominant methods of economics as having a universal purchase on access to understanding the economic aspects of human life. An essential task today is to overcome the economic logic that permeates all aspects of existence and yet remains unquestioned in the terrains of knowledge production.

1.4 Signpost

> If we want to start something, we must ignore that our starting point is, *all efforts taken*, shaky. If we want to get something done, we must ignore that, *all provisions made*, the end will be inconclusive. This ignoring is not an active forgetfulness; it is, rather, an active *marginalizing* of the marshiness, the swampiness, the lack of firm grounding in the margins, at beginning and end.
>
> (Spivak 1999: 175, emphasis original)

> *You know this is not your story, but you must claim entrance into this story with a difference*. Those two things together: strategic identity reactively claimed, negotiable for struggle..., and a catachrestic relationship to the nation-state format. ... These are things that can work but if the project succeeds, they work within the circuit of a telematic society where there can be, or there already is, access to political teaching of this kind of stuff.
>
> (Spivak 1991: 241, emphasis added)

To invoke my own positionality overtly at this point – I have never experienced the story of economics as my story. As a woman from a 'Third World' country, engaging with economics both over 'there' and over 'here', I have experienced extreme dissonance with the truisms of the discipline. However, the act of faith demanded by my academic performance in economics, was also matched by an unsatisfaction with the wider 'disciplined' separation of the various contexts (economic, the political, the social, the moral, the legal, and so on) in modernist knowledge. Thus, the fault lines that I turned to in order to explore my discontent were inevitably those that cut across and not simply within disciplines. I have in mind the impact of feminist theory, poststructuralist, postcolonial, ecological, deconstructive work which challenges not simply the organisation of disciplinary knowledge, but also its insularity, its ability to be adequate, its terms of access, and its inevitable involvement in the context of its generation. Accordingly, these were all important handles for my endeavour. Appropriating Derrida's words 'in a certain spirit of Marx' (*The Spectres of Marx* 1994), my endeavour here is 'in a certain spirit' of these ethical and political vocabularies. Within economics, these lines of thought are very much a promise of the future, but an urgent and ethical promise. Combining the many forces of disciplinary segregation, institutional pressures, and ethical political imperatives has meant that heterodox scholars in economics have explored alternatives, but the conversations have a long way to go, especially regarding genuine discipline-challenging endeavours.

Amariglio (1988) once argued that an economics influenced by Foucault would look to deconstruct economic discourse as a human science. This would mean that economic discourse would not crave scientistic unity following from application of methodological and epistemological principles. Instead, by rejecting the subject/object distinction and historicising the will to truth which is the source of this distinction, the claims of rationalism and empiricism to certain or even approximate knowledge would be rejected. Also, by adopting the archaeological approach rather than traditional histories of ideas, excavations would not treat economic knowledge as a progressive, continuous, unified strand consisting of common concepts, authorial intentions, accumulation of facts, and so on. There would be space for seeing dispersion and discontinuity, and an avoidance of teleology and essentialism. Finally, such an economics would be forced to admit its intersection by relations of power. As Foucault argues (1980: 291), identification of the knowledge-power (*pouvoir/savoir*) nexus reveals the linkage of truth claims with systems of power:

> [T]ruth isn't outside power, or lacking in power: contrary to a myth whose history and functions would repay further study, truth isn't the reward of free

> spirits, the child of protracted solitude, nor the privilege of those who have succeeded in liberating themselves. Truth is a thing of the world: it is produced only by virtue of multiple forms of constraint. And it induces regular effects of power. Each society has its regime of truth, its 'general politics' of truth: that is, the types of discourses which it accepts and makes function as true; the mechanisms and instances which enable one to distinguish true and false statements, the means by which each is sanctioned; the techniques and procedures accorded value in the acquisition of truth; the status of those who are charged with saying what counts as true.

In such an interrogation of how discourses are harnessed to powerful social forces and in the name of scientific objectivity have come to constitute regimes of truth, we realise the urgency of locating all knowledge of economic life in human history, culture and power relations. This present book is an attempt to actuate these principles.

The attempt to examine the link between the preservation of structures and the structures of knowledge is also an invitation to think the violence of knowledge. One cannot represent all of one's concerns – the trouble with universalistic aspirations of (economic) knowledge; the lineage of modernist knowledge in enlightenment tensions; the paucity of axiomatic modelling that passes for most economic theory; the difficulty of even heterodox economics in coming to terms with the contextuality of all knowledge; the writing out of the subaltern and the submerging of difference in modernist narratives; the need to challenge the economism of contemporary life; the linking of questions of theory with questions of practice to demonstrate the theory/praxis divide as being unsustainable; highlighting the violence enacted by the dominance of concepts of the individual, the nation-state, the economy, liberal democracy, when their interested alignment is not questioned; the need to think not only knowledge, but also thinking itself 'Otherwise' – and also represent them adequately under the institutional constraints of present enactment. But, despite the shaky starting point and the inconclusive end that Spivak's words alert us to, the endeavour must be indispensable, even if problematic. As Connolly puts it (1991: xi):

> The will to system is a lack of experience, to say the least. To say more: within the academy it is a consummate form assumed by the will to dominate. A better alternative is to confirm simultaneously the indispensability of interpretation and the limited, porous, and problematic character of any particular effort.

And further (39),

> [t]hese microstrategies of academic containment, like their world historical predecessors, revealed how fragile and established the structure of faith is, how compelling its maintenance is to the identities of the faithful, how difficult it is to keep defeat by demonstration, reason, and evidence alone, how indispensable a discursive field of contrasts, threats, and accusations is to its internal organisation. These strategies disclose, as does their reversal, some elements in the enigma of identity in its relation to the other.

The idea that economics is what it is, and everything else is a reaction, needs subverting. Making strange the question of how we identify the economic is also at the same time a questioning of the nature of knowledge, the purpose of theory, and one's own status as supposedly foreclosed by the abstractly rational and essentially individual self.

In today's presence, I find that a re-memorising of the economic is crucial. This is not simply a 'CNNtelepoliticsGoldCardtransnationalfrequentlyflyerhome-shoppingworldbeatprogrammedtradingHungarianhiphopcrackinBenares' story (see Csicsery-Ronay 1997). The blippy digital circuits of transnationality and hyperreality have their counterparts in the innumerable who die for want of water in the heat, starve because of policy-induced famine, struggle every day simply in order to survive, lost in prisons, hospitals, in cities, by the wayside – invisibilised. When I turned to economic theory, it was because I thought a study of the economic (those crucial terms of production, distribution, and consumption, structures of work and reward, an ethical obligation to the Other) would tell me more. I found empty diagrams, foolish assumptions, and painful generalisations (on unravelling this, see Kurien 1996), passing as science – (the unstated completion) – of capitalism and neocolonial exploitation. Even more surprising was the widespread belief in the unquestionability of the economic logic, or, alternatively, an exhausted despair at its unassailability. Economics haunts me, but I believe, '[a]gainst the grain of... [its] universalising moment, however, is written the story of its own impossibility' (Sorensen 1999: 91).

Consider the following sentiment of Žižek (2002: 15)

> On the one hand, politicians have abandoned the economy as the site of struggle and intervention; on the other, economists, fascinated by the functioning of today's global economy, preclude any possibility of political intervention... yes, the economy is the key domain – the battle will be decided there; one has to break the spell of global capitalism – but the intervention should be properly political, not economic. ... In the end, the universal appeal to 'freedom and democracy', the belief that they will save us from the abuses of capitalism, will have to be challenged. Liberal democracy, in truth, is the political arrangement under which capital thrives best.[28]

The intervention does need to be one which is *properly political*, a political that washes into the economic in every sense. This is far from what can be said for the attempt at hand. But all beginnings have to be made...

28 Žižek goes on to discuss an image of a solid gold hammer and sickle studded with diamonds, the advert for an internet broker called Self-trade. The caption underneath reads, 'and what if the stock market profited everybody?' The strategy of portraying the stock market as the egalitarian communist agenda in which everybody can participate, works because 'the hammer and sickle invokes the hope that "history would eventually be on the side of those struggling for fraternal [*sic*] justice"' (2002: 15).

Part 2

Rooting and routing economics

2 Enlightenment epistemology and the subject-world of economics

Commerce gives Arts, as well as gain:
By Commerce wafted o'er the main,
They barbarous climes enlighten as they run....
Planets are merchants; take, return,
Lustre and heat; by traffic burn:
The whole creation is one vast Exchange.

(Young, in Myers 1983: 17)

2.1 Introduction

My main aim in this chapter is to 'root' the epistemological inheritance of economics in the enlightenment tensions over knowledge, thus demonstrating how the endeavour of economics is not a universal and timeless objective science, but a 'routed' body of knowledge whose underlying foundations in theory and explanation are necessarily structured by the contingent emergence of ideas in a geohistorical-temporal-ideological context in line with a wider discursive fixing of objectivity and representation in knowledge. Such a positioning of economics does not take it as a 'given', but seeks to investigate its 'coming into being', thus rendering everything open to question and nothing sacrosanct. This is important since it allows us to zoom out of the narrowly defined contestations at play in a discipline solely in the present, and to take a panoramic view of the epistemological transitions that have structured a body of knowledge so that it comes to be recognised as economics, and carries the weight of what that signifier has come to mean.

Looking at economics as a *social science* immediately raises the question of what conception of knowledge and the justification of knowledge claims, what conceptual apparatus or set of beliefs one *needs* to carry in order to see the endeavour of economics as legitimate. Economics as a body of knowledge is a 'kind' of discipline relying upon a 'particular' version of what counts as knowledge, how one approaches it, and what procedures are involved in justifying knowledge claims of this sort. I will argue that this 'particular' version of knowledge owes substantially to the Enlightenment and subsequent negotiations (of both academic and non-academic nature) and is, in fact, inseparable from the episodes and narratives of Western enlightenment modernity.

The epistemological status of contemporary mainstream economic thought cannot be considered in isolation from the context in which such knowledge foundations *came to be*. What come across as tensions in the epistemological fabric of contemporary mainstream economics as a social science, are *symptomatic* of the various difficult negotiations that have *always* been a part and parcel of any endeavour to create 'scientific' knowledge about the social world. This being the case, such tensions are especially accentuated in the case of economics, owing to its very peculiar traversing of the terrain between the *desire* for scientific objective knowledge like that (presumably) obtainable in the natural sciences, the shifting balances in the *interests* served by such knowledge (e.g., at different times, the monarchy, the parliament, the colonial administrators, the new class of experts, the corporations, and so on), and the inherent difficulty of carving out a suitable external unchanging realm of subject matter to be designated as 'economic'.

A set of themes around knowledge (I will elaborate these themes later) *which began to be understood in a particular way following on from the European Enlightenment can be termed as 'enlightenment epistemology'*. The endeavour of economics, I argue, relies upon this enlightenment epistemology and hence any inquiry into its coming into being necessarily involves engaging with the wider issues of the enlightenment era. Several key thinkers whose work was influential in what became known as the Enlightenment were also important in the newly coalescing field of classical political economy, and in the subsequent centuries the critics of the Enlightenment also criticised the forms that economic organisation took (e.g., industrialisation) and the role of political economists in this. Economics being a child of the Enlightenment, such an engagement as that in this chapter will interleave several branches of thought.

Therefore, *instead of* starting *from* the notion of a positive science based on analysing individual choice (which is the theoretical ground afforded by mainstream economics) *and then* seeking to interrogate its methodology and perhaps deliver an epistemological critique of it, I will proceed by *locating the situatedness of the enterprise of economics in the Enlightenment*, and *demonstrating how the negotiations writ into its constitution have necessarily meant that it be viewed as a positive science based on analysing individual choice*. The advantage of questioning the standard starting point in this manner is that it offers an unpacking, a re-memorising, of the construction of that fiction which passes for truth.[1] Attempting to trace such a speculative genealogy (although fragmented and incomplete) of a set of disciplined knowledge claims allows asking not only the question, why is economics the way it is?, but also the questions such as how

1 What, then, is truth? Recall the inimitable Nietzsche (1873):

> Truth is a mobile army of metaphors, metonyms, anthropomorphisms – in short, a sum of human relations which have been enhanced, transposed, and embellished poetically and rhetorically, and which after long use seem firm, canonical, and obligatory to a people: truths are illusions about which one has forgotten that this is what they are.

did we come to recognise a set of claims as economics? and, how can it be linked to other similarly negotiated abstractions and knowledge formations?

2.2 Enterprise of economics

The phrase 'enterprise of' is used to preface economics because the aim here is not to interrogate the *disciplinary method* of mainstream economics by pointing out either its absences or excesses. The methodological critiques often question the view of economics as a systematic universal social science with a legitimacy based on factual truth status, but this evaluation automatically imports unexamined notions of what counts as fact, science, and so on, into one's account. Further, because the methodological critiques often start from an unquestioned separation between method and theory in social science, they are faced with the problem of remaining within the confines of mainstream method and thus cannot address questions not translatable into that format, and at the same time they are faced with the unanswerable charge of 'then what', for criticisms of method do not then make clear how to proceed from method to substantive theory. In contrast to this, my focus here is an epistemological interrogation of the *institutionalised and situated enterprise of economics*, aiming to uncover the presumed picture of knowledge widely prevalent in *structuring* the discipline and *forming* its practitioners. It would serve to demonstrate the contingencies of this picture, the things that need to be held in place for this picture to make sense. These things may be underlying, unstated, and implicitly assumed. An epistemological interrogation can further elaborate the difficulties generated by conforming to such a picture of knowledge and can outline alternative frameworks of thinking about knowledge creation and justification.[2]

To mount an epistemological critique, it is not necessary to characterise schematically 'all' of the endeavour of economics across space and time.[3] Some clarification of terminology in relation to economics is needed however. As discussed in the introductory chapter, by contemporary mainstream economics I will denote principally the neoclassical school of thought and extensions and variations on similar themes (game theory, new classical economics, experimental economics). Implicit in these different methods is mathematical formalism and determinism. Histories of economics trace the origins of neoclassical thought in what became known as the marginalist revolution in economics, occurring towards the end of the nineteenth century. The key figures recited in this regard are William Stanley Jevons, Carl Menger, and Leon Walras.[4] Subsequently, such

2 For example, by postulating that economic theory creates rather than reflects realities, one can arrive at radically different paths of inquiry. I will take up this theme later.

3 Heterodox economists of various stripes are, of course, a significant minority within the discipline. In this text, I draw upon and engage their work when necessary; however, they are not the focus of my interrogation since they remain marginalised within the discipline. For a recent discussion about heterodox economics, see Lawson 2006.

4 They are credited with simultaneously coming up with the basis of the neoclassical doctrine. The contributions most recited are Jevons' *Theory of Political Economy* (1871), Walras' *Éléments*

a neoclassical conception of economics became entrenched, a process in which Alfred Marshall played an important role at the beginning of the twentieth century.[5] According to Perelman (1996: 14–16), Marshall was influential in the changeover of terminology from 'political economy' to 'economics'.[6] In this he was motivated by the desire to affirm the scientific status of political economy by dropping the signifier 'political' (which had resonance with *polis* or community as a whole) and thus restricting its scope to a more scientific sounding econom-ics (like physics). In the period around the Second World War, a great influx of engineers into economics combined with the increased need for institutionalising economics in the face of the Cold War meant that neoclassical formalistic rigour gained firm ground (see Mirowski 1991a). The Walrasian general equilibrium framework reformulated by Arrow and Debreu (1954) became the cornerstone of theoretical analysis. In America, Samuelson's rendering of economics became standard,[7] and even the intellectual challenges posed by John Maynard Keynes were first assimilated (although partially) and then 'watered down' following the breakdown of the macroeconomic consensus in the 1960s.[8] A certain amount of disciplinary soul-searching has always been intrinsic to the endeavour of economics, yet there are many histories of dissent that remain to be written.[9]

Standard accounts of development of the discipline sometimes locate a radical rupture in the transition from classical political economy to neoclassical economics ('the marginalist *revolution*'). There are many good reasons to differentiate

d'économie politique pure, ou théorie de la richesse sociale (1874), Menger's *Grundsätze* (1871) and *Untersuchungen* (1883). However, this was not a sudden ruptural event, as Blaug (2001: 159) points out, the marginalist revolution had a history in Cournot (1838), Dupuit (1844), von Thünen (1852), and Gossen (1855).

5 Though it should be pointed out that Marshall's style of economics was very different from that of the later neoclassicals. See Perlman (1996).

6 The story that Perelman (1996) tells is as follows: 'at the time, Sir J. R. Seeley (a historian) was appointed by the then Prime Minister Gladstone (1869) to Regius Professorship in Cambridge and he considered political economy as within the scope of his subject owing to the policy role of his Chair. Marshall deeply resented that anyone could aspire to speak of 'political economy' and hoped that the newly christened 'economics' would deter any but the scientific experts to comment on it'. According to Perelman, although writers like Sturtevant (1877) and Macleod (1878) had used the term economics before, Marshall was important in reconstituting the discipline.

Later, Lionel Robbins differentiated economics from political economy thus: 'Political Economy in my vocabulary is not scientific economics, a collection of value-free generalisations about the way in which economic systems work.... it consists of prescription rather than description' (in Sassower 1985: 15).

7 His textbook *Economics* (1948) became a classic, even to the extent of generating a two-volume response titled *Anti-Samuelson* (Linder, 1977). For a recent rhetorical reading of this textbook, see Klamer (1990).

8 It is widely agreed that the micro-foundations of macroeconomics as presented in the neoclassical format are far from adequate. One interesting piece on the problems in the aggregation of representative individuals in the economy is Kirman (1992).

9 One such example is the current work of Lee (2002), who writes about the suppression of heterodox economics dissent in the United States and United Kingdom. In this, he provides a telling account of the fate of non-mainstream economists during the McCarthy era in the United States.

between these two paradigms. Classical political economy was characterised by 'big' concerns pertaining to material prosperity in a good society – the relationship between the state and the market, the ways and means to ensure survival for large sections of the population, the manner in which commerce promoted well-being, and so on. These practical questions were often articulated not solely by an expert class of specialist knowers, but rather by 'men of the world' who were also often engaged in or connected to business and trade. In contrast, by the last decades of the twentieth century, analytical rigour had become a supreme virtue, often leading to hyper specialisms in formally characterising the economy in mathematical terms. This situation remains so today.

Undeniably, the change in emphasis and the choice of language that occurred with the shift to neoclassicism was significant, but the fundamental grounding in enlightenment epistemology remains unchanged. For, although the neoclassical phase was marked by a massive shift in its language of scientific representation, achieved in a large part by borrowing metaphors from mid-nineteenth-century energetics[10] (Mirowski 1989), the underlying model of knowledge was not radically affected. While concerns such as the distribution of well-being in society *per se*, concepts such as use-value, and extensive debates over the benefits of industrialisation, gradually dropped out with the acceptance of neoclassical economics, there were also underlying similarities between the classical and neoclassical research programmes. To mention a few such continuities, the way in which nature was incorporated into economic thought as an external provider was not challenged by the neoclassical framework where nature's bounty was still read as free goods. Similarly, the position of the social scientist in its claims to obtaining privileged knowledge about an external world was not undermined by any serious interrogation. The status of science, if anything, became even more overvalorised. Likewise, the entrenchment of liberal democratic industrial capitalism is gradually near complete. In fact, the prominent figures of classical political economy[11] – Adam Smith, Thomas Malthus, David Ricardo – have remained influential and

10 Mirowski's arguments cannot be summarised here. However, see table 5.1 (1989: 224) for comparisons between mechanics and economics, so that 'energy' gets translated into 'utility'. See also Schabas (2005).

11 I have not mentioned Karl Marx here. To a great extent, Marxism has provided a viable way of opposing mainstream economics. Yet, belief in modernism and teleology remain central to the Marxist project in its unreconstructed forms (see Caute 1973). Kanth (1997b: 82–93) provides an account of both capitalism and socialism as 'having joint provenance, philosophically, in the dialectic of the European "Enlightenment" '. He astutely points out that both Smith and Marx shared a 'confident historical materialism, with its inevitable correlates of both determinism and reductionism' (91). He further mentions reductionism, linearity, and progress, along with anthropocentrism, as features of Marxist thought. On the other hand, Marx as an antidote to bourgeois political economists (see Freedman 1961), was well aware of the interests that come into play behind what seems to be a scientific economic model (Sassower 1985: 163). Moreover, in recent times, anti/non-determinist and postmodern moments in marxist thought have been developed by various authors, such as Resnick and Wolff (1982), Amariglio *et al.* (1996), Ruccio and Amariglio (2003).

the particular intellectual agendas set by their work have not been diminished by the newer frameworks provided by neoclassical theory and its variations. It is thus the case that I will view the transition from classical political economy to neoclassical theory (and subsequent mainstream economics) as a mutation rather than a radical rupture.

With this in mind, I will now proceed to discuss the themes structuring enlightenment epistemology. The aim of discussing the enlightenment epistemology is to enable the characterisation of the social scientific endeavour of economics in such a way as to highlight *a certain general way of understanding* some key elements which hold together the disciplinary narrative. I will then argue that the received manner of understanding notions such as explanation or formalism results from *methodological* compromises *necessitated by the underlying enlightenment epistemology*. This understanding functions as the crucial joints in an installation without which it would not hold up at all (let alone hold up to scrutiny).

2.3 Enlightenment and epistemology

The Enlightenment is a vast and complex canvas which does not lend itself to any easy categorisation. It can be and has been conceptualised in different ways, and two prominent ways of invoking the concept are – to designate a historical and chronological period primarily in Europe as a time which was marked by the rise of modernity and its visions of progress; or, the term enlightenment can be used to signify a set of ideas which importantly marked a significant departure for ways of knowing the world (Hibben 1910; Berlin 1956; Hampshire 1956; Hampson 1968; Hankins 1985; Schouls 1989; Porter 1990, 2000; Outram 1995; Yolton *et al.* 1995; Israel 2001). These two senses are interlinked, but I will refer mainly to the epistemological sense of the enlightenment.

The enlightenment dialectic is fascinating, for although in some measure the tensions between affirming and rejecting, accepting and remaking ideological matrices have been (and are) a feature of every time and place, the environment in which such tensions were enacted in the period around eighteenth-century Europe were to be succeeded by numerous significant developments, including colonialism, imperialism, slavery and racism[12] – which are often signalled as deviances from the promises of modernity. But this view is sustained only if one starts from the premise that the enlightenment inaugurated the *exercise of Reason*

12 It is often seen as a paradox that the period marking the official abolition of slavery also denoted widespread racism. See Sharpe (1993: 5–6) for a discussion of this. She notes (paraphrased) that 'Nancy Stepan writes of the apparent paradox that just as the battle against slavery was being won by abolitionists, the war against racism in European thought was being lost in the first half of the nineteenth century. In the second half, racial explanations were particularly forceful because they sanctioned *both* the management of the free slaves *and* the expansion of empire.' This is not surprising if one bears in mind that, during the period of the slave trade, the slaves were not seen as human beings but as commodities, and once the trade was abolished, the erstwhile commodities began to be seen as inferior human beings.

in a knowable world, so that episodes which did not reflect such universal Reason can be seen as anomalies. This unqualified sense of seeing the enlightenment as the exercise of Reason in a knowable world is not a starting premise if one recognises the particular environment of the enlightenment in which the tension-ridden blending of conflicting persuasions took place. As only *a* way of making sense of the world, the enlightenment ideology has no prior claim on being universally privileged to deliver 'the promises of modernity'. It may instead be especially susceptible to what are often understood as 'its contradictory and illegitimate offsprings'.

What follows now is a discussion of some significant themes of enlightenment epistemology as they impacted on the notion of knowledge in the disciplinary narrative of economics. These are – the work accomplished in the realm of economic representation by the use of the machine metaphor; the status of theory and practice; the role of theory in characterising the play of forces in an external world; the (dis)embodied entity of the individual knower and its tensions with otherness; and, finally, the structuring of the realms of the general and the particular.

2.3.1 The work of the machine metaphor[13]

To the extent that we can reconstruct important themes of the enlightenment, it must be noted that to a significant degree there was a focus on *knowing*, on making sense of the world. Extreme importance was given to the possibility of understanding both the natural world and human nature by scientific methods. Underlying this belief in the ultimate knowability of the world if approached by proper scientific methods was an equally interesting notion of machines, a notion that was crucial for schematising comprehension. By using metaphors of *machines*, complex notions such as 'nature' or 'society' could be rendered comprehensible in an analogous format. Such a mechanistic rendering (crafting) of entities served many purposes. Consider the following quote on nature from Robert Boyle (in Dunthorne 1991: 9), '. . . like a rare clock . . . where all things are so skilfully contrived, that the engine being once set a-moving, all things proceed according to the artificer's first design'. There was a close correspondence between the notion of a *system* and that of a *machine*. Smith writes (in Coleman 1995: 132, emphases added):

> Systems in many respects resemble machines. A *machine is a little system*, created to perform, as well as to connect together, in reality, those different movements and effects which the artist has occasion for. A *system is an imaginary machine* invented to connect together in the fancy those different movements and effects which are already in reality performed.

13 See Black (1962) for a discussion of the functioning of metaphors and their relations to models. In economics, the influence of metaphors within the field is much debated on every side; see McCloskey (1986); Klamer and Leonard (1994); Biccheri (1988); Henderson *et al.* (1993); Ellerman (1991); Browne and Quinn (1999); Lagueux (1999).

So, the notion of *viewing* something *as* a system is closely tied to comprehending the *mechanistic* nature of systems. When considered in relation to social science, this leaves open the possibility that the machine will *eventually* produce outcomes that are good and well and proper. Even if this is not the case immediately, there are the famous 'unintended consequences' – that somehow (Deus Ex Machina) there is an invisible order which will produce beneficient outcomes (on this latter, see Ullmann-Margalit 1978). This is also helpful if conscious efforts to create change are to be kept within limits or undesirable extensions of philosophical ideas are to be contained.

An example of this is provided by Smith in his account of the *impartiality* of the impartial spectator.[14] Smith focuses on the relation between 'agent' and 'spectator', such that moral evaluation is practically achieved by imagining an 'impartial spectator'. The relation between the agent and the spectator is asymmetrical but governed by a feeling-with which Smith terms 'sympathy'. The impartial spectator sympathises with the agent and the motivation for this sympathy is the pleasure that arises from the perfect coincidence or harmony of sentiments. Note that impartiality here is defined as, 'to be prepared to act against that which we might unreflectively feel to be in our own private interest, unless on independent examination that interest is justifiable' (Griswold 1999: 140). Impartiality does *not* require 'that as agents we treat ourselves as mere parts of the moral universe on an exact moral par with each of the other such parts' (ibid.), what Smith calls 'universal benevolence'. Thus, and this is crucial, it does *not* require that one's own interests be subsumed under some greater interest (like that of the state); impartiality here takes the path between selfishness and universal benevolence. For, according to Smith (in ibid. 141, emphases added), '*the administration of the great system of the universe*, however, the care of the universal happiness of all rational and sensible beings, is the *business of God and not of man*'. And further, '[t]o man is allotted a much *humbler department*, but one much more suitable to the weakness of his powers, and to the narrowness of his comprehension; the care

14 This refers to Smith's work in the *Theory of Moral Sentiments*. I do not feel that a discussion of Smith's ideas here should necessarily be restricted to his work in the *Wealth of Nations*, simply because my object of investigation is economics as a social science. Smith's ideas in the *Wealth of Nations* are part of his larger philosophical project and it is equally untenable that there was a radical split between *WON* and *TMS*. I agree with Tribe (1999) in his assessment of *Das Adam Smith Problem* (i.e., the supposed incompatibility of human psychology underlying Smith's two works, see Sassower 1985 for a survey), which is better understood as two distinct forms of rhetorical strategies rather than divergent theories of human motivation. On Smith, see also Clark (1993); Shapiro (1993); Brown (1994a); Walsh (2000); Rothschild (2001). Finally, Mizuta and Sugiyama (1993) provides international perspectives on Smith, including the reception and influence of his work in Germany, America, France, Italy, India, China, Japan and Russia. Grampp (1951) traces the influence of Stoic thought upon Smith so convincingly that often Smith seems to be mouthing Cicero (on conceptualising materialism, advocating private property, desirability of self-interest, a teleological notion of explanation, seeing the acquisitive instinct as natural, as psychological datum) in fashioning the classical concept of the 'economic man' who was a conceptual device, a prescriptive guide (like the moral hero of the Stoics), and a typical individual.

of his *own happiness*, of that of *his family, his friends, his country*'. Thus, it is only by pursuing our self-interest in an enlightened manner that we can play our humble role in the great system of the universe whose invisible order is ultimately entrusted to higher powers.

Let us consider just a few other implications of the machine metaphor ('machine is a little system, system is an imaginary machine'). Machines have parts, but the sum of those parts is more than the parts themselves, it is a 'whole' – the way the parts are set up in a machine produces ultimate benefits that *could not have been* produced had the parts not been set up in that particular way. When we view systems in the existence of Nature, State, Society, Market they are like imaginary machines, and certain questions take a back-seat in this conception. For instance, it draws attention *away* from striving to change the 'system', a telling example of which is provided in the *laissez-faire* doctrine where it is argued best not to interfere with *the economic system*. Similarly, the hierarchies of social order in an imaginary machine become just 'different' systemic levels, each serving its purpose in the larger scheme of things. But this does not encourage us to ask the question – whose ends does the machine (State, Nature, Society, Market, conceptualised thus) serve? More pertinently, when we view 'the economic *system*', what conceptions of human beings, material interactions, and ultimate benefits are we locked-into? The focus on systems and mechanistic aspects of machines leads to a craving for systematising the social, carving out objective slices such as the 'economy', denying ambiguity inherent within the 'economic', fostering calculationism, and requiring formalisation at the level of representation which is aided by mathematics (a preferred language which satisfies these impulses).[15]

Further work accomplished by using the machine metaphor can be evident if one considers the way in which the notion of machines can be used to service the ideals of 'efficiency' or 'rationalisation' of systems. The understanding that one has of an efficient and rationalised system, especially a rational and efficient economic system, is far from innate or universal. As Porter (1994: 128–172) discusses, there was an intense debate in nineteenth-century economics on 'rigor' and 'practicality' as rival ideals of quantification.

First, there was the response to the deductive writing of political economists such as Ricardo, Jean Baptiste Say, Marx, whose work was seen as 'theoretical'.

15 It is not impossible to conceive of machines in other (less restrictive?) ways. As a contrast to the enlightenment ideals of the system and machine, consider recent poststructuralist work by authors who have appropriated a very different sense of the machine metaphor, such as Deleuze and Guattari (1983), Haraway (1985). Their work engages the machine metaphor at the human-machine boundary; however, their purpose is not the old one of distinguishing the machine and the human and putting this classification to work – rather, it is to blur this boundary and use this re-imagination for critical purposes. The 'cyborgs' in the age of globalisation and the 'desiring machines' of capitalism are an anti-enlightenment postmodern subversion carried out with due intent. Even popular culture contains echoes of some of these reimaginings – a Citroen Picasso car advertisement (UK television) presents a world of playful machines that draw upon the car body while the human factory manager is not looking, thus redoing the usual watchful-machine and error-prone-human coding.

It was considered lacking in rigour by people like William Whewell, who wrote a mathematical exposition of Ricardian economics in order to expose its errors of reasoning which would become apparent in the light of mathematical rigour. Porter writes (134) of the admiration Whewell had for Bacon and induction, and his desire to help the work of his friend Richard Jones,[16] a great advocate of statistical factuality (and induction), which motivated his project 'to join political economy to mathematics and thereby to "make nonsense of it"'. Subsequent neoclassical economics has retained the Whewellian ideas about mathematical rigour as a way of exposing theoretical excesses (see footnote 10 in Chapter 1), but not so much the inductive statistical components. Thus, today it is common to find the argument that the rigour of mathematics is a guard against theoretical excesses, but the purpose for which that argument was originally made (i.e. to further inductive statistical work) is forgotten.

Second, there was the economics of engineers and physicists (first in France, and then Britain) who were more interested in quantifying economic magnitudes in *practical* terms, drawing upon scientific vocabularies of the effectiveness of engines.[17] Drawing upon Norton Wise, Porter writes (142–143, emphases added),

> Here was a form of economic reasoning and, more crucially, a *system of economic practice that would permit scientists to judge* the productivity of machines and labour, *as well as to improve* them. In this economics, statistics of factories, workers, and production meant something. *Quantification could aid administration, could guide the improving activities of engineers and reformers*...this formulation permitted a clear distinction between useful work and waste, and indeed gave a quantitative expression of efficiency.

Third, there was the economics of mathematised utility, with pioneers in Cournot,[18] and then Walras. Porter gives an account (147–153) of how Walras's

16 Porter (1994: 133) informs us that Jones was largely responsible for the organisation of section F., Statistics, of the British Association for the Advancement of Science. This section F. in turn formed the kernel of the Statistical Society of London, ancestor of the modern Royal Statistical Society.

17 Typical examples of such practical calculation are provided by attempts to determine the 'optimal mix of machine labour with human labour'. Porter (143) cites some examples of James Thomson (engineer and brother of physicist William Thomson) – one interesting instance is Thomson calculating to decide whether it was energetically advantageous to boil urine as fertiliser, thereby producing an increase in food for human workers, or to employ the coal fire directly for productive work.

18 In the words of Porter (ibid., 148–149)

> As Claude Ménard [1978] points out, Cournot's strategy of economic mathematization depended on excluding history, with its irrationality and perpetual disequilibrium. Cournot was willing to pay the price of mathematical rationality by excluding the whole domain of *économie sociale*, all the complications that would be as mud to the pellucid waters of pure economic reasoning. The 'logical reconstruction' effected by Cournot's mathematical approach was made possible by his willingness to assume pure rationality and not limit himself to what could be ascertained empirically or applied to policy. Real economic decisions, he conceded, involve so many complex factors that practical sagacity outweighs scientific apprehension.

general equilibrium theory was understood as mathematics, but failed to generate interest as economics in the Circle of Actuaries, or, engineer economists. History decreed otherwise. Samuelson (1952: 61, second emphasis added) approvingly says:

> We may say of Walras what Lagrange ironically said in praise of Newton: 'Newton was assuredly the man of genius *par excellence*, but we must agree that he was also the luckiest: one finds only once the system of the world to be established!' And how lucky he was that 'in his time the system of the world still remained to be discovered.' Substitute '*system of equilibrium*' for 'system of the world' and Walras for Newton and the equation remains valid.

He implies that Walrasian general equilibrium theory was a discovery – of a system that already existed fully formed waiting to be uncovered. This is in sharp contrast to Mirowski and Cook's (1990) assessment of Walras's economics and its relation to mechanics.

Underlying their differences, the approaches to quantification had a shared reverence for mathematical analysis since the language of mathematics enabled simplification, erasure of lived history, and mechanistic representation.

2.3.2 The status of theory and practice

The tensions in the enlightenment thinking between 'theory' and the 'world' continue to impact deeply on economic (as on social scientific) thinking. Let me consider the issues arising from this in some greater detail. Recalling the earlier discussions on Smith, for him as for many other Enlightenment thinkers, theory and practice are separable. In fact, as we saw earlier, 'man' is probably better off taking care of his immediate self, family, and country, something to which he is more suited, than to engage in philosophical speculations. Note that this implies some sort of a split between the requirements of philosophical speculations and those of 'everyday life' (such as taking care of oneself). Such a postulation is well in line with the Enlightenment thrust of valorising, at least for the greater part of humankind, the ordinary life. This affirmation of the everyday life, the commonplace, and the ordinary is an important part of the Enlightenment. In the case of Smith, 'the vision of the dignity of ordinary life' (see Griswold 1999: 13, 174) is an important theme to be defended.[19] However, theory is not utterly humbled by this affirmation of the commonplace and the everyday business of life.

19 Griswold points out that Taylor (1989: 14–15) sees (a) the affirmation of ordinary life or the life of production and the family, (b) autonomy, and (c) the importance of suffering – as major themes of Christianity, especially (a) which 'comes to receive new and unprecedented importance at the beginning of the modern era, and which has also become central to modern culture [being] one of the most powerful ideas in modern civilisation'. In my view, it is no coincidence that the rise of modernity and that of capitalism can be read in parallel, and likewise that the importance of suffering is enacted in accounts of capitalism going through the recurring crises which enable it to proceed. Along similar lines, see Kanth (1997a, b).

On the contrary, theory comes unsutured from a direct link to an apparent world. It is not replaced by practice, a practice which is rooted in the 'world', a physicality. Practice is mediated by the materiality of the world, and its necessaries and urgencies for which theory is no substitute. As *Candide*'s closing words remind us: 'Excellently observed... but let us cultivate our garden' (Voltaire 1759). But even then the linkage between theory and practice is more complex, and one of the tasks of theory is to make sense of the world. The enlightenment impulse is to explain the extraordinary and the unfamiliar in terms of the obvious and the familiar, and theory can play a part in this.

Theory retains its classical sense of superior reflection. In the platonic sense, 'theoria' is a way of viewing the world. According to Griswold, Smith uses the term philosophy 'in senses that are perfectly familiar to us today'. What is this sense of philosophy? He answers (1999: 22), ' "Philosophy" can here mean a comprehensive account of things taken as a whole, the speculative effort to provide an explanatory system.' However, he notes that on other occasions [in *WON* I.i.9], Smith also uses the term in less familiar senses (22, emphases added), ' "philosophy" *includes the ability to understand* the structure of a thing or process *in order to improve* it: for instance, he [Smith] speaks of a "philosopher" as thinking of a method for improving the machine used in an industry'.

In Smith's vision, theoretical and moral matters are insulated. In *TMS* (III.2.19–23, Griswold 1999: 176), Smith remarks on the contrast between bitter 'literary factions' and equanimity of mathematicians and scientists. Clearly, part of the vision of the philosopher is to service the sublime to political, moral, and economic effect. Theory can result in practice, but theoretical speculation in the enlightenment era is apparently not the territory for everyone.

It is the philosopher or the theorist or the scientist who can create theoretical knowledge – and further, in the debates in economics in the nineteenth and twentieth centuries, we can see at least two senses of such 'theoretical' knowledge. One of the senses in which 'theory' in economics was seen as being excessive was a deductive, wordy, and often imprecise philosophical speculation such as that attributed to the later classical political economists. While such theory located economic thought (and thus 'the economic') in the world around the writers – in ongoing debates over taxation or production or trade, it was *not* empirical in a quantifiable (measurable) sense, and thus was not quite claspy when it came to designating the difference between what could be 'objectively' confirmed and demonstrated and what was 'mere' opinion or value judgement. The second sense in which 'theory' in economics was recognised, related more to the 'abstract', a mathematical, self-referential system where 'the economic' was located in a highly idealised version of the world. This was *not* straightforwardly empirical either – however, it could be *applied* to count as empirical work, but this is questionable. It is pertinent to the way in which these tensions were written into enlightenment conception of theorisation.

The role of the theorist, philosopher, or scientist in the enlightenment conception is a curious mix of emphases. The various pulls that the theorist needs to balance are only matched by the external world, which is itself extremely movement-oriented, by which I mean that it is a *continually balancing* system. There are, constantly, mechanisms in operation that interact and counteract to produce eventual harmony. In order for theory to do justice to this continually balancing external system, it also needs to reflect these forces, to represent them and by representation to enhance understanding, and eventual comprehension, of this complex reality. On this account, while the materiality of the world allows practice to be identified, theory needs the mind – in cognition, Reason, comprehension, imagination, and vision. Let me now discuss how this account – relating to theory as characterising a continual movement or pull of forces – was and is important in structuring knowledge in economics.

2.3.3 The play of forces in theory

The metaphor of 'play of forces' is a significant structuring device in much theory and economic theory is an attempt to best categorise these diverse opposing and interacting forces which can be conceptualised to eventually produce an equilibrium. Then, it is this promised equilibrium state which needs to be reached by manipulating these forces in the world 'out there', and often this is what economic policy aims to do. This manipulation of the forces imagined in theory constitutes application of the theory to the world, the practice. It remains, however, that, regardless of the intentions of the theorist, or the desire for pure forms of theory – no account is meant to be (or admittedly capable of) characterising the play of forces in a *universal* manner. The representations can at best be partial, as even the modernist freeze-frame technique cannot translate the whole of the presumed system into its representation. This being the reason why the famous 'ceteris paribus' (other things being equal) is needed to fix the situation. Theory must remain partial, although this does not deter its universalisation in the enlightenment epistemological schema.

Thus, we have numerous accounts of the economy demonstrating how partial equilibrium can be reached in the individual markets (a comparative static analysis), famously represented by the demand and supply curves intersecting in the Marshallian cross diagram. In this framework, the diagrammatic visual representation plays a crucial role in structuring understanding. It is not just an additional adornment, but very much the stuff of which the concept of equilibrium is operationalised in the context of economic theory. On the other hand, we have the highly stylised axiomatic mathematical formulation of the whole economy, the general equilibrium. However, these two accounts are not integrated, and as De Vroey (1999) argues, do not stand in a relationship of continuity. His thesis being, 'the generalisation of the Marshallian market does not lead to a Walrasian economy or, conversely, the Walrasian economy is not composed of Marshallian markets' (320), and that 'they are two disjointed theoretical constructs' (327).[20]

20 According to de Vroey (1999: 331), the point here is not just semantic since 'the frontier between semantics and substance may be thin'.

While mathematics proper is rather a late arrival on the scene,[21] it is more the tendency to grasp and represent the play of forces in theory that has structured economic and social knowledge since the enlightenment.

An early example of the 'interacting forces' schematology can be read in Smith. According to him, pleasure and pain inflect the passions in varying ways and degrees. This has echoes with the later Benthamite calculus of pleasure and pain, neoclassical ideas of utility and disutility, and perhaps even modern-day ideas of costs and benefits. In the context of the actor and the spectator, the spectator's willingness to sympathise with the actor's passions, to approve or disapprove of them, varies. He describes it as follows ([*TMS* VI.iii.14] Griswold 1999: 124):

> In some passions the excess is less disagreeable than the defect; and in such passions the point of propriety seems to stand high, or nearer to the excess than to the defect. In other passions, the defect is less disagreeable than the excess; and in such passions the point of propriety seems to stand low, or nearer to the defect than to the excess.

Others have noted the way in which the commerce of passions in Smith resembles a continual search for equilibrium. For instance, Heath (1995: 466) discusses how in Smith's account, when both the actor and the spectator engage the sympathetic imagination, mutual sympathy results, which is the equilibrating mechanism to ensure correspondence and social harmony. Similarly, Griswold (1999: 102–103) points that Smith often writes as though sympathy between persons is an ongoing process of adjustment, a continual search for equilibrium. He further comments how this is a process with analogies in the economic sphere, not only with respect to the search for equilibrium in supply and demand (as expressed by price), but more generally with respect to the importantly rhetorical dimension of selling and buying.

Thus, it may be argued that what economic 'theory' is and does, follows closely the enlightenment conceptions of theory. For instance, theory as something which is superior knowing, split from practice, and has a role in providing a system of explanation, is recognisable in economics. Likewise, economic theory, even when necessarily partial, needs to reflect the play of forces in the external world, which can be conceptualised to eventually produce an equilibrium.

2.3.4 The (dis)embodied knower

The next issue is that of embodiment in relation to enlightenment, epistemology, and economics. Embodiment, which is a great help in affirming the radical physical separateness of individual human beings, and allows the identification of bodies as coherent and separate *mind-containers*, needs to be surpassed (or at least negotiated) for successful theory. This can be seen in several ways. To begin

21 On this see Mirowski (1991a). Recall that the mathematisation probably begins in earnest with Cournot and then Walras.

with, there is one strand of ideas relating to embodiment that I should mention first – this relates to the way in which embodiment affects subjectivity. There is a vast feminist literature that uncovers how historically at least since Descartes, mind-body dualisms have played an important role in structuring knowledge, and, through it, social orders. This separating out of the 'pure' mind from the 'lower and baser' body is an attempt to arrive at a 'higher' knowing, a knowing free from captivity within situatedness. Resonant with this is the idea of the extent to which embodiment affects subjectivity; in the case of men embodiment does not affect their capacity for dispassionate and higher knowing, while in the case of women, their bodies overwhelm their mind, and thus leave them susceptible to the corruption of corporeality.[22] There is a body of work that traces the links between women and nature, and the construction of gender in the Enlightenment era, and the relationship of feminism and Enlightenment (see Lloyd 1993; Kramnick 1995: 560–628; Outram 1995: 80–95; Yeo 1996; Israel 2001: 82–96; Soper 2001). These are not the immediate focus of my argument here.

2.3.4.1 The signifier individual

> While I think; here I lie under a haystack. ... The tiny narrow space I occupy is so minutely small in comparison with the rest of space where I am not and which has nothing to do with me; and the portion of time in which it is my lot to live is so insignificant beside the eternity where I have not been and will not be. ... And in this atom, in this mathematical point, the blood circulates, the brain works, and wants something... how disgusting! How petty!
>
> (Turgenev 1861)

The notion of the individual that structures enlightenment epistemology is one that has been quite powerful, especially in social sciences like economics. Theory, which is not seen as directly anchored in the materiality of the world (unlike practice), is often seen as arising in response to sense-stimuli. The mind of the individual is designated as the site where the complexity and franticness of external chaos is filtered, arranged, and resolved into theory. This individual then

22 The limitation of women's cognitive capacities has been declared by many dead greats. Code (1991: 9) gives the examples of Aristotle, who contended that women's deliberative faculty is 'without authority'; Rousseau, who maintained that young men and women should be educated differently because of women's inferiority in reason and their propensity to be dragged down by their sensual natures; Kierkegaard, who saw women as merely aesthetic beings; and Nietzsche, who considered women Dionysian (sensuous) creatures as opposed to the male Apollonian (intellectual) domain. More recently, Szabados (1997) examines the significance of Wittgenstein's misogyny. Code (1991: 10) also gives the example of Wilhelm von Humboldt, who sums up this line of thought by claiming that women lacked 'analytic capacity which draws a strict line of demarcation between ego and world; therefore, they will not come as close to the ultimate investigation of truth as man.' For a contemporary investigation of body, passions, and citizenship in the US context, see Phelan (1999).

needs to be an identifiable unit in the larger scheme of things, a fully formed subsection of the systemic whole, capable of interacting with its environment in such a way as to translate some representation of that outside into the inside of the mind in a communicable format. However, these translations never completely substitute for the superior invisible order or the design of the system as a whole. There is always a residue, that does not get completely filtered between the system of the world, and the individual who is the subsection. It is this stubborn residue that lends credence to the necessity and existence of the higher order, which is variously God, Nature, or in some accounts even an imagined and idealised intermediate entity such as the impartial spectator or the ideal observer. Typically, these higher-order entities have more or greater comprehension of the systemic whole, something which is in part ensured owing to their perspective, a vision above all individual visions, a One to Many interaction. Also typically, these higher-order entities are in some way unfettered by contaminating and limiting embodiment such as that of ordinary, same, average, and common individuals.[23]

Now, what are the requirements and peculiarities that arise from this picture? The creation of knowledge is represented as attempts by individuals to grasp and translate ever greater amounts of the corpus of the system of the world. In the natural ('exact') sciences, this means the dis-covering of the immutable laws of nature, laws which govern how the system of nature operates. In the social ('inexact') sciences, at least two major problems are immediately apparent.[24] The first relates to isolation of unique and yet meaningful control contexts, and the second is the inherent unpredictability of the 'social'. Given that the standards for what counts as knowledge have developed in close relation to the successes of the natural sciences, it becomes necessary to devise ever newer methods to approximate those standards. These methods cover a wide range of spectrum, from utilising mathematics to manipulate symbols designating the complications arising from individual human interactions, to shifting what is meant by the characterisation of theory, to (regardless of the problems cited earlier) systematically represent freeze-framed sections of the social world in thought-experiments and then regard the conclusions derived therein as universally applicable (and accordingly translated into practice) by drastically undervaluing the possibilities of difference.

The idea of the individual is intricately linked to the idea of knowledge and its making. Later in the book, I will critique this essentialist view of identity as it obtains in economics. In effect, this powerful notion of the individual has served to act as the marker of all knowledge and judgement. The ready identifiability of

23 One such example within economics could be the Walrasian auctioneer (a disembodied entity with higher-order knowledge) who is required to oversee the *tâtonnement* process leading to equilibrium.

24 Of course, one way to side-step the issue is to assert that social and natural sciences are the same thing. Consider Samuelson (1952: 61–62): 'There are no separate methodological problems that face the social scientist different in kind from those that face any other scientist. It is true that the social scientist is part of the reality he describes. The same is true of the physical scientist . . . we find no differences in kind'.

this notion is ensured by the biological fixing of embodiment in personhood with its attributes of the radically split body carrying its own fully formed mind. Multiply this discrete entity many times over and we have the 'social'. Further, in order to comprehend the surrounding sociality, the individual has only to best understand itself ('Know then thyself... the proper study of Mankind is Man'),[25] something made tractable by the proposed sameness of all individuals. However, this does not necessarily imply that the mind of the individual is rational or self-transparent (in fact, thinkers such as Smith believed that it was ambiguously neither). In order to arrive at better self-knowledge, the individual (in Smith's account, the actor) uses the judgements of others (Coleman 1995: 133). But who is 'the Other' in such a picture?

2.3.4.2 Self and the Other

This is an important question, for it helps to reach at the heart of the self-other tension in enlightenment epistemology. What do we mean by 'an Other?' If we answer this question in terms of difference, that the Other is someone radically *different* from the self, then it is not possible for the self to grasp the Other. For if the Otherness of the Other is completely comprehensible to the self, then there would be no reason to call it the Other on these terms. Clearly, this is an account of Otherness which will *not* hold well in the picture of the individual and of knowledge outlined earlier. This is because it would render fundamentally unstable the *very join* of all knowledge – the knower. And it is precisely this point which *permits a crucial critique of enlightenment epistemology and of social science derived from it*, as I will elaborate later in the book. The inability of enlightenment epistemology to come to terms with *radical otherness* is evidenced

25 Perhaps some lines from Alexander Pope's *An Essay On Man* (1733–1734) will serve to illustrate.

> The glory, jest, and riddle of the world!
> Go, wond'rous creature! mount where Science guides
> Go, measure earth, weigh air, and state the tides;
> Instruct the planets in what orbs to run,
> Correct old Time, and regulate the Sun;
>
> ...
>
> But when his own great work is but begun,
> What Reason weaves, by Passion is undone.
> Trace Science then, with Modesty thy guide;
> First strip off all her equipage of Pride,
>
> ...
>
> Mere curious pleasure, ingenious pain:
> Expunge the whole, or lop th' excrescent parts
> Of all, our Vices have created Arts:
> Then see how little the remaining sum,
> Which serv'd the past, and must the times to come!

in the very way it is always possible to (claim to) see things from the Other person's point of view. This self-confident belief is at the heart of a cherished and superior rationality which is available to the Enlightenment knower and him alone. This same faculty is denied to the Other (backward peoples, savages, children, and so on) whose existence only serves to validate the self. This interrogation of enlightenment epistemology and modernist knowledge in relation to questions of radical difference and Otherness will follow in Chapter 3. For now, the question of what we mean by 'an Other' must be answered so that the Other is subsumed to the comprehension of the self (i.e. it is not a radical Other) in line with enlightenment epistemology.

In these terms, the Other who is really important is the idealised intermediate entity. The entity that spectates, observes and whose judgements or approval matter. This idealised entity need not necessarily be designated as God; in fact, in enlightenment thinking it rarely is. In Smith's account, for example, there is an asymmetry between the actor and the impartial spectator such that it is the actor who needs to view himself from the eyes of the spectator to obtain his approval, whereas the spectator out of sympathy looks at the actor's situation and approves; this mutual adjustment is motivated by the pleasure attained by a harmony of emotions. Thus, as Griswold (1999: 105) points out, Smith's view is that we always see ourselves through the eyes of Others and are mirrors to each other. The theory of moral sentiments is about the actor-spectator relationship, but it is the spectator who judges. His act of 'spectating', of being able to spectate, is what lends him superiority. Further, in spite of the radical separateness of embodiment, it remains possible to 'see' things from the other person's point of view. The theme of seeing, or vision, can be linked to the notion of perspective.[26] The theorist's vision, like the perspective of the philosopher, remains composed by the act of spectating or observation.

Another way in which difference is undervalued relates to the theme of the 'average' as 'the standard'. In line with the affirmation of ordinary life discussed earlier (in Section 2.3.2), the average standard which, as Heath (1995: 450) writes, '(almost) everyone expects (almost) everyone to employ in forming moral judgments', will be the standard of the common people. This will 'either underweight or exclude those valuations unique to a certain (minority) class or institution'. The 'strange' or the 'different' could be an error or anomaly. Coleman (1995: 135) sees Smith's concern with the normal or the average as indicative of two things. First, it makes contact with certain ideal or non-real entities (he gives the example of 'natural price'), and secondly, it falls within a deep manifestation of rationalism,[27] 'to explain the strange in terms of the mundane'.

26 As Griswold (1999: 138–139) tells us, Newton had written on optics. Smith values George Berkeley's *New Theory Of Vision* (1709). Thus, Smith compares the process of making correct visual judgements to that of exercising balanced moral judgement – the idea that just as gauging the correct proportions of various-sized objects requires a 'transporting... in fancy', similarly evaluations of Smithian Passion require a leap of imagination to the impartial spectator.

27 Coleman sees Smith as making an impartial synthesis between rationalism and anti-rationalism.

Coleman (ibid.) gives an example of the idea of the 'middle form' in Smith, the aesthetic norm which was beautiful, as opposed to monsters, 'the singular and the odd'. Monsters thus serve to *de-monstrate* the norm by exhibiting their oddness and singularity. This desire to sweep difference under the epistemological carpet is common to Enlightenment theorists such as David Hume (cf. Ferreira 1994).

It is a tension which runs deep through to present-day social scientific theorising. On the one hand, there is a desire to find general universal laws and regularities in confirmation of the sameness of 'human nature' – a powerful basis on which arguments can then be marshalled to legitimate ideas of control or even emancipation. On the other hand, there is the endless realm of perpetual lurking differences just around the corner – which liberal progressivist ideologies even now manage to cast into the enlightenment blackmail of either-or (see Foucault 1984: 32–50), so that the differences are either indications of backwardness or primitiveness (advance or progress), or a sign of debilitating and dangerous relativism. I shall discuss this in greater detail in the next chapter.

Staying for the moment with Hume, for him, we should not accept 'travellers' tales', since the commonplace of one society can easily be made to appear strange by the tales based on a foreigner's eye. Now, this is important – since, the Humean story that there are some general principles which are legitimised by experience rests on delegitimising 'travellers' tales', on the writing out of difference, of radically different perspectives.[28] While the Enlightenment treatment of *difference* is not necessarily unprecedented, it has been uniquely influential.

To recap my arguments so far, I have made the case that there was a particular confluence of the structuring elements of enlightenment epistemology such as invisible orders, theory-practice split, celebration of the average and the commonplace, mechanistic view of the world, and the like, which was especially pronounced in eighteenth-century Europe. These themes have been understood in that particular way since, and have been extremely influential in undergirding the edifice of 'social science' as a particular way of knowing, and 'economics' as one significant constellation in this universe.

2.3.5 The general and the particular

> [The fragment] is simultaneously in the whole and it is in each part. ... A fragment... involves an essential incompletion
>
> (Manjali 2001: 117)

28 This is related in Coleman (1995: 67). Other Enlightenment figures such as Voltaire did write *Persian Letters*, based in part on how French society could be made to look strange from the eyes of Turkish travellers. But these Persians are a French man's construction, so in a way it is only making Hume's point. The theme of the '(ig)noble savage' runs through the Enlightenment and after. Daniel Defoe's *Robinson Crusoe* is one example (favourite of economists, though not for all the right reasons; see Kaul 2002c ; Grapard and Hewitson 2007). For an account of *Social Science and the Ignoble Savage*, see Meek (1976).

In a large part, the debates around the salient structuring elements of enlightenment epistemology can be seen as arising from a tension between conceptions of the 'general' and the 'particular'. The '*part*icular' arises from 'part', of a presumed whole, and the terms general and particular rely on each other for their meaning and comprehension. To wit, if accounts of knowledge were to be created which made sense *not only* to the experiencer who was relating these accounts, but in a more *general and universal way* to everyone when faced with that account, then this required the *manufacturing of a consensus on understanding the world and knowledge* in some way. Therefore, the observed particulars must be assimilated in such a way as to blend in with the general telling of an account of knowing. What will be deemed as a *worthy* 'particular', or a singled-out instance or specificity seen as inviting consideration, will depend significantly on what is allowed to be seen as such within the epistemological structuring. Similarly, the way in which knowing coalesces into disciplinary knowledge will depend on the interests served by drawing the boundaries in specific ways.

A tension between the general and particular is, however, of a nature that cannot be said to have been resolved, only negotiated. For there is an inherent instability in the partitioning of general/particular which will resurface in any telling. For instance, it has been argued that one of the inherent tensions of enlightenment and post-enlightenment cosmopolitanism is the 'attempt to grasp the unity of mankind without working through the relation of part to the whole' (Bhabha drawing upon Schlereth [1977] 1996: 201). As a social science following on from the enlightenment, economics has had its share of this tension, but has remained principally a deductive enterprise, with or without mathematics. This may be owing to the nature of a 'science' of 'society' – a body of knowledge that has claims to provide *control* over the *understanding* of certain social interactions (as exemplified by the phrase 'science as *systematic knowledge*'). It is easier to achieve such systematic understanding (or epistemic control) by *establishing generalities* and then seeking to rein or tie them in, than it would be by engaging in an (in)finite study of particulars which may not satisfactorily add up, leaving the possibility of an anarchy, the epistemic riot of interpretation.[29] The establishing of generalities allows particular particulars to be identified and sifted, and enables the 'disciplining' of comprehension, psyche, and even desires.[30] The appeal to the general can thus be read against the grain as the invitation of repressed particulars.

Let me make two points relating to the Enlightenment negotiation of the general/particular. First, Enlightenment thinkers linked the 'general' to that which arises from experience. General rules thus arise out of experiences, but not everyone's experiences could give rise to general rules. In a remarkably

29 One might also add, all ideas are cumulatively built but singly discarded.

30 In 1881, Henry James wonders, 'How can places which speak so to the imagination *in general*, not give to it the particular thing it wants?' (Preface to the *Portrait Of A Lady*, emphasis original).

self-referential gesture, we see that Hume writes out traveller's tales – *the generalities were to be valued universally, but were not universally derived.* Further, in order to be able to string one's experiences into generalities, among other things, one needed to possess Reason. Again, not everyone was thought as being capable of possessing Reason – the philosopher-spectators certainly thought themselves as having a greater claim to Reason and understanding.[31] By ruling out certain forms or certain actors' testimony as possibly valid enough to be generalised, the dangers of the epistemically rioting particular were somewhat averted. However, this was not achieved without making 'difference' the perpetual remainder; aversion to anomalous particulars also wrote out undecidability.

Second, the notion of 'essences' is another favoured stop in the travels between the general and particular. Coleman (1995: 73) discusses the Enlightenment penchant for the general man. He draws upon Carl Becker and other twentieth-century historians to argue that enlightenment history was not interested in the diversity of humankind's experience; it was interested in explaining its general character; they were searching for 'general man'. Becker (1932) writes:

> Man in general, like the economic man, was a being that did not exist in the world of time and place, but in the conceptual world, and he could be found only by abstracting from all men in all times and all places those qualities all men shared (in Coleman ibid.).

Recall the account given (some paragraphs earlier in Section 2.3.4.1) of the 'individual'. This concept of the individual which functions as the very join of enlightenment epistemology is not an account of an *actual* individual. Consider Bulgakov (2000: 256, emphasis original)

> [Political Economy] replaces the individual personality as the universal actor, as the living source of all that is new in history, with the *economic machine* postulated by Bentham and reminiscent of the contemporary automatic dispenser: if you deposit a coin, it will produce a candy or a piece of soap, but no more. All constructions of the economic man, whether individual or collective, are in fact based on the image of an economic machine.

Rather, the signifier individual was an essence which plays an important role in the Cartesian framework (the self-transparent thinking and knowing being of *Cogito Ergo Sum*). While the essence of what it meant to be an individual was elevated, this did not necessarily imply individualism straightforwardly, since not everyone could aspire to be the 'individual' of Enlightenment knowledge.

In this discussion about essences, it is perhaps worth speculating on the relations between the philosophical (and social scientific) faith in essences of

31 Diderot writes, 'There are some readers whom I do not, and never shall desire. I write only for those with whom I should enjoy conversing. I address my works to the philosophers; so far as I'm concerned, there is no one else in the world' (in Dunthorne 1991: 17).

social entities and the valorisation of the experimental method (following Bacon). Science, as the ultimate human endeavour to translate the book of 'nature', was (and still is) about getting at the very heart of the unknown ('mysteries of nature').[32] The notion of experimentation, examining and analysing, is spurred by the desire to extract – to squeeze the essentials, the vital core, the kernel, the basic essence – out of any process. When this logic is approvingly applied to social science, the essences do not emerge at the end of a process of understanding (since outright experimentation is largely not possible), but are *prefigured as the very beginning* of any process of understanding. Nietzsche (1873) describes the formation of concepts thus:

> Every word immediately becomes a concept, inasmuch as it is not intended to serve as a reminder of the unique and wholly individualised original experience to which it owes its birth, but must at the same time fit innumerable, more or less similar cases – which means, strictly speaking, never equal – in other words, a lot of unequal cases. Every concept originates through our equating what is unequal. ... [We call a person honest.] ... We know only numerous individualised, and thus unequal actions, which we equate by omitting the unequal and by then calling them [honest] actions. In the end, we distill from them a *qualitas occulta* with the name of 'honesty'.

'Essences' thus become serviceable to 'generalities', which are the concatenations of abstract concepts (such as the general man arrived at by abstracting out all wo/men) on which to build social science.

The role of the theorist (*qua* economist) in this context is not easy as it involves constantly accommodating the observed particulars into the generalities of the prefigured essences. Keynes (1924), in writing on Marshall, contemplates the 'rare combination of gifts' that the 'master economist must possess' (in Wilmore 2002). Keynes writes (emphasis added),

> he [master-economist] must be mathematician, historian, statesman, philosopher – in some degree. He must understand symbols and speak in words. He must *contemplate the particular in terms of the general, and touch abstract and concrete in the same flight of thought.* He must study the present in the light of the past purposes of the future.

Thus we find a curious juxtaposition of the mechanistic with the hermeneutic, especially when considered in the light of the role of the theorist

32 Much of this world-view is still enacted every time the media in the twenty-first century relates the attempt of heroic scientists to decode the human genome – the 'book of human nature'. Not so long ago, research into female sexual arousal was reported along the lines of 'If you don't know how the machine works, you can't fix it when it doesn't' ('Love rats point to female sex drug' 2002). More recently, the Japanese health minister said: 'Because the number of birth-giving machines and devices is fixed, all we can ask is for them to do their best per head' ('Japan women called child machines' 2007).

(scientist/philosopher/economist). There is one conception where the world is a system of many forces, like a machine with its movements which lend themselves to comprehension by the scientist seeking after objective truths to string generalities out there, and there is another conception where there is an appeal to the knower to 'understand' the particulars of world by imbuing them with 'meaning' derived from experience. To conclude, this overlay is insufficiently negotiated in the enlightenment.[33]

2.3.6 The section revisited

Until now I have discussed enlightenment epistemology through various *themes* which have served to structure knowledge, such as the importance of machines, the invisible order, the affirmation of ordinary life, the theory/practice split, the status of embodiment, the signifier individual, the self/other tensions, and the negotiations of the general/particular. These discussions have in turn attempted to set forth the *salient emphases* of the enlightenment epistemology on: explaining the unfamiliar in terms of the familiar; the possessing of Reason; the world as a system existing already performed; the possibilities of observability, discreteness, comprehensibility, measurability, and commensurability in relation to knowledge; the notions of essences or ideal-types; the notions of average; the significance of generalisations. In what follows, I will consider aspects of the subject-world of economics and characterise its imprints in enlightenment epistemology.

Before proceeding to this next section, it is important to point out that my consideration here is limited to locating the epistemological structuring of economics in the methodological compromises necessitated by the various emphases of enlightenment epistemology. But there is another avenue of inquiry not fully explored by this, and this is the curious relation of the Enlightenment age to the marketplace (on related themes, see Delany 1999; Gagnier 2000). As many authors have noted, enlightenment ideas gained ascendancy in the commercial climate of early capitalism, and the avid consumers of enlightenment ideas have been identified as the rising middle classes. These consumers were also the intended target of the principal enlightenment authors, and are sometimes explicitly identified as being so.[34] The texts of the Enlightenment period were thus often in a symbiotic

33 Put another way, there is an insufficient negotiation of the hermeneutic moment in enlightenment epistemology. For instance, appeals to the Reason of a transparent self for the accomplishing of higher goals requires a well-grounded hermeneuticist understanding (of the self, of the world, of the importance of striving for ideals), *but* this vast importance of the *actual processes* of understanding is at the same time negated in favour of a mechanistic systemic (machinic) world-view, where the 'familiar' is the 'obvious'.

34 Dunthorne (1991: 17) quotes the characteristic remark of Lord Chesterfield, 'All reasoning is thrown away upon the people; they are utterly incapable of it.' By people, Chesterfield means the masses. Dunthorne (18) further comments: '[f]rom sociological point of view, in short, the Enlightenment was an elite addressing elites.' Also recall Diderot's comments from footnote 31 earlier.

relationship with the publishing industry of the times. Dunthorne (1991: 18–20) mentions the popularisation of scientific theories in simpler versions, the development of serial publishing, and the unworried attitude of the authorities towards the trade in literary smuggling (the high price of banned texts in the market confined circulation to the educated and well-to-do clientele). Enlightenment conception of knowledge did not demand ascetic self-denial as the path to higher forms of knowing (as perhaps elements in the medieval scholastic tradition did). Quite the contrary, it commercialised (among other things) appeal to ethics by 'selling' enlightenment culture as the 'in' thing to the consumers with increasing wealth. The sphere of knowledge was thus not separated from concerns of 'materiality', but interlinked.

Finally, I will move on, but pause just to venture a hypothesis – that the particular forms of knowledges (both of science and of society) arising in the Enlightenment age, and structured by enlightenment epistemology, share the Enlightenment era's relationship to the marketplace. The disciplines that were institutionalised based on these particular forms of knowledges all share this genealogy, and thus rest on an unexamined 'economic logic' of the marketplace as it was understood at the onset of modernity. This includes economics, which is *not* a study of the logic of the marketplace, but a no-holds-barred affirmation of it, which successfully places it as the *beyond of investigation*.[35] Thus, even the most pertinent and extensive critiques of modern disciplines (like economics) take an understood 'economic logic' for granted, and therefore do not excavate the precise ways in which this logic came to be established in the last few centuries, radiating outwards from Western Europe. This is a concern which motivates the present work, and is a pertinent strand running through this text.

2.4 Subject-world of economics

I now consider the subject-world of economics and unpack some of its received understanding to demonstrate how this is firmly linked to the underlying enlightenment epistemology. It is extremely important to emphasise that I am *not* undertaking to deliver a methodological critique of economics in the following sections. Where relevant, I will refer to the literature in the field of economic methodology, but this is *not* the focus of my endeavour. This is because a large part of the methodological literature takes the body of knowledge titled 'economics' as given, whereas it is precisely *this grounding* of a body of knowledge *as*

35 Consider Bulgakov (2000: 258):

> Political economy was born under the star of commercialism, that is, of completely practical motives, of the need to figure out the complexities of the economic mechanism. It is the child of capitalism and is in turn the science of capitalism; it provides instructions for proper economic behavior.

economics with its associated (and accepted) characteristics that I wish to interrogate.

2.4.1 Questions and the aim of economic theory

Let us start by considering the following closing remark of McLachlan and Swales (1978: 21, emphasis added):

> Our present aim...to suggest that economists should seriously consider the *question of what the aim of economic theory should be and why it should have that particular aim*. Without acceptable answers to these questions the promulgation of economic theories seems pointless.

There are at least two (relatively) recent notable attempts to ask such fundamental questions. The second one is by Mirowski (1994b: 50–74), and, like the first one, it is titled, 'What Are The Questions?' These questions require a rethinking of the very basis of economics, and much of this book takes on their spirit. The questions that Mirowski discusses are as follows:

Question 1: What are the standards?
Question 2: What is so 'social' about social science?
Question 3: Are we constituted by our subject matter?
Question 4: How are we so pure?
Question 5: Why does much economics look like bad applied mathematics?
Question 6: Is experimentation really impossible in economics?
Question 7: What is neoclassical economics, anyway?

The first article of the same name was by Joan Robinson (1977: 1318–1339), a fascinating piece with these words on the very first page, '...there is no such thing as a "purely economic" problem that can be settled by purely economic logic...'. Mirowski summarises the signal topics that Robinson's 'characteristically uncompromising essay' broached as follows:

1 To what extent is orthodox economics driven by ideological error, and why does it persist?
2 Does the subject matter of economics change too frequently to underwrite its putative 'laws'?
3 Why cannot neoclassicals adequately encompass the passage of historical time in social life?
4 What is economic growth for, or what can we hope to achieve as an affluent society?
5 Why does so much of economics take the organising principle of the nation-state for granted?
6 And finally, to what extent can the evolution of economic explanation be comprehended as the 'choice' of (in)appropriate methods, for instance, opting for mathematics instead of participant ethnology?

And one can only agree with Mirowski (50) when, immediately after, he writes

> But now, Robinson is dead, deprived of the Nobel Prize that was rightfully hers; and I glance at various recent books with 'Philosophy' or 'Methodology' yoked to Economics in their titles, or at the journals *Economics and Philosophy* or *Methodus*, or attend various conclaves of economists and philosophers, and, by and large, those questions are no longer on the agenda. Perhaps some of my colleagues think that is just as well, bidding good riddance to what they perceive as naive rubbish. But some, myself included, feel that what we have left is diminished, desiccated, and not a little sad.

Another way of going about it is that adopted by Garfinkel (1981), who considers, 'if social science is the answer, what is the question?' Analogously, we could ask, 'if economics is the answer, what are the questions?' There is a whole range of issues involved here, and before I proceed, let me attempt to tease out some of them. There is, first of all, the issue of the questions that need to be posed to any body of knowledge, questions (at their broadest) as to what that knowledge is about. Further, in *what way* can these questions be posed, that is, which aspects of the claims to knowledge can be contested, against what, and how? There is the related concern about the questions that *cannot* be asked legitimately of a body of knowledge, questions that are either non-translatable (meaningless) or enforced as illegitimate within a particular paradigm. The (contemporary) dominant view of science and social science is one where there is a *process of inquiry* to arrive at newer and/or better understanding of phenomena deemed to be of interest. Albeit simplified, this is not an oversimplified rendering of what most people see anything with the signifier 'science' as doing.

Let me illustrate. It is extremely useful to be faced with this reverse genealogical questioning to realise that a body of knowledge currently titled economics is *not* a response to the same set of questions which have remained universal, eternal, and fixed. Rather, the nature of questions has changed (and will continue to change) over time, and at any given time there will always be a contested boundary between questions that are addressed and those that are not. This is in the very nature of power relations that constitute the questions of interest in the creation of knowledge. Now this may seem like an obvious enough point. But, when one confronts last century's most commonly accepted definition of what economics is, one realises the need to foreground this crucial point about the contingency of knowledge. Robbins (1932, in Stigler 1984: 301) defined economics as 'the science which studies human behavior as a relationship between scarce means which have alternative uses'; the conjunction of endless human wants and scarce resources with alternative uses. This places economics as a scientific response to the eternal fixed questions of how to satisfy endless human wants in a world of scarcity. This belief in the 'prevalence of scarcity – always and everywhere' has become an article of faith almost beyond assessment (economic scarcity, unlike physical scarcity, is defined to exist perpetually, since, no matter how much the resource, human wants are always endless). Wennerlind (2000) develops the argument on the historical specificity of scarcity, linking it to the rise of capitalism. He argues that scarcity is not a universal pre-existing condition, but rather a societal condition created by the confluence of a particular set of historically specific institutions, and the result of rules of conduct prescribed by economic theory in its quest for efficiency, utility, and profits. Therefore, 'by assuming that scarcity is perpetual and ahistorical, modern economics becomes relevant as "cosmology" ' (ibid.: 4). This focus on a purportedly scientific response to universal scarcity obviates consideration of situations of extreme plenty *coexisting* with those of extreme deprivation, as a rational organisation of resources under the world-view of economics.

2.4.2 Grounding explanations

> Explaining metaphysics to the nation
> I wish he would explain his Explanation
>
> (Byron 1824)

We can view this example in terms of Garfinkel's notion of *explanatory frames*, 'a model or paradigm of a form of explanation and an object to be explained' (1981: 7). We need a concept of explanatory frames because we realise that 'there are not only different explanations but different conceptions of what explanation *is*' (ibid.: 4, emphasis original). Thus, with reference to the explanatory frame of contemporary economics, we can figure out what would and would not count as an explanation and of what, to be seen as legitimate. But further, it allows us to see the particular grounding of the explanatory frame *itself* in historical, temporal, and ideological terms. The concept of explanation provides a good handle to refer to the subject-world of economics. Explanation is most often cited as the aim of theory. But, just as there is debate over the exact status of theory (and its aims), similarly there is much debate over the nature of explanation. What do we mean by explanation in the social sciences?

There can be different understandings of what one means by an explanation (what counts as having provided a satisfactory explanatory account), and the particular questions and *kinds* of questions (e.g., the 'why-questions') considered significant. The particular form of explanation that is most often the (unstated but understood) aim of theory in economics is – deductive explanation. However, this by itself does not tell us much. It is important to attempt to understand *why and how* this particular form of explanation came to be centre stage in economics. This will involve providing different prominent accounts of explanation (Aristotelian, Galilean or Newtonian) over time, and the particular rendering of the concept of explanation by theorists (Duhem, Mill) following on from the Enlightenment, and subsequent twentieth-century theorists (Hempel).

The motivations which played an important role in the way the (eventually prominent deductivist) concept of explanation was grounded in economics were also extremely influential in the *related developments* of the rise of formalism and the associated role of mathematics. In what follows, I will trace the epistemological basis of these developments.

To begin with, let me revisit the relation between explanation and the nature of questions. Garfinkel (ibid.: 7) writes:

> Explanations are sometimes answers to explicit questions. ... But often there is no explicit question at hand, and in those cases it can be very instructive to perform a kind of diagnostic inference and ask what question the explanation is really answering. ... The emphasis on questions, and on ferreting out the implicit question behind an explanation, is crucial. ... Attending to the questions rather than the answers and looking for the implicit question hiding behind the answer are a useful device for analyzing explanations and understanding historical shifts.[36]

The shifts in explanatory frameworks are marked not just by the answers that they give, but equally by the questions that they ask. To illustrate this, Garfinkel (7–10) gives the example of the shift from medieval to Newtonian theories of motion. In relation to an object in motion, the medieval physicists asked the question, 'Why does it keep moving?' and provided the answer in terms of force called 'impetus'. Newton rejected such forces, and did not offer an alternative explanation for why the object keeps moving. Instead, on his explanation, things do not need anything to keep moving, and this question was mistaken. According to him, an object in motion just tends to remain in motion unless acted on by an outside force. The shift to the Newtonian explanatory frame marks the shift to the question '[w]hy the motion of an object *changes*?' Drawing upon Toulmin (1961), Garfinkel writes that, in the Newtonian explanatory framework, 'the body's motion is treated as *self-explanatory*'. It is this self-explanatory aspect which signals that one has *reached the outline* of the explanatory frame in use. Thus, this could be formulated in very loose terms as – understanding usually presupposes further implicit understanding.[37] It is important to understand that there is some eventual basis for knowledge claims and it is not clear that this basis is explainable in some final sense (as we shall see later, it can be inexplicable or self-explanatory). However, the relation between explanation and questions can be seen in the light of the 'why-question' (i.e. explanation as an answer to the why-question) and its distinguished history.

36 Soon afterwards, Garfinkel (1981: 8) provides this very interesting quote from Marx: '[f]requently the only possible answer is a critique of the question, and the only solution is to negate the question'.

37 Cf. Whitehead (1933: 197), 'No science can be more secure than the unconscious metaphysics which it tacitly presupposes.'

2.4.2.1 Causality and explanation

Now, causality and explanation are not the familiar territory in relation to economics.[38] John Hicks[39] in his unconventionally titled book *Causality In Economics* (1979), writes (1):

> Causality and economics, which I have joined in my title, are words that are not often found together. Causality, the relation between cause and effect, is thought to be the business of philosophers; economists, though they often talk about effects and sometimes (perhaps less frequently) about causes, are usually content to leave the question of the meanings of these terms to others. I have come to think that this is a pity.

Hicks is just the person to begin from, because as a prominent economist and economic historian writing in the latter half of the twentieth-century, we find in his accounts of causality, explanation, theory, science – the negotiations of these themes as they have been constituted historically, with the special accommodations necessitated in the light of enlightenment epistemology in economics.

Hicks describes 'Old Causality' as a system of thought in which 'causes are always thought of as actions by someone; there is always an agent, either a human agent or a supernatural agent' (ibid.: 6). This way of looking at causes and effects in a theologico-legal manner was almost universal until the eighteenth century: 'it originated in a time when men understood very little of the things that surrounded them' (5–6). He observes that in the literature of the seventeenth and eighteenth centuries, this Old Causality broke down as questions began to be raised about the moral quality of the supernatural actions.[40] Hicks writes that the solution to this was found by the Enlightenment philosophers such as Hume and Kant (and Gibbon), who provided the 'New Causality'. The *Old Causality* was based on an association between *Causality* and *Responsibility*, and this needed to be rejected. In the system of thought referred to as the *New Causality*, *Causality is a matter of Explanation*. This is an important change as, 'when we explain, we do not necessarily praise or condemn' (7). Clearly, Hicks is setting up a contrast between the pre- and post-Enlightenment notions of causality, to argue that, following on from the Enlightenment, causality was tied to explanation. But what is the significance of this?

> Causation can only be asserted, in terms of the New Causality, if we have some theory, or generalisation, into which observed events can be fitted; to suppose that we have theories into which *all* events can be fitted, is to make a large claim indeed. It was nevertheless the claim that thinkers of the eighteenth

38 The recent critical realist work in economics is an exception to this; see Lawson (1999a).

39 Hicks was jointly (with Kenneth Arrow) awarded the Nobel Prize for Economics in 1972. His major texts include *The Theory of Wages* (1932), *Value and Capital* (1939), and *Capital and Growth* (1965). See Hahn (1990) for a survey of Hicks' work as a theorist.

40 He gives the examples of Milton's *Paradise Lost* and Voltaire's response to Pope's *Essay On Man*.

> century, dazzled by the prestige of Newtonian mechanics, were tempted to make; not, even then, that knowledge of 'natural laws' was already complete, but that it was on the way to completion; a complete system of natural law seemed just round the corner. … But just because it is incomplete, it is capable of being improved. And there are no bounds to the improvement that one may attempt to undertake; there are no events which one may not attempt to explain.
>
> (Hicks 1979: 8–9, emphasis original)

The New Causality (as Hicks calls it) was a product of the enlightenment epistemology – with its faith in the complete *system* of natural laws composing an *invisible order* to the *machine*like universe, the belief in the value of *generalisations*, and *comprehensibility* of knowledge. To assert causation was no longer to imply the responsibility in terms of a human or supernatural agent; it was *simply an application of theory*, an exercise in explanation.

But if causality is understood as an exercise in explanation by Hicks writing in the twentieth century, '[i]n a statement of causality, theory is being *applied*' (1979: 8, emphasis original), then *how and where does this notion of explanation come from*? I argue that, from its Aristotelian origins, explanation slowly underwent changes into, *first*, a Newtonian (also alternatively called Galilean) format which was adopted by the Enlightenment until the eighteenth century, and by the classical tradition of economists. *Then*, in the nineteenth-century, it was given an empiricist cast by Mill, a format which was adopted by twentieth-century positivists, and by the neoclassical tradition of economists. All this while the concept of explanation accumulated heritage which was Aristotelian in origins, but mutated through the Enlightenment and the nineteenth- and twentieth-century renderings.

Harking back to the debate over the general/particular (Section 2.3.5), Coleman (1995) presents the contrast Smith made between explanation by general principles and explanation by specifics in terms of 'Newtonian' and 'Aristotelian' methods. He quotes Smith (137, emphasis added) thus,

> … in Natural Philosophy or any other Science of the Sort we may either like Aristotle go over the Different branches in the order they happen to cast up to us, giving a principle commonly a new one for every phaenomenon; or in the manner of Sir Isaac Newton we may *lay down certain principles known or proved in the beginning from whence we account for several Phenomena connecting all together by the same Chain*. – This latter we may call the Newtonian method is undoubtedly the most Philosophical, and in every science whether in Moralls or Natural Philosophy etc., is vastly more ingenious and for that reason more engaging than the other.

Smith favours the Newtonian method, or explanation by general principles.[41] Now, modern economists and methodologists alike don't speak very much about

41 According to Coleman (1995: 137), 'Smith did not seek to derive all from one principle; but neither is he content to derive all from many.'

explanation, and, no doubt, if they were queried on this, at least some of them would respond with the Wittgensteinian dictum (whereof we cannot speak, thereof we must be silent).[42] However, it is still interesting to trace the epistemology of that 'cannot'.

Referring to the title of Smith's book, *An Inquiry into The Nature and Causes of the Wealth of Nations*, Hicks writes that he must have been thinking in terms of the New Causality (i.e. link of causality with explanation instead of responsibility). And so we find, '[e]conomics, ever since that day, has been committed to the New Causality, to the search for "laws", or generalisations, on the basis of which we can assert something about the causes of events' (1979: 9). In understanding further this commitment evidenced in economics to a particular form of theory – generalisations, employing deductivist mathematical formalised models, and its basis in influential notions of scientific explanation (see Chapter 1) – we need to journey from Aristotle to Mill and forward.

2.4.2.2 Aristotle on explanation

So, how can we interpret Aristotle on explanation?[43] To begin with, for Aristotle there are different kinds of knowledge – not only is there scientific or theoretical knowledge, but he also admits of practical and productive knowledge.

Aristotle has a doctrine of causes (*aitiai*) which sets out four causes of (or explanations for) things – the matter, form, goal or end, and motion-originator of the thing. Now, although Aristotle wrote of these four things as 'causes', the sense of the word *aitiai* in his time was much wider than the current understanding of what we mean by a 'cause'. In contemporary philosophical accounts of causation, the idea of an efficient cause relates principally to a succession of cause and effect in the sense of the fourth Aristotelian cause (the motion-originator). Therefore, contemporary scholars regard Aristotle's doctrine as setting out not just four causes, but four explanatory principles.

42 Hahn replies in this fashion to Backhouse in the issues of *the Royal Economic Society newsletter* (1992). First, Hahn, as a retiring Cambridge economist in his 'Reflections' (1992a), advises young economists that economics is not in a crisis, and that one need not worry about methodological discussions. He writes, 'Here is an old man's advice – don't worry. If you are very able and creative you will be heard and reap the benefits. If you are not, then you don't deserve to and there are many other attractive opportunities besides academic economics.' Subsequently, Backhouse (1992) asks the question in an article 'Should We Ignore Methodology?' and Hahn (1992b) replies: 'Answer To Backhouse: Yes.' In his answer, Hahn quotes Wittgenstein, and further writes, '. . . [a]s for them [young economists] learning philosophy, whatever next? Philosophers themselves tell us that theirs is not a 'linear' subject. The same questions have been debated for thousands of years. They form schools. Schools of economics are bad enough. Add to that schools of economic philosophy and we can pack in. (There is no reason of course why one should not read philosophy for recreation).' Indeed!

43 I will mainly follow the reading of Aristotle (and later Mill) after David-Hillel Ruben 1990 – hereafter DHR (77–109 and 110–154). Please note that my reasons for bringing in Aristotle are sharply divergent from the attempts to argue for a 'return to Aristotle' for a 'moral' economics (on this see Crespo 1998; van Staveren 2001).

Thus, to know something is to have an explanation for it, to have grasped the 'why' of it. Aristotle is offering a classification of different 'kinds' (*topoi*) of explanation; it does not mean that every thing has an explanation in each of the four senses, just that these four kinds of explanation exhaust the concept of explanation, or what it means to have grasped something in the fullest possible way. We can see that Aristotle has a very wide concept of explanation, or what it means to have explained or gained knowledge of something. But what is this concept of explanation based upon? If these four kinds of explanation are non-arbitrary, then they must have some grounding basis.[44] The grounding basis is – Metaphysics.[45]

The general Aristotelian account of explanation places a reliance on obtaining knowledge about something in terms of being able to 'explain' it. When it comes to *scientific* knowledge (episteme), the requirements of explanation are different than for general knowledge.[46] With Aristotle, 'science' has already become a special knowledge requiring a special notion of explanation. He writes (DHR 1990: 96 [*Posterior Analytics PA* I, 2, 71b8ff.]):

> We suppose ourselves to possess unqualified scientific knowledge of a thing, as opposed to knowing it in the accidental way in which the sophist knows, when we think that we know the cause on which the fact depends, as the cause of that fact and of no other, and further, that the fact could not be other than it is . . .

Possessing 'unqualified scientific knowledge' for Aristotle requires both knowledge of the bare fact (knowledge *that*), as well as knowledge of the reasoned fact (knowledge *why*). So, scientific knowledge of something involves being able to give an explanation of it, but also being able to know that it could not have been otherwise. DHR (96–97) sums this up as,

A :x knows that the reasoned fact that p (knows why p) iff,
(1) for some q, x knows the bare fact that q is the explanation of p, and
(2) (x knows that?) ~p is impossible.[47]

44 DHR writes (84), 'Aristotle appeared to have some reason for thinking that these four modes of explanation were exhaustive of the sorts of explanation there are: "It is evident, then, even from what we have said before, that all men seek the causes named in the *Physics*, and that we cannot name any beyond these" (*Metaphysics* I, 10, 993a 12–15).'

45 Aristotelian theory of explanation is 'ultimately grounded on and to be justified in terms of metaphysics' (DHR 85). To understand this metaphysical basis of Aristotelian explanation, one needs to appreciate what Aristotle means by 'Substance', and this is defined by Moravcsik as 'a set of elements with a fixed structure that moves itself towards self-determined goals' (ibid.). It is easy to see that each of the four factors in the definition of substance correspond to the four elements of explanation – the element, the structure, the motion originator, and the goal.

46 This is in contrast to Plato, for whom explanation whether in science or generally must have the same requirements.

47 'x knows that' is placed in brackets with a question mark because this is ambiguous in Aristotle's text.

The special requirements of explanation are (A1) that one has an explanation of what one knows, and (A2) that one knows the necessity of what one knows. Such scientific knowledge has as its objects *laws* which can be deductively demonstrated. With regard to *scientific knowledge, Aristotle has a deductivist theory of explanation*. For Aristotle, a scientific explanation must therefore be as an argument, a *demonstration* – a deductively valid syllogism from necessary premisses to a necessary conclusion.[48]

There is, then, a *trilemma* about explanation (and about epistemic justification) which can be stated (DHR: 103, emphases added) as follows,

1 either explanations *regress ad infinitum*, or,
2 there is some *circularity* in explanation, so that something can be part of the explanation for itself, or,
3 there must be some *ultimate* explanans which is itself inexplicable or self-explanatory.

According to Ruben, Aristotle's theory (like Plato's) agrees with the third alternative, that there are ultimate explanantia which are *self-explanatory*, that there is such a thing as '*non-demonstrable understanding*'. Recap – *scientific* knowledge (*unlike* general knowledge) involves knowledge of *laws* to be attained by *deductive* explanations which are *syllogistic* forms of demonstrative reasoning fulfilling certain special requirements. But, the *ultimate* first principles of such scientific knowledge are *self-explanatory*, and *not* further *explainable*. How then do we get to these ultimate first principles of science?

One possible interpretation of arriving at the ultimate first principles relies upon obtaining them by a *process of induction* (epagoge) from *particular instances* (DHR: 100, 104). However, even if we get to know the primary premisses by induction, these particular instances cannot provide the explanation for the ultimate principles of a science. Rather, it is the ultimate principles which explain the particular cases. Aristotle does *not* believe that the 'particular' can be 'explained' in scientific knowledge. The objects of scientific knowledge are 'laws', but, in order to produce scientific knowledge of such laws by deductive demonstrations, it may be possible that the ultimate first principles are arrived at by a process of induction from particular instances (the particulars which do not explain, but are themselves explained by the general laws).

Let me sum up some *important trails* here. For Aristotle,

- There is more than one kind of knowledge; especially, there is scientific knowledge, but also there is practical or productive knowledge.

48 Further, such syllogisms must meet the following six requirements: the premisses must be (1) true, (2) primitive, and (3) immediate. The premisses must be (4) prior to the conclusion drawn from them. They must be (5) explanatory of the conclusion, which itself must be true. And finally, (6) they must be more familiar (in nature and to us) than the conclusion.

- The requirements of scientific explanation are different from those of general explanation because scientific knowledge involves knowing both the explanation of a thing and the necessity of that knowledge – that is, knowledge of the bare fact as well as the reasoned fact.
- Scientific explanation is deductivist, so that it is a demonstration of a deductively valid syllogism from necessary premisses to a necessary conclusion, and must in addition obey six stated conditions, one of which requires that the premisses must be more familiar than the conclusions in nature and to the knower (i.e. a move from familiar to the unfamiliar).
- This leads to a trilemma of explanation (and of epistemic justification), so that explanation must either infinitely regress, or be circular, or ultimately self-explanatory or inexplicable.
- The ultimate self-explanatory first principles of a science can be seen to be the result of a process of induction (epagoge) from particulars.
- The object of science is not to explain the particulars, but to explain as necessary the general laws of which the particulars may be an instance.

Now, there is a *tension* between the general and the particular that has been inaugurated in the context of scientific knowledge. The particular instance in some way contributes to the first principles of explaining general laws in scientific knowledge, but it is the general laws which explain the particular cases. Also, because the first principles of science are arrived at by a process of induction (epagoge), they cannot be *a priori*, and so are not necessarily self-evident.

2.4.2.3 Aristotelian versus Galilean traditions

In what sense can the body of knowledge we now recognise as contemporary mainstream economics be said to be Aristotelian in its epistemological inflections? Economics (including classical political economy) uncomfortably saddles the intersection of practical and productive knowledge with (aspirations to be) scientific knowledge. Historically, the spheres of operation of these two kinds of knowledge were seen as separate and separable, but the enlightenment emphasis on 'scientific' as a criterion for all knowledge, and the successes of natural sciences, set in motion a vigorous intellectual ferment to align the 'social' with the natural sciences. Such an alignment, although never completely effected, was nevertheless attempted repeatedly. Mathematical formalism in the late nineteenth and then twentieth centuries, although neither necessary nor inevitable (and always much resisted; see Mirowski 1991a), provided great service in giving a successful appearance of such an alignment, especially in economics. Being a deductivist system, mathematics (and associated mathematical models) could provide an intellectually convenient bridge in the uneasy crossing of the general/particular divide in economics, by reinforcing the Aristotelian idea of explanation of general laws, rather than particular instances, as being the objects of scientific knowledge.[49] Except, unlike Aristotelian first principles of science, which are composed of non-demonstrable understanding, are self-explanatory but are *not a priori*, the first principles of economic science are often curiously *a priori*.

Von Wright (1971) provides a contrast between two main traditions in the history of ideas – the Aristotelian and the Galilean. He mentions that contrasts between these two traditions are often made by characterising the Aristotelian tradition as having a view of scientific explanation which is teleogical and finalistic, so that this tradition focuses on human efforts to 'make facts teleologically or finalistically understandable' (2–3). The Galilean tradition, on the other hand, conceives of scientific explanation as causal and mechanistic in its attempts to focus on human efforts to 'explain and predict phenomena' (ibid.).[50] The next important thing to note is the relation of *positivism* to the Galilean tradition. While positivism is a term that can be (and has been) used in many senses, I will draw upon Von Wright's careful characterisation of positivism as, 'an entire intellectual tradition extending from Comte and Mill not only down to the present-day but also upward in the stream of time to Hume and the philosophy of the Enlightenment' (4).[51] What are the important features of positivism so understood? Von Wright identifies them as follows – methodological monism or the belief in *the unity of method* amidst the diversity of the subject matter of scientific investigation; exact natural sciences, especially mathematical physics, as the *standard or ideal* of perfection to which all knowledge must aspire; a view of scientific explanation which is in some sense 'causal' so that it places an emphasis on explaining individual instances by subsuming them under hypothetically assumed more *general laws* of nature, including human nature;[52] and a characteristic attitude towards 'finalistic explanations' (these are defined as

49 Of course, I am not suggesting that all economists since Aristotle, and especially enlightenment onwards, were consciously taking up Aristotelian ideas. Rather, I am attempting to trace a certain epistemological inheritance in what became known as economics.

50 An important caveat is *not* to assume that the Aristotelian tradition has ancient roots while the Galilean is a relatively recent one. Von Wright (1971: 2) is of the opinion that while there may be some truth in this characterisation, the Galilean tradition can also be said to have an ancestry going back beyond Aristotle to Plato.

51 The sense of positivism linked with a phenomenalist or sensualist theory of knowledge, and modern positivism with a verificationist theory of meaning, he sees as more appropriate for Mill. For Comte, he finds the characterisation of positivism linking it with a 'scientistic' and 'technological' view of knowledge and its uses, as more appropriate. He draws an interesting comparison between Comte and Bacon as 'missionaries of technological attitude to knowledge', writing that, 'both contributed greatly to the creation of a certain "scientistic climate of opinion", but next to nothing to the *actual* progress of science' (Von Wright 1971: 171, emphasis added). Note that von Wright is *able to make* a distinction between prevailing scientism and actual progressive science.

52 In this context, consider the following remark by Mill (Von Wright 1971: 172 fn. 15 [Mill 1843, Bk. VI, Ch. iii, Sect. 2]), 'The science of Human Nature may be said to exist, in proportion as the approximate truths, which compose a practical knowledge of mankind, can be exhibited as corollaries from the universal laws of human nature on which they rest'.

'attempts to account for facts in terms of intentions, goals, purposes,' ibid.) which involves either *rejecting* them as unscientific *or* attempting to purge them of their ' "animist" or "vitalist" remains' and *transforming* them into causal explanations.

One is perhaps not surprised that these features of positivism resonate rather well with the body of claims that we have come to recognise as economics.[53] Contemporary mainstream economics owes a lot to the positivist mutations of the enlightenment, especially the vigorous epistemological refurbishment in the late nineteenth century. This refurbishment was part of the general intellectual climate which in turn was affected by many influences such as industrialisation, imperialism, Victorian mores, and developments in the natural sciences (especially those made possible by examining, experimenting, analysing – dissecting nature, mapping society – thus furthering the earlier enlightenment impetus to map the world, secure Reason, 'torturing nature's secrets out of her').

Let us return to the fourth feature of positivism identified earlier, namely its attitude towards Aristotelian (or finalistic) explanation. When faced with a theory of explanation – which ultimately relied upon non-demonstrable understanding, or self explanatory (though not *a priori*) first principles of science which could perhaps be had from particulars by induction, but could not be explained without the general laws – the empiricist alternative (which had been emphasised by enlightenment epistemology) is either to reject explanation as an unscientific concept, or, to reconstruct it in line with empiricist principles. Both these options were explored. Ruben gives the example of Duhem, who chose the first route; and Mill, who chose the second.

In his *The Aim And Structure of Physical Theory*, Duhem defines 'to explain' as 'to strip reality of the appearances covering it like a veil, in order to see the bare reality itself'. Explanation is for him a metaphysical idea which transcends experience and could result in subordinating physical theory to metaphysics. What then is the purpose of physical theory for Duhem? The answer (DHR 1990: 113, emphasis added) is:

> . . . the aim of physical theory is merely to summarise and classify logically a group of experimental laws 'without claiming to explain these laws'. Having rejected explanation as a legitimate aim of science, Duhem claims that *'A physical theory is not an explanation. It is a system of mathematical propositions, deduced from a small number of principles, which aim to represent as simply, as completely, and as exactly as possible a set of experimental laws'* (Duhem 1977: 19). Since explanation is connected for Duhem with a non-empirical conception of reality, it has no place in science.

Duhem's idea of a physical theory is reminiscent of a mainstream economic theory, *except* that, for him, the system of mathematical propositions deduced

53 In fact, these are some of the principal characteristics of contemporary mainstream economics – the neoclassical method (applicable anywhere any time), its mathematical ideal type in The Model™, and its underlying deductive nomological (see Section 2.4.2.5) mode of explanation.

from a small number of principles represents – a set of *experimental* laws. An economic theory of similar format will *not* claim to represent experimental laws, because conventionally experimentation is seen as impossible in economics. The current sub-field of experimental economics[54] notwithstanding, experimentation has *not* historically had many adherents. Perhaps the enlightenment impetus to explain the general man, the high values placed on the search for uniformities of human nature, and the perpetual difficulty of dealing with 'difference' – ensured that the experimental basis of empiricism never took a stronghold in the set of ideas which coalesced as political economy or economics.

Mill, a significant precursor of modern economics, now enters this discussion as a late-nineteenth-century figure who is important in the epistemological redoing of explanation. Mill was part of an empiricist tradition (Hobbes, Bacon, Locke, Berkeley, Hume) which sought to criticise or reformulate concepts or ideas which could not be traced directly to experience. The Aristotelian concept of explanation was rejected by Smith as we saw before, but it was not until Mill that it was explicitly addressed. How did Mill see explanation?

2.4.2.4 Mill on explanation

Mill holds a deductivist account of explanation along with a reductivist account of deduction. But what does this mean and imply?

For Mill, explanation does *not* reveal deeper mysteries of nature,[55] and he does not want to explain in any final sense. Explanations, according to him, need *laws*, which he sees as *uniformities*. He makes the distinction between uniformities of coexistent phenomena and those of successive phenomena – simultaneous or successive uniformities. If the uniformities of successive phenomena are to be causal, then they are *invariable and unconditional regularities of experience*. Mill *rejects* any non-empirical idea of causation as metaphysical.

He differentiates between the ordinary and scientific meanings of explanation. The difference lies in ordinary explanation replacing the unfamiliar by the familiar, and scientific explanation (or explanation in science) replacing the *familiar by the unfamiliar*. So that in science (DHR 1990: 114 [Mill 1970: 310–311], emphases added),

> [explanation] resolves a phenomenon with which we are familiar into one of which we previously knew little or nothing. . . . It must be kept constantly in

54 Even here it is *not* clear that 'experimental economics' is an attempt to secure empiricist epistemological underpinnings for economics as a social science. A lot of experimental economics literature is principally oriented around testing neoclassical assumptions about human behaviour in simulated laboratory conditions. For a survey of sources on experimental economics, see Kaul (2001a).

55 According to Mill (DHR 1990: 113 [Mill 1970: 310]), the 'word explanation is here used in its philosophical sense. What is called explaining one law of nature by another, is but substituting one mystery for another, and does nothing to render the general course of nature other than mysterious: we can no more assign a why for the most extensive laws than for the partial ones.'

> view, therefore, that *in science*, those who speak of *explaining* any phenomenon *mean* (or *should* mean) pointing out *not some more familiar, but merely some more general phenomenon*, of which it is a partial exemplification…

These remarks represent the apotheosis of standing at the juncture of familiar/unfamiliar and general/particular (see Section 2.3), with both the Aristotelian ideas on general and scientific explanation, and the Enlightenment empiricist (in some part in Galilean/Newtonian) tradition, as well as the earlier rationalism/antirationalism tensions in Smith and Hume. Thus, one can already see with Mill the many intellectual traditions at play, influential in the putting together of 'science' with the 'unfamiliar'.

Ruben comments that while Mill often talks about 'events and facts as what explain and are explained' (115), *facts did not figure* in Plato's or Aristotle's ontology of explanation. What is one to make of the notion of a 'fact'? Further, '[w]hatever facts are, they are not events or even patterns of events, although there is the fact that some event occurred, or the fact that some law or pattern of events obtains' (ibid.). For Mill, both particular instances (or individual facts) as well as general laws are explained by an explanation. He is thus of the opinion that (DHR: 116 [Mill 1970: 305], emphases added),

> *[a]n individual fact is said to be explained by pointing out its cause, that is, by stating the law or laws of causation of which its production is an instance.* Thus a conflagration is explained when it is proved to have arisen from a spark falling into the midst of a heap of combustibles; and in a similar manner, *a law of uniformity of nature is said to be explained when another law or laws are pointed out, of which that law itself is but a case, and from which it could be deduced.*

Mill's usage of the notion of a 'fact' is both *symptomatic and constructive* of a larger role that the epistemological unit of a fact has played in modernity. Poovey (1998) provides a *History of the Modern Fact* (subtitled: *Problems of Knowledge in the Sciences of Wealth and Society*), in which she addresses the peculiarities of the 'modern fact'.[56] She sees the category of the factual in most modern sciences in the West as positioned between the phenomenal world and systematic knowledge, as a result of which, 'the epistemological unit of the fact has registered the tension between the richness and variety embodied in concrete phenomena and the uniform, rule-governed order of humanly contrived systems' (1). Poovey's focus in providing a history of the modern fact is Britain from the late sixteenth to the early nineteenth century, and, in this context, she sees Mill's elevation of deduction over induction[57] in the emergent social sciences as an important move. This metatheoretical gesture owed to a recognition of the *tension*

56 For a contemporary take on 'facts' and their relation to knowledge, see Baillie *et al.* (2004).

57 Along with McCulloch's 1825 taxonomy of knowledge and Herschel's 1830 attempt to deal with the problem of the fact in natural science (see Poovey 1998: 3, 264–325).

between observed particulars and theoretical or systematic knowledge as a problem that required a professional (or disciplinary) solution (3, 317–325).

One relevant thread of Poovey's argument can be understood as follows. At the beginning of the period roughly understood as the enlightenment, Bacon was important in elevating the observed particular, from which one could move to making generalisations which constituted systematic knowledge. However, induction was anything but unproblematic, and one can see Hume's philosophical formulation of the problem of induction in the 1740s as a belated effect of Bacon's empiricism. Poovey points out that although Hume himself did not see this problem as particularly troubling (14), his formulation of this tension between the observed particulars and systematic knowledge allowed the peculiarity written into the modern fact to be conceptualised as such. In the nineteenth century, Mill (and others such as McCulloch and Herschel) were important in the formulation of a disciplinary solution to this problem; it was a solution which involved, 'turning the task of knowledge production in the rapidly professionalising sciences over to so-called experts' (3). These experts eventually introduced the formulation to gradually elevate 'rule-governed, autonomous models over observed particulars' (3). This reformulation (akin to what I have called epistemological redoing/refurbishment in line with positivism) occurred at different moments in different disciplines, but as a result it was ensured that (Poovey 1998: 3, emphasis original):

> After the late nineteenth century, at least in the natural and social sciences, expert knowledge producers sought not to generate knowledge that was simultaneously true to nature and systematic but to *model* the *range of the normal* or sometimes simply to create the most sophisticated models from available data, often using mathematical formulas.

Poovey is providing an epistemological account of *why and how* the important changes that occurred in the nineteenth century in the understanding of *what it meant to create knowledge about the world, and how it could be done*, could be linked both to – a history of the modern enlightenment concept of a *'fact' and its peculiarities* which stemmed from an inherent tension between the world and its representation, and – to the *methodological compromise* of creating taxonomies of knowledge, classes of experts, usage of statistics, and mathematical modelling as an effective solution. This rise of disciplinarity and scientism is something that is otherwise just usually stated but not genealogically excavated; for instance, von Wright (1971: 7) states that, the 'application of mathematical methods to political economy and other forms of social study was an inheritance of the eighteenth-century Enlightenment which found favour with the nineteenth-century positivists'.

Given that Mill was an influential figure in effecting the methodological compromise following on from tensions in enlightenment epistemology, his rendering of the concept of explanation is a very good example of the varying pulls that he sought to characterise. Mill has a deductivist theory of explanation, but also has a peculiar account of deduction. He writes, '[i]t must be granted that in every syllogism, considered as an argument to prove the conclusion, there is a petitio principii' (DHR: 110). Mill sees deductive inference as circular, and as founded upon some sort of non-deductive inference, so that *deduction cannot advance knowledge*.[58] When he has such an epistemically downgraded and reductivist account of deduction, then might one not expect him to relate explanation to induction instead? Yet this is *not* what he does, and the odd conjunction has been noted. Even though Mill believes that by inductive inference one *can* actually move from known truths to those unknown, in the same way that he believes predictions as being capable of advancing the predictor to new knowledge about the conclusion, his account of explanation remains deductive, and this is because he is attempting to *epistemically downgrade explanation from its non-empiricist pretensions* (DHR: 130–131, 137). Mill does not see explanation as being able to answer the why-question; we can *never ever really know*, all that we can do is to *fit facts into wider patterns* by deductive arguments (137). This is exactly the state of the discussion in contemporary economics, which does not really care much about *what one does when one explains*; all that one can do as a good scientist is to fit patterns by deductive mathematical models.

Further, Mill's account of causation is deterministic, so that there is a cause for everything that happens, and every such cause is a determining cause. Explanation involves fitting a universally general fact (or a uniformity) into the more general law or uniformity of which it is a special case. The derivative laws are themselves dependent upon a plurality of ultimate laws with *no further explanation*. However, for Mill (unlike for Aristotle), since there is no non-demonstrable understanding, these ultimate starting points are inexplicable rather than self-explanatory. In this way, there is a double ultimacy of inexplicables – there are *laws* for which there is in principle no explanation; and there are *particular brute facts* for which there is in principle no explanation. Then, the causal laws explain by either resolving the effect of the causes into separate laws of the causes which contribute to it, or demonstrating an intervening uniformity linking two uniformities, or by subsuming laws into a more general law – resolving individual particulars or uniformities under more general laws.

Finally, Mill also originates the 'symmetry thesis', the idea that explanation and prediction are symmetrical, so that they are both identical in content of their product, which is a deduction. This is another lasting influence of Mill on economic thought. As late as the second half of the twentieth-century, debates in economic methodology discuss this concept[59] (see Blaug 1980a, b; Rosenberg 1992).

58 Mill writes, 'nothing ever was, or can be, proved by syllogism which was not known or assumed to be known, before' (DHR: 131 [Mill 1970: 120]).

59 It is a flawed concept in many senses – one, it relies upon construing explanations and predictions as arguments; two, Hempel, who provided an influential account of explanation drawing upon Mill in his later work (DHR: 146 [Hempel 1965: 367, 376]), admits that at least the second part of the symmetry thesis (that every successful prediction is a potential explanation) is open to question.

Let me now sum up the important trails below.

- Mill has a deductivist account of explanation, but a particular account of deduction, so that deduction cannot advance knowledge.
- This does not immediately tail in with his account of inductive inference, which he believes can lead from known to unknown truths.
- However, Mill has introduced the notion of the 'fact' in relation to explanation, so that he can say facts explain facts.
- There is a history of the notion of 'fact' in Enlightenment epistemology, which originates in a general/particular tension from Bacon onwards, a problem of induction recognised by Hume.
- Subsequently, in the nineteenth century, a methodological compromise was effected which involved Mill elevating deduction over induction, as witnessed in his account of explanation.
- The notion of explanation is thus epistemically downgraded, to effect a compromise to the problem of the modern fact.
- Explanation is no deep demystification, only the fitting of uniformities into patterns of more general uniformities, at the base of which there are ultimately inexplicable facts and laws.
- This can also be understood so that the fitting of facts into patterns by deductive arguments can lead to gaining new knowledge of patterns in nature itself.
- This cementing of a deductivist basis for explanation paves the way for abstractions such as nature, society, and so on, to be thus incorporated into models of a pared-down notion of knowledge which does not aim to represent knowledge as being both true to nature and systematic, but a deductivist modelling of abstractions.
- This deductivist modelling of abstractions as a basis for 'theoretical' knowledge in economics changes the very notion of theory and transmogrifies it into contemporary 'The Model™'.
- This transmogrification of what one would mean by the term economic theory, and its peculiar way of carrying out associated roles – to describe, explain, and predict the world, as conceptualised in the formalised model, is a legacy of Aristotelian ideas inflected through the enlightenment, and nineteenth-century methodological compromises effected as resolution to tensions in enlightenment epistemology.
- The result is a positivist social science with theoretical understanding constituted by modelling abstractions in a deductivist mathematical format. As I argue later, all of this requires the fixing of individual choice as the focus of analysis, and characterisation of individual choice in a way as to make it mathematically tractable and commensurable. It further requires abstractions to function in a credible way, a task for which the role of metaphors is crucial.
- Underlying this is a picture of the subject-world of economics as it has been epistemologically structured in a temporal-historical-ideological way. But, *because* the particularity of these genealogical inheritances is insufficiently

uncovered, and often goes unstated, the enterprise of economics appears to be a plausible representation of a coherent universal system that exists already performed, which the Economist as a theorist renders understandable by simplifying it using mathematical tools. This is challengeable on the account that I have provided.

2.4.2.5 Hempel and the types of explanation – IS and DN

According to Hempel, basic scientific explanation is of two types – a) the deductive nomological (DN) type of explanation, and b) the probabilistic statistical or the inductive statistical type (IS) of explanation. They are both ideal-types in being idealisations/models or rational reconstructions by the standard of which actual explanations can be judged, and are found wanting in some or other aspect. Hempel does not aim to provide a plausible account of how scientists actually explain; rather, the purpose is 'to indicate in reasonably precise terms a logical structure and the rationale of various ways in which empirical science answers explanation-seeking-why-questions' (Hempel 1965: 412).

The deductive nomological type of explanation has a significant role for laws, so that on a DN account we can expect the explanadum event (that which is to be explained) to occur by the reason of explanans (that which explains) made up of particular facts and uniformities expressed by general laws. This can be roughly expressed as:

> An explanadum event E can be said to occur from,
> Particular circumstances such as C_1, $C_2 \ldots C_N$, in accordance with,
> General laws such as L_1, $L_2 \ldots L_K$

Causal explanations (which are answers to the 'why E' question) are thus DN in character.[60] The DN model has also been called the 'covering law' model, such that an event is considered as being explained only if all possible occurrences can be subsumed under more general covering laws. It is easy to see the link between Hempel's DN ideal type of explanation and Mill's empiricist rendering of explanation. This is not surprising, since Hempel is an empiricist and believes that empirical phenomena is basically the same in all areas of scientific inquiry, so that 'scientific' explanation of empirical phenomena is in some sense a complete explanation.

The inductive statistical explanation (which was a later addition) relies upon laws of probabilistic statistical type, so that it is an assertion that, given certain conditions, an event of a particular type will occur with a certain degree of statistical probability. Within IS explanation, the logical occurrence of the explanadum event E is not deductively implied, but a high likelihood (inductive probability) is conferred upon it.

60 This does not imply the reverse – that all DN explanations are causal.

First, as many have argued, Hempel's account of explanation is based on his view of explanation as nomic expectability; that is, to show that, given the circumstances, an event is to be expected. This means that his view of explanation is closely tied to prediction, so that a complete explanation is a potential prediction. Second, Hempel argues that the DN or IS explanatory schema relies upon resolving explanations which rely upon means-ends situational calculations conducted by an agent into either DN or IS explanations (Ruben 1993). This implies that scientific explanation does not need to take into account the particular/specific dispositional features of the agent, such as rationality or explicit deliberation, in order to explain an event. This is because explaining the behaviour of an agent A in a situation C by saying that, in a situation of type C, the appropriate thing to do is X, does not explain A's in fact having done X which is, according to Hempel, a necessary condition for an explanation. To explain the underlying rationale, one needs to say the following:

> A was in a situation of type C
> A was disposed to act rationally
> Any person who is disposed to act rationally will, when in a situation of type C, invariably (with high probability) do X.

And so the explanans again explains the explanadum by a DN or a IS type of explanation. The Hempelian idea here is that we can sensibly formulate an ideal type explanation by subsuming elements of explanations which account for an individual's behaviour in a particular situation by attempting to reconstruct their *own* deliberations, under explanations which rely upon more general laws that all agents act in accordance with. Particular meaning and individual intentionality are erased in favour of a similarity of agents acting in accordance with a uniformity of laws.

It is here that recognising the positivist empiricist enlightenment epistemological intellectual heritage of Hempelian ideas becomes pertinent. The role of laws is significant only if they are seen to be uniformly operant. Invoking laws to explain particular facts, as Mill (and later Hempel) did, needs to subsume them under even more general laws, for which ultimately there is no explanation. The role of the social scientist then is to formulate theories which are now attempts to 'model of the range of the normal' (Poovey 1998), as it is perceived. The access to facts and general laws on which to base explanation in this positivist empiricist enlightenment epistemological tradition[61] cannot be grounded on any

61 The alternative view to positivist empiricist enlightenment epistemology is a view characterised as anti-positivism, one strand of which is the hermeneutic tradition. This tradition is characterised by emphasis on the contrast between the sciences that Windelband (1894) calls – 'nomothetic' (sciences which aim at generalisations about reproducible and predictable phenomena, the search for laws) and those that are 'ideographic' (sciences which want to grasp the individual and unique features of their objects, the descriptive study of individuality). Linked to this is the contrast drawn by the German historian-philosopher Droysen (1858), between 'Eklaren' or explanation and 'Verstehen' or understanding (for the source of both citations, see von Wright 1971: 5, 172).

non-demonstrable understanding, because that would be harking back to Aristotelian metaphysics. On the contrary, there has to be some perceived empiricist basis for them. I say 'perceived empiricist basis' because it is not clear that the basis (at least in economics as a social science) is in fact empiricist. For instance, in economics, contemporary theory as The Model™ relies upon what are *a priori* assumptions, but these are defended as being based upon some self-evident uniformities of human nature.

Further, numbers in the form of statistics are harnessed as providing evidence to testify to the overall uniformity of human behaviour. Thus, basing the theory (an effort to model the range of the normal) on the typical individual economic agent with certain (*a priorily*) assumed characteristics is seen to be empirically validated in the epistemological strength emanating from the law of large numbers. How did it come to be thus? It is here that the role of statistics in generating the realm of the average or the normal was important in the late nineteenth century. Recall my discussion earlier (Section 2.3.1) on Whewell and Jones (Porter 1994). Further, Poovey writes (1998: 325, emphasis added),

> ... whereas British philosophers since Hume had asked how one could reason from observed particulars to final causes or from observed particulars to general laws, *after statistics began to be equated with the law of large numbers*, philosophers as well as ordinary readers began to ask how one could conceptualise free will, given that the *regularities that emerge from 'numerical calculations'* seemed to leave so little room for volition, for morality, or for ethics of any kind.

For Hempel, 'scientific' explanation of empirical phenomena accommodates explanation in social science. Relying upon the positivist tradition of Mill and his predecessors and successors, it is this aspiration to a covering law ideal type of explanation that one finds in contemporary economics. The fact that actual explanations do not exactly conform to the ideal type does not affect the deep-set aspiration of mainstream economists as social scientists to attempt to approach this ideal with formalised mathematical models so as to permit such approximations.

2.4.3 The section revisited

I have relied upon secondary sources in my discussion of some philosophers and economists (Smith, Aristotle). This is because I am not disputing what Smith or Aristotle actually said. Rather, my concern is to read meaning into the way their work has influenced others along the line. For example, I do *not* provide a history of explanation, even though it might seem that I am looking at a few accounts of explanation in a chronological order. What is novel here is not what Aristotle or Mill or Smith said about explanation or science; the novelty lies in the way I trace a particular contemporary version of explanation in economics back into time and signal how different parts of it were sourced from different influences. In making these connections lies the aim of this endeavour. Also, I refuse to be daunted by the size and enormity of some of the issues dealt with in this book. Can one say anything about the Enlightenment (let alone trace some themes in enlightenment epistemology) in a few pages? Would it not need several books to make each of the points in this chapter? Perhaps, but to conclusively prove beyond any doubt each of my points has never been an aim. Knowledge as earnest speculation deserves to be recognised too. In Derridian terms (1989), I am setting forth a 'theoretical jetty', to an as yet unnamed address.

It is time to start pulling together the various threads in the complexly layered itineraries that I have attempted to present. I have argued that the contemporary epistemological structuring of economics reflects methodological compromises necessitated by tensions in the underlying enlightenment epistemology. Thus, I did not begin from *economics as it is* to argue its shortcomings, a strategy pursued at many levels by numerous critiques/assessments of mainstream economics. I will now relate some other elements of the subject-world into the picture presented earlier. They should be seen as issues arising from and useful in the service of fixing my arguments until now. In this, I will revisit some theorists and themes discussed earlier in order to pull together and conclude.

2.5 The theory and science of economics

Earlier, I had discussed Hicks on causality and explanation. In the light of the arguments that followed it, I can now revisit Hicks' view of theory, the theorists, and science – in economics. He writes, '[c]ausality, of whatever kind, is always a relation, a relation between facts. And yet it appears to be a theoretical relation. How can there be a theoretical relation between facts?' (1979: 27). Subsequently, he provides an answer which most economists would agree with. Hicks recognises that theories on which assertion of causal relations must be based cannot be purely deductive, so that if the theory is not pure theory (purely axiomatic) and if it is to be applied to facts, then it must begin from some proposition or propositions which are inductive. Can one link empirical association between characteristics with the demand for Reason (that they be brought into a logical system)?

He believes that there is 'plenty of experience in science (and even in economics)' (29) to show that a statement of association, even if purely inductive in character, can in its capacity as a proposition have implications in the logical sense, some of which may be testable. And if the test is successful, then a logical bridge has been built between two inductions, and the logical coherence of this bridge strengthens confidence in the induction. Although he gives an example from Newtonian theory, it is his belief that, '[t]he pattern of deductions serving as a bridge between inductions is, however, general. The chain of deduction may be short or long, simple or complex' (32).

According to him, a theory that is 'properly established' must have been based on some evidence and all that new evidence can do is to show that its field of application is narrower than had been thought. And, as with most economists, this leads him to argue that there is no reason to abandon the theory until 'a new theory has been developed with a wider field of application' (34). The whole process of theorisation is for him like the image of 'rungs on a ladder; the investigator climbs from one to the next' (34). I wanted to get to this crucial point in order to ask the question that Hicks asks himself, '[b]ut where does the ladder start?' (35).

He answers, '[t]hey are pure inductions, which are not verifications of some hypothesis, derived from results which have been already obtained' (35). But he simultaneously explicitly rejects the Baconian heresy which claims that such inductions can be obtained by a mere collection of facts, without an ordering principle. Thus, these pure inductions are obtained not from collecting facts, but are made available from the 'work of *classification* which has to be performed before the inductions can be made' (35). In relation to this work of classification, he writes (ibid.: 35–37):

> It is a work which from one point of view is external to the science in which the inductions will be used; for it is a work which must be performed before the 'climbing' can start. But from another point of view it is the first stage of the science.... When these classifications are first formed, the science is still in the future; so we should not be surprised to find that as they start they are unscientific. Their purpose, at that stage, is not the advancement of science; it is something quite different. The primitive classifications which led to astronomy were made, in the first place, by astrologers. ... There is a somewhat similar relation of alchemy to chemistry. ... In a similar way the medical sciences begin with empiricists ('quacks'). One of the chief sources of primitive inductions is the practical arts. ... Looking back, we can reckon a classification as better if it led to inductions that were more fertile, so that they could be used as primitive inductions for a (later) 'ladder' of development.

Thus, writing towards the end of the twentieth-century, Hicks embodies the epistemological spirits of foregone stories. He retains an Aristotelian love of generalisations,[62] an awareness of the Humean problem of induction which stems from Bacon's overvalorisation of the deracinated particular, a Millean empiricist rendering of explanation in facts, and the consequent methodological compromise of creating a taxonomy of knowledge along with a special class of experts who 'do' science. This is the coming to a full circle of an important strand of my argument, which sought to show that the epistemological inheritance of economics is geohistorically-temporally-ideologically located and not universal. Challenging the self-image of economics as a universal neutral science, we see that economics is a contingent disciplinary coalescing whose coming into being

62 Hicks's ideas behind a ladder of science can be compared with the following quote on Aristotle (DHR: 104),

> For Aristotle, in the finished setting out of the science, each generalisation should be immediate; each generalisation should follow immediately from its predecessor in the inferential chain. If it does not, then there are some further premisses on which the truth depends, or through which the truth is mediated, such that those premisses have not yet been incorporated into a science.

cannot be seen in isolation from the rise of disciplinarity and scientism themselves as ways and means of creating systematic knowledge from observed particulars to serve the interests of administration.

Hicks further writes[63] (ibid.: 37),

> [h]ow does all this apply to economics? . . . Just as the first steps towards the natural sciences were made by non-scientists, so the first steps towards economics were made by non-economists. Administrators, calculating imports and exports; accountants, calculating profits and incomes and drawing up balance-sheets; it is from the work of such practical people that economics begins. And just as in the natural sciences, the first step towards science proper is the refinement of unscientific, or semi-scientific, classifications, so there is in economics the corresponding proceeding, the refinement of the practical concepts so as to fit them better to be tools of thinking.

In addition to confirming my previous arguments, we can see that this highlights another peculiarity – divergence of the commonly understood practical content of economics, and its scientific aspirations. As I mentioned before, economics straddles the inconvenient juxtaposition of (what is understood as) practical knowledge with (what is understood as) scientific knowledge. This has often meant that *practical quotidian economic experience has come to be defined by its scientific construal.*

Meanwhile, where does the ladder of science get us in economics? Not very far,[64] and Hicks attributes this to the fact that economics is in time, in the way the natural sciences are not. This is worth commenting upon since it highlights an interesting point – success in economics is perceived to be like climbing the ladder of science in the way that natural sciences do. Thus, while for Friedman (1953) judging the success of economic theory by its comparison to reality seems unpalatable because realism is unattainable,[65] economists are not usually averse to somewhat unfavourable comparisons with the status of knowledge in natural sciences, as it can indicate relative mathematical progress given the 'problematic' status of their subject matter.

63 Compare the quotes from Hicks (1979) contained in these pages to Huxley's statement in his essay *Heaven and Hell* (a sequel to the famed *Doors of Perception*) first published in 1956: 'However lowly, the work of the collector must be done, before we can proceed to the higher scientific tasks of classification, analysis, experiment and theory making' (1994: 61).

64 See Hausman (1989) for an argument that explanatory progress *has* occurred in economics. He judges cumulative explanatory progress thus. By discovery of new laws and new 'facts' (economists have come to recognise new regularities; he defers the question on whether these can be seen as laws), by correction of errors, by recognising the relevance of already known facts and generalisations, growth of systematisation, increasing conceptual articulation and clarification (early classical economists failed to understand marginal concepts, now we do), 'deepening' or 'superseding'. I do not agree with his account.

65 Even Samuelson felt compelled to disagree with Friedman on the 'realism of assumptions' issue. For a compelling critique of Friedman on explanation and the nature of economic theory relevant to the tone of my arguments here, see McLachlan and Swales (1978).

2.6 Mathematical formalism, representation and the moralisation of objectivity

The mutations of enlightenment epistemology in the nineteenth-century corresponded roughly to the transition from classical to neoclassical economics. Neoclassical economics is famous for the positive-normative distinction,[66] first articulated by John Neville Keynes (1891: 34–35, 46); it is also known for its methodological individualism,[67] and mathematical formalism. I will comment on this last as a way of concluding.

Hicks again says it for most economists when he writes that (1979: viii, emphases added),

> [t]here is much of economic theory which is pursued for no better reason than its intellectual attraction; *it is a good game*. We have no reason to be ashamed of that, since the same would hold for many branches of pure *mathematics*.

Mathematics is perhaps a link in the cherished association of economics with the natural sciences. How did it come to be thus? I am going to briefly discuss this along two lines – one relating to the ideal of objectivity, and the second to a history of mathematical expression in economics. I will not engage with the 'standard' arguments on should economics as it is have more or less of mathematics, is mathematics just another language, is there more to formalism than mathematics in contemporary economics.[68]

66 Following on from this, the mainstream idea that economics ought to be about 'positive' and not the 'normative', is itself normative. Weston (1994) argues in favour of retaining the positive/normative divide as a conceptual distinction (which will not cause economics to be value free). The reasons? As follows: to keep the questions distinct ('attach an asterisk to ethical questions because there isn't time to discuss them in undergraduate classes'); to issue a caution about credentials so that economists cannot abuse their credentials to advance certain ethical arguments; to maintain a scholarly environment; to promote the norm of objectivity. See Walsh (2000), who discusses Putnam to underline the positivist insistence on sharp dichotomies such as science/ethics, science/metaphysics, analytic/synthetic – which serve to deny entanglements such as that of fact and value. See also Wilson (1997) for a discussion of morality and economics, and Machan (1998) for an argument that ownership or property as a moral-political concept is the normative basis of economics. However, it can be argued that the liberal ideology of property and person is neither natural nor neutral; for its unravelling in the face of race slavery; see Kawash (1999).

67 Garfinkel (1981: 16–19, 52–53) compares individualism in social theory to microreduction in physical science. He quotes Arrow (1968) on reduction: 'A full characterisation of each individual's behaviour logically implies a knowledge of group behaviour; there is nothing left out. The rejection of the organism approach to social problems has been a fairly complete, and to my mind salutary, rejection of mysticism.'

68 For a detailed discussion along these lines, see Weintraub, Dow, Chick, Backhouse, Krugman in *The Economic Journal* 1998 (451: 1826–1899). On the related question of the status of models in economics, see Morgan and Morrison 1999; Little 1995. And finally, McClelland (1975) examines causal explanation and model building in history, economics, and the new economic history.

2.6.1 Objectivity and representation

Daston and Galison (1992) examine the nineteenth-century fixing of a particular form of objectivity – mechanical or non-interventionist objectivity. This form of objectivity is different from other components of the conglomerate notion of objectivity (such as aperspectival objectivity).[69] Of course, the attempts of scientists, artists, social scientists, theorists since the early Enlightenment were always oriented towards being 'true to nature'. However, Daston and Galison, through their study of scientific atlases produced during this period, argue that, in the nineteenth-century, a particular form of being *true to nature* emerged, which was conceptually distinct from earlier such attempts. It was conceptually distinct in three ways – a) in its methods, which were mechanical; b) in its morals, of self-restraint; and c) in its metaphysics, which was individualised (see ibid.: 84). This argument is pertinent for my discussion here because the influences that were at work in science and art during this period were also the ones influential in the shaping of what was to become the social science of economics. The disciplinary terrains were not marked out as they are now, and indeed, the *very basis of what it meant to be scientific about the social realm* was being worked out.

2.6.1.1 Until the nineteenth-century: representation as interpretation and mediation

Thus, the argument of Daston and Galison is that, *until* the second half of the nineteenth-century, the scientific ideal was one of *interpreting* nature to produce *representations* which were both reflective of the *ideal essence* of nature as it

69 The relations between objectivity, representation, and maintenance of social orders are complex but open to historicisation and criticality. Aperspectival objectivity can be traced to the origin of Western perspective in the Renaissance painters such as Brunelleschi, Donatello, Masacchio and Alberti. This way of having a centrepoint or vanishing point of entry into the painting was later mathematically formalised by Desargues (Zeeman 2002). This story of the illusionistic perspective as an arch-trope is undone in Damisch (1994 [1987]). Later, the Enlightenment produced pictures in boxes with an eye-hole so that the perspective could be fixed for view in a manner difficult for paintings. Te Heesen (2002) unfolds the story of an eighteenth-century picture encyclopaedia in a box. The box had images from nature, history, myth, and so on, to demonstrate to children the proper way of collecting, storing, and ordering knowledge – 'epitomising Enlightenment concern with the creation and maintenance of an appropriate moral, intellectual, and social order'. Henderson (1995) discusses the role of Maria Edgeworth in the nineteenth century in introducing children and young people to economic stories which taught them the virtues of – division of labour ('The Cherry Orchard'), rational consumer behaviour ('The Purple Jar'), and work and thrift ('Lazy Lawrence'). Belsey (2002) discusses the relation between perspective vision and the Lacanian Real, and the many ways in which truth was 'conjured into being' in perspective painting, the nineteenth century novel, thus raising questions of the screened relation between cultural forms and the real or real-ism. Similarly, Grootenboer (2005), in her study of seventeenth century Dutch still-life, contends that perspective as a language of the image determines perception so that painting is a form of thinking. Finally, for a discussion on the implication of perspective in relation to economics, see de Sousa Santos (2001a, b) on debating knowledge and responses by Pieterse, Wagner, Caraça in the same issue (*European Journal of Social Theory* 2001).

ought to be, and were also systematic in the interests of creating knowledge. For instance, 'typical' phenomena was the focus of consideration – the *typus* or 'archetype' served the function of being that which was *drawn from all observed particulars* but would *not* be observed in its entirety in any *one particular*.

The role of the theorist, artist, scientist, social scientist was an important one in order to mediate between the grand system of nature, and its true representation, where *truly representing* meant being able to *distil the essence* from the perfection of nature, or in the case of the social scientist, to *discern the essential meanings* from the vast systems of human interaction, in order to then represent this essential meaning in a *general form*. No doubt that individual instances would not conform to this essential and ideal archetype, but this archetype is the *systematic* representation of the external world. Another thing to note is that the archetype is not seen as something that wholly transcends experience; in fact, Daston and Galison provide the example of Goethe (87–88), who is writing before the advent of mechanical objectivity, and for whom, 'the act of "definition" [is] required to distil the typical from the variable and accidental [and] is not a slide into subjectivity but rather a precaution against it.'

The enlightenment tensions are in full view here. In order to understand the external system, generalisations are required, but with a somewhat empirical basis; however, observing the deracinated particulars simply will not serve the purpose, for there is no guarantee that they are not an anomaly, so the generalisations must be reflective of the essential ideal which will be derived from and tested by observation but against a definition. The act of defining serves a crucial purpose – it guards against endless subjective variations, it provides the basis for a somewhat empirical anchoring, and it can be seen as being both systematic and true to nature at the same time. Besides the typical and the ideal, there was also the concept of 'characteristic' – which attempted to locate the 'typical' in an individual, and, along with the concept of the 'ideal', served to *standardise the phenomena*. Daston and Galison give several examples to illustrate their arguments, and I am drawing upon a much pared-down version of their ideas to suit my purpose here, which is to argue that a similar process was at work amongst the early social scientists.

As an example, consider Hicks' discussion of Smith (1979: 39–49), where he is attempting to examine if Smith's theory in the *WON* (he refers to 1976: 31) can be seen as a form of the bridge of deduction bridging inductions. If improvement in productivity comes about with a division of labour or specialisation, Smith also recognises that this division of labour is limited by the extent of the market. Restrictions can also be naturally imposed, so that places with easy access to water transport should have a locational advantage. My interest here is in one particular aspect of the way Smith argues. In order to structure his argument, Smith assumes that relative advantage implies relative wealth, something that Hicks calls the *Economic Principle* (he points out that this is wider than the profit motive). The idea is that, 'people would act economically – when the opportunity of an advantage was presented to them, they would take it', and further, '[t]he people of Britain, of Holland and America, about whom he [Smith] was largely thinking, did seem to behave like that' (Hicks 1979: 43). This usage of the economic principle *as a defining characteristic serves to standardise the working objects* of Smith's argument. It is important to point out that this economic principle is not seen to be empirical in any provable sense; however, '... the application of the principle to different times and places is to that extent an empirical matter... the principle was one of definition, or classification' (ibid., 44). Now, Smith's designation of the economic principle as a rather non-empirical defining characteristic of people's behaviour, to which he believes most people in most places at most times would conform if there are no obstacles, achieves a standardisation in terms of both being 'typical' and 'characteristic' (and also perhaps 'ideal' since conformity to this principle brings wealth in Smith's perception).

Like the other enlightenment scientists and artists, Smith is also committed to his role as a social scientist which involves representing the system of human interactions systematically, and being guided by the ideals of creating knowledge in the image of the typical, the characteristic, and the ideal, as manufactured by the careful interpretation (hermeneutic mediation) of the external system of nature and human interactions. *Qua* social scientist, for Smith, *interpretation is not ruled out* – rather, careful interpretation ensures a standardisation of the working objects of social science in order to create systematically objective and meaningful knowledge from the welter of particulars.

2.6.1.2 Nineteenth century onwards: representation and the effect of moralised objectivity and mechanised science

Now, and this is the second part of my purpose here, in the epistemological mutations of the late nineteenth-century, there emerges a different kind of ideal, in part due to what Daston and Galison call the *moralisation* of objectivity, and the *mechanisation* of science. The problem was not the earlier one of a 'mismatch between world and mind', but rather 'a struggle with inward temptation' (1992: 82). Briefly, this can be explained as follows. The fascination with the machine, and the ideals of the machine, has always been part of the enlightenment,[70] but in the late nineteenth (and then twentieth) century, this becomes particularly pertinent as machines (especially those of visual representation such as the camera, the x-ray machine, the microscope, and so on) are now celebrated as the paragon of certain human virtues. What humans lacked, the machines had in abundance. They offered 'freedom from will', accuracy, and eternal vigilance – '[t]he phenomena never sleep, and neither should the observer' – and, most of all, the release from intervention by attributing meaning ('for theory and judgment were the first steps down the primrose path to intervention', 83).

Machines had the advantage of being seen as devices to enable 'nature to speak for herself' in the 'language of the phenomena themselves' (81). The previous

70 A recent book by Wood (2002) titled *Living Dolls: A Magical History of the Quest for Mechanical Life* traces the history of the 'romance of the machine encouraged by the Cartesian view of life as mechanism' (Connor 2002). In addition, this cultural fantasy with automatons is gendered and raced.

attempts of theorists, scientists, artists, and social scientists to interpret nature and the world were seen as interested intervention, something that could be avoided by the machines, which could not and did not have any reason to lie. The scientist should then aim to be dutiful, self-restrained, alert, and patient – embodying the ideals of the machine. Such heroic self-discipline and moralised vision of self-restraint would go well with the Victorian temperament. Science and morality were united in their condemnation of the mere undisciplined human as prone to excesses, inconstant, and incapable of grasping nature. The machines on the other hand were seen to operate *in a vacuum of meaning*; the enforced amenability of nature to machine enacted by human intervention was ignored.

This was an ideal at work in what was to become neoclassical economics. A large part of the appeal of the machines lay in their visual representation of the truth of nature. This is an extremely interesting conjunction because of the way the visual imagination was crucial to the Victorians. Douglas-Fairhurst (2002: 153), in reviewing Flint's (2000) *Victorians and the Visual Imagination*, writes of how, in a terse exchange at the end of Conan Doyle's *A Case of Identity*, Watson queries Sherlock Holmes on how he was able to read a great deal in someone which was quite invisible to him. Holmes replies, 'Not invisible but unnoticed.' There are two ideas at work here: one relates to how what one sees may not always be true, and the other relates to how certain kinds of observation (noticing) count for an accurate representation. The mechanical reproduction of an image through a machine like the camera is not only a true representation of the object or event, but also a more trustworthy one when compared to a human rendering of the same object or event. The eye has to be habituated *to see* things in the scientific manner, and from the late nineteenth-century onwards this often meant *seeing differently. The machine ideal, moralised objectivity, visual imagination, and science together played a great role in motivating formalism in economics.* The symbols, illustrations, diagrams and graphs are now seen to *represent the phenomena* in a way that one learns to recognise as accurate, and minus the interference of the theorist. The earlier classical political economy writers interpreted in accordance with a different ideal; now, their words were seen as inevitably theirs, while the symbols were seen to capture the phenomena.

Even though the science of political economy would unfortunately not admit of machines in any direct sense,[71] the machine ideal and its correlate of visual representation without any interference of the theorist could be admitted into the new sense of theory transmogrifying into a model with mathematical symbols and graphs standing in for the objects of study. The words are now seen as imprecise, while the symbols and graphs represent accurately and without any argument over the content of what is meant by the theorist (see Sassower 1985: chapter 4;

71 However, the pervasive influence of machines perhaps was even more intrinsic to the development of economics in the twentieth-century – Mirowski, in his (2002) *Machine Dreams: Economics Becomes a Cyborg Science*, links Cold War history, history of the computer, with the history of the postwar economics profession in America.

Szostak 1999). This is paralleled by the rise of statistics, the important epistemological role played by numbers in the aggregate, which are now seen to state unequivocally (Poovey 1998). The important census undertaken in Britain in 1851 is bringing new categories into being, literally constructing concepts, and their realities. Out of this a new type of epistemological entity is emerging – that of the 'average' (see Cooper 2001, 2003). For instance, Bulgakov (2000: 251–252, emphasis original) in his *Philosophy of Economy* writes,

> the individual exists for political economy only as the *average* specimen of a social type. ... This peculiar and as yet poorly understood logic of political economy's basic concepts – by means of which multiplicity is compressed into unity, isolating selected aspects of phenomenon – is analogous to the method of statistical collectivities. ... Thus we might say that the magnifying glass of political economy sees both more and less than the naked eye. ... The overwhelming significance of statistical observation in political economy makes sense in light of its fascination with collectivities, with the general, the typical, the average.

The average is different from the typical or the ideal in an important sense – the means of accessing the average are essentially those of cataloguing, classification, categorisation, taxonomy accomplished by statistics, mathematics, and visual reproductions representing phenomena – all (apparently) without any hermeneutic mediation or interpretation. The theorist, scientist, social scientist needs to be a repository of readiness to let the world speak for itself, without attributing any additional meaning through interpreting in words.

2.6.2 Fixing the world for mathematical formalism

But this extraordinary documenting of social science through the methods and ideals of natural science was not immediate, unproblematic, or complete. The residue of the social has galled many economists as social scientists, but at the same time has also provoked evermore creative means of justification for translating excesses of meaning into graspable formulations. It is this point that I want to link to the history of mathematical expression in economics. As I have argued earlier, the epistemological structuring of economics is not separate from the wider debates of the times, and if the content of economic analysis needed to reflect positive scientific mathematical professional methods in the late nineteenth-century, then the world needed to be fixed in a commensurable way in order for this account to make sense.

I agree with Mirowski (1991a) when he writes that the onset of mathematisation of economics that is associated with the marginalist revolution, and fully flowered in the postwar period, was *not* cumulative, inevitable, or natural (145).[72]

72 Many think otherwise. Writing in 1952, Samuelson believed that the problems of economic theory are 'by their nature quantitative questions whose answer depends upon a superposition of many

Mirowski locates two inflection points or major discontinuities in the history of mathematical economics. The first one occurs after the middle of the nineteenth-century, when a large number of economists adopted a single mathematical metaphor – of equilibrium in a field of force, to translate potential energy as utility. However, by the early twentieth century, this neoclassical marginalist revolution based on analogies from physics was meeting widespread resistance in its social mechanics. The second quantum leap in the application of mathematical discourse to economic theory is identified in the decade 1925–1935 (see ibid.: 149–151), and involved a new generation of economists applying more up-to-date mathematical techniques and metaphors to the neoclassical program.[73]

Samuelson's Nobel prize-winning lecture, published in the *AER* (1972), is titled 'Maximum Principles in Analytical Economics', and the very first line goes, '[t]he very name of my subject, economics, suggests economising or maximising' (249). In the same paragraph, he recalls the Cambridge economist Pigou once having asked the rhetorical question, 'Who would think of employing an economist to run a brewery?' and answers, '[w]ell, today, under the guise of operational research and managerial economics, the fanciest of our economic tools are being utilised in enterprises both public and private.' No doubt, he is right. The 'application' of the 'tools' of economics is *de rigueur* in government, enterprises, and most realms of human interaction. However, the nexus between the expert knowledge of economists and the political power of the administrators coexists with the widespread evidence of a disjuncture between the views of economists and

different pieces of quantitative and qualitative information. When we tackle them by words, we are solving the same equations as when we write out those equations' (63–64). Contrast this with Krugman: 'Without doubt there is too much mathematics in the economics journals, because mathematical elaboration is a time-honored way of dressing up a bad idea' (in Szostak 1999: 88). Bulgakov (2000: 253–259) critiques 'deductive' political economy thus,

> [it] is completely constructed on a particular representation of a typical or average form of behavior, any departure from which is seen as accidental or irregular. ... We mustn't of course deny the scientific utility of ready-made theoretical models within certain limits. ... It is nonetheless clear that modeling and modernisation, which to many constitute the quintessence of the scientific approach, sometimes obscure historical reality in its colorful individuality, even though the stylization of history according to the tastes of contemporary political economy – the application of ready conceptual schemas and orientations – can be convenient... [it] can, however, be as dangerous as it is convenient, and we may one day be forced to rid historical science of these modernising weeds.... Collecting facts with no guiding aim in mind is not science at all but a mere scientific game.

73 Unlike the first wave of mathematisation (which was composed of economists borrowing metaphors from physicists), the second wave involved physicists, engineers, and mathematicians themselves moving into economics. Mirowski names several of these – Frisch, Koopmans, Tinbergen, Allais, Arrow, von Neumann, Evans, Davis, Wilson. New formalisms which had evolved in physics (he gives the examples of stochastic formalisms, improved mathematics of vector fields and phased spaces, linear algebra, and constrained optimisation) were applied, so that,

> [the] net result was a new discourse self-consciously patterned upon the rhetoric of the scientific research report, *shifting the intellectual centre of gravity from the book or essay to*

'laypeople' on the economy (see Sassower 1985: chapter 5; Blendon *et al.* 1999; Caplan 2002). The appeal of the formal methods lies in their being able to provide answers, so that when the administrators require 'expert' opinion, they turn to social scientists. Economists, especially, are valued for their formal mathematical procedures which seem to give accurate representations of average entities. Especially from the nineteenth-century onwards, the ability to render the world of human interaction comprehensible in mathematical terms in line with the mechanistic ideals and the appeal of visual representation, required important changes and fixing in how we see the world. Contrary to mainstream beliefs (see Samuelson 1952; Debreu 1984), nothing about the world, or its social scientific representation in economics, is inherently suitable to mathematical formalisation. Like any other attempt at representation, doing so imposes its own peculiar adjustments.

All means of creating knowledge are *not only* attempts to view certain given objects in a particular way, but are ways of constituting the *what and how* of the objects of knowledge. And each such structuring imposes its own givens in terms of subjects, objects, acts, and themes which need to be unproblematically accepted for the resulting enterprise to make sense. In the case of mathematisation of the economic discourse, I agree with Mirowski that it 'should not be traced to the natural quantification of commodities, but rather should be explained empirically by changing social perceptions of the symmetries and invariances read into market activities through the instrumentality of social institutions' (1991: 155).[74]

> *the journal article constructed around a mathematical 'model'*, eschewing the earlier discursive mode of expression accessible to economist and non-economist alike.
>
> (Mirowski 1991a: 153, emphasis added)

I should remark that this has had repercussions within the profession. Economics departments within the United Kingdom, for instance, routinely prefer research output in the form of articles in 'high-ranked' (largely orthodox) journals at the expense of books/research monographs. This is in marked contrast to humanities and other social sciences where books are valued highly. Also unique to economics is a classification system (JEL codes, see http://www.aeaweb.org/journal/jel_class_system.html) that codes all research articles under pre-defined categories.

74 He further gives the following example to illustrate his point (ibid.),

> The reason that modern economic actors express prices as ratios is that the following regularities are being projected onto their quotidian exchange activities:
>
> 1 The commodity preserves its identity through the exchange process;
> 2 Buying nothing should cost nothing;
> 3 The order in which the items are presented for purchase should not influence the amount paid in the aggregate;
> 4 Dividing the aggregate into subsets and paying for each separately should not influence the sum paid;
> 5 The net result of buying an item and then returning it should be zero;
> 6 Everyone should pay the same price for the same item.

The above regularities which are projected for tractable abstraction and perhaps reflect the nature of market activity in some market structures will not stand up to scrutiny for anyone who takes one stroll through the popular Janpath Bazaar in New Delhi in India (see Kaul 2004b). The locatedness of mathematical expression, and its epistemological appeal, is tied to a desire to make uniform, standardise, make commensurate the welter of human particulars.

2.7 Conclusion

The enlightenment epistemology has fixed for view the world in a particular way, and in many ways economics is the *social science par excellence*. In this chapter, my aim has been to interrogate the epistemological tensions behind how the social science of economics came to be. I have argued that these tensions have always been part and parcel of any endeavour to create scientific knowledge about the social world, stressing that in the case of economics its geohistorical-temporal-ideological situatedness meant that they were especially accentuated. Some of the important themes of enlightenment epistemology that I have discussed are: the work of the machine metaphor; the status of theory and practice; the play of forces in theory; the signifier individual; relations between self and the Other; and the general and the particular. I then related these considerations to the subject-world of economics, pointing out that the body of knowledge currently titled 'economics' is not a response to the same set of questions which have remained universal, eternal, and fixed. Rather, if we genealogically excavate the concept of explanation, we find that its mutations and inflections indicate the changing ways in which what counts as knowledge and the terms of access to it have been understood. This is also crucial for unconcealing how the notion of a theory operates in economics – its current form as generalisations employing deductivist mathematical formalised models has its basis in influential notions of scientific explanation and its relation to scientific or theoretical knowledge (as opposed to practical or productive knowledge). And thus we find that the transmogrification of theory into a model can be seen as the blending of an Aristotelian love of generalisations, an awareness of the Humean problem of induction (stemming from Bacon's overvalorisation of the deracinated particular), a Millean empiricist rendering of explanation in facts, and the consequent methodological compromise of creating a taxonomy of knowledge along with a special class of experts who 'do' science.

The scientific ideal of being true to nature previously meant the theorist interpreting the world to produce systematic representations in the interest of creating knowledge which was 'typical', 'ideal', and 'characteristic'. This ideal underwent changes in the nineteenth-century, in part due to the moralisation of objectivity and the mechanisation of science, and what emerged was the ideal of non-interventionist representation (to create knowledge 'in a vacuum of meaning'), for which the entity of the 'average' was more suitable. This valorisation of the average, diminished interpretive role of the theorist, and adoption of visual representative techniques such as diagrams and mathematical formalism was also a significant influence upon what came to be economics. However, this fixing of the world in a particular way for certain kinds of knowledge to be deemed scientific was not immediate, unproblematic, or complete. The accumulated epistemological heritage of what we see as economics testifies to its tension-ridden theoretical and scientific status.

In the next chapter, I will analyse the question of 'difference' in the modernist rendition of knowledge of which economics is a part. This then becomes a statement to the effect that in order to interrogate the problems of economics as a social science, one can do a lot by focusing on epistemology; but in order to do even more, one has to move beyond the question of economics as a problem of modernist knowledge to the question of modernist knowledge itself in its relation to its Other. To put it bluntly, I am not content with examining and interrogating economics as a social science from a perspective delimited by historical methodological or philosophical guidance. The problems of knowledge in a modernist social science like economics are also those that it shares with social science in general. Social science here signals Western modernist politically interested body of knowledge that has refused to recognise its own provincialism, epistemic violence, or complicity with the dominant regimes of power. It is thus that I will turn my attention to foregrounding the role of history in the conception of knowledge sanctioned by modernism, and argue for thinking knowledge *Other*wise.

Part 3

Issues of knowledge and difference

3 Modernist rendition of knowledge and the question of difference

> Thus the science of economy, or political economy, is also a dogmatically conditioned branch of human knowledge . . . the outcome, in our time of scientific specialisation is a peculiar but characteristic dogmatism of specialized sciences. We require the effort of philosophical analysis to free ourselves of this. We must begin to doubt that which is unusual or improper to question, we must look with the naïve eyes of a foreigner or a savage, for whom starched collars and white cuffs, self-evident for us, seem peculiar, and who asks about their true purpose.
>
> (Bulgakov 2000: 42–43)

3.1 Introduction

My aim in this chapter is to examine the questions of difference in relation to the questions of knowledge. Until now I have traced the influence of some tensions in enlightenment epistemology on the subject-world of economics, but an acknowledgement of the geo-historical-ideological-temporal locatedness of the enterprise of economics is also at the same time an avowal of its imbrication as a contingent episteme in the modernist constellation. One can then no longer sustain the claim that the scientific character of economics is a natural norm, or even maintain that this claim is separable from the strategic adoption of methods in social science, or from the way in which science itself was instituted as a legitimating ideology of the modernist era.

Economics today is universalist in line with the generalising impulse of the Enlightenment; it is peculiarly rationalist, it is eurocentric, it has tended to push differences of gender, race, class, culture, ecology, sexuality under the epistemological carpet, it has striven for crafting an 'economic' that is split, separate, and explainable in its totality. This category of the economic is seemingly unable to be juxtaposed with identity, and it is not enough to continue to critique economics on the theoretical terms afforded by disciplinarity. Instead, the thrust here is to be *able to think* economics as a social science *Other*wise.

The 'Otherwise' referred to here can be understood thus. Every systematic structure, for its own comprehensibility (i.e. in order to be seen as a *structure* in the sense of something which structures), relies upon a fundamental and founding move – that of making impossible, to a large extent, the possibility of thinking its *own structurality*.[1] This is because thinking the structurality of the structure is already a *thinking against* the norms of comprehensibility flowing from an ordered systematisation. Further, this thinking against, or to put it more completely – thinking *against the grain* (thinking *Otherwise than*), is also the prelude to situations where one can attempt to face up to all that which a structure needed to omit in order to establish its structurality as a structure. One must clarify that the omissions are not always identical in their content or in the ways/processes by which they are written out. However, it is important to continually think against the grain precisely because it is important to confront the Other to every present, and to let its Otherness (in a word, difference) disrupt the comforting self-identical lullabies of the Same. Therefore, it is not enough to start from a social science like economics and to point out its errors and omissions in however detailed a manner. It is also crucial to be able to think its structurality, and to disrupt its genealogical heritage, by interspersing it with its constitutive exclusions.

The moves that I will make in this chapter are as follows. I will begin by alluding to the status of Time and the Other in modernist knowledge. Next, I will argue that political economy as a precursor of economics was not simply a discourse about a crafted-out and split realm which could be universally perceived as the economic. Rather, as will emerge from my discussion of Jean-Jacques Rousseau's discourse on political economy, its situatedness was tied to concept resonance with European discourses on virtue, nationality, government, masculinity, under the overarching theme of modernity. Underlying the dilemmas of modernist knowledge in general, and specific social sciences like economics in particular, is the binding conceptual-glue of the idea of 'human nature'. In a critical vein, I will present the case that appeals to human nature have almost always functioned as the authority of a transcendental pretence, which remains narrowly provincial while claiming to be universal. In this process, difference remains the perpetual remainder. One way of situating this in modernist knowledge is to consider the potent tension between Reason and history. Even when a compromise is sought which combines the forces of Reason and history, such as with the Hegelian dialectic of world history, it actively needs to position an Other (in Hegel's case, Africa) in order to derive its own coherence.[2] This is symptomatic of an inability to negotiate the problem of difference in modernist discourses of science or society. In those cases where difference is actively engaged, the terms of engagement are woefully inadequate. For instance, nineteenth-century Victorian race debates demonstrated the inability to see the Other as anything but a *limit-phenomenon* in the context of knowledge.

1 This resonates with Derrida's work. Consider the term 'Hauntology' (a play on the worded certainties of 'ontology') which owes to him (1994) – so that to haunt does not mean to be present, but absent neither. According to Derrida, '. . . it is necessary to introduce haunting into the very construction of a concept. Of every concept, beginning with the concepts of being and time.' Thus viewed, *every concept is an attempt to continually exorcise its own disjointedness*.

2 Marx's 'Asia' or Mill's China or India could number among other such examples.

In view of this, the need is for *reconstellated genealogies of the present*. This will be addressed by arguing for a postcolonial intervention in epistemology, an intervention that allows questions of difference to be placed at the heart of self and identity in order to disrupt the modernist disciplinary logic that relies upon creating knowledge based on manufacturing conceptual abstractions and universalising their essence. This would allow the connections to be made between interrogating the notion of economics as a modernist science, with excavating how economics was sanctioned as a societal mechanism – a practice – of management, of colonisation, of organising what now came to be seen as 'economic' experiences under the lengthening shadow of modernity through which everything continues to be filtered.

As a result, in the next part of the book I will be able to juxtapose issues of identity and the economic, as a prelude to imagining the writing of economic theory an*Other* way.

3.2 Time and the Other of modernist knowledge

Modernity is an over-imagined historical construct.[3] The linkages between modernity and the period of the Enlightenment have to be acknowledged. One could say that the Enlightenment was the intellectual counterpart of modernity as the political, economic, and cultural transformation that radiated outwards from Western Europe especially after the eighteenth century. But at the same time it is important to realise that the Enlightenment was *not* simply the theory to the praxis of modernity. Rather the *designation as Enlightenment* of a certain chronological period – which was seen to be marked by a confluence of advances in knowing (many of these advances in knowing relied upon crucial changes in the way they articulated what it means to know) – is extremely important in *engendering a subjectivity* which came to be understood as *modernist*. This modernist subjectivity is deeply implicated in the themes and emphases of enlightenment epistemology. For now, the *world was to be manufactured* in the image of science and the individual knower. It is the very *self-conscious belief* in the value of these *totems of modernity* that is most striking in retrospect. Modernism is not a mere

3 Since the concept of modernity is available for utilisation in various ways across the disciplines, it has been given many enduring meanings. In the historical sense of periodisation, the moderns have sometimes sought to designate themselves in relation to the ancients or sometimes the medievals (Yolton 1995: 25–27). In other historical accounts, modernity is inaugurated in roughly the sixteenth century, in the compass-map-globe quests of the white, Western European male adventurer, as the advent of a new kind of knowing anew (see Hall 1992). Still other accounts focus upon the links of modernity with a period of state governance, secular humanism, scientific advances and instrumental Reason in Western Europe. In addition to this, modernism as a rationally ordered ruling ideology of contemporary secular, capitalist, liberal, democratic nation-states is counterposed with traditional systems of state and market governance mixes which are seen as inefficient and ineffective, breeding anachronisms. For work on the characteristics of modernity, see Latour (1993); Heller (1999); Delanty (2000); Venn (2000).

historical curiosity, soon to be surpassed, but is a potent (if not always productive) method of sweeping order into the business of knowing the present in presence of the past.

As the Enlightenment luminaries set about their task of interpreting everything as if *no* interpretations had existed before, it was also a desperate attempt at coming to terms with their present as they faced it. It was a present laced with ideas of instrumental rationalisation of society, secularisation, and the emergent capitalist relations of production. Amidst all this, many *reconciliations* had to take place between entities that were inherited, those that were constantly invoked, those that existed, and those that had to be fashioned. Some of these entities were – God, Sovereign, Individual, Nature, Nation, Science, Facts, Machines, and Economy. It is important to realise that these were *not* ideas or even physical formations that existed fully formed only to be grasped and explained and understood. Rather, these were the very bricks of the new modernist structure that was going to be vastly influential in the Western world view and incredibly disseminated in the rest of the world. These were constructs that were formed over periods of time and in no particular organised discipline; it is only later that they come to be associated with one or another relatively 'autonomous' spheres of inquiry (aka 'disciplines').

To begin with, modernist knowledge has always functioned by designating its history and its Other. One can never be modern without having been something else.[4] In a trivial sense this gestures to a 'Whiggishness'[5] in the way the very idea of modernity is written and understood, but it is important to reiterate that *modernity's necessity for a history*, any history, is also in effect *its impossibility of ever being anachronistic*. The carving of the modern era in the telling of history indicates the way a master concept like modernity is ensured that it is *in time, in step with time, its time*. There is always a before, and an after tainted by its before. Those ideas, subjects, civilisations that are counterposed with modernity are always ranked in modern time, the time of the self-conscious emergence of the modern Western European self whose knowledge of *its world* has since then served to function as knowledge of *the world*. Such self-conscious emergences are further foreclosed in the modern account, so that retrospective beginnings cannot be rewritten for non-modernist anachronisms.[6] In other words, *the modern has an exclusive purchase on splitting the melon of time*. With Arnaud (in Bachelard 1969: 137 [1950: 127]), it merrily declares, 'Je suis l'espace où je suis' (I am the space where I am).

4 Indeed, for some, one can never be modern, fullstop. See Latour (1993).

5 Blaug (2001: 151) writes of the origins of the term 'Whig interpretations of history' after the title of a 1951 book by the English historian Herbert Butterfield, which attacked the dominant tradition of English historiography depicting the history of England as a story of steady progress towards the liberal ideals represented by the Whig party.

6 Consider the following (Anand 2007, Chapter 3, emphasis added)

> *Chronopolitics*, or the politics of time, has played an important role in Western representations of the non-Western Other. The Other has been imagined as socially and culturally backward

The modernist era has been the story of an infatuation with the compilation of time; the modern Western European self compulsively needs *to archive its contemporaries*. Latour says it (1993: 97, emphases added):

> The great divide between Us – Occidentals – and Them – everyone else, from the China seas to the Yucatan, from the Inuit to the Tasmanian aborigines – has not ceased to obsess us. *Whatever they do, Westerners bring history along with them in the hulls of their caravels and their gunboats, in the cylinders of their telescopes and the pistons of their immunizing syringes*. They bear this white man's burden sometimes as an exalting challenge, sometimes as a tragedy, but always as a destiny... In Westerner's eyes the West, and *the West alone, is not a culture, not merely a culture.*

Thus, modernist knowledge is not simply the West writing its own history, but also the history of its Others' histories. It is this that makes anthropology viable – the ability to write not just one's own history and culture, but to write it so that it includes the compiled and concise writing of every Other's being. What needs examining is the belief that the Other has surrendered its identity to be bound and placed on the shelf of a modern library.[7]

It is no surprise then that Western anthropologists abroad have been able to seamlessly bind the entirety of foreign exotic cultures in the single anthropological monograph.[8] But this ability to generate authoritative knowledge abroad cannot

> (in time) – medieval (feudal like pre-Renaissance Europe), archaic (like ancient Egyptians or Mesopotamians), pre-historic (primitive), or simply beyond the matrix of time (timeless). The colonial journey and travel of contemporary Western commentators is figured as proceeding forward in geographical space but backward in historical time... The Other is both a prisoner of time (frozen in a certain stage of history) and an escapee (outside the time grid, timeless, outside history). The West is [seen as] the present, the now and it has the duty/right to bring Progress to the Other.

See also McClintock (1995).

7 Interestingly, speaking of libraries, one is reminded of Macaulay's lines (in Southard 1997), '[he has] never found one among them [Orientalists, an opposing political group] who could deny that a single shelf of a good European library was worth the whole native literature of India and Arabia'. For Macaulay it was 'no exaggeration to say, that all the historical information which has been collected from all the books written in Sanscrit language is less valuable than what may be found in the most paltry abridgments used at preparatory schools in England'. Note Southard when he says, '[w]hile all colonizsers may not have shared Macaulay's lack of respect for the existing systems of the colonized, they do share the idea that education is important in facilitating the assimilation process.'

8 Latour writes (1993: 14),

> Every ethnologist is capable of including within a single monograph the definition of the forces in play; the distribution of powers among human beings, gods, and non humans; the procedures for reaching agreements; the connections between religion and power; ancestors; cosmology; property rights; plant and animal taxonomies. The ethnologist will certainly not write three separate books: one dealing with knowledge, another with power, yet another with practices. She will write a single book, like the magnificent one in which Philippe Descola attempts to sum up the constitution of the Achuar of the Amazon region...

be replicated at home. If there were to be an anthropology of the modern world, it would mean analysing the very constitution of the principles of organisation, and justifying their existence. While everything else is compared to the standards of modernity, it is difficult and dangerous to undertake an analysis of the construction of those standards. Such an interrogation could even result in the realisation of recognising oneself as different, as another, just an Other.[9]

And conventionally, when the anthropologists investigate at home, they confine themselves to the marginalised groups of society seeking to explain their 'irrationalities' and 'excesses'. For instance, in nineteenth-century Britain, working class women and the Irish were frequently the subject of ethnological scrutiny (see also Latour 1993; McClintock 1995). This anthropological and ethnological agenda in the West was closely tied to the expectations of the science of political economy (see Darity Jr. 1995), since some Others were seen as not being capable enough of judging their own best interest or making rational choices. Dimand (2001) gives the examples of William Stanley Jevons (one of the founders of the neoclassical marginalist 'revolution') who, like Nassau William Senior, did not believe that English working class or the Irish made rational intertemporal choices: deploring the 'ignorance, improvidence, and brutish drunkenness of our lower working classes', which led them to save too little and marry too early. Similarly, John Rae and Irving Fisher (famous economist and also founder of the American Eugenics Society in 1923) also attributed lack of foresight and will-power to particular ethnic groups. Dimand (2001) quotes Fisher from *The Theory of Interest* [1930: 374–375] as well as from *Elementary Principles of Economics* [1912: 404]

> The communities and nationalities which are most noted for the qualities mentioned above – foresight, self-control, and regard for posterity – are probably Holland, Scotland, England, France, and the Jews, and among these peoples interest has been low... among communities and peoples noted for lack of foresight and for negligence with respect to the future are China, India, Java, the negro communities in the Southern states, the peasant communities of Russia, and the North and South American Indians, both before and after they had been pushed to the wall by the white man.

9 The despair at this possibility is characterised by Ricoeur (in Sharpe 1993: epigraph) as,

> When we discover that there are several cultures instead of just one and consequently at the time when we acknowledge the end of the sort of cultural monopoly, be it illusory or real, we are threatened with destruction by our own discovery. Suddenly it becomes possible that there are just Others, that we ourselves are an 'Other' among others. All meaning and every goal having disappeared, it becomes possible to wander through civilisations as if through vestiges and ruins. The whole of mankind becomes a kind of museum.

If one cannot preserve a monopoly on identity, then we must all be specimens in a museum. The imperial gaze is relentless.

3.3 Rousseau's discourse on political economy

Knowledge in social science is thus also a movement in history, in time, and place. Concepts do not function in isolation but make sense in a mesh of other interrelated and connected systems which lend them credence and credulity. In this sense, political economy is not simply the reference to a pre-existing economic system of production, consumption, and distribution, but is tied into the wider European discourses on the individual, the sovereign, and the state. I term this ability of a concept like political economy to function successfully as owing to the sedimentation of *concept resonance*.[10]

As an example, let me discuss Rousseau's discourse on political economy[11] which is in line with his wider objective of negotiating the relations between the individual and the state, a purpose for which he puts his notion of the 'savage man' to use. Rousseau advocated a social constitution of individuality – the civilised man was socially constituted and did not precede society. But, the civilised man was not necessarily the pinnacle of humanity. He sketched out the differences of the civilised versus the savage man. While the civilised man is '... always moving, sweating, toiling, and racking his brains to find still more laborious occupations ... in drudgery to his last moment, and even seeks death to put himself in a position to live, or renounces life to acquire immortality' (in West 1996: 27–28), the savage or natural man is 'healthy and vigorous, has little foresight or fear of death and has no command, because little need, of language ... exists without morality ... has a healthy "love of self" ... celebrates the simpler and healthier existence of the peoples colonised or enslaved' (ibid.: 28). In other words, the natural and savage man (humanity as lived outside Europe, modernity's *contemporary archives*) is where we started from: we were good, healthy, and simple, innocent, primitive, and happy. Now, modern civilisation in Western Europe has made us hard-working, competitive, tired, jealous, and unequal, but also virtuous, honourable, moral, and responsible. Yet, Rousseau is not advocating a return to the 'state of nature'; he is very aware of the complexities of modern nexus of individual-society-sovereign and reconciles it in his notion of the 'general will'. For Rousseau, civilisation meant that individuals transit from being primitive to being modern in societies

10 By concept resonance, I mean, that there is a non-arbitrary correspondence, an aligning of certain inflections of concepts such as the individual, society and sovereignty so that these particular understandings holistically provide an ideological umbrella for working out further concepts.

11 This choice of Rousseau needs further explanation. If Rousseau's thought was an important influence on the idea of the socially constituted individual, it was also a particular way of placing the subjectivity of the modern western European subject, and its relation to its Others. Rousseau's conceptualisation of the terms of the individual, society, and sovereign nexus was also an important strand of thought for later reactions to the Enlightenment modernity. While Rousseau does not fall within the canonical history of economics, yet as an enlightenment thinker his discourse on political economy illustrates the fluidity of knowledge categories not yet sedimented into disciplinary boundaries. Moreover, his discussions embody several themes and emphases of enlightenment epistemology – for example, the conflict between the general and the particular, the notion of machines, plays of interacting forces, invisible orders, and the like.

governed in accordance with a general will, and what they lose in natural liberty, they gain in civil and moral liberty.[12]

In his 1755 *A Discourse On Political Economy*, Rousseau starts by distinguishing between the 'general' or 'political' economy, and the domestic or particular economy. He postulates a great difference between the two, simultaneously differentiating between 'public economy' (which he sees as his subject and also calls it 'government'), and the supreme authority, which he calls 'sovereignty'. He further compares the body politic to an organised living body resembling that of man:

> The sovereign power represents the head; the laws and customs are the brain, the source of the nerves and seat of the understanding, will and senses, of which the judges and magistrates are the organs: commerce, industry, and agriculture are the mouth and stomach which prepare the common subsistence; the public income is the blood, which a prudent *economy*, in performing the functions of the heart, causes to distribute through the whole body nutriment and life: the citizens are the body and members, which make the machine live, move and work; and no part of this machine can be damaged without the painful impression being at once conveyed to the brain, if the animal is in a state of health.

This body politic is also a moral being possessed of a will – the general will, 'which tends always to the preservation and welfare of the whole and of every part, and is the source of the laws, constitutes for all members of the State, in their relations to one another and to it, the rule of what is just or unjust'. His concern is with joining together governance and justice, the rule of law and the freedom of Reason. Governance is invoked as an abstract general principle regarding which the 'Legislator' needs to take into account '. . . for every need of place, climate, soil, custom, neighbourhood, and all the rest of the relations peculiar to the people he had to institute'. Already, a particular form of understanding the being of people in the world – a form involving a State, sovereign and executing legislators, citizens, and body politic – is being placed as the unquestioned basis from which further rules of regulating this 'system' can be derived. Further, Rousseau places an extreme stress on maintaining authority by internalising the ideas of citizenship and patriotism. 'The most absolute authority is that which penetrates into a man's inmost being, and concerns itself no less with his will than

12 See West (1996: 30) on this, where he gives a quote from Rousseau to say,

> The passage from the state of nature to the civil state produces a very remarkable change in man, by substituting for instinct in his conduct, and giving his actions the morality they had formerly lacked. Then only, when the voice of duty takes the place of physical impulses and the right of appetite, does man, who so far had considered only himself, find that he is forced to act on different principles and consult his reason before listening to his inclinations.

with his actions.' However, like Adam Smith's 'sympathy', Rousseau's virtue stops short of embracing humanity. He writes,

> [i]t appears that the *feeling of humanity evaporates and grows feeble in embracing all mankind*, and that *we cannot be affected* by the calamities of Tartary or Japan, in the same manner as we are by those of *European nations*. It is necessary in some degree to *confine and limit our interest and compassion in order to make it active*... it is proper that our humanity should confine itself to our fellow-citizens,... greatest miracles of virtue have been produced by patriotism... makes it most heroic of all passions...

This is an instructive lesson in understanding the foundational 'humanity' of enlightenment modernity – it is a limited fund of humanity affected by distance, dissimilarity, but also racial difference (European nations are likely to be dissimilar as well, but they still fall within the ambit of the 'mankind' destined for 'humanity'), and therefore needs to be distributed prudently.[13]

The love of country is situated as the fount of virtue: '[d]o we wish men to be virtuous? Then let us begin by making them love their country'. In this interesting way, by linking up happiness with virtue, virtue with citizenship, citizenship with patriotism, and country with governance, and governance with the general will, he moves towards justifications for taxes by the state.[14] Indeed, for him, the instant of birth of the child is the inauguration of the moment of citizenship, and 'ought to be the beginning of the exercise of our duty'. The laws of both infancy and of maturity are necessary because, '[f]amilies dissolve, but the State remains'. He envisages each house as a school of citizenship with the 'unlimited power of *fathers*' (emphasis added).

Now, witness the ways in which patriotism, authoritarian governmentality, civic constitutionalism, European provincialism, and patriarchy meld into

13 More than two centuries later, the 'critical' theorist of enlightenment and modernity, Habermas, diagnoses the sickness of modernity as not a fatal one. Venn (2000: 28) sums up Habermas's views on this by saying, 'What is needed is for "Europe" [...] to realise that the illness is self-inflicted, aggravated by bad theoretical prognoses in conditions of unfettered capitalist development,' so that '"Europe could draw *from its own* traditions the insight, the energy, the courage of vision" to cure itself' (1987: 367, original emphasis). Venn (68) writes of this 'revealing slip, consistent with his [Habermas's] neglect of difference. ... There is no recognition in his [Habermas's] analysis of the mutations in modernity in the context of its implantation in the colonies and the varieties of modernity that have developed today.' However, the irony is that, shortly afterwards, Venn himself argues that a consensus on normative issues outside of Europe is difficult to achieve, and gives the example of 'the customary sexual mutilation of girls in many Muslim communities' (28), an issue which has become *the new Sati*. On the politics of Sati, see Narayan (1997), Spivak (1988). For the weaving of the politics of Sati into a literary narrative, see the novel *Rich Like Us* by Nayantara Sahgal (1985), especially Chapter 11.

14 Rousseau writes: 'There can be no patriotism without liberty, no liberty without virtue, no virtue without citizens; create citizens, and you have everything you need; without them, you will have nothing but debased slaves, from the rulers of the State downwards.'

Rousseau's discourse on political economy.[15] Indeed, two things can immediately be said about this bringing together. First, it has always been a feature of modernist renditions that they are all brought together in the name of the general man.[16] In the split between theory and praxis, often praxis is designated by interaction with a brute materiality of the physical world, while unified accounts of this interaction provided by the theorist constitute theory. The unity of the diverse ideas that are reconciled in recitation constitutes the power of theory, a power deriving from the proposed interrelation between many knowings, an interrelation thus permitting transcription into control and legislation. Second, the very fact that Rousseau chooses to bring together these competing signs under the umbrella of political economy is remarkable. Political economy is then not far from designations of virtue, power, government, nation, and man. Its situatedness remains tied to *concept resonance* with European discourses on virtue, nationality, government, masculinity, under the arched theme of modernity. Yet, in the light of my discussions about the status of science, the latter-day universalisation of the development of a provincial discourse on political economy (later, economics) is an affirmation of the West not being a culture, Science not being an ideology, and the Other as *not* capable of systematic and coherent management of any kind (management of passions to lead to virtue, management of authority for proper governance,[17] management of the boundaries for sovereign nations,[18] management of sexuality to produce proper masculinity, management of subsistence – perhaps the idea of management itself).

The reason why I have stressed on management as a means to control in my discussion of political economy is because, in the context of Rousseau,[19] wise and good governance approximates economy. Economy, 'which means rather the prudent management of what one has than ways of getting what one has not', so that the prudent administrators can fix the system of the economy by balancing the needs of the present against the needs distant from now, '. . . just as a mariner when he finds the water gaining on his vessel, does not neglect, while he is working the pumps, to discover and stop the leak.' Already, the manufactured notion of the economy linked to the body politic of the individual State, is being sedimented as a system that exists out there fully performed, nonetheless in need of balancing, repair, and management.

15 This concept resonance is not out of date today. Consider the following comment on feminism made by Pat Robertson (right-wing US politician) in 1992: 'Feminism encourages women to leave their husbands, kill their children, practice witchcraft, destroy capitalism and become lesbians.'

16 Lyotard tellingly said, '"Man" is but a sophisticated knot' (in Venn 2000: 21).

17 Now we know that this is why the international financial institutions such as the IMF, the World Bank, and Western governments continually recycle the rhetoric about promoting 'good governance' in the 'Third World'.

18 The non-Western and non-modern governments' and societies' incomplete incorporation into the full functionality of the idea of 'sovereignty', works even today to their loss, as they have to make their case in terms of the grand narrative of sovereignty, or nationalist resistance.

19 Rousseau even makes use of the notion of 'ceteris paribus' in his discourse on political economy.

At several places in his text, Rousseau invokes China – as a place where the Prince maintains his authority by deciding against his officers in any dispute between them and the people, as a place where the peasants pay no taxes yet best cultivate (along with England and Holland with little peasant taxes), also as a place where,

> the taxes are greater and yet better paid than in any other part of the world. There the merchant himself pays no duty; the buyer alone, without murmuring or sedition, meets the whole charge; for as the necessaries of life, such as rice or corn, are absolutely exempt from taxation, the common people is not oppressed, and the duty falls only on those who are well-to-do.

Then, as now, Europe is exhorted by the example of China.[20] There are also examples of the 'classical civilisations' of Rome and Greece. Rousseau's treatment of the Others of Europe is a *complexio oppositorum*, complex and contradictory.[21]

3.4 Subjectivity of modernist knowledge and the transcendental pretence

> The West is a name for a subject which gathers itself in discourse but is also an object constituted discursively; it is, evidently, a name always associating itself with those regions, communities, and peoples that appear politically or economically superior to other regions, communities, and peoples... it claims that it is capable of sustaining, if not actually transcending, an impulse to transcend all the particularizations.
>
> (Sakai 1998, in Chakrabarty 2000: 3)

If Rousseau's political economy is underwritten by enlightenment epistemology, it is also an indication of the extent to which the general man of civilised society drew his appeal from the Cartesian subject. The common thread was the application of Reason. Whether in philosophical meditation or in everyday conduct, Reason played an important part as a distinguishing feature of human nature. There were differing views on the extent to which Reason was influenced by passions, or the role it had in guaranteeing access to rational knowledge, but it was commonly held that the Cartesian subject with a Kantian mind[22] was the ideal subject of

20 Witness the current panic in Western media over China's 'rising' status vis-a-vis Europe. In making these facile comparisons between a country and a continent (see Lewis and Wigen 1997), the unstated fear is of a 'non-Western power' overturning the familiarities of the international relations arena.

21 In the case of China, Rousseau typifies the Enlightenment brand of fascination mixed with revulsion when it comes to looking beyond. If the Chinese taxation system is an example worthy of emulation, the Chinese people themselves are surely not. '[T]here is no sin to which they are not prone, no crime which is not common among them' (in Clark 1997: 53).

22 From Descartes onwards, the mind was split from matter, the thinking being who is capable of doubting its existence, must therefore exist (cogito ergo sum). The world was not a teleologically unfolding purposive experiencing, but a vast realm of matter that needed to be observed, analysed, and understood by the dint of a labouring, reasoning, and scientific human mind functioning like the most perfect machine imaginable, attributing causes to effects. With Kant, this pure Reason is

social science. This conscious knowing subject is the benchmark for all knowledge, always and everywhere. The disciplinary structuring of modernist knowledge in its various forms performs the act of shoring up all the world as it appears to this knowing subject. Descartes (1641) in his *Meditations on First Philosophy* recalls Archimedes, 'Archimedes, in order that he might draw the terrestrial globe out of his place, and transport it elsewhere, demanded *only that one point* should be fixed and immoveable.' It is this one point that was to be the lever for moving everything else. The Cartesian cogito, the I that exists because it can doubt its own existence, like the Archimedean lever, is the centre-pin that moves everything else, and thus manufactures the world in its image. The Cartesian cogito is, above all, a being with Reason.

This knowing being inhabits a dualistic world which is split from itself. Also, an important part of the legacy of the Cartesian subject is its inability to conceive of an unassimilable Other whose difference cannot be reduced and explained to its irrationality, insanity, or inability. When the Other is invoked in canonical modernist meditations, it is called forward as if in a Court to testify to its difference, and thus mark out its own irrationality, insanity, or inability. Therefore, it is an important part of this modernist enlightenment (and also the semi- or counter-enlightenment strains inhabiting its folds) that the relation between the self and Other, even when conceptualised, remains an enactment within the consciousness of the knowing subject.

This self knows no Other, and the centrality of its subjectivity forms a large part of the epistemological thrust from the 'Cartesian doubt to the Hegelian absolute'. Solomon (1988) captures this self-referential subjectivity by calling it the 'transcendental pretence'. Referring to the 'practical and political dangers of a viewpoint that is so universally projective and self-congratulatory' (4), he points out that this is linked to the European self-image of which science and knowledge, along with the romantic imagination, are important ingredients. Let us consider his views on what the transcendental pretence is.[23] He writes (7):

> The transcendental pretence is the unwarranted assumption that there is universality and necessity in the fundamental modes of human experience. It is not mere provincialism, that is, the ignorance or lack of appreciation of alternative cultures and states of mind. It is an aggressive and sometimes arrogant effort to prove that there are no such (valid) possible alternatives. In its application the transcendental pretence becomes the *a priori* assertion that

critiqued, and a synthesis is sought between empiricism and rationalism. The empiricist bases too much on experience (impression, sensation, observation) and neglects the contribution of human mind itself, the rationalist relies too much on *a priori* knowledge and neglects the role of experience. The need is for realising the boundaries of knowledge, and for creating its firm foundations. Kant's '"Copernican revolution" in metaphysics' seeks to do justice to both these objectives. This is achieved by his being a transcendental idealist and empirical realist at the same time. All human knowledge is to be made sense of in terms of the human mind – a mind which can know things in the world of phenomena, or the world as it appears to us, however, also a mind which cannot know the world of noumena, or the world of things in themselves.

23 In the light of Solomon's views on the transcendental pretence, it really *is* interesting that when discussing Rousseau's influence, he writes, 'it came to influence half of the civilised [*sic*] world.'

> the structures of one's own mind, culture, and personality are in some sense necessary and universal for all humankind, perhaps even 'for all rational creatures'. In the realms of morality, politics, and religion it is the effort to prove that there is but one legitimate set of morals (the middle-class morals of Europe), one legitimate form of government (the form of parliamentary monarchy that ruled most of Western Europe), and one true religion, to be defended not just by faith and with force of arms, but by rational argument, by 'reason alone'.

Sometimes taking the form of 'human nature', this transcendental self is presumed to be timeless, universal, identical, and embodied in everyone. Relating the story of its discovery, Solomon (16) finds that Rousseau, '[s]trolling in solitude through the lush forests of St Germain during early adolescence of the modern age, made [the] miraculous discovery...[of] his self'. Rousseau's self was also the soul of humanity (to him). Soon, Kant could say, '[a]s Newton was the first to discern order and regularity in nature, Rousseau was the first to discover beneath the varying forms human nature assumes, the deeply concealed essence of man and the hidden law in accordance with which providence is justified' (in ibid.: 16). Indeed, one could argue that it is this very unquestioned transcendental pretence (how ironic that the 'transcendental' ideals of the foundations of 'universal' knowing were put forward by a white European man, Kant, who never in his life left the port of Königsberg)[24] that provides the grounding legitimacy for universal modernist disciplinary knowledges. Economics as the universal scientific study of human societies could not ever purport to provide rational explanations of all human choices without being bolstered by the transcendental pretence, and associated principles and assumptions about human nature. It is for this reason that economics is a Western science, its most notable practitioners prior to the twentieth century, geographically concentrated in Europe. I should add that the attempts by historians to dig up ancient economic traditions in all civilisations and at all times does not serve as a counter-argument to my point here. For, I'm not saying that prior to the Western Europe of enlightenment times (and except for ancient Greece and Rome), no societies organised production, consumption, or exchange. That would refer to a notion of economy (and economising) which is not the invention of economics. Rather, it is the particular confluence of ideas on the economy (around the autonomous and insatiable

24 Solomon (1988: 7) writes about 'the white philosopher's burden',: '[p]hilosophers who never left their home towns declared themselves experts on "human nature", and weighed the morals of civilisations and ' "savages" thousands of miles beyond their ken', and gives the example of Kant. On the relation between philosophy, modernity, and colonialism, see especially Eze (1997). In his introduction to this brilliant critical reader on postcolonial African philosophy, Eze points out the dire provincialisms of the European greats – Hume, Kant, Hegel, Habermas, and many more. Kant draws upon Hume to state: '[t]his man was black from head to toe, *a clear proof* that what he said was stupid' (7), and, in his *Observations on the Feeling of the Beautiful and Sublime*, provides a hierarchical chart on the different 'races' – 'STEM GENUS: *white brunette*, First race, very blond (northern Europe), Second race, Copper-Red (America), Third race, Black (Senegambia), Fourth race, Olive-Yellow (Indians)' (7).

individual freely choosing in the face of scarcity which forms the basis of understanding human behaviour), which emerged from a modernist disciplinary structuring[25] to provide the basis for a universal scientific study, that is actually located and contingent. It is further tied in to equally located and contingent ideas on governance, morality, patriarchy, sovereignty, and so on.[26] Finally, none of these ideas would have seemed sensible or credible as the basis for a universal social science, had it not been for the lure of the transcendental self, arrogantly reincarnated as human nature, but based upon a narrow model of Cartesian subjectivity. A model of subjectivity that has at its very core the picture of the transcendental self, a being in the world, that seeks to know the world; the world which in concentric circles radiates outwards from this knowing being. A crucial element is that, although there are numerous other people, the transcendental self is identically incarnated in each, so that one can always know other people from the inside. This means that essentially everyone is the same, operates on the same logic, and can only be located at different places on the same grid – a grid which we can study/map. If there are anomalies, that is, people, patterns, societies, then they must be irrational, insane, or unable. Then the question is, can they be made rational, sane, and able, or, are they simply the damned?

Further, only by seeing knowledge as separate from ethics, politics, strategy, subjectivity, Reason, and being, will we see it as scientific, rational, and universal, because it will seem to emanate from a supposedly transcendental pretence, and can then be 'applied' as praxis to specific contexts.

3.5 Reason, history and the Hegelian dialectic

If one takes the conventional picture of the modernist subject-world, with the Cartesian subject at its centre, and the world of everything else all around it, one returns to the tension with meaning. The Cartesian subject 'I' which is at

25 This structuring of ideas may itself have been motivated by responses to problems of knowledge, its categorisation and management in the interests of the eminent social orders. See the discussions in Chapters 1 and 2.

26 It is especially tied in to imperialism, colonialism, and the empire. The colonial and the economic have always worked in tandem to propagate the logic of the capital to serve vested interests. Joseph *et al.* (1990) give an example of how the conceptual framework of the economic was constructed so that colonial ideology could be defended and extended within it. The Kikuyu of Kenya were being encouraged to grow coffee rather than maize around the same time as the Malays were discouraged from planting rubber and encouraged to concentrate on cultivating rice. The reason given was similar in the two cases – that the farmers would be better-off if they followed these economic prescriptions. Yet, the motivation was different in these two cases (3):

> In the Malayan case, the volume of rubber production had to be controlled to safeguard the profit margins of European plantation owners and/or avoid rice imports that would be needed if there was a significant shift from rice to rubber cultivation. In the case of the Kikuyu who had to share their land with the white settlers, the need to bring them into the money economy, as either labourers or small producers of cash crops was felt to be paramount.

centre of the whole enterprise of knowing, is itself left unexamined and untheorised. The subjectivity which forms the basis of the transcendental pretence is a knot. A universal self that knows the world, and at the same time is identical to every other self in that world. Further, as Code (1991: 5) points out, for each knower, the Cartesian route to knowledge is through private, abstract thought, through the efforts of reason unaided by the senses or by consultations with other knowers. 'Reason' itself is conceived as autonomous and unassisted by the senses, enabling the independent quest for certain knowledge undertaken by rational beings.

The tension between the (conscious) part and the (knowable) whole, the general and the particular, resurfaces as the divide between the self and the world, which is the master divide and simultaneously structures the difference between theory and praxis. If the self is a part of the world that knows itself and through itself knows the world, then the very question of the Other will cause it to unravel, because the concept does not make sense within this picture of the self and the world. The face of the Other will introduce limitations on knowledge, the reining-in of subjectivity, detranscendentalisation of the self, and the spectres of heteronomy, alterity, mysticism – that is, a complete alienation of this rather mechanistic picture of rational understanding and mediation between the part and the whole.[27]

If, on the other hand, one takes the picture that is amended to include history and particularity of society and culture, it may seem that it can account for the self's encounter with the Other in a productive way. However, what treatment is accorded to difference within the dialectic of world history? In order to answer this question, I will examine the pre-eminent synthesis of Reason and History effected in Hegel's rational dialectic of world history.

Hegel's grand speculative enterprise draws up the connections between individual consciousness and universal consciousness in the philosophy of world history as unfolding stages in the dialectic of the spirit (Geist) as the progress of freedom. This dialectic of world history spirally ascends from the 'stationary' Orient to Europe, not just as an unfolding of the absolute spirit but also as its realisation. He combines and welds together the history of all peoples in all the world into the architecture of Reason itself; Reason that culminates in a present, spreading back its tentacles to trawl through an infinite realm of the 'before',

27 A rational attempt at dealing with this is made within hermeneutics. For instance, a Gadamerian approach to hermeneutics, will reject the divide between subject and object, and also reject the possibility of contemplating a being removed from temporality or context. Instead of focusing on the attenuated Cartesian picture where the subject constitutes meaning from the world (in many variations with emphasis either on pre-given categories or sensations), we find that 'the hermeneuticist comes to appreciate the availability of meanings already in the world, and [interprets] these meanings' (Solomon 1988: 170). The emphasis is not on method, but in the realm of practice and on the historical context. Thus, comparing multiple interpretations, even in the face of differences, will lead to an eventual 'fusion of horizons'. Here, the radical challenge posed by an unknowable Other to the conscious Cartesian subject, is recast as a situation with multiple subjectivities, interpretations, which then find satisfactory resolutions in ethical conversations. This rendering demonstrates the hermeneutic faith in Reason and hope for future (172). See also Bleicher (1980).

catching resonances to designate a finite 'after' to the present. History is extremely important for Hegel. It is within the particular situated communities, its cultures, values, and practices, that the individual can be free or ethical. The individual for Hegel is not only the disembodied mind of Cartesian thought. The pure logic of a universal absolute is nonetheless empirically situated in time and space, and the Hegelian oeuvre was to provide a narrative of the development as progress of this absolute spirit in history and culture. Further, the historical unfolding of Reason is not its truth at any particular moment, but, the dialectic of overcoming through contradiction. Through the dialectic of history, the spirit comes to realise itself on the unfolding path of progress and Reason. As West (1996: 38) puts it, '[h]istory can be reconstructed as a dialectical progression of structures of consciousness or "spirit", embodied in particular historical societies. ... [T]he overall direction of the spirally ascending dialectic can be understood as the progress of freedom.' So that, Hegel becomes 'the architect of the dream of an absolute metanarrative of the historical unfolding of an always unitary reason' (Barnett 1998: 2).

The Hegelian system is an enterprise made solely of mirrors – in the house of Hegel, wherever one looks, one cannot escape one's own presence. And, at the same time, this presence provides the anchor for viewing anything else for as far as one can see in any direction. In this house, it would be impossible to argue the possibility of a shadow which cannot be reflected in the mirrors. By definition of the way in which it is set up, the Hegelian dialectic of world history as the unfolding of the spirit on the way to its self-conscious progress of freedom, is a story where the tension between the opposing poles of the dialectic is always productively materialised toward betterment.

Hegel stands for the snowballing of Enlightenment ideas to the point where the self-realisation of modernity becomes a celebration of European (Germanic) present as the peaked culmination of everything everywhere at all times. As Spivak puts it in another context (2000: 43), 'the triumphalist conviction that history happened in order to produce my kind.' To confront Hegelian modernity, it is indeed important to be able to *think* the possibility of a negative which is not made productive by its sublation into dialectical narrative recognition. The thinking of such a negative is intimately tied up to thinking alterity. The rational resolution of every opposite finds home in Hegel's house of mirrors precisely because those admitted into it have never really confronted an Other which is incapable of being reflected.

Such an Other has to be staged, as a negative which is unassimilable into the dialectic of presence in history. But this Other cannot be seen within Hegel's mirror; rather, it is Hegel that needs to be brought into view and confronted with all that he could not see, or chose not to see. What seems the infinity of systematic modernity, may only be the reflective depth of mirrors to the subject in history. Without the interweaving mirrors, the subject cannot be constituted. This unconstitutable subject, which is perhaps the ethical metaphysics of deconstruction, is the route to generating disrupted memories of modernity.

Anti-Hegelianism will not do, because the opposite of modernity is also defined by it. Rather, a calculated remembering of the erasures of modernity, its many forgettings, needs to be carried out. Foucault (in Barnett 1998: 2–3, emphases added) deliberates the specifics of such a 'calculation',

> [b]ut to truly escape Hegel involves *an exact appreciation of the price we have to pay to detach ourselves from him*. It assumes that we are aware of the extent to which Hegel, insidiously perhaps, is close to us; it implies a knowledge, in that which permits us to think against Hegel, of that which remains Hegelian. We have to determine the extent to which our anti-Hegelianism is possibly one of his tricks directed against us, at the end of which he stands, motionless, waiting for us.

Foucault is right, modernity's bankruptcies call for costly rememberings. These rememberings need to comprise of visits to the scenes where modernity's knowledge was constructed, and an examination of the procedures by which it was made possible.

Bernasconi (1998) takes a long journey back to bring Hegel to the Court of the Ashanti. He examines the role that 'Africa' played in Hegel's world. In order to situate his dialectic of world history, Hegel needed to place Africa as the outside of the progress of Reason. Bernasconi draws upon Hegel to demonstrate how in his world history's court of judgements ('Weltgericht'), he found Africans to be 'barbaric, cannibalistic, preoccupied with fetishes, without history, and without any consciousness of freedom... lack[ing] any integral ingredient of culture (Bildung)' (41). In fact, Bernasconi reiterates a summary of the portrait of Africans that emerges from Hegel's *Lectures on the Philosophy of World History*. This is as follows (1998: 50):

> First, Black (*die Neger*) are a childish people in their naivety (*Unbefangenheit*). Second, they allow themselves to be sold without reflection as to whether or not this is right; they feel no impulse (*Trieb*) towards freedom. Third, this childishness is reflected in their religion. They sense the higher, but do not retain it. They transfer the higher to a stone, thereby making it into fetish, although they will throw it away if it fails them. Fourth, although good-natured and harmless when in a calm condition, they commit frightful atrocities when suddenly aroused. Fifth, although capable of education (*Bildung*), as evidenced by their grateful adoption of Christianity on occasion and their appreciation of freedom when acquired, they have no propensity (*Trieb*) for culture (*Kultur*): their spirit is dormant and makes no progress.

Now, at this point, note that my argument is not that Hegel, like a large number of his contemporaries (also his predecessors and successors), was simply a 'racist'.[28] Rather, my aim is to argue that the status of Africa is crucial to Hegel's account

28 See Taiwo (1998) for a statement of Africa's challenge to philosophy and the need to exorcise Hegel's ghost.

of the dialectic of world history. Even as it was placed outside Hegel's system, it can be read as the fulcrum to the Hegelian meditations on progress of Reason in free and ethical societies.

No doubt, it is not common to read the 'dead greats' in this way. In fact, the strategies of reception of earlier theorists range from either ignoring their 'inconvenient' views by arguing their irrelevance or insignificance in the larger scheme of things, or excusing their 'inconvenient' views as only to be expected given their locatedness in an earlier time which is characterised by ignorance, intolerance, and prejudice. This is not something I agree with; let me explain why. If one takes the first route, and argues for the intricacies of Hegelian notions of political economy, ethical life, and freedom in society, without paying attention to the rest of his structure, then that is a reading of Hegel which ignores the *very ways* in which Hegel was able to say what he said. But, there is a vast and implicit gesture of epistemic violence in assuming universal relevance in readings of Hegel today, while not attending to the 'outside' of his structure. Thus, for example, if one is convinced that the dialectic of world history was in fact operant as Hegel argues, one would, no doubt, attempt to 'lift' those 'backward' societies and economies out of their thraldom from 'our' 'advanced' perspective. This is only too prevalent in the history of apologia for colonialism, and now in the rationale for neo-colonialism. However, on the other hand, if one takes the second route, one is arguing that we should not 'hold against' the dead greats their inconvenient views, because such views are only to be expected in that time and place. But, this is itself a Hegelian move that implicitly assumes progress in history, towards the benevolence of Reason. Further, it accomplishes the feat of, at the same time, casting critical consideration of inconvenient views as a gesture of 'holding against', and suffocating any examination of the 'how' or 'why' of the operation of such views. This latter is especially important. It is crucial to try to understand the ways in which considerations of race not only provided the justification for imperialism, but also functioned from within to generatively write narratives of modernity. It is the interrogation of the appeal of such narratives – that can be approached by deconstructing the desires behind the setting up of categories (such as race or gender) – and the ways in which they interacted. This is necessary to confront the logic of power behind the historical desires of modernity.[29]

Thus, Hegel was *not* simply describing Africa to the best of his knowledge in order to create a disinterested narrative of pure Reason. In fact, Bernasconi's research (1998: 45–48) would seem to suggest that Hegel was not even being completely true to his sources, especially Bowdich and Hutchison. For instance, Hegel reports that the Ashanti King inherits all the property left by his deceased subjects (where Bowdich mentions gold), or that the King of the Ashanti washed the bones of his dead mother in human blood (where Hutchison specifies rum

29 See Young (1995) for a discussion of colonial desire and racial theory in relation to Victorian imperialism.

and water), or that Ashanti chiefs were said to have 'torn their enemies' hearts from their bodies and eaten them while they were still warm and bleeding' (where Bowdich's accusation of cannibalism is unsubstantiated), or that at the end of public festivals, 'a human being is torn to pieces; his flesh is cast to the multitude and greedily eaten by all those who can lay hands on it' (source unknown), or that the Dahomey King has 3333 wives to produce children who could be sold as slaves (this was in Bowdich as the number of wives of an Ashanti King). Even Hegel's sources were exaggerating and embellishing their accounts, but Hegel was not simply conveying anecdotal disinformation; he was creating knowledge of 'Africa' and 'Africans' *without* which he could not have argued that instinct and respect are not universal human characteristics (ibid.: 46).

In fact, anecdotal disinformation was only too common, then as now.[30] The point is not that Hegel did not know enough about Africa, or that his sources were inaccurate and prejudiced, but that Hegel's 'Africa' provides him with an understanding of his 'Europe'. His 'being' is predicated upon there being his 'Others' – Others who are caught in the extremes of their climate, are incapable of achieving spiritual consciousness, are uniformly unchanging, are 'dominated by passion, savage, barbaric, and hence, most importantly for his discussion of history, at the first level (*Stufe*)' (ibid.: 52–53).[31]

Hegel is especially important for my discussion because of his influence upon political economists. Larrain (1994) provides some distinct examples of instances where Hegel's ideas were influential in the thought on political economy. Hegel distinguished between the world-historical peoples who were culturally developed and could contribute to the progress of world history by building a strong state, and the people without history who were spiritually and physically weak and whose destiny was to be subject to the civilising mission of the former. Likewise, most political economists (J. B. Say, Malthus) saw colonialism as necessary for bringing about progress in the stagnating 'savage nations' possessing an 'inferior civilisation'. John Stuart Mill believed that 'backward societies have a very weak "effective desire" to accumulate, to work harder and to save' (19). James Mill's description of the moral character of Indians and Chinese impressed Ricardo, who wrote: '[w]hat a frightful obstruction to improvement does the immoral

30 Even Hegel's sources such as Bowdich (author of *Mission from Cape Coast Castle to Ashantee*) were inaccurate. Bernasconi (ibid.: 45) writes, 'the copy of the treaty that Bowdich negotiated with the Ashanti was different from that which he deposited on his return.' Further, Bernasconi (50) points out that several of Hegel's chosen sources, such as Dalzel and Norris, wrote to further the pro-slavery cause, while the situation might have been different if he had relied upon anti-slavery authors such as Benezet.

31 As Larrain (1994: 19–22) points out, these Others include people of South America who are 'physically and spiritually impotent' and where 'even the animals show the same inferiority as the human beings'. For instance, in Paraguay, 'a clergyman used to ring a bell at midnight to remind them to perform their matrimonial duties, for it would otherwise never have occurred to them to do so'. China too represented a stationary nation which did not contribute to the progress of world history.

character of the people of India present!' (ibid.). The beliefs of even Marx and Engels belied Hegel's influence.[32] And thus,

> For Hegel it is the Spirit as it manifests itself through the primacy of historical nations, among which the Prussian state has pride of place; for classical political economy it is the bourgeoisie as the representative of Britain, the first capitalist nation; for Marx and Engels it is the proletariat of Britain. The emancipating subjects may be different but they all represent the highest stage of historical reason as it is given in western Europe, and it is from there that they should carry out their mission.
>
> (ibid.: 23)

This lineage is not by any means 'over'. As Franco (1988: 504) argues, metropolitan discourses on the Third World adopt either of the three devices: (1) exclusion, as the Third World is irrelevant to theory; (2) discrimination, as the Third World is irrational and its knowledge is subordinate to the rational knowledge of the metropolis; (3) recognition, as the Third World is only seen as the place of the instinctual.

The possibility of the Other is not confronted in its radical plurality, and multiple random scattering. The Other remains captive as a spectral possibility within the logic of the self-same subject in whose certainties there linger anxious hauntings, forcing it to cast its tyrannous net ever wider. The disjointedness at the very core of this anxious haunted subject needs addressing.

The status of the Other in the modernist subject-world is: 'the Other of the Same'. Irigaray used this concept to designate the way in which 'Woman' as the alternative to the conventional male subject has functioned. She provided an influential critique of Simone de Beauvoir's account of Woman in terms of 'the Other of the Same'. Woman is 'the necessary negative of the male subject, all that he has repressed and disavowed' (Whitford 1991: 24–25), and her access to universal subjecthood is based upon claiming sameness to the supposedly universal male subject, and repressing any social and symbolic representation of otherness and difference.[33]

The way in which the Other is confined to being the 'Other of the same' is also linked to Irigaray's critique of the Hegelian account of women's role in the maintenance of society. As Whitford explains (161, emphases original),

> For Hegel, men operate within the domain of the universal and the ethical (as citizens) but also have their *particular* needs attended to within the family.

32 For instance, Marx following Hegel's remarks on Latin American creoles in his comparison of Mexicans with the Spaniards, writes 'the Spaniards are completely degenerated. But in the presence of a Mexican a degenerated Spaniard constitutes an ideal'; and, Engels found the conquest of Algeria by France, 'an important and fortunate fact for the progress of civilization' (Larrain 1994: 20).

33 In contrast, Irigaray argues not just for an equality based on claiming sameness but the recognition of women's difference and 'for symbolic forms which correspond to women's specificity, the need for an *identity*' (in Whitford 1991: 160, emphasis original). Whitford (162) clarifies further that Irigaray's concern is with the way in which 'what she calls "the people of men" has appropriated women's bodies, children's bodies, nature, space, symbolism, the divine and representation in general'.

> Women do not have this dual possibility; their particularity is subordinate to the needs of the family and the state. ... While men can be spirit (universal), the family represents 'nature'. So long as women are confined to the family, their access to the universal is derivative, via the husband or son, rather than direct. ... For Irigaray, Hegel 'does not succeed in thinking the family other than as *one* substance'; he does not consider the possibility of the woman who is not subordinate to the family. As a result, the maternal genealogy is condemned by the patriarchal state ... with the backing of patriarchal and monotheistic religion.

The universal 'spirit' manifests itself yet again in the domain of the male; women function as subordinate to this logic as 'Others of the same' (recall the discussion of non-European Others, especially 'Africa' above). The concept resonance here between European 'universal' spirit, male citizens, family, nation, and the state is reminiscent of Rousseau's characterisation.

3.6 Human nature and the question of difference

> Yet hierarchies of gender, nationality, sexuality, class, race, etc. continue to trouble the waters of consensus and disrupt agreement on what it means to be fully human.
>
> (Williams 1993: 150)

The inability of enlightenment modernity to face up to difference, to the Other, is vastly apparent. This has been a continuing story. The terms on which the Other is encountered remain violent, exclusionary, assimilative, and negating. The question of difference in modernist knowledge is particularly problematic. This is because on the one hand the legitimacy of a body of knowledge as social scientific derives from its grounding in human nature, and on the other hand, the positing of human nature as the basis for grounding knowledge has always been the universal*isation* of a narrowly provincial transcendental pretence. The question of difference is a challenge to modernist knowledge precisely because it threatens the coherence of its constitution which owes to its narrowly defined subject which knows no Other. At best, the Other can be a testimonial of the limits of modernist knowledge, functioning as a limit-phenomenon, but there is no engagement with difference which questions the self. Of course, modernist knowledge functions as if none of these tensions exist. Apparently scientific discourse on society (such as that of economics) relies heavily upon eliding the question of difference while at the same time being ever more method-driven in its appeal to scientificity.

However, as Williams notes (1993: 145), the 'forefathers of neoclassical economic theory were also the children of an imperialist world, one in which enslavement, colonisation, genocide, and the discourses thereof were formative of self, norms, values, political means, and ends'. It is then no surprise that 'as the brainchild of Western man's philosophical traditions, *homo economicus* bears the markings of his fathers' gendered social and cultural lives' (ibid.). Economics is thus an ideology which disguises its particularity under the signs of objectivity and generality (see Milberg 1993). Heilbroner (1990: 104) gives two instances of this. The first is a statement by Milton and Rose Friedman that the distribution of wealth may be 'unfair', but life is unfair in the unequal distributions of talent. They write, 'the inheritance of property can be interfered with more readily than the inheritance of talent. . . . But from the ethical point of view, is there any difference between the two?' The second is the response of Robert Lucas to the question of whether government might not be an instrument for the redress of social injustice: 'That wouldn't be anything like my view. I can't think of explaining the pharoahs as being in existence to resolve the social injustice in Egypt. I think they perpetrated most of the social injustice in Egypt.' As Heilbroner goes on to discuss, it is unclear that inequalities of talent can be applied the term 'ethical', and inequalities of wealth are social differences to which ethics addresses itself. Similarly, Lucas's selection of pharoahonic Egypt to illustrate government and justice is ideological. Thus, viewing economics as ideology allows a challenging of 'the sheer facticity of the economy' thus changing 'the observer's view of the economy from that of a system to that of a regime' (ibid.: 107).

This draws attention to the mixing of power and interest in the questions of political economy. At present, viewing certain questions as 'economic' is only made possible by disregarding this. In the late twentieth century, different disciplines (economics, politics, literature, anthropology, philosophy, and so on) act like so many windows of the modernist structure that looks upon essentially the same 'human condition'.[34] The question of difference within a purportedly universal human nature is galling. This is not surprising if we consider the ambivalence of human nature in founding modernist knowledge.

Let us examine a nineteenth-century example that illustrates the narrow terms of the debate over encountering difference. Hall (2002) discusses the relation between the Metropole and the Colony in the English imagination between 1830 and 1867. She describes how 'the empire' was central to English domestic life and popular consciousness and mentions the shift in perspective from an earlier missionary paternalist type to the more vociferous and biologically racially determinist discourse of difference. The earlier missionaries such as Knibb delighted in 'pleading the cause of the injured, the degraded and the oppressed', and believed that a proper subjectivity could be provided for the (erstwhile) slaves by adopting the Christian vision. On the other hand, after the abolition of slavery, Victorian imperialism betrayed its more overt racial obsessions (see Young 1995). Robert Knox argued that 'Race is everything', and Thomas Carlyle argued differential treatment for different races.[35] Now, after the 'Indian mutiny' of 1857,

34 However, these windows are all on the foggy side of the building – the side which faces the social, the messy human. If you want a really good view, you have to move a few floors up towards a satisfying analysis of the essentially unchangeable nature of the world of objects, the physical world – the exact sciences. Or so they say.

35 Hall (2002) quotes Carlyle on considering black people as born servants, in his imagination like animals, 'sitting yonder with their beautiful muzzles up to their ears in pumpkins, imbibing sweet pulps and juices; the grinder and incisor teeth ready for ever new work'.

and after the brutal repression of rebellion by Governor Eyre in Jamaica in 1865, the debate in England took the following form. On the one side there were the 'liberal intelligentsia' comprised of Thomas Huxley, Charles Darwin, Charles Lyell, and led by Mill. On the other, defending Eyre, were Carlyle, supported by Charles Dickens, John Ruskin, Charles Kingsley, and Alfred Tennyson. While the former argued that they were concerned with legality not race (loving the law, not the negroes), the latter maintained that 'Eyre was a manly hero who had saved Europeans from "black unutterabilities."' The debate was anchored around the question of whether 'these' people could be made civilised like 'us'.

Dickens, who was so concerned about the impact of industrialisation, and is still brought forward as a role model to illustrate resistance to the excesses of industrial economy (see Henderson 2000), is the person raging at ' "that platform sympathy with the black – or the native" and the indifference to what went on at home – as if "New Zealanders and Hottentots... were identical with men in clean shirts at Camberwell" ' (Hall 2002). The enlightenment humanism in its hollowness is perhaps the biggest modernist myth, systematic in its manufactured method, perpetuating via disciplinary knowledge. And Ruskin, who loved Utopias and saw 'political economy not as an abstract, mechanistic and self-referencing system, justified by "arithmetic", but a set of ideas focused upon the problem of economic behaviour and justice within given social settings' (in Henderson 1995: 116), is also the person leading nineteenth-century critics of art and design against the figure of the arabesque in architectural or interior design, 'because it was Islamic or, more generally, "eastern" '.[36] The continuing inability to face up to an Other takes many variations.

Political economy was never far from these concerns. James Hunt, who was the founder of the Anthropological Society (as a means to conduct empirical anthropology, rejecting theory, unproved hypothesis, and popular superstitions, and based 'on actual demonstrable facts, and arguing solely from the logical inferences from such data', in Rainger 1978: 52–53) and a believer in polygenetics, had this to say about political economy:

> That the *science of political economy must be based simply and solely on the facts discovered by the anthropologists*. ...Now a social science cannot be based on mere philanthropic theories. In other words, *social science must be*

36 In a remarkable study of Gilman's arabesque wallpaper (referring to Charlotte Perkins Gilman's *The Yellow Wallpaper*) and its implication in the culture of nineteenth-century imperialism, Roth (2001: 148) writes of Ruskin thus, 'He regarded arabesque as an "Oriental" writing that "proved" that eastern races were inherently superficial, fanciful, and cruel: "The fancy and delicacy of eye", he wrote, "in interweaving lines and arranging colours – mere line and colour, observe, without natural form – seems to be somehow an inheritance of ignorance and cruelty, belonging to men as spots to the tiger or hues to the snake" '. Turns out, Gilman, sometimes recorded as an early feminist (she wrote *Women and Economics* in 1898), herself adopts white supremacist attitudes at home while setting utopian fiction abroad (Roth 2001: 145). The yellow wallpaper can thus be read for its *yellowness*, and for its *arabesque* wallpaperness (the infinity of pattern defying a finite economy of negotiation with the infinite).

> *based on the facts of human nature as it is, not as we would wish it to be.* ... We are the students and interpreters of nature's laws, and it is our duty carefully to ascertain what those laws are, and not attempt to raise up in the name of 'social science' a code of morals based upon an assumption of human equality and consequently equal human rights, because we know that human equality is a mere dream and all systems based on it are mere chimeras.
>
> (in ibid.: 61, emphases added)

Either 'human nature' is rejected in favour of racial superiority and the stereotyping of difference, or narrowly provincial Western experiences are falsely universalised under the domain name of 'human nature'. Further, all of this is carried out under the signifier 'science'. There is no place for a genuine Otherness.

Even when the Other is admitted into comprehension as an unknowable and radically separate alterity, a dilemma arises. This is a dilemma around moral responsibility; consider Strugnell (1996: 180), who discusses the philosopher of alterity, Levinas, to say, 'the tension between a "pure Otherness, separated, in some way, from any whole", identified by Levinas, and his acknowledgement that its mortality is nonetheless his business, is revealed as a contradiction'. This is the unravelling of humanism around Reason in the face of the Other. Either Western enlightenment humanity is to be happily waved off on its path to negating, assimilating, violently excluding the Other, or, if the possibility of 'alterity' (radical Otherness) is to be seriously admitted, then further concern cannot be expected.[37]

In modernity, which is constituted around its subject, the Other is only introduced as a play within unitary consciousness; that is, when it is not being materially vampirised.[38] The debate, in this knowledge, which is at once and already a form of ethics, politics, strategy, subjectivity, Reason, and being, is then cast as – whether they (the insufferable Others) belong perpetually on the outside, or can they be brought in?

And so, the costly rememberings of modernity's bankruptcies need to face up to examining the procedures of modernity in its claims to its many knowledges. A modern writing of history is premissed upon a fundamental denial of coevalness to the Other. The disciplinary construction of modern knowledges such as anthropology (for a critical undoing of anthropology, see Fabian 1983), political economy, sociology, Darwinism, history, literature, and natural science, is underwritten by enlightenment epistemology.

37 In addition, the ethical standard of a Levinasian ethics is open to the problems of maintaining a generalised Other. Irigaray writes (in Whitford 1991: 182), this can 'give rise to an infinite series of substitutions, an operation which seems . . . non-ethical. No one can be radically substituted for the other, without depriving the other of identity. Even a substitution which is authorized by proxy is questionable, given the irreducibility of each.' This leaves the way open for everything to 'slide in this historical and genealogical deracination. There is no longer any irreducible difference of the other'. As a result, ethics may become indistinguishable from what can be seen as a 'kind of formalism or a disordered drift' (ibid.).

38 Sardar (1992: 515–516) describes Europe's encounter with the Other in metaphorical terms as vampirisation – the relationship where the vampire has insatiable desire and can survive only by a never-ending supply of victims, the victims are enticed and penetrated, subsequent to which the victim is physically and mentally possessed.

The effect of the inability of modernist knowledge to engage with difference is especially acute for those at the receiving end of this knowledge. The science of political economy has accomplished the functioning of unrestricted greed. Right from the hagiography of 'Columbus the great', glory is closely tied to god, gold, and greed.[39] This has undergone mutations in the service of trade, commerce, and, often, development. While the subject at the heart of knowledge is thus constituted, its Others are designated as uneducated, uncultured, and uncivilised (Hegel's *das ungebildete*), although with a manufactured and understood multiattribute hierarchy generally in place. While uncultivated Europeans will still have a taste for freedom (see Heller 1999), Hegel's uneducated included 'among others, the poor, Arabs, savages, children, and the mad' (in Bernasconi 1998: 58).[40]

3.7 The postcolonial moment in epistemology

> [D]riven by the subaltern history of the margins of modernity – rather than by the failures of logocentrism – I have tried, in some small measure, to revise the known, to rename the postmodern from the position of the postcolonial.
>
> (Bhabha 1994: 175)

I earlier defined the postcolonial moment in epistemology as the placing of difference at the heart of self and identity in order to disrupt the modernist

39 See Sardar (1992) on this. He draws upon Bishop Bartholomew Las Casas's *Historia des la Indias* to point out features of the model of colonial governance employed by Columbus. In relation to gold, he writes, '[e]very Taino over the age of fourteen was ordered to supply the governor with a hawk's bill full of gold every three months. Those who did were awarded a token to wear around their necks; those who did not had their hands cut off and were left to bleed to death; the deserters were hunted down and killed' (ibid.: 502). God also usually had a part at least in the earlier stages. An excellent illustration is Robinson Crusoe. For a reconstruction of the reality behind Crusoe's tale, see Souhami (2002).

40 I say that the multiattribute hierarchy is generally in place, because it functions like a sort of scale where the sum total depends on all the beads in all the rows of the Abacus. An example of this hierarchical scale can be seen at work in Aristotle's *Politics* when he remarks,

> The freeman rules over the slave after another manner from that in which the male rules over the female, or the man over the child; although the parts of the souls are present in all of them, they are *present in different degrees*. For the slave has *no deliberative faculty* at all; the woman has, but it is *without authority*, and the child has, but it is *immature*.
>
> (in Code 1991: 9, emphases added)

Or, to take a recent example, after the terrorist attacks on the World Trade Centerre towers in New York, on 11 September 2001, and in the aftermath of the US bombing attack on Afghanistan. there were numerous programmes on television in 'the West', discussing the issue of how do we tell 'our children' about what happened. That the rare reportings of the horrible plight of the Other (Afghan) children was crowded out to select alternative media, probably confirms Rousseau's remarks (see above, the discussion of his discourse on political economy) on the limited and geographically specific store of sympathy, at least for a significant section of the population.

disciplinary logic that relies upon creating knowledge based upon manufacturing conceptual abstractions and universalising their essence.

Let me clarify a few things. To begin with, I could be asked, why the 'postcolonial' moment? This can be interpreted in several ways. For instance, it could mean, why go further? Why not say that the subject is dead, and this is enough – why this fascination with 'post-al politics'? Does not my cup overflow? In my argument, therefore, the Other of enlightenment modernism is not a fixed and stable category of exclusion whose origins can be foundationally traced. It is the very unravelling of the illusion that enlightenment modernism *ever was*, and also at the same time it is a demonstration of the grasping power of this illusion in disciplinary knowledge (see Said 1978). Indeed, the whole thrust of this book has been that one cannot begin from the discipline (say, economics) in order to undo the seams where it is sutured together. Rather, one has to confront its coming into being in a strategic manner in which one never suspends the suspicion over its existence.

It is, therefore, an unfamiliar theoretical geography which can let monsters erupt (unfamiliar because it is a theoretical geography which is not 'proper' theory, method, history, philosophy, anything – it questions the status of 'proper' as a rational economic production). It will not be a simple matter of mapping exclusions from an Archimedean point because the geography of studying boundaries as already marked out depends on imagining a prior unbounded coherence. The act of mapping, connoted as it is to imperial surveying, relies upon the comprehension of a structure which cannot be further interrogated. Structures have to be situated in place (placed) before they are destabilised, and it is the traces of the act of differentiating excesses to create meaning that require attention.[41]

I will now turn toward a discussion of the much-anticipated (and already inaugurated) postcolonial moment in epistemology. I would like to argue for the postcolonial moment in epistemology – because, the globe extends beyond Europe; because, there might have been people before the Greeks; because, the dilemmas of the un/folding Western European subject (the w.e/'we') are not exhaustive of me. In short, because, there are *many*. Many traditions, languages, philosophies, ways of thinking, writing and being and saying so, but also *saying*. Totality must be resisted. Like the example of obscure Jude's little child's scrawl,[42] the graffiti on the walls of history – in one ink, should not testify to murder, even as suicide. It should not read – 'Done because we are too menny.' Some of us had to die. Difference must not be surrendered. A continual assertion of alternatives to that which is dominant is necessary to breathe multiply against the suffocation of the One.

41 This attention to textuality is not at the expense of giving up any 'real' concerns. Reality exists in language, with language. There is no other way of accessing it. However, if the comprehension of materiality within language resonates so well with the immediate physicality of our being in the world, then this should not be a problem. The material concerns of our physical being in the world are undeniable, but no less, and no more, real than anything else. In sum, the real is not a terrifying spectre in my account.

42 This refers to *Jude the Obscure* (1895) by Thomas Hardy, in which the eldest child of the protagonist kills himself and two younger siblings on purpose, leaving behind a note that said 'Done because we are too menny [*sic*].'

On the other hand, the question could be why the 'post' of 'colonial', specifically? To this, I have the following to say. I do not believe in the lexicographical understanding of 'post' as that which comes after, as a temporal prefix. Numerous writers have defended or chastised the 'post', attempting to locate what 'exactly' it means, and its 'precise' relation to the other 'posts'. For me, to forcefully recognise the postcolonial only as the hyphenated post-of-colonial is a significant blunting of a term connoting a constellation of ideas which are urgent and crucial. This is because the 'postcolonial' is not, in my view, a fashionable-lefty-third-world kind of lit-crit badge! The reason I have chosen to take the longer, tortuous, definitely 'non-mainstream' attempt to theorise the violence of the modernist scientism of economics is because I want to make the connections between strands of thought such as the following.

There is the notion of economics as a science. This is located in the establishment of the conceptual idea of what a science is and does – something which is not universal. On the contrary, this is historically, temporally, geopolitically, ideologically, located and contingent. Enlightenment epistemology underwrote such a universalised idea of 'science', and further, made its formalistic emergence possible in the nineteenth-century mutations of responses to the problem of knowledge, of which economics is an example.

Now, there are also implications of the above. That is, how economics was sanctioned as a societal mechanism – a 'practice' – of management, of colonisation, of organising what now came to be seen as 'economic' experiences under the lengthening shadow of modernity through which everything was filtered. By the same token, a knowledge management exercise feeds and feeds off other knowledges and means of access to them. These strands are intimately connected. The belief that calls for an uncritical acceptance of the split between theory and praxis, is the same as that which painstakingly ensures the pigeonholed separation between the economic, the political, the cultural, the scientific.

Thus, modernist knowledge needs to be haunted by a postcolonial memory, a re-membering, which can be instigated by placing the question of difference at the heart of the story. When one re-members, one does not simply recall – to re-member is to put it all together again. This putting together all over again is not a temporalised recitation of what happened after what. Rather, it is first of all an undoing of the present. Think of it like this. There is a present (it could even be doubly metaphorical, so one can even think of a present as that which one holds, an uncertain gift).[43] In order to re-member the present, one has to not undo simply the present, but also undo oneself. As one rethinks all the trajectories that led to the here-and-now, as one undoes all the strings of the uncertain gift that one holds, it dissolves the coherent continuity of the grid of comprehension. Now, as the closures of the present moment are revisited, its coherence (and one's own) is undone. We have, therefore, an implicit unravelling in any re-membering.

43 The word 'present' can stand in for a gift. Present, in time, can also be seen as an (uncertain) gift. Further, a gift unsettles the logic of economism. Yet, if economy is the dialogue between the infinity and finitude, then an economy of the gift is impossible. But if this is speaking in the spirit of Derrida, there is also Mauss. O'Neill (2001: 41–48), following Mauss, would rather not endow

In this way, the postcolonial moment in epistemology is immediately also the *interpellation of knowing with re-membering*. For, after all, *how does one know in the face of memory*? This is an important question because, trawling through the backyard of Western enlightenment modernism, one finds that this question has been erased from significance by the positing of science as universal memory. But since no erasure can be traceless, the haunting comes back. And one can interrogate the *how* of one's knowledge by undoing the coherence of oneself (untie the strings of the uncertain gift, the present) in the face of memory, by re-membering differently, with *difference*.

At once, many issues arise. Modernist enlightenment epistemology sought to explain 'the unfamiliar in familiar and everyday terms'. For Smith, monsters served the purpose of *de*-monstrating Others. Now, by remembering difference, the move is to make the familiar unfamiliar. This is what is underway when I speak about the attempt to enculture, historicise, politicise the 'economic' context. What this calls for is a translation – not of terms, but of oneself. The 'I' that stands between theory and praxis, needs to 'see' differently. Hume's disregard for travellers' tales will not do. Instead, theory itself will have to travel.

3.8 Conclusion

Fukuyama's *End of history and the last man* (1992) presents Hegel's dialectical history to interpret contemporary historical events as the ultimate 'triumph' of liberal democratic capitalism. As Derrida argued, Fukuyama's eschatological announcement of the end of history is based upon reducing the singularity of events to 'historical empiricity'.

Spanos (2001) brings into relief the imperialism of Fukuyama's metaphysical ontology (the hegemony and mediatisation of this representation). In his critique of Fukuyama, Spanos argues that to an extent the impasse of emancipatory political practice in the post-Cold War period is in some significant degree '*an impasse of thinking itself*' (35, emphasis original). My link to this argument is exactly this focus on the relevance of re-thinking, and thinking Otherwise. Along with Spanos, I would argue for a *reconstellated genealogy* to 'instigate a rethinking of the relay of *practical* historical imperatives precipitated by the post-Cold War global occasion' (41, emphasis original). His project, which is 'to make visible and operational the substantial practical role that ontological representation has played and continues to play in the West's perennial global

a philosophical pedigree to the 'free gift', making the gift both voluntary and obligatory. He writes, 'today, as we give less to the poor, by refusing them work, reducing their wages, and withdrawing welfare, market theorists rationalise the withdrawal of the gift and articulate an ideology of the free gift – the gift that obligates neither the donor nor the donee.' Boundas (2001: 2) summarises O'Neill's belief in the significance of Mauss, according to whom, 'social life involves a meta-gift, that is, an inalienable surplus of labour and service, incapable of being reduced to the calculation of contracts'. See Shershow (2005) for debates on work and the gift that lead to his vision of a community of 'unworking' which relies upon a fundamental being-in-common, eschewing both production and progress, and the ethic of liberal generosity.

imperial project', therefore requires this (21–46, emphasis added):

> need to reintegrate theory and practice – the ontological and the socio-political, thinking and doing – and to accommodate the present uneven balance of this relationship to the actual conditions established by the total colonization of thinking in the age of the world picture,... [T]his reconstellated destructive genealogy will show that the 'triumphant' liberal democratic/capitalist polity rests on a fabricated ontological base that privileges the hierarchically structured binarist principle of principles – that *Identity is the condition for the possibility of difference and not the other way around* – and that, therefore, this polity is imperial *in essence* as well as in its multi-situated political practices.

Modernist knowledge has consistently striven to elide the question of difference. But, difference is a slippery slope. When it is not attended to at all, it does not go away – rather, it remains beyond the boundaries, returning a silent powerful gaze. Thus we find that the repressed of the Cartesian remainder has returned. On the other hand, when one attends to difference, but only by making *identity as a condition for the possibility of difference* – then, it is no longer clear where to draw the boundaries of difference. This situating of difference as the latent monster that will not go away, is not merely literary or poetic-philosophic, it is political and ethical (in short, it is not 'merely theoretical', but also practical – of course, it is another matter that the divides between literary, poetic-philosophic, political, ethical, or even the economic, are sustained by the originary act of splitting theory from praxis, itself a most important systematic policing of the differentials). Just as the Queen in Alice's adventures in Wonderland had only one way of settling all difficulties ('Off with his/her head'), modernist disciplinary knowledge can only keep up its house-of-cards façade by denouncing critique as 'airy-fairy'. The remarkable fairytale is the way in which modernist abstractions stick as 'real', while the hard work of uncovering and blowing apart concepts such as the sovereign individual subject, the nation-state, culture, is dismissed as 'theoretical'.

Recent critiques of modernist knowledge in the form of feminism, poststructuralism, postmodernism, deconstruction, and postcoloniality have attempted to grapple with the dehiscence in modernism, inaugurating newer handles to subjectivity such as the theorising of desire and scrutiny of modes of representation. However, within modernist knowledge, even critique is subject to pigeon-holing and neutralisation, and the thrust has been to limit participation in these multiple theoretical theatres. The privilege of multiple attendance is taboo, and this ghettoisation of critique is itself an effective strategy of policing the channels through which responses to enlightenment modernism can be conducted. In accordance with these views, I shall not definitionally clarify each of these terms, attempting to set their boundaries and locate their emphases. Modernist lexicography in all its strategic inadequacies is the place for that.[44]

44 How do I support this assertion? Well, lexicography is the ultimate modern art of taxonomising comprehension, at the same time blunting it irrevocably. One can imagine the whiteness of the

Many alliances can be made under the shadow of the subject, but, as long as they are made *under the shadow of the subject*, they will impose the same neurotic insistence on affiliation ('identification') as the unexamined precondition for concern or political ethics. Finally, if the call of difference prevails in an absolute sense (and there is no inkling of danger of this being the case in the world today), then it means that difference, like a monster, has erupted from within identity itself. Such difference is not a theorisation of the Other, it is, instead, a stepping beyond ever being able to define the self. In which case, thinking is 'questioning and *putting ourselves in question* as much as the cherished opinions and inherited doctrines we have long taken for granted' (Heidegger 1968: xii, emphasis added).

Knowledge creation is then no longer a prelude to effectively intervening in the world, but is itself an intervention whose effectivity relies upon an ethics which is experienced in its enactment. Or, that knowledge creation is *already* a form of ethics, politics, strategy, subjectivity, Reason, and being. It is in this spirit that I will go on to juxtapose the 'economic' with identity next.

page as set into the authority of the black marks in the middle, the margins, and here, down below, the footnotes. The footnotes are for paraphernalia, so the conventional wisdom goes. But, two or three things I know about meaning insist otherwise. The origins of the word 'paraphernalia' indicate that it was used to designate the property that remained under a married woman's own control – since when did we come to understand that as being (or, more importantly, why is that) insignificant? Now, to the inadequacy of lexicography. Royle (2000), in an article titled 'What is Deconstruction?', brilliantly takes apart the *Chambers English Dictionary* definition of the term. I will not repeat the Chambers definition here, but instead recall the hypothesis Royle offers for its awfulness, 'your definition is haunted by the anxiety that, with deconstruction, the very possibility of a dictionary explodes' (ibid.: 2). The rest of Royle's text discusses deconstruction, text, and contexts, and offers alternatives. The next question is, why are these inadequacies of lexicography *strategic*? Let me now give an example of my own (telepathy, perhaps, but I had formulated this example from Chambers too, and before setting eyes upon Royle 2000) to illustrate what I term (yes, even the footnote can be a place for naming: it was in footnotes that Kant declared the exceptions of Reason, and the American Declaration declared the limits of freedom, see Ellerman 1991: 559) 'lexical politics'. The *Chambers Dictionary* (1999), which claims to be '*The* Authority on English Today' (emphasis original), defines the word 'Hottentot' as,

> **Hottentot** *n.* one of a dwindling, nomad, pastoral, pale-brown-skinned race in SW Africa (resembling Bushmen and Bantu), calling themselves *khoi-khoin* (men of men); their language; a barbarian; a member of any black or coloured people (*old derog*);... [the rest of the entry refers to non-capitalised meanings relating to a fish, fruits, animals, etc.]

Note the way in which the entry is phrased, with the usage 'calling *themselves*', '*their* language'. It does not begin to mention that Hottentot is '*our* old derogatory' term for the '*khoi-khoin*' people. In other words, Hottentot is the term for people who *call themselves khoi-khoin*, rather than, it being our derogatory term for the *khoi-khoin*.

This is a lexicographic entry strategic in its politics – making strategically invisible a politics enacted in history over Saartje Baartman (1789–1816), a native Khoisan woman who was exhibited in Europe as an ethnological and sexual freak to curious Europeans to support their ideas on African race and sexuality (the 'Hottentot Venus'). She later drifted into poverty and prostitution and died. Her remains (her brain, genitalia, were bottled as scientific specimens), until recently at the Museum of Mankind in Paris, were returned to South African government on 3 May 2002, as a result of talks initiated in 1995. The *Los Angeles Times* reports a leader of Griqua Heritage as '[t]his is not the coming of one person – it is the coming of a nation' ('A S. African Native's Homecoming' 2002). For more on this, see Hall (1997).

Part 4

Juxtaposing questions of identity and the economic

> It wasn't only wickedness and scheming that made people unhappy, it was confusion and misunderstanding; above all, it was the *failure to grasp the simple truth that other people are as real as you*. And only in a story could you enter these different minds and show how they had an equal value. That was the only moral a story need have.
>
> (McEwan 2002: 40, emphasis added)

In Parts 1 and 2, my concern was with the possibility of social science, and the particular form of theorisation that is involved in being scientific about the economic realm in the social, and how this theorisation in economics relates to the methodological compromises necessitated by an underlying enlightenment epistemology. In Part 3, my aim was to examine the questions of difference in relation to the questions of modernist knowledge, demonstrating how the transcendental pretence that has functioned under the sign of human nature has taken for granted a particular version of subjectivity which was also influential in the discourses on political economy. In contrast, the postcolonial moment in epistemology allows us to think beyond the disciplined categories of knowledge which have situated the Other as a limit-phenomenon.

In linking up the concerns raised by an exploration of the theoretical status of economics and its imbrication in the wider modernist elisions of difference, it becomes imperative to examine the links between identity and the economic. Accordingly, in this Part 4, I will approach the issue of identity and economics. In Chapter 4, I will examine the 'essentialist individual' view of identity which is dominant in economics and mainstream social science. I will discuss several critiques of it, and then reflect on other ways of thinking identity which arise from assessing the limitations of these critiques themselves. The action in this chapter can be seen as the setting-up of a contrast between different versions of identity – the 'essentialist individual' notion of identity as followed in economics, and as a response to the problems inherent in this view, the version of identity as a matter of politics in relation to inalienably situated subjects. This second version can provide the resource to envision what I will term the 'politics of identity', and which avoids the pitfalls of standard 'identity politics'.

In Chapter 5, I will discuss and critique the two relatively rare instances where famous economists have attempted discourse on identity. The first of these is a straightforward economic model where identity is introduced as a variable into utility function, and, in the second, identity is seen as an important matter but it is nonetheless subsumed by the overarching dynamic of rational universal Reason.

In Chapter 6, I will introduce the 'concentric mode of identity' which is deployed by not only the abstract essentialist view which underlies the economists' discussions, but also by prominent cosmopolitan accounts such as that of Nussbaum. I will present critiques of thinking identity in this manner, and link back to the 'politics of identity' view discussed earlier. Drawing upon the work of Bhabha, I will argue that a productive way of thinking about identity is to formulate it as translational experiencing. This 'translational mode of identity' not only avoids the difficulties associated with conventional identity politics, but also enables us to affirm the ethical importance of being always-already different. Following on from this, I will transpose the discussion to considering how the divide between identity and economic as separable rests upon a presumed separation between the spheres of culture and economy. This then allows economics to function as the science of economy and a representation of the category economic; however, the very basis of economics in a fixing of value is always the fixing of values in translation. I will explain this and theorise the slippage between the categories of economics, economy, and economic. I will conclude by making the case that a translational view of identity in relation to the economic makes it imperative to envision the writing of economic theory an*Other* way.

4 Identity problematics

4.1 On identity

> I know who I am and I know where I am from.
>
> (US Senator Robert Dole, in Smith 2001: 32)

> To those critics who are so pessimistic about our economy, I say: Don't be economic girlie men!
>
> (Schwarzenegger 2004)

The question of identity can be approached in many ways, for many strategic reasons (see Shotter and Gergen 1989; Corbey and Leerssen 1991; Lash and Friedman 1992; Harris 1995; Hall and Du Gay 1996; Woodward 1997; Du Gay *et al.* 2000). The question of identity has been discussed by framing it in terms of whether identity is mostly a fixed, self-same continuity over time, or whether it is something that 'comes about' at a point in time, and so is not predetermined or always present, but happens. Also, one can contrast the personal identity of the 'I' with the collective identity of the 'we'.

Here, I need to make a distinction between identity as it is tied up with the supposed epistemological subjects and agents which are the objects of inquiry, and identity as an aspect of subjectivity. While the first raises questions of identity as a construction within the production of knowledge, the second relates to an experiential dimension of identity. These notions are inevitably connected, but my discussion will be more pertinent to the exploration of identity and difference in relation to knowledge production in a social science like economics.

Within economics, the 'subject' of knowledge is seen as being abstract and universal. In line with modernist social science in general, the aspirations of disciplinary knowledge imply that the universal subject is an essence distilled from all the particularities of time and place. This essentialist individual view of identity plays an important part in economics, and identity is seen as a fixed and continuous sense of self of an abstract rational individual. However, as I will go on to explore, there are many ways of problematising this construction. The essentialised and universal subject of social scientific inquiry, available to be understood through formalist methods, is not simply a convenient way of enhancing scientific knowledge, but a very particular view of identity in relation to knowledge. This view crucially depends on identifying individuals as isolatable units, employs a notion of choice which is problematic, and does not adequately reflect the reality of human existence. These are some of the many critiques that have justifiably been levelled at the abstract essentialist view of identity in economics. In what follows, I will summarise these criticisms, and then discuss the ways in which we can go beyond basing knowledge on the study of abstract essentialised individuals, to thinking about knowledge in relation to 'standpoints' and identity politics. While standpoint theory and identity politics are able to go some way towards accommodating difference in relation to knowledge production, I will also highlight some limitations of these endeavours, and argue for maintaining a position which may be called the 'politics of identity'. Such a way of rethinking identity in relation to knowledge can provide us with ways out of the 'difference conundrum' where either difference is added on or it is excluded.

4.2 Abstract essentialist individual identity

> [T]he private is measured by and contains within it the possibility of the social. The seemingly concrete individual is predicated by the possibility of abstraction.
>
> (Spivak 1999: 178)

The most important component of the essentialist version of identity is continuity and sameness. Identity, on this account, becomes a corroborative seamlessness whose clarity and stability is not subject to question. Also, this ties in rather well with the personal account of identity as originating from the personal I. In practice, the sum of these two views is often traced back to the Cartesian self and the Kantian subject with transcendental pretence. This self-aware subject is necessarily an individual who is the basic conceptual apparatus through which everything else is filtered. This individual self is the bounded container of autonomy, rationality, and Reason.

This essentialist individual mode of identity underlies, apart from several other ideologies, liberal individualism. Connolly (1991: 73–74, second emphasis added), in his discussion of liberal individualism in relation to identity, rightly points out that,

> individual*ism* presupposes a model of the normal or rational individual against which the conduct and interior of each actual self are to be appraised. ... [T]he doctrine of the steadfast individual (the autonomous agent, the self-interested agent, the normal individual) easily becomes ... a doctrine of *normalization through individualization*. ... The theory of the normal individual establishes its parameters of normality not so much by specific argumentation as by omissions in its generic characterization of the individual.

The ideal subject of knowledge is pointed out not by careful distinguishing of its outlines, but rather by positing a 'legitimate' version of identity. This normalising of essentialist individualism is not just a fictive exercise, but also an important political move. It limits the terrain of explanation and fixes the basic atomic structure concept of abstract individual identity that has to be mobilised in order to create meaning in a social science like economics. For instance, it both structures and confines what can be seen as political, and how. As a result (ibid., emphases added), the

> tendency is to *reduce the political to the juridical* – to condense most issues of politics into the juridical category of rights, justice, obligation, and responsibility and to treat the remaining issues instrumentally as *contests in which individuals and aggregations compete within juridical rules to advance their 'interests' or 'principles' by rational means.*

Within essentialist individual mode, the legitimate conceptualisation of identity is one based upon basic uninterrogable units who interact in accordance with pre-understood rules in predetermined ways.

The work done by the idealisation of the abstract individual as the basic anchor of knowledge can be seen in two different ways. The position of the knower and the object of knowledge are both idealised in the image of the abstract individual. The social scientist is seen as the collector of knowledge, who, in order to better theorise and augment the store of knowledge and create 'good' science, should try to approximate as closely as possible the characteristics of an ideal abstract individual in pursuit of knowledge. Analogously, the object of knowledge, or what knowledge is about, is also seen as graspable in terms of the abstract individual. These two positions are seen to be reflected in each other whereby the ideal pursuit of knowledge requires abstract individual-type social scientists to engage in the study of their subject matter which is characterised in terms of abstract individuals like themselves. There is a strong normative aspect to this idealisation, since it is believed that good knowledge is one that is available universally in terms of abstract individuals, and in order to reach such knowledge, the social scientist has to approximate the position of an abstract individual knower.

This view of identity as an attribute of self-aware subject individuals acting in their self-interest in conformity with the ideas of rational choice and economic principle is the basis of the economic agent, '*homo economicus*', as conceptualised in mainstream economic theory (see Folbre and Hartmann 1988; England 1995). In this scenario, the economic agents are usually by definition rational, self-interested (thus profit-motivated), utility-maximising (thus constantly calculating), amoral, disembodied[1] and disembedded, abstract individuals. As a Hobbesian mushroom, this *homo economicus* (HE) is the quintessential Rational Economic Man (REM). As Hollis and Nell (1975: 54–55, emphasis added) write, HE is an abstract being:

> His is the behaviour to be predicted; he is the bearer of economic variables. Unlike the man in the street, he never misses an opening, ignores a price

1 See Kaul (2001b) for an elaboration of this theme. Cf. Amariglio and Ruccio (2002).

> change, overrates the short-run or turns a blind eye to the unquantifiable. Every model predicts the rational response. Rational economic man is both the average and the *ideal.*

Identity of the *homo economicus* signals a 'stable core of the self, unfolding from beginning to end through all the vicissitudes of history without change; the bit of the self which remains always-already "the same", identical to itself across time' (Hall 2000: 17). REM's identity is seen as a possession, an essence, abstract, and naturally fixed, *not* at all as contingent, processual, contextual, and in flux.

Thus, in order to understand the 'market' as an economic phenomenon, one would resort to a thought process whereby numerous similar self-aware subject individuals (further assumed to be acting in their self-interest, a motive deriving from human nature, and reminiscent of the transcendental pretence) interact and transact in goods and services together. Similarly, to understand any other social process or institutional setting, the explanation would begin from an abstract individual who is the self-aware subject and rational agent.

Within the essentialist individual mode, the having of identity is grounded in the exercise of choice. There is an important role for a subject who is capable of conscious choice in a radical sense. This is because in this act of choosing, the subject of knowledge seemingly locates its identity firmly and irrevocably. The 'I' of identity is a conscious self-aware subject, who not only is always able to calculate the possible outcomes of alternatives and then make the rational and free decision (exerts choice), but also serves as *the theoretical boundary within which responsibility for actions can be fixed.* The ability to then exercise conscious rational and free choice, for which responsibility can be located, gives us *the* model of subjective identity which *is the condition for any identity.*

But this focus on the role of choice in constructing the identity of the free and rational economic agent does not clarify what counts as a free choice. Knowledge production in mainstream economics takes the following form. We assume the existence of an abstract essentialist individual being able to maximise its utility, or rank order its preferences[2] over a bundle of goods in a way so as to give us 'well-behaved' (convex to the origin of X-Y axis, not cross each other, etc.) indifference curves. Further, there exist externally given constraints, which do not influence preferences, and the indifference curve and the budget constraint are matched at the beautiful and aesthetic tangency on the graph.[3] The basic neoclassical microeconomic conceptualisation of consumer theory is mirrored in

2 The typical economist's answer to 'where do the preferences come from?' is that you need to go to psychology for that. As if, the separability of disciplines in the modernist rendition of knowing and being can somehow deny that all these structures of knowledge share their common bases in Cartesian subjectivity, enlightenment epistemology, and modernism.

3 Of course, there are complications. But, basically: 'Consumers demand. Producers supply. Self-interest being ever present. Markets oblige. Everything else *is* a complication.'

production theory,[4] and the competitive markets match demand and supply to ensure equilibrium. Finally, mathematical proofs ensure that under certain conditions the whole economy (a mathematical system) equilibrates to a perfect and brilliant humming aesthetics.[5] This abstracted essentialist individual economic agent is like the one point that Archimedes wanted, and Descartes craved, to be able to accomplish everything else.

4.3 Critiquing the abstract essentialist individual view of identity

> The challenge is to recognize ourselves for what we are, and not for pale, essentialist shadows.
>
> (Smith 2001: 46)

The next question is, what can we make of the essentialist individual version of identity? I now want to critique this view of identity, especially as it underlies much of economic theory.

First, if the basic premise of knowledge in a social science is the idea of a universal subject like the rational economic being, then the actual study of people can only proceed by ignoring all the ways in which they are not like the rational economic beings. We have a trajectory that begins from a desire for universal knowledge, for which it requires conceptual abstractions, which in turn limit the inquiry to formalist modelling. The formalism and universalism of a social science like economics feed upon each other. Lawson (1997) explains this problem of method in the following way. Mainstream economics is based upon a method of deductive closed systems modelling in order to obtain conclusions of if-this-then-that type. However, this presumes that the world is a closed system within which

4 So budget lines becomes iso-cost lines, indifference curves become iso-quants, marginal rate of substitution (MRS) between the choice of goods for the consumer becomes marginal rate of technical substitution (MRTS) between factors of labour and capital for the producer, and so on. For confirmation, browse through introductory chapters of any economics textbook.

5 As Klein (1998: 189–190) summarises (referring to Arrow and Debreu 1954, which stated the general conditions for the existence of equilibrium, the 'existence proofs'):

> An Arrow–Debreu economy consists of a finite number of units executing production plans and a finite number of units realizing consumption plans. Such production and consumption plans are always expressed as real, finite-component vectors of commodities. . . . A competitive economy is one in which each agent takes prices as given and these are independent of the agent's individual choice decisions. Evidence of the consistency of a competitive economy is the existence of a competitive or Walrasian solution for such a system.

On the other hand, macroeconomics has the share of the messy questions of trade, employment, inflation, exchange rates, business cycles, growth, but there are no 'microfoundations' of macroeconomics, and, in any case, macroeconomics too proceeds from the assumption of the 'representative agent'; see Kirman (1992).

we can postulate event regularities, and is not suited to grasping the reality of an open system such as the real world where conclusions of if-this-then-that type are not sustainable. As a result, economic theory based upon the assumption of abstract similar and universal rational economic agents both requires and is required by formalism.

Second, the identity of the economic agent as universal subject which underlies knowledge production is not simply an abstraction, but also an important and political construction. We can see this in two different ways. The abstract individual economic agent is both *an individual*, and a *particular type* of individual. Thus, while the first criticism (see the earlier paragraph) draws attention only to the way in which this abstraction serves the ends of formalism and universalism, we can broaden this critique by focusing on the way in which this view of the identity of the subjects of knowledge is limited to their being individuals of a particular type. What at first seemed to be a convenient fiction manufactured in the interests of knowledge production, is actually an interested construction that serves particular ends. For instance, as feminist economists have argued, though *homo economicus* is deemed to be an abstract individual, a being without a body, this abstraction is based upon a normalisation of gendered (masculine) and raced (white) Enlightenment rational man.[6] A focus on this version of identity simultaneously obscures from view not only the constructed nature of the individual subject, but also confirms it as *the* model of ideal identity which must be aspired to by everyone.

Let me now give two examples of the consequences that can result from unquestioningly keeping with the view of identity which is limited to individuals of a particular type. The first example is to draw attention to the link between this notion of identity and the conception of an individual as an isolatable unit. Given that this view of identity places a premium on the sense of continuity and sameness, the notion of an 'individual' seems to fit in naturally since it ostensibly provides a way of thinking a coherent and continuous I which fixes continued self-aware identity. In the context of economics, the single unit of the individual is used to signify a core stable essence which is determinate and not subject to interpretation. The study of any situation can proceed as if between different individual actors, and the conclusions can then be applied to situations where the actors may be different people, groups of people, or countries. The problem arises because on this account there is no way of paying attention to the significance of sociality which is not fixed by simply individuals. The social becomes just an aggregation of individuals, and nothing more. We have a billiard-ball-like model of interactions, with no insight on the processual nature of how social outcomes come about. We study human behaviour and social processes by taking a 'snapshot'

6 England's (1993) work on the separative self in neoclassical economics, Grapard's (1996) work on the 'benevolence of the (famous Smithian) butcher's wife', Feiner's (1999) portrait of HE as a young man, and especially Hewitson's (1999) deconstruction of Robinson Crusoe as the REM – all have dealt with the androcentric character of *homo economicus*.

of situations where there are essentially similar individual actors who take upon identities A or B (for instance, consumers or producers), and then the hypothesisations of their interactions can be universally generalised.[7] This format of comparative statics[8] in economics is a social scientific gloss that serves as an excuse for obliterating serious consideration of how meaningful knowledge can be generated about the widely divergent social contexts in which processual identities are continually discovered and enacted upon.

An example of extremely simplistic characterisation of interactions is to assume that there are two units (for instance, country A and country B) and under certain conditions certain outcomes (e.g., the benefits of free trade) will mathematically hold. Lifting the conclusions of this study to talk about two nations (which are now thought of as two countries from the economic world) and argue for certain policy measures, does not allow power differentials to become visible. This is very destructive, for instance in international negotiations (climate change, aid, trade related, etc.), where all nations are assumed to be like abstract isolatable individuals, the ideal concept of a nation; so we have a situation with power imbalances – hundreds of delegates (lawyers, scientists, negotiators) representing the powerful matched by the meagre resources of another nation. As Bhagwati (2001: 29) asks, '[w]hy not get a rich country to give the poor countries against which it is bringing the case a sum that matches its own estimated legal expenses, so that the contest is equal?' A different way of going about the situation would be to realise that the linkages and similarity of interests are not always bounded by geography, so that one begins by starting from the imbroglio where interests are multiple and variously aligned, there is an enormous diversity of actors, and actions have real-time consequences. A 'snapshot' will not do, and neither will it help to carry out the two-stage routine where, first, we get conclusions on the basis of the essentialist individual abstract economic agent, and then attempt to graft this upon a 'messy real world'. There is no substitute for making way through the various interpretations that exist of the materiality of the world,[9] and understanding how inalienably situated people navigate processually through its various complexities.

The second example alludes to the consequences of not realising that this model of identity does not simply posit any individual as the marker of knowledge, but a particular type of individual. An essentialist abstract self-aware

7 For instance, the way in which economists have continued to study discrimination as the outcome of interactions between groups such as W and N (white and 'negro', as in Arrow 1995 [1972]) or W and B (white and black, as in Coate and Loury 1993). See also Arrow (1998).

8 In comparative static analysis, one of the 'other things being equal' parameters is altered to see its effect on equilibrium price and quantity. So, what would happen if something was altered in equilibrium one – the new equilibrium would be equilibrium two. Bear in mind, the analysis is *not* about the process (the 'how' of change) but about two states of a hypothetical system.

9 I am not arguing that there is a brute materiality that is not available to interpretation. But neither am I arguing that materiality does not matter. In my view, attention to (what appears to be) materiality and to which we might only have discursive access is still an important part of our work.

subject individual rationally acting in its self-interest, not only normalises such behaviour, making the political into the juridical, and is unrealistic as the basis for social science, but, is also representative of the patterns of behaviour following from the privileges that accrue to masculinity in society. The white heterosexual middle-class able-bodied Anglo-Saxon man (and this 'incidentally' fits the description of a typical economist) is perhaps most representative of the economic agent in the economic world. Feminist economists have pointed out how this version of identity has excluded people for whom relationality is not an option but a part of their life (see England 1993; Ferber and Nelson 1993, 2003; Strassmann 1993a; Folbre 1994; Kuiper and Sap 1995; Grapard 1996; Hewitson 1999). Women, who are in almost every society in the world, expected to be the most 'natural' caregivers and mitigate the excesses of the economic agent by situating them in a wider context of non-market social glue, most obviously do not fit into this view of identity. Their difference is to be claimed as a deviance from the individualised norm of abstract essentialist identity.

Third, partly as a consequence of the critiques above, one of the most common ways in which the view of identity underlying economic theory is rejected amounts to saying (in many different ways as evidenced by the various heterodox schools of thought) – economic theory is not realistic, its underlying notion of how people are and how they behave does not match up with the reality of people's lives. The abstract essentialist version of identity based upon a self-aware coherent sameness of self-interested individuals does not do justice to how people actually are. People do not behave like standard economic agents – people don't always know what they want, cannot always decide the order of their choices, are not insatiable, often go out of their way to help others (see Sen 1977), are not completely motivated by self-interest (see Ferber and Nelson 1993), often contradict themselves, and so on. Human beings are multidimensional, and cannot be flattened out into fictive rational economic agents.[10]

Fourth, another way of critiquing the view of identity underlying economic theory is to focus upon the role that is played by employing the notion of 'choice'

10 However, it should be pointed out that this realist critique of economic theory, while useful, remains limited to the extent that it relies upon a correspondence theory of truth. Claiming that economic theory does not reflect the reality of people's lives, presents the issue in terms of a misplaced or 'wrong' theorisation which excludes certain aspects of reality. Then the way forward is to analyse the ways in which there is a 'mismatch' between the theory and the real world so that we can then augment the theory in order to make it better or more correct against some verificatory external reality which remains brutely available and unaffected by interpretation. But, critiquing economic theory for its realism does not go far enough in interrogating the privilege available to the social scientist from whose transcendental perspective reality is admitted as uncontested data from which to postulate ontology. This approach forecloses the exploration that economic theory is not just a 'mismatch' which can be corrected but a power-laden production of knowledge which needs its 'constitutive outside' in order to function and at the same time creates its own real. Taking this further would mean admitting the contested nature of reality itself whose perception is the effect of power-laden processes of representation. The consequence in this case would not be additive but transformatory, requiring us to link up the exercise of power in relation to the construction of economic knowledge. See Kaul (2002b).

in the theoretical explanation of social outcomes. That is, the theoretical recognition of individuals in an economic explanation occurs only through their individualised free choices, whether as consumers or as producers. But, as I explain below, there are enormous implications of the way in which the concept of choice is utilised to fix the identity of economic agents in the economic world. Let me start with the question – how much is the essentialist individual conception of identity dependent upon the capacity of this self-aware rational subject to be able to choose? By choice I don't mean that general sense of doing one thing rather than another. Rather, what I wish to interrogate in the abstract essentialist individualist version of identity is its need for coherence of the subject that is most manifest in the strong sense of a decision, 'free choice'.

The relation between identity and choice is clear in economics in a dense filling-in of the economic agent with conscious choice which is both free and rational, and justifies the outcomes in terms of responsibility for having made that choice. Let me elaborate this. For the purposes of economic science, one takes as a starting point any social outcome (say, unemployment or discrimination). Then, one proceeds to explain it (i.e., constructs a model) as having occurred as the consequence of conscious purposive rational and free choices made by self-aware responsible essentialist individual subject economic agents. This rational choice type of explanation[11] for social outcomes is seen as an example of the scientific economist uncovering causal connections between choices and outcomes. This is seen as merely 'positive' economics (as opposed to 'normative' economics). When prescriptions resulting from such models or explanations are utilised, the outcomes can be quite stark. For instance, take the case of women earning less than men: one can 'explain' this as their rational and free choice to have babies and so lose a few years of productivity, in response to which the rational and free employers view them as potentially risky and, accounting for their lesser productivity over the lifetime, pay them less. Take another case: black people earn less then white people; one can 'explain' this by some employers having a 'taste' (a term used by Becker of the Chicago school) for discrimination, which will in time and with competition prove to be costly to sustain, and so wage gaps will decrease as the competitive markets will force the discriminating employers to realise the increasing costs of their otherwise rational decision made in accordance with their 'tastes' (for the bleak ways in which economics and discrimination intersect, see Darity Jr. 1995). Or even, the gendered division of labour within the household, the asymmetry between husbands' and wives' share of housework can be 'explained' by referring to the specialisation of women in household production in the light of which it is a rational choice for a household to have an asymmetric gendered division of labour to maximise total utility.

11 For a critique of rational choice theories which unpacks the four basic assumptions – that individuals act on the basis of self-interest; that interpersonal utility comparisons are impossible; that tastes are exogenous to economic models and unchanging; that individuals are rational – see England (1995).

Now, at first glance, the economist as scientist might argue that these justifications are not ethical but explanatory. However, this needs to be problematised. Consider the practical consequences of operationalising the prescriptions following from these models. Two that Jameson lists as his 'favourite' are: oppressed minorities only make it worse for themselves by fighting back; and, 'household production' in Becker's sense is seriously lowered in productivity when the wife has a job (1991: 260–278). Some economists have even argued that discrimination could benefit those who are discriminated against by forcing them to accumulate more 'human capital'.[12] As Bergmann (2002: 65–66) explains by example,

> Glenn Loury published a theoretical paper in the *AER* [*American Economic Review*] on affirmative action. There were several very complicated diagrams in it that purported to show that under certain assumptions, affirmative action could be harmful to its supposed beneficiaries. The main idea of the paper is this: if a black man is unable to get a job as a truck driver because he is discriminated against, he might become a lawyer instead. But if things changed and truck driving is opened to blacks, he wouldn't become a lawyer. So affirmative action prevents the acquisition of human capital. Loury ignores the possibility that the man turned away from trucking might be unemployed or might take up a life of crime. Of course it is possible that affirmative action could do more harm than good for other reasons, but you would never know for sure using a complicated diagram. This is an empirical question.

In fact, Coate and Loury (1993: 1239, emphasis added) conclude with stating the 'important practical application' of their results thus: 'if one objective in the fight against discrimination is to break down stereotypes, then it will sometimes be better to encourage disadvantaged workers *to supply greater efforts, than to bribe or coerce employers into promoting these workers*.' In the light of these examples, the standard response, that the economist is simply uncovering causal regularities between choices and outcomes, and that the ethical aspect only attaches to otherwise 'scientific' conclusions in the political domain, is untenable. Economic theorists functioning under the cover of mathematical method do still state their results in practical terms.

12 Justifying or explaining away discrimination as being favourable to the discriminated is not very different from the oft-expressed sentiment at the turn of the twentieth century in the United States regarding slavery being beneficial to the 'negroes' and its abolition having had an adverse influence on them. For instance, in 1891, one of the reasons that Francis Walker, the first president of the American Economic Association, offered for what was seen as the declining black share in the US population, was the competition from the 'vigorous, resolute white element' (see Darity Jr 1995: 39). Moreover, if economists have argued discrimination as being favourable to the discriminated, they have also argued against affirmative action for being discriminatory. A very recent example of this is the American Economic Association (AEA) refusing to list University of Vermont's tenure-track job opening for an economist because it included the words that the University 'welcomes applications from women and underrepresented ethnic, racial and cultural groups and from people with disabilities'. While it allows the listing of citizenship restrictions in adverts by government agencies, the AEA saw this reference to welcoming diversity as discriminatory since it listed particular groups. See Jaschik (2006).

The next question is the extent to which governments can intervene to minimise unequal or discriminatory social outcomes or more generally intervene in market for achieving desired policy outcomes. Even at this stage, economists write out not simply the ideological rationale for government intervention, but also claim a theoretical rationale against government intervention. So that not only on normative, but also on positive terrain, the economists explicitly argue against government intervention. Let me give an example. The 'new classical economics' (mainstream macroeconomics) relies upon the idea of 'rational expectations' (leading to a Nobel prize for the economist Lucas), which serves to demonstrate the irrelevance of government intervention. Fine (1999: 408–409, emphasis added) explains this as,[13]

> the idea that, in effect, each economic agent acts upon the same, consistent economic model, fully deploying the information available. This simple, wildly unrealistic, assumption raised dramatic implications – that all previously estimated macroeconomic models were inappropriate for policy making, and *government could not effectively and systematically intervene to shift the path of the economy*. Economic fluctuations became understood primarily as the consequence of responses to shocks by optimizing and efficient economic agents who would neutralize systematic government intervention by anticipating its intended impact.

Therefore, social outcomes are 'explained' as a result of rational choice by individuals, there is no regard to the simplistic assumptions of the model when policy prescriptions are put forward, and, at the same time, this is matched by an argument for the irrelevance of government intervention at the macro level since people's expectations are rational and would neutralise government intervention. Again, the crucial assumption that economic agents are optimising, efficient, and similar generic individuals is left ungrounded. As a result, the basic idea remains the same. Take any outcome, and explain it as having occurred as a result of conscious and rational choice by free economic agents. Where this is a bit more difficult in the face of continued empirical evidence, bring in 'technological change' as a determinant.[14] Generally, never question the competitive wisdom of 'free markets', since there is nothing better to start an explanatory account than the freely choosing abstract universal self-interested rational utility-maximising economic agent. Governments, or regulatory agencies, should not 'interfere' with the free choices of economic agents. Moreover, even when governments or bureaucracies are created, they are no different from economic agents in pursuing

13 Further, he argues that the professions' embrace of rational expectations not only considerably ratcheted up the levels of mathematical and statistical techniques required, but also served the crucial function of rescuing the discipline from the analytical stagnation attached to the Keynesian/monetarism debate.

14 Galbraith (2000) in his discussion of 'how the economists got it wrong', gives as one of his examples: the pet rationale of economists when explaining rising pay inequalities – they stem from technological change. Never mind that the diffusion of technology speeded up after 1994, while pay inequalities declined at this time, after having increased in the 1980s.

'rent seeking behaviour'. The concept of choice is further linked to the idea of 'willingness to pay' as a measure of valuation. As a result, in 'the conventional model differences in income for personal services reflect ultimately the willingness of the community to pay for such services as derived from market desires and preferences', and the net outcome is that '[i]nequality in non-property incomes thus derives a substantial measure of functional sanction' (Galbraith 1970: 477).[15]

All of this suggests that this notion of 'choice' is problematic. Not only is it unjustifiably serviced as being rational in the interests of accounting for and maintaining hierarchical social outcomes, it is also debatable whether it is 'free' in the way assumed by economists.[16] If the choice is one between starvation and exploitation, I would not consider it a choice in the sense that the notion of choice is grounded for the individual essentialist view of identity. Further, I cannot accept the logic of a system of understanding economic outcomes which does not take into consideration the historical ways in which those starting points came to be. I am referring here to way in which mainstream economists start from 'initial endowments', taking them as 'given', a move which makes it impossible to account for history. And, finally, to start from any social outcome and justify it as the logical result of conscious free and rational choice by economic agents is a sure way of never challenging the *status quo*. A system that produces 'caviar for the rich before milk for the poor' is not simply producing outcomes in line with 'effective demand' or 'willingness to pay', and requires not just theoretical justification and explanation, but change. However, it becomes impossible to conceive of change if the model is presented as being the description of an inevitable outcome of people's choices, when it is in fact an interested and problematic refusal to step outside a particularly narrow method, by economists who are ideologically complicit with the *status quo* (also recall Heilbroner's discussion of Friedman and Lucas's ideology, referred to in Chapter 3). Multiply this need for change many times over for every concept that is uncritically harnessed in the service of social scientific justification for capitalist liberal democratic outcomes, and it is no longer curious why the essentialist individual version of identity is not enough.

So, let me return to the general account of the relation between identity and choice that gives us the 'I' as the model of subjective identity which *is the condition for any identity*. Here, choice is not a happening, but rather a conscious act of the subject who is both rational and free. There is no place for undecidability within the 'moment of choice', or the possibility that the very idea of choice as an *originary moment* is an illusion useful for sustaining a particular version of identity. There is no choice in the sense of 'the choice' envisaged in this version of identity.

To sum up, the essentialist abstraction of this view of identity can be critiqued for its feeding into formalist simplification, interested construction of the particular

15 Galbraith suggests moving away from assuming consumer sovereignty to account for producer sovereignty, which makes this income inequality, at least in part, the product of bureaucratic design, tradition, and self-arrangement.

16 The economists' favourite illustration of Robinson Crusoe and Friday hardly shows any recognition of the extent to which Friday was not 'free'. See Grapard (1995); Samson (1995); Kaul (2002c).

individual economic agent, its 'unrealism', and its deployment of the notion of choice in theoretical explanation. All of these draw from thinking of identity as the self-same continuity over time of an abstract individual agent capable of being located as the origin of the 'I'. This 'subject' of knowledge is part of a picture of knowledge creation where the economist as social scientist produces simplified theories about the world by assuming it to be full of such abstract similar subjects. The demarcations on this account of knowledge are quite clear – there is the social scientist, the external reality, and the subjects of knowledge who are all alike. The production of knowledge involves a neutral scientific exercise whereby the social scientist applies a method to reality in order to theorise it. The application of proper methods will result in proper science. Admittedly, this picture of knowledge creation linked to the abstract individual of the liberal tradition has been extensively critiqued and relegated in some branches of social study, but within economics it retains its fervour.

My interrogation of the place of 'difference' in the creation of knowledge about the social world means that I find this picture of knowledge in economics extremely inadequate and problematic. The most important problem that I have with the view of knowledge creation underlying the identity of the universal subject of economic theory is to do with the treatment of difference. Within the essentialist view of identity, the place of the Other is a perpetual remainder which destabilises the whole picture of knowledge creation. Difference is either ignored, or excluded, or assimilated, or considered as being the 'Other of the same' (as discussed in Chapter 3).

If knowledge creation is a political endeavour, then we need to pay attention to the implied picture of knowledge creation for the ways in which its claims can be justified. In other words, we need to examine more closely the politics of knowledge creation, and in this endeavour we can start by destabilising the view of identity which underlies economic theory, as a prelude to thinking about identity of the subjects of knowledge in ways that have a more productive relation to difference. But, before launching into ways of rethinking identity in relation to knowledge, I want to briefly consider what possible justifications could mainstream economics offer for maintaining its viewpoint. This is because one might ask, given all these criticisms, how could the mainstream still hold on to such a model of knowledge? To this end, I will now set up a possible dialogue between a mainstream economics perspective and a critical response to it. In this exercise, I will draw from some of the critiques that I have already mentioned earlier, and also link back to some of the points made in previous chapters.

4.4 The orthodox and the heterodox: a possible dialogue

> Although the rational-discursive day-time I is the sharpest expression or symptom of life, it *grows out of* the depths and has its roots in the darkness of the night-time, dreaming I; the personality is immeasurably deeper and broader than its consciousness at any given moment.
>
> (Bulgakov 2000: 53, emphasis original)

4.4.1 The case for orthodox economics

To begin with, let me put forward a possible perspective from the point of view of mainstream economics and social science. To the extent that mainstream economics is aware of some of the critiques levelled at it, but still continues to theorise in the same manner, a possible response could be the following.

Of course, not everybody can be a rational-selfinterested-utilitymaximising-calculating-amoral-disembodied-disembedded-abstract-economic-agent-individual all of the time. We all do depart from this baseline, and some more than others. However, first, this is not a bad approximation to make, because most of the people most of the time do behave *as if* they were conforming to the characteristics outlined earlier (see Friedman 1953). It is a moot question whether they in fact conform in their heart of hearts, but as long as we perceive them to be behaving as if they conform (and action is more important than talk),[17] we are on safe ground.

Second, the main purpose of theory is good explanation and prediction of economic reality (see Klein 1994). So, going by the law of large numbers, what most of the people seem to do most of the time is good enough subject matter to attempt explanation and try predictions.

Third, such a characterisation of the identity of the economic agent is important in order to make considerations of behaviour tractable for mathematical formalisation using modelling methodology. So, if one did not make these assumptions when trying to study economic behaviour or social processes, how would one be able to put the determinants of human action in equations, how would we approximate the language of science, how would we get all those neat and aesthetic diagrams and equations?

Fourth, if one were to give up the modelling methodology, and try to understand human behaviour and social processes *in their context*, how would we generalise enough to do 'proper science'?

Fifth, if we didn't do proper science, we wouldn't be able to serve as the hand-*maidens* [*sic*] of governance by providing answers to 'what if' questions. Economics would, by a single stroke, lose both its claims to science, and its claims to practicality. For all the arguments in favour of greater realism, where would we be then?

4.4.2 The case for heterodox economics

Let me now put forward the arguments against the mainstream point of view.

First, to reiterate – people are *not* rational-selfinterested-utilitymaximising-calculating-amoral-disembodied-disembedded-abstract-economic-agent-individuals. More importantly, assuming that people are so disguises the political and power-laden nature of this construction itself. While seemingly a universal assumption, this manner of characterising people is itself particular and located in the way that it serves to detract attention from the operation of power differentials.

17 As McCloskey and Klamer (1995: 191) put it, '[e]conomists view talk as cheap and culture as insignificant.'

Further, people are *not* rational-selfinterested-...not because they *cannot manage to be* thus all of the time, or for some, at any time. This is because, to people untutored in economics, this starting point does not make sense at all. Not because they can never act in their own interest as they perceive it at the moment, or because they are 'irrational', but because this conception of human identity as a basic uninterrogable unit to explain behaviour and social processes, seems itself an irrational thought-experiment in the face of enduring complexity, fluidity, impermanence and variation in human behaviour. If this means that a focus on complexity will detract from the benefits of excessive simplification, then 'it is better to be vaguely right than precisely wrong'. As I have argued until now, this way (i.e., abstract, essentialist, universalist, and formal) of conceptualising the form and content of knowledge is immensely steeped in its origins in enlightenment modernism and the consequent trails of valorising a particular narrow segment of human experience (in accordance with class, gender, geography, morals, governance, nationality, and race) at the expense of silencing its radical Others. At this point, it must be emphasised that I am not arguing for the incapability of the Others of enlightenment modernism to subscribe to this version of knowledge and behaviour. This is *emphatically not* a plea for those who cannot grasp instrumental rationality or enlightenment ideals or self-interested profit motives. This either/or question, something Foucault terms as the 'blackmail of the enlightenment' (1984: 32–50), is unproductive. The Others are not geographically determined happy community-oriented innocent tribes in faraway places who just cannot be self-interestedly rational in the manner of the individual economic agent. Freedom or rationality of the individual are not European belongings. However, the particular ways in which they have been invoked in the version of human identity employed in economics, are tied to located intellectual legacies. Further, because the conception of the economic agent is generously inapplicable and seemingly irrational to people everywhere, it is not a good baseline.

Second, this version of identity as a thought-experiment (i.e., assuming that the basic unit of knowledge is an abstract essentialist individual) *cannot* be defended as necessary for the theoretical purposes which are seen as being mainly to explain and predict reality.[18] This is because explanation and prediction have long been undermined by social theory as the unquestioned aim of theory. Even within economics, it is fairly well accepted now that economic theories have not done a good job of any predictions.[19] Methodological attempts to diagnose why this is

18 Of course, there is the argument that reality itself is a construct, but until now within economics (whether mainstream or heterodox) this argument has not had much impact. In Chapter 7, I put forward this view and analyse its implications in detail.

19 Therefore, the line 'an economist is someone who will tell you tomorrow why the things he predicted yesterday did not come true today' (the signifier 'he' is apt in that sentence because most economists are men). A few words from Keen (2001: 4, emphasis original):

> Though economists have long believed that their theory constitutes 'a body of generalisations whose substantial accuracy and importance are open to question only by the ignorant or the

the case point toward the culprit of complexity and inherent unpredictability in the world. This leaves us with explanation. As discussed in Chapter 2, there can be and have been various ways of understanding what we do when we explain. None of the many things we might do when we explain necessarily require one to start from the premise of identity outlined earlier. It is only when the explanation is implicitly oriented toward putting the determinants of human action into equations to construct models and diagrams that can be applied 'universally' that one is concerned about the mathematical (and more generally, formalist) tractability of human behaviour.

Third, there is no justification for an unquestioned *a priori* overvalorisation of understanding human behaviour and social processes in formalist terms using modelling methodology. This is the argument that the nature of reality is open-ended and unlike the closed systems studied by the natural sciences (see Lawson 1997; Fleetwood 1999). Therefore, the methodology of formalist modelling cannot begin to approximate the complex richness of human behaviour, for the understanding of which we need to proceed differently.[20]

Fourth, given that there is no reason to adopt formalist modelling methodology, and many good reasons to proceed from more realistic bases of human behaviour, we cannot justify adherence to this version of identity. And, there is no doubt that understanding human behaviour and social processes *in their context* would definitely mean that one *cannot generalise universally*, as is permitted in the abstract formalist modelling methodology at the moment. Now, to those who wring their hands in despair worrying about how one can do 'proper science' – without the trappings of aesthetic equations, models, diagrams, universal applicability – consider the following arguments (drawing upon Chapter 2). The idea of a 'proper science' as something which comprises of aesthetic equations, models, diagrams, universal applicability is not itself universal. Systematic knowledge is not mortgaged to the language of mathematics, or, universality. Further, the belief in these characteristics of 'proper science' is itself traceable to the successes of natural science (especially physics) in general, and as far as economics is concerned, mid nineteenth-century energetics in particular (on this, see Chapter 2, and Mirowski 1989, 1991a, b, 1994a, b). Thus, there is no reason to believe that the study of human behaviour and social processes should conform to the methods used for the study of inanimate matter. Also, science itself is not a pure, higher order, dispassionate, innocent way of knowing (see Longino 1990; Flax 1992). The practice of science is tied to history, ideology,[21] and culture – it is

perverse' (Robbins 1932), for over a century *economists* have shown that economic theory is replete with logical inconsistencies, specious assumptions, errant notions, and predictions contrary to empirical data.

20 For instance, Lawson suggests instead to aim for contrastive explanation (explanation by comparison), looking for demi-regularities rather than explanation of the form if x, then y.

21 The dominant view is that science is not an ideology; if it is, it is not true science. As Latour (1993: 93) characterises it, '[o]nly what breaks forever with ideology is scientific.'

tied to the representation of science not being an ideology, of West not being a culture.

In addition to these critiques, I would like to add further points which are useful for questioning the mainstream. If economics cannot be a 'proper science' (noting, however, that proper science itself is not proper science either all the time), it would not have a claim to privileged service as the handmaiden of administrative governance and social management. This is indeed the case. But, consider the implications of this. To begin with, one would be able to comprehensively overhaul the basis of what counts as 'the economic', paying attention to what 'the economic', in fact, designates. Next, acknowledging the inextricably normative context of human behaviour and social processes could lead to a serious consideration of the important issues – such as, systematic and structural inequalities, deprivation, injustices – whereby the politics of knowledge creation in the academy, its role in the preservation of structures of governance, and its dissemination via trans-contextual management applicability, are all seriously questioned. Finally, the universality of economic knowledge as neutral representation will be questioned in its construction and applicability. One might even dis-cover the extraordinary parallels between the wannabe 'proper science' of economics (classical political economy/marginalist-neoclassical economics/neo-liberal economic view), and the unrolling of Western (mercantile/industrial-imperial/postindustrial-neocolonial) capitalism (see Dowd 2000). And what is more, we can explore alternative ways of writing 'the economic'.

To sum up, economic world is anchored in the abstract essentialist individual version of identity that underpins reified models such as the *homo economicus* (the REM), and critiquing this view of identity is a step toward recognising the violent gestures inherent in this conception. This is a violence which is enacted materially so that structural inequalities, injustices, and deprivation are perpetuated while economic theory is unable to analyse them in any but the most simplistic terms based upon the abstract essentialist individual version of identity. This means that such material violence is often justified as the random outcome of rational-self-interested- ..., agents freely interacting and transacting. However, in addition to this, I would argue that it is also important to recognise violence at the epistemic or the representational level where recognition as rational-self-interested- ..., agents is withheld from most 'Third World' people and governments, who then need to be advised, taught, even coerced by 'advanced' Western economic agents such as governments or international financial institutions.[22]

So, the purposes served by the essentialist individual view of identity include the following – the terms of access are predicated upon an ideally abstract

22 It may be argued that in the name of increasing productivity, often unprivileged sections of the so-called First World countries are also disciplined in a similar manner. However, the extent to which full recognition as rational agents is withheld from them is probably systematically limited in the 'first world'.

individual embodiment (which is patterned after privileged masculinity); it fixes responsibility in choices which are seen as rational (this naturalises outcomes, thus often perpetuating inequalities); the assumption of sameness and definiteness mostly does away with the need to consider difference in relation to identity; and, all this theoretical incomprehension goes along with practical non-redressal. Finally, this view of identity 'fixes' difference as its Other in an extremely political manner while claiming to be a neutral category.

4.5 Rethinking the relation of identity and difference in knowledge

Until now I have discussed the ways in which knowledge production in economics relies upon the underlying model of an abstract essentialist individual view of identity. The idealised economic world gives voice to supposedly universal truths based upon the viewpoint of the 'universal knowing subject'. Economics as a social science is not unique in this, but while the debates in feminist theory have influenced most other disciplines to a significant extent, within economics the influence of feminist thought still has a long way to go. In what follows, I want to examine some of the ways in which feminist theory has attempted to respond to knowledges based on the universal subject.

One of the most prominent critiques of the liberal individualist or abstract essentialist view of identity and the corresponding structuring of knowledge can be said to be the epistemology of standpoint theory, and its political correlate in identity politics. Starting from the view of knowledge from 'nowhere', feminist standpoint theory relies upon the idea that all knowledge is from 'somewhere'.[23] In other words, the most important point of departure of feminist standpoint theory from the earlier models of knowledge is to argue that the subjects of knowledge are not disembodied and disembedded abstract agents, as is often presumed in disciplinary knowledge, but that we can only have knowledge from particular subject positions. Knowledge is no longer universal but *situated and perspectival*. Having its origins partly in the Marxian project and in large the project of feminism, the criteria for what counts as knowledge in standpoint terms is not simply what we know in the classical sense, but includes 'seeing, tasting, feeling, and thinking' (Hartsock 1997: 370). What we know is not universally available from any and every subject position, but it is crucially linked to who we are and where we are situated in a wider totality of social relations. In this sense, the categories of gender, race, class, are not additional empirical data which can

23 This is not to say that all feminist standpoint theorists agree. There are indeed different versions of standpoint theory, for instance, ranging from those inspired by object-relations theory (associated with Chodorow 1978), to those influenced by Marxism. Some early works include Smith 1974; Hartsock 1983; Harding 1986. My purpose in discussing standpoint theory or identity politics here is not to summarise these vast fields, nor even to discuss them generally, but to draw the insights that are relevant to my arguments.

be added on to abstract universal knowledge, but rather our gender, race, class, and other aspects of our identity determine what we know.

The forcefield of social relations is always determined by the criss-crossing flow of power, and the discourses of the oppressed are different from those of the dominant groups. At this point, we can clearly see the way in which feminist standpoint theory is not only a project of knowledge gathering, but is seeped with political considerations. The having of knowledge is made always-already political on this account. Even further, most standpoint theorists argue that it is not only that knowledge differs according to situation and perspective, but also that knowledge from the perspectives of the oppressed allows us to generate better accounts of society which can then be used for bringing about greater emancipation. Therefore, those who are oppressed under the current system of power relations in society have perspectives on society which are not only different from those of the dominant group, but are better because they afford a view from the 'outside within'. This is not the same as saying that the knowledge of the oppressed is better just because they are 'oppressed'. Harding (1997: 385) explains this in relation to modern science. She writes that when one asks questions about standard accounts of the growth of modern science, for instance, starting from the lives of people who suffered from that growth and from the associated European expansion that made it possible and benefited from it (thus taking into account the resources of postcolonial science studies and the critiques of development, and feminist work in these areas), then one arrives at better accounts of the growth of modern science than if one had restricted oneself to northern and northern feminist science studies. This is not because 'poor, Third World women are "more oppressed"', but because 'thought that begins from conceptual frameworks developed to answer questions arising in *their* lives starts from outside the Eurocentric conceptual frameworks within which northern and northern feminist science studies have been largely organised' (ibid., emphasis added). When we look at theorising in this way, '[s]tandpoint theories are technical theoretical devices that can allow for the creation of accounts of society that can be used to work for more satisfactory social relations' (Hartsock 1997: 370).

An important aspect of standpoint theory is the way in which it conceives of the identity of the subjects of knowledge. The subjects of knowledge are not simply individuals as isolated subjects, but collective subject positions. As Hartsock puts it, 'the subjects who matter are not individual subjects but collective subjects, or groups' (ibid.: 371). The central aspect of identity that underlies knowledge is not the identity of the individual subject of knowledge, but the collective identity of a social group which comes into being over time through the sharing of experiences. For standpoint theory, it is not the isolated experience of individuals that is crucial, but rather the study of how certain social experiences 'come to belong' to certain social groups in ways that individuals of a particular group are likely to experience systematic similarities in their negotiation of the asymmetric power relations in society. This is not to deny that individual experiences can be different, but the emphasis here is on the group-based experiences and commonalities. Hill Collins (1997: 375) gives the example of the African-American experience with racism to illustrate this point. She argues that African-Americans as a 'stigmatised racial group' existed long before she was born and will probably continue after she dies, and no doubt her individual experiences of institutionalised racism as an African-American are unique, but nonetheless, the types of opportunities and constraints that she would encounter on a daily basis will be similar to those that confront African-Americans as a group.[24] What this means is the following, '[r]ace, gender, social class, ethnicity, age, and sexuality are not descriptive categories of identity applied to individuals. Instead, these elements of social structure emerge as fundamental devices that foster inequalities resulting in groups' (ibid.: 376). In this way, standpoint theory aims to make visible the workings of power which are disguised in the universalist account. And so, 'standpoint theory concerns the commonality of experiences and perspectives that emerge for groups differentially arrayed within hierarchical power relations' (ibid.: 377).

The conceptions of knowledge and of identity that structure standpoint theory find their political expression in 'identity politics'. If we think back to the abstract essentialist view of identity and the liberal individualist types of knowledges that it structured, then we can recall that, in those frameworks, the political is reduced to the juridical. As Connolly argued (1991: 73–74), most issues of politics are condensed into the juridical category of rights, justice, obligation, and responsibility, and the remaining issues are treated 'instrumentally as *contests in which individuals and aggregations compete within juridical rules to advance their "interests" or "principles" by rational means*' (ibid., emphasis added). On this view, politics is the result of constituencies of neutral abstract individuals coming together based on their shared interests. Political mobilisation has to do with common interests, and there is no great role for who one is in terms of identity affiliations. In contrast, the notion of identity politics as the political correlate of standpoint epistemology enshrines a very different view of politics.

Within identity politics, politics is not the arena where abstract individuals who share interests, compete. The focus is shifted to the question of shared identities. That is, on this view, politics is an effect of shared identities, something that has given rise to numerous debates in the last decade. For even when theorists are agreed on the idea that politics can be seen as an effect of shared identities, it is not clear how these shared identities come into being. Are we simply born naturally aligned to some groups and not to others, or do we have to work in thought and action in order to realise that we belong to a certain group? Most standpoint theorists now hold the view that we do not automatically have the situated and perspectival knowledge of the identity groupings to which we belong. For instance, not all women will possess the feminist standpoint simply because they

24 Hill Collins further adds, '[a]rguing that Blacks as a group come into being or disappear on the basis of my participation seems narcissistic, egocentric, and archetypally postmodern. In contrast, standpoint theory places less emphasis on individual experiences within socially constructed groups than on the social conditions that construct such groups' (1997: 375).

were born biologically women. Or, there is no simple trajectory from one's less privileged subject position as a woman in the totality of social relations to the feminist standpoint. However, this does not detract from the conceptualisation of knowledge as being based upon and shaped by the experiences of exclusion, and the relation between knowledge that is produced and those whom the knowledge is supposed to be about. The position of the 'collective subject' (e.g., woman) of identity in a particular situated relation to knowledge is not merely the aggregation of the individual subjects (e.g. individual women), but the constitution of the collective subject is the result of 'a complex interplay of "individuals" and larger-scale social forces' (Hartsock 1997: 372).[25] In other words, the constitution of the collective subject of standpoint theories requires 'an always contingent and fragile (re)construction/transformation of [these] complex subject-positions' (ibid.). Hartsock quotes Weeks as follows, '[t]he project of transforming subject positions into standpoint involves an *active intervention*, a conscious and concerted effort to reinterpret and restructure our lives. ... *A standpoint is a project, not an inheritance; it is achieved, not given*' (ibid.). Thus, politics involves the assertion of shared identities, but the standpoint of the shared identity is not something given naturally; rather, it has to be realised and achieved. According to Hill Collins (1997: 380), this realisation can come about through the process of 'consciousness raising'. Similarly, Hartsock (1997: 372) also draws upon Sandoval's (1991) notion of 'oppositional consciousness' in order to illustrate how subject positions of those who are less privileged can be used as effective sites of resistance once they are self-consciously recognised by their inhabitants. Sandoval's example in this case is to see US Third World feminism as a model of oppositional political activity. If the world is viewed as a kind of 'topography', then the points can be defined around which 'individuals and groups seeking to transform oppressive powers constitute themselves as resistant and oppositional subjects' (in Hartsock ibid.). Then, the subject positions of the oppressed, if self-consciously recognised by their inhabitants, can be transformed into effective sites of resistance through the operation of what Sandoval calls a 'differential consciousness', which, operating like a clutch of an automobile, allows the driver to engage gears in a 'system for the transmission of power' (ibid.).

Identity politics as an advance on the earlier notions of politics in relation to knowledge has become a central issue for feminist theory.[26] The appeal of identity politics can be understood, as Smith (2001: 37) puts it, because, 'part of the process of identity politics is a battle to assert the salience and meaning of a given

25 Hartsock draws upon Gramsci in her discussions about rethinking the nature of identity. She takes from Gramsci the idea that our capacity to think and act on the world is dependent upon other people who are themselves also both subjects and objects of history. And so, the idea that the individual is a synthesis of the social relations and the history of the social relations, a 'précis of the past' (1997: 372 [Gramsci 1971: 353]).

26 The reader may notice that I have not referred to economics ever since the close of discussions on the abstract essentialist individual view of identity. This is *not* an oversight. Rather, feminist economics as the only subfield of economics that might want to engage with standpoint theory or

identity'. Not only is standpoint theory responsible for the appreciation of a situated and perspectival nature of knowledge (which is at least initially a great improvement on the abstract universal presuppositions of knowledge-type thinking), but also its correlate of identity politics is responsible for thinking politics as something determined by the identities of the political actors involved. Because there is a great thrust on recognising the experiencing of identity in collective similarities, especially those similarities of experience which result from exclusion or oppression, identity politics serves an important function when strategic visibility in the political arena is at stake. An example of this is the way in which the assertion of the identity of woman as a political move (owing to systematic similarities between the experiences of women as marginal groups in society) results in the strategic visibility of women as important political actors. Smith (ibid.: 44) argues that another possible reason for the appeal of identity politics lies in its basis in essentialism. That is, the 'simplicity and non-reflexive nature of the discourse allows it to work equally well on both sides of potential line of division'.

Thus, we begin to see the ways in which identity politics might be open to difficulties. An important difficulty, and one that has just been aforementioned, relates to essentialism. Put another way, the collective subject positions of standpoint theory which provide the basis for identity politics face the following problem. The constitution of the collective subject position will require that it be a relatively stable ground from which politics can ensue. This will mean, first, that differences of experience within a collective subject position will need to surrender their salience, and, second, that the collective subject position as a shared identity will rely upon the idea of identity *itself* as a stable and shared continuity which can provide the basis for political action. In both cases, the discourse of essentialism functioning both normatively and descriptively is not transcended.

Further, although standpoint theory as a response to universalist knowledge is undoubtedly welcome for the way in which it is committed to a linking of knowledge with knowledge- producers, an espousal of situatedness, and a bringing into relief of the relations between power and knowledge, ultimately, however, its wider pedigree in modernism comes to the fore in the way in which it conceptualises truth and identity. This is related to the homogeneity of the collective subject position, but also to the way in which it is assumed that we can identify social or material positions which give us privileged knowledge, and that, even though these knowledges are from particular situations, they can yield up knowledge which is 'good' for everyone.

identity politics, at present, does not have many such intersections. An exception might be Barker and Kuiper (2003). Hewitson (1999: 87) speculates on the possible reasons for this:

> [T]he lack of feminist work [in economics] which is in fact underpinned by feminist standpoint theory may simply be due to the immaturity of the field of feminist economics as a whole, practitioners of which are still to a certain extent assessing alternative feminist theoretical works and their implications. There may also be some hesitancy over how actually to implement the research project based on feminist standpoint theory…

So, the issues that arise from identity politics afford no easy capturing. The responses to feminist standpoint theory and identity politics are varied. This is because there are those who find the idea of knowledge being multiple, situated, and perspectival as troubling, because it no longer provides the grasp that the modernist universal knowledge promised. Such theorists are anxious to ask the question, 'but if this is the case, then how will we be able to arbitrate between knowledge claims, and decide which claims are better than others?' Similarly, people may also find the idea of identity politics troublesome because it involves a radical redefinition of politics as something which is dependent upon and determined by identities. Their worry is that the political arena will become a contest amongst multiple identity groupings, and that, as these groupings of the different identities proliferate, it will be difficult to achieve coalitions or solidarities which are crucial for political action. As a response, those who find standpoint theory and identity politics problematic in the ways mentioned, can advocate a renunciation of identity politics. An example is Hekman, who raises the problems I have mentioned with standpoint theory and identity politics, and argues for saying no to identity politics, in order to develop an alternative epistemology which will allow us to retain the powers of arbitration between competing knowledge claims.[27]

27 There are many others who give variants of the same response. I am not discussing Hekman's position here, for many reasons. To begin with, her position is not clear. She seems to see herself as a sometimes-postmodern (but not poststructuralist) feminist epistemologist. She critiques standpoint theory for its conception of knowledge as multiple, situated, and perspectival because it does not allow her to arbitrate between knowledge claims. However, responding to her critique of feminist standpoint theory, Hartsock, Hill Collins, Harding, Smith (all standpoint theorists) point out that she does not understand the way in which the standpoint in feminist standpoint theory is not simply an aggregation of individuals, but involves group experiences, thus misrepresenting and misunderstanding all their respective positions (see Harding, Hill Collins, Smith, Hartsock – all 1997). In a detailed exchange between standpoint theorists in the journal *Signs* (1997a, 1997b), Hekman completely leaves out questions of power in relation to questions of knowledge, and argues that the way forward for feminist analysis requires a paradigm shift involving a return to Max Weber's 'ideal type' methodology. Two things need to be said about this. First, Hekman's case for the adoption of Weberian methodology is unpersuasive and sketchy. As Smith (1997: 393) says, 'the oddest thing is to find Hekman restoring us to the law of the father: Alfred Schutz, Michel Foucault, and, finally, Max Weber.' Second, in relation to the value of feminist analysis for economics, the adoption of an ideal type methodology is far from useful since most mainstream neoclassical economics already relies upon 'ideal type' methodology.

Now, Hekman's (1999a, b) problems with identity politics are even more complex. She worries that identity politics makes for too many differences in the political arena, and wants a resolution of the paradoxes of identity. A resolution which for her demands that identity politics be given up. Repeatedly in her discussions of identity politics and standpoint theory (1997a, 1997b, 1999a, 1999b), she keeps arguing and demanding in the name of a 'WE' – a 'we' that is having problems because it cannot determine what knowledge is superior in the face of multiple knowledges, a 'we' that is having problems acting politically because it does not know who it is any more in the face of so much multiplicity (for instance, she asserts that 'I need to know who I am before I can choose and act, politically or otherwise,' 1999a: 9). In fact, Harding (1997: 386) terms this stance of Hekman, the 'administrator perspective' and writes that Hekman's responses to identity politics and

Another response is the postpositivist realist reclaiming of identity from what is perceived to be an unhelpful debate between the essentialists and the postmodernists (Mohanty 1997; Moya and Hames-Garcia 1997; Moya 2002). This postpositivist realist position, which draws upon the pragmatist and analytical philosophical tradition, sees itself as providing a way of distinguishing between different kinds of identity. They have, in common with standpoint theory, a focus on the significance of experience, and a faith in the knowledges of the dominated as being better, but at the same time they view identity politics as inherently essentialist. The 'postpositivist' designation owes to their recognition that fact and values cannot be easily separated, that knowledge is theory-laden, and that objective knowledge is not unmediated, context-transcendent, or subject-independent. The 'realist' designation stems from their emphasis on the constant striving for objective knowledge, albeit fallibilistic, and a desire to judge well by being able to abstract from relevant cultural particularities while appreciating the situatedness and embodiedness of knowledge (cf. Engelstad and Gerrard 2005). No doubt their motivations in this project are partly practical and pragmatic (they refer repeatedly to their commitment to progressive politics and to multiculturalism as a goal of educational and political institutions); however, their characterisation of postmodernism is clearly problematic. Postmodernism does not imply throwing identity overboard, as it were; neither does it mean an utter discounting of experience. Moreover, the postpositivist realists constantly conflate linguisticality with discursivity when discussing postmodernism, so that the postmodernist call to attend to discursive construction comes across as merely the instability of language. Mohanty (1997) argues that realism about identity requires identities to be seen as complex theories about, and explanations of, the social world. There is a focus on being able to arbitrate between competing accounts of the world and good identities are simply good explanations. Yet the basis upon which these arbitrations are to be carried out is seen as self-evident. Moreover, in light of the realist concern with the ways in which resources accrue to identity

standpoint theory arise from her Eurocentric reaction, frustrated as she is by 'too many axes of analysis' and an 'inability to speak for certain categories of women'. Similarly, Hartsock (1997: 367) finds in Hekman, 'a kind of American pluralism that prefers to speak not about power or justice but, rather, about knowledge and epistemology'. My own reading of Hekman (see Kaul 2002e) corresponds to Harding and Hartsock, and, in my view, part of her trouble with multiple knowledges and identity politics stems from a frustrated Eurocentrism unable to speak in universal terms any longer. In her introduction to *Feminism, identity and difference* (1999a), despite the title, she makes no attempt to consider any Third World feminists, but continually laments (in the face of poststructuralism) her inability to have a coherent identity, and power of epistemological arbitration. Her ultimate aim is to apply what I would call a *diagnostic approach* to the question of difference. For instance, in her book titled *The future of differences: truth and method in feminist theory* (1999b), the very first chapter is called 'the *problem* of difference' (emphasis added), wherein she repeatedly asserts that feminists should 'get on with the task of devising a theory and method for differences' (7), and that 'the politics of difference provides no way of justifying the eliding of some differences, the emphasis on others . . . provides no method of argumentation by which this and other issues can be decided. Jettisoning the modernist metanarrative of logic, the politics of difference offers no viable replacement' (21).

categories (and in relation to structures of inequality), it becomes even more important to deconstruct the stability or availability of these categories.[28] Finally, contrary to postpositivist realists, poststructuralist views on identity are not necessarily politically disabling. Indeed, I now argue that the poststructuralist position can allow us to conceive what may be termed as the 'politics of identity'.

4.6 The politics of identity

> In this exchange, there would be 'no geometry, no accounts'. It would be beyond the calculable and measurable, beyond the *quantitative*: like 'the first instants of love' or like *admiration*, perhaps. And this text too, like so many others, is written under the sign of love: that which does not calculate, does not ask what it risks, gives without guarantee, does not seek to protect itself. The possibility of stepping outside the circle of the 'proper' is presented here as risking life itself – in order perhaps to have it more abundantly?
>
> (Whitford with Irigaray in quotes 1991: 164)

A poststructuralist view worries neither about the multiple, situated, and perspectival knowledge positions, nor about the proliferation of different identities in the political arena, but questions the very idea that identities can precede politics. That is, it does not see politics as either the effect of shared interests or the effect of shared identities, but questions the mutually constitutive and problematic nature of both identity and politics. On this response, the proliferation of difference is not something to be feared as that which would put an end to identity and politics, but rather seeks to destabilise identity as something that can be immune to the effects of difference. It is this view that I wish to formulate, discuss, and contribute to.

The question of identity is intrinsically born out of the question of difference. The sense of seeing/experiencing something as 'different' to the same is closely tied to defining and acknowledging one's sameness in relation to difference along certain parameters. There are immediately two ways of thinking this. The first can be summarised in the words of Spanos (2001: 41), where *identity is the condition for the possibility of difference*. I agree with his assessment of this view of difference as a 'hierarchically structured binarist principle of principles' which forms

28 Young (2002) argues that the postpositivist realists are only ostensibly opposed to postmodernism but produce a similar ideological effect which is the 'suppression of the political economy of identity'. He finds that this project is insufficiently materialist and mystifies the class logic of social relations: 'identity is not the cause of distribution patterns but its legitimation'. According to Young, Mohanty's theory offers only a liberal political project, and that 'reclaiming identity is nothing more than an updating of humanism'. I agree with Young in his critique of the postpositivist realist project, but would contend that the poststructuralist position may be formulated to address his concerns about the political economy of identity (this would mean addressing first the cultural/economic separation and then an interpellation and deconstruction of the inevitability and universality of economic logic, thus challenging the scientistic insularity of the processes through which inequalities are effected and perpetuated, and so undermining the master narrative of economics).

the 'fabricated ontological' basis for a ' "triumphant" liberal democratic/capitalist polity' which is 'imperial *in the essence* as well as in its multi-situated political practices'. In other words, on this view, identity pre-exists difference so that being acknowledged as different relies upon first being identified as different from the same. The difference is a categorisation claimed in direct proportionality to its deviance from the same. The identity of the same, or the very basis on which the category of identity itself is made operational, remains unquestioned.

It is this conception of identity and difference that operates both in the abstract essentialist individual version and the standpoint version of identity. Difference quickly becomes translated into Otherness, which is called upon to verify sameness. Indeed, difference serves the purpose of 'identifying' and making coherent the self, or making coherent one's understanding of collective experiences. In this scenario, the calls to accommodate difference are not so much a concern with Otherness, as they are the response to collating one's own identity in a crisis. Likewise, the collective experiences which are redeemed as a feature of the group identity are claimed as coherent in relation to their 'difference' from other stable identities. In Butler's words (1990: 121), '...identity categories tend to be instruments of regulatory regimes, whether as the normalizing categories of oppressive structures or as the rallying points for a liberatory contestation of that very oppression.' What are the implications of this? Can we think of difference without starting from its relation to other pre-existing identities?

This is the second way of thinking the relation between identity and difference, where *difference is the condition for the possibility of any identity*. On this account, difference is not something that has to be claimed from a pre-existing identity of the same, but rather, *difference is the most fundamental undifferentiated excess from which the concept of identity is fashioned*. Any identity is a continually structurally contingent attempt in the face of universal difference. This way of conceptualising identity is an affront to the imperial liberal democratic capitalist polity where difference cannot pre-exist identity, since this possibility would make *every* identity open to question, and not just some different ones. It is also quite clear that this is a radical move and critics of various stripes (including some postmodern or feminist ones), while criticising some aspects of the essentialist individual identity or standpoint-inspired identity politics, may not be at ease with questioning the basis of a pre-existing 'identity' itself in the face of difference. If we do not take the having of stable identities as the starting point of our thought about the world and of the possibility of politics, then we can reimagine the nature of identity and of politics so that difference becomes integral to knowledge.

The thinking of difference as the condition for the possibility of any identity involves a destabilisation of identity as something which is a stable belonging or recognition. It also leads to a challenging of the view where identities precede politics, because if (as I will argue) identities are unstable and constructed, then they cannot function as affiliations which exist prior to the political arena. In contrast, identities then become discursive constructions which arise in and through politics, or, as Butler puts it (ibid.: 148), 'the deconstruction of identity is not the deconstruction of politics; rather it establishes as political the very terms through which identity is articulated.'[29] There are many consequences of this view for the importance of knowledge in relation to 'different' subjects, since the subjects of knowledge can then be seen as being *constructed as 'different' in the political process of knowledge creation*, rather than the received view where knowledge creation functions neutrally in relation to subjects who are 'different' (i.e., different from some standard normative identity conventionally ascribed to the 'valid' subjects of knowledge). Therefore, let me now argue for moving beyond identity politics to what I call the 'politics of identity'.

Contrary to some disciplinary thought, identity is not like a name tag with affiliations that can be taped on to each isolatable individual person and groups (where groups themselves are seen as an individual unit). Rather, identity can be thought of as something that arises in sociality, is shaped by the surroundings, is affected by interactions, and changes in multiple and contradictory ways. Instead of taking identity as a 'given', if we consider it as something which is socially and politically constructed (and not simply recognised or claimed), then (following Butler 1990: 25), it can be seen as something that is 'performatively constituted by the very "expressions" that are said to be its results'. This allows for considering identity as 'always mobile and processual, partly self-construction, partly categorisation by others . . . [it] is a creolized aggregate composed through bricolage' (Malkki 1992: 47). Further, discussing identity in terms of identification, Hall (2000: 17) argues that, though not without its determinate conditions of existence, including the material and symbolic resources required to sustain it, identification is in the end conditional, inevitably lodged in contingency: 'Identification is, then, a process of articulation, a suturing, an over-determination not a subsumption.'

Because standpoint theory starts from the point of there being different subject positions in relation to knowledge, it does not adequately raise the question of how these different and reasonably stable subject positions came to be recognised. Analogously, identity politics requires that politics be an effect of shared identities, but begs the question of how identities can themselves be dynamically constructed in the political arena, in fluid and contradictory ways. In all of this, *identity itself as a concept is not politicised*. But, if we think of identity as a mobile performative constitution subject to over-determination and suturing, then it can be creatively reimagined and reconstructed as the politics of identity.[30] The politics of identity is an attempt to make visible the basic agonisms which are functional at the moment in which identity coheres. That is, at the very root

29 To quote Butler again (1992: 13, emphasis in original), the 'epistemological model that offers us a pregiven subject or agent is one that refuses to acknowledge that *agency is always and only a political prerogative*.'

30 The phrase 'politics of identity' has been used by some authors to denote something similar to identity politics (or the politics of identity and difference), and has also been used to denote the renewed interest in and relevance of categories such as race, class, gender, sexuality, in social theory or cultural geography. In contrast to these connotations, I am arguing for the availability of a radical analytic of interpretation and conceptualisation in the phrase 'the politics of identity', something which is not within the ambit of the designation 'identity politics'.

of the designation of identity lies the long trek between an 'I' and a 'we'. Most modes of thinking about identity derive their legitimacy and functionality by making invisible any trace of this difficult train between the I and the we. Whether individual or collective, identity remains subordinate to a logic of fixing responsibility in 'difference'. But, the generally unquestioned contours of this logic of fixing responsibility in difference evade the questions of how identity itself is fixed for difference to be recognised. *The politics of identity is a politicisation of identity which gathers in its train a rethinking not just of politics but also of identity.*[31]

This involves stressing on the constructedness of any identity category, and loosening the recognition of identity politics as the political coming together of people who have essentially similar identities, in favour of considering identity as a fluid and constructed contingent process of discovering with shifting and multiple alliances. The difference between identity politics and the politics of identity can be seen as a function of the extent to which differences should be allowed to matter, and what response should be undertaken in the face of the worry engendered by a recognition of the multiplication of identities. While identity politics is seen as divisive and requires the bridging of gaps between the different identity constituencies, the politics of identity is a call for making difference 'foundational' to the having of any identity in the sense that there exists an ethical responsibility inherent in the comprehension of any identity (whether I or We) which realises the suturing functional at the moment in which identity coheres. This making/thinking of difference as the condition for the possibility of identity confronts us with a radical alternative where identity becomes *irreversibly politicised*. What Butler (1992: 15) writes about the subject and deconstruction is applicable to my stance on identity and retheorising it in the light of difference:

> To take the construction of the subject as a political problematic is not the same as doing away with the subject; to deconstruct the subject is not to negate or throw away the concept; on the contrary, deconstruction implies only that we suspend all commitments to that to which the term 'subject', refers, and that we consider the linguistic functions it serves in the consolidation and concealment of authority. To deconstruct is not to negate or to dismiss, but to call into question and, perhaps most importantly, to open up a term, like the subject, to a reusage or redeployment that previously has not been authorized.

This politicisation of identity constructs it as a *contingent structure whose structurality is always open to question in the face of difference, a difference not from something but everything as different*. The politics of identity is therefore always-already also the politics of difference.

31 Todorov (1984: 249) wrote: 'We want equality without its compelling to accept identity, but also difference without its degenerating into superiority/inferiority.' My addendum to this in differentiating the notion of the politics of identity is this – who poses this demand to whom?

The implications of this politicised identity – the politics of identity – are enormous. The very grounds on which identity is claimed become open to interrogation, revision, and change. This is not something that has been taken on board in standard disciplinary knowledge because the openness and variation in identity are hard to reconcile with the neutrality and universality of knowledge that applies in relation to those identities. Let me briefly consider some immediate implications of the politics of identity.

First, it entails the recognition of *all* (and not only some) identities as being the result of *contingent* manufacturing. If identity itself is a politicised performance, then no identity is secure against which the Other or different identities can be claimed in reaction. Thus, we need to challenge the conventional view where some identities (the meta-identities) are open to question, but not others. In this conventional view, identities can be questioned only until such questioning does not threaten to destabilise the 'strategically important' identities. For instance, the idea that the identity of women in relation to knowledge should not be questioned when it comes to differences between women. So, some feminists and feminist economists would have all the women be good champions of the feminist cause, and not let the issues of difference matter when it comes to claiming the different identity which is most important – as women.[32] Another example is where claiming some identities becomes problematic if they 'interfere' with other strategically important identities. Bramen (2002: 3), in her discussion of Rorty [2000: 101], notes that, according to him, 'to take pride in being black or gay is an entirely reasonable response to the sadistic humiliation to which one has been subjected. But in so far as this pride prevents someone from also taking pride in being an American citizen... it is a political disaster.' Recognising that it is *all* and not some identities that are contingent and 'fixed' in the face of difference, will mean that all identities become open to question and being politicised.

Second, the politics of identity draws attention to thinking about identity as a political construct. Identity is a construction within knowledge producing texts and is therefore tied up with relations of power and exclusion. This is important because a politicisation of identity which stresses upon the constructedness and fluidity of identity can be misunderstood as a claim that identities are simply ludic performances – fluid and flimsy. I am not asserting that identities cannot be freely chosen, but the claiming of an identity also relies upon its recognition within the context in which it is being claimed. Not everyone can equally withhold recognition, and the constraints in the experiencing of identities are inevitably greater for some.[33]

32 This brings to mind the difficulties that black or third world or lesbian feminism poses to the dominant Western feminism which deploys the category 'woman'. Consider the following: 'There are some less auspicious developments as well. For instance, there is some dissension between African-American and white feminists. The more sensible ones in both camps recognise that they are natural allies against a model that is white and male' (Ferber 2002: 49–50). This leaves the question of black males unutterable.

33 For instance, my remarks on feminism might be taken to be designating 'Third World feminism', or the voice of a 'woman of colour'. Also note that this range of signification within which

As Taylor puts it, 'since identities are formed dialogically in social contexts, they require recognition from others, not denial or misrecognition, and hence withholding recognition can be a form of oppression' (in Sayer 2000: 183). The way in which differences are fixed for view in relation to identity is political. This power of signification is observed by Butler (1992: 17–18) as follows:

> The violence of the letter, the violence of the mark which establishes what will and will not signify, what will and will not be included within the intelligible, takes on a political significance when the letter is the law. . . . So what can this kind of poststructural analysis tell us about violence and suffering? Is it perhaps that forms of violence are to be understood as more pervasive, more constitutive, and more insidious than prior models have allowed us to see?

This importance of signification extends to the way in which 'different' subjects are constituted as valid subjects of knowledge. Constructions of identity are produced in relation to knowledge and are inflected through power.

Third, as mentioned before, the politics of identity is also the politics of difference, since identities are only contingently formed out of the undifferentiated excess of difference. Conventionally, difference is either seen as a threat to the coherence of identity, or as an additive advantage in knowledge production (difference as more data, a better picture). Thus we have, within feminist economics, an attempt to create better knowledge by adding women's experience in order to get a more complete picture. In this case, the supposed connection between women's experiences and their difference from the abstract essentialist individual version of identity (rational economic man) has been questioned. But, feminist economics has been unable to move beyond claiming difference under the sign of 'woman', to question the grounds of the processes by which difference has to be claimed – namely, the process of identification and assimilation.[34]

Therefore, the move from identity politics to the politics of identity is not one of merely identifying positions and their access to knowledge. Rather, it is about recognising that identity categorisations are constructed within texts and discourses and are linked to power and privilege. Instead of privileging some identities as allowing access to additive better knowledge, the task is to interrogate texts for the multiple ways in which they construct identity categories and to make visible the arbitrariness of these constructions. The politics of identity is then a method

identities, opinions, and politics can be expressed, is systematically wider for some. Thus, an Indian commentator on German philosophy or Renaissance art might be perceived as anomalous, whereas an English commentator on Indian feminism or Middle East/West Asia politics is *de rigeur*. This asymmetry in the range of how something can become someone's issue is an arena of constant contestation.

34 That is, despite the extreme usefulness of feminist critiques in economics in stressing the identity 'woman', it is also important to recognise the diversity and difference within that category, and attend to the problematics thus raised in the way that the wider feminist movement has sought to do (see Mohanty *et al.* 1991; Lennon and Whitford 1994; Alexander and Mohanty 1997; Gedalof 1999; Ahmed *et al.* 2000; Alsop *et al.* 2002).

for interrogating any coherence in the arising of identities, so that the responsibility for identity is not fixed in difference. This requires us to need a plurality of theories in order to examine the processes by which 'difference' itself comes into being.

Linked to the difference conundrum in knowledge (i.e., where difference is only seen as exclusion or addition) is the worry engendered by identity politics – an infinitely multiple world where it would be impossible to admit difference while claiming solidarity. Lawson (1999b: 49) warns of the dangers of 'a world of universalised difference'. He writes, 'in an awareness that the existence of multiculturalism or of differences in general, need not in any way undermine or contradict [such] emancipatory practice,' so long as we focus on the commonalities of human nature and needs. One could go much further in thinking identity politics as a route to the politics of identity, so that identity is not the result of pre-formed political actors carefully and consciously deciding what to contest for, from an *à la carte* menu of identities. Politics of identity is about politicising the identity question – about treating identity and politics as mutually constitutive – while identity politics is generally seen as politics based on given identities. The politicisation of identity is not an option but a way of living in the liberal polity that forces a terrain of contestation where one is seen as having chosen one's identity in order to then politicise it, while all the time that choosing and politicisation are not separately available to many actors. For example, 'Third World women' do not choose their identity as 'Third World women' before they digress from the universalist claims of feminism in order to argue for differences.

The operationalised logic of comprehension in capitalist imperial liberal democratic polity means that, in order to be different, often one just has to *be*. Hasty and misjudged calls to undermine the recognition of difference are common both to the liberal left and the conservative right. But this is not to say that solidarity is not an extremely important ingredient of emancipatory sentiment. It is, and is definitely worth imagining. However, one needs to move beyond the possibility of recognising political action as being confined to acting *only* on common needs – 'my issue' is the world. Imagining such political action is not just to 'build bridges' between different constituencies, but involves a *radical rethinking of the very principles on which different constituencies are organised and recognised.*

As a summing up, consider the following. Identity as a continuous politicised processual construction which grounds the sociality of life differently everywhere, is captured well in the statement of Subcomandante Marcos (partly[35] in San Juan Jr 1999: 19), head of the Zapatista rebellion in Chiapas, Mexico:

> Marcos is gay in San Francisco, Black in South Africa, an Asian in Europe, a Chicano in San Ysidro, an anarchist in Spain, a Palestinian in Israel, a Mayan

35 Several modified versions of this statement are available from different online sources; some have Marcos giving more examples and others have him giving different ones. The gist remains the same. For more, see Marcos (2001).

> Indian in the streets of San Cristobal, a gang member in Neza, a rocker in the National University, a Jew in Germany, an ombudsman in the Defence Ministry, a communist in the post-Cold War era, an artist without gallery or portfolio, a pacifist in Bosnia, a housewife alone on Saturday night in any neighbourhood in any city . . . a dissident among free-marketeer economists. . . . So Marcos is a human being, any human being, in this world. Marcos is all the exploited, marginalized and oppressed minorities, resisting and saying 'Enough!'

So far, the questions of identity have been linked to economics only through the abstract essentialist individual discussions. In the next chapter, I will consider in greater detail two relatively rare and illustrative cases where the questions of identity have been juxtaposed with economics.

5 Economics and identity

Do I contradict myself?
Very well then, I contradict myself,
(I am large, I contain multitudes.)
(Whitman 1990: 78)

5.1 Expanding 'Economics Inc.' (Economics Incorporated)?

Frankly, economists are not interested in identity. It seems, I am sure, to most of them, a completely alien concept – adapting the words of a famous song, 'what's identity got to do with it'.

Further, the discussion of new topics as an academic exercise in economics happens when it is seen as the extension (or application) of the economic method (rational choice theory, cost-benefit analysis, game theory, modelling human behaviour as an exercise of utility maximisation) to 'new' pastures.[1] The merits of interdisciplinarity are summed up in the interesting phrase usually adopted: 'economics imperialism' (see Stigler 1984; Hirshleifer 1985; Radnitzky and Bernholz 1987; Swedberg 1990; Ingham 1996). This refers to the 'colonisation' of other social sciences in the explanation of human behaviour following economics, for instance, '[t]here is only one social science. ... Thus economics does really constitute the universal grammar of social science' (Hirschleifer 1985: 53). And Dasgupta (1998: 24) proudly writes, 'Modern economists have demonstrated the power of their discipline by crossing into law, political science, anthropology, demography, ecosystem ecology.'

Discussing the question of economics as colonising the other social sciences, Fine (1999: 413) believes that this is based upon simply extending the notion of

1 As Thompson (1997) notes, there is a preference in economics for 'new' as a prefix as opposed to 'post' (schools of thought such as – neoclassical, new classical, neo-liberal, new home economics, new institutionalism, new growth theory, new political economy). Fine (1999: 421) remarks that this excludes post-Keynesian economics, which is perhaps a significant exclusion in the light of the greater radicality of the 'post' to the 'new'. The American poet Frank O'Hara once said, ' "New" is an old word, let's get a new one.'

rational agents to all domains.[2] And he argues that, increasingly, the barriers between other social sciences and economics are lessened as the method of economics – peculiar form of methodological individualism (behaviour reduced to utility maximisation), analytical focus around equilibrium, uncritical use of ahistorical and asocial concepts (capital as physical object, utility, commodities as goods, production as a technical relation between inputs and outputs, and so on) – is universalised. He gives the example especially of the notion of 'human capital' which has played an important part in Gary Becker's new home economics (incidentally, Becker is seen as a paradigmatic 'postmodern' economist by Jameson 1991), and is now spearheading 'the assault of the economic approach upon other social sciences' (Fine 1999: 414). This notion (and variants such as personal capital, social capital) has been picked up by the World Bank and used as the 'missing link' in explaining economic development and performance – past, present and future (ibid.: 416–417, emphasis added):

> In this way, issues such as the environment, community, gender, conflict, ethnicity, customs and culture are *incorporated into* economic analysis. The World Bank has even set up web site for social capital. … [S]ocial capital is colonizing the theory of development just as economics is colonising the notion of social capital. The promotion of social capital by the World Bank is part and parcel of its move towards what has been termed the post-Washington consensus, a more state-friendly stance than the previous neo-liberal Washington consensus.

Another example of this can be seen in the World Bank policy research report (2001) on 'Engendering Development', where the Bank wants to make a case for the importance of gender equality in development.[3] But, as Bergeron (2002) discusses, the approach adopted is narrowly economistic, and qualitative evidence is not seriously admitted into the discussion. In this way, economics is seen as the provider of tools and concepts (a disinterested method) which can then be unquestioningly applied to any situation. '[This] is not so much an exercise in critical interdisciplinarity (challenging the assumptions of neoclassical economics) as expanding the toolkit of an existing discipline' (ibid.; see also Bergeron 2000, 2005; Kaul 2002a; Herrera 2006). As a result, any analysis becomes about translating its scenario in economic terms. Inevitably, these terms are such that there are no proxy variables for history or culture, and so these 'non-salient' attributes are allowed to drop out of the analysis. As far as the overall outcome of such expansion of (what I would term) 'Economics Inc.' for the other social

2 Not only can this rational agent model be used for understanding aggregations of choices made by individuals, but it can also be turned inwards to rationally explain the various ostensibly conflicting selves *within* the rational agent in the process of decision-making. See Elster (1986).

3 This report generated a lot of discussion at the International Association for Feminist Economics (IAFFE) conference in 2002. There were many critical assessments of the report, and a book-length response can be found in Kuiper and Barker (2006).

sciences is concerned, Fine believes it 'to intensify the features of economics' influence – the reductionism, eclecticism, empiricism, unevenness, ignorance, parasitism, contempt *and* critical, at times futile, conceptual reaction' (1999: 415, emphasis original).[4]

And thus, as the uncritical use of ahistorical and asocial concepts from economics is universalised, there is a corresponding careful guarding of the basic premises of economic logic as being scientific, timeless, and universal. The strategy for this guarding is a combination of stifling interdisciplinary dialogue by the adoption of unjustified mathematical formalism and at the same time pointing out the obviousness of economic postulates based on human nature such as scarcity, self-interest, greed, importance of incentives. There are numerous implications of this. Economics functions as an ideology of market capitalism, and further asserts that the *identities of the actors who play certain roles at the micro and macro levels are of no concern*. Literally anyone (person or nation) could take on any role, so that the specificity of history or the politics of identity becomes a farce in a world where anyone could rationally grow, develop, trade, and prosper. The effectiveness of this strategy is clear in the way in which it often spellbinds its critics as well in their homage to the god they seek to dethrone. At the same time, the timelessness or universality or scientificity of the basic building blocks (such as human nature, scarcity, incentives) can easily be problematised. As argued in Chapter 3, 'human nature' is another name for the historically situated 'transcendental pretence' in modernist disciplinary knowledge. Scarcity is a scare-spectre of capitalism usefully employed to divert attention from the political nature of the choices made (on scarcity and greed, see Wennerlind 2000, also refer back to 2.4.1 in Chapter 2). Finally, the importance of incentives was not discovered by economics, but operationalised in such a way as to make its ethics unquestionable.[5]

Referring to economics as it is studied, in his review of conservatism's best young economists ('Delta Force'), Warren (1994, emphases added) writes

> *The creeping rot of multiculturalism, feminism, de-constructionism, and other fashionably radical intellectual trends has spread to nearly every branch of study* in American universities. *But economics appears to have developed an immunity to such diseases*. It is one of the few disciplines in which radical Left ideology has failed to take root. Market capitalism – anathema to the bulk of the professoriate – flourishes in economics departments, where Keynesians have been unable to prevent the growth of various offshoots of classical free-market thought. *This lack of political correctness* is one of the reasons why U.S. economics programmes are considered to be among the best in the world, while humanities and most other social sciences attract *fewer foreign students*.

4 Even fairly well-converted supporters of rational choice axioms such as the political scientist Keohane (1988) lament about economists not really conversing with them, but preaching and dominating the conversation.

5 Given all this, it is telling that it is the students of the discipline who are at the forefront of pedagogical revolt today (the post autistic economics movement @ http://www.paecon.net).

This illuminates the rationale for my arguments beautifully, linking up economics with the 'creeping rot of diseases' of multiculturalism, feminism, de-constructionism, market capitalism, pedagogy, political correctness, foreign students. In Warren's view, economics is the 'science' of market capitalism resisted by 'ideology'. The diseases that have contaminated all other knowledge, economics has been immune to. The inoculation against 'multiculturalism, feminism, de-constructionism' – reflect, for a moment, that all Warren's diseases are intimately related to questions of the politics of identity and the fixing of difference in knowledge – has been achieved by *lacking* 'political correctness' (which I define as: not so much the "restriction of the sayable" but rather *the politicisation of saying which questions the grounded privilege of utterability*).[6] As a consequence, more 'foreign students' are attracted to the study of the science of market capitalism in American universities in an era where its dominance goes serially unquestioned.

It is a legitimate question to ask of every theoretical premise, 'what does it take for granted?' The important questions in the interrogation of knowledge are not just the details of its edifice, but an examining of its unstated basis. And thus, thinking the structurality of the structure is also to ask the question, 'how is the legitimate ground of theoretical contestation constituted?' The questions of 'why is there no talk of identity in economics?' and, 'why would economics talk about identity?' are interlinked in the politics of knowledge creation about the economic.

It becomes interesting, therefore, to now confront two pioneering instances where economists[7] George Akerlof and Rachel Kranton (2000), and Amartya Sen

6 Political correctness, defined by Martin Amis (2002) as 'the restriction of the sayable', is an interesting issue in relation to identity. Amis celebrates the retreat of 'the PC'. Unable to bring himself to say 'politically correct', he nonetheless denounces it as being the 'lowest common denomination'. He is thankful that, 'PC, having made its gains in *the restriction of the sayable*, is now in modest retreat. And it is true that the expansionist phase, with its denunciations, its invigilations, its organised execrations, seems to have run its course.' My point is this. The signifier 'political' is a powerful construction which opens up everything to question. The political is automatically the contested, opening up the carefully sutured-together closures of taxonomised difference. No wonder then that the politicisation of language hits where it hurts – and the 'PC' is resented with a liberal/conservative vengeance that wants to claim as uncontested and prior some terms of identity from which everything else can then be problematised. The PC is not so much the 'restriction of the sayable' but rather the *politicisation of saying* which questions the grounded privilege of utterability.

And so, consider the following illustrative application. At an economics seminar that I attended, an economist presenting intergenerational transfers model in terms of fathers and sons (in economics, the transfers between generations is conventionally studied in a fathers-and-sons-type setting), when questioned about the possibility of mothers and daughters, had this to say, 'now this is as PC as we are going to get'. Now, it is clear from the work of feminist economists that, in fact, intergenerational transfers and the relative altruism of fathers and mothers differs, so that within the institutional setting of a typical family, women are much more likely to have less discretionary income and leisure, lower bargaining power, and a disproportionate share of costs of raising the next-generation (on this, see Folbre 1994, n.d.).

7 Sen was awarded the Nobel Prize in 1998 and Akerlof in 2001. Though they are not 'typical' economists in the sense that Akerlof has worked at the intersection of economics and psychology,

(1999) have spoken of identity and economics.[8] But before this, let me give an example of what I *don't* mean by my discussion until now. McCloskey is a well-known 'postmodern neoclassical freemarket feminist economist' (see McCloskey 2000). Christensen (2001) assesses McCloskey's memoir *Crossing*, which describes the experience of her transition from a man (Donald) to a woman (Deirdre). In her reading, Christiansen finds 'a bewildering lack of self-consciousness regarding the implications of McCloskey's transition experience for the neoclassically based, individualistic economic theories s/he has espoused all his/her professional life' (2001: 113). In other words, McCloskey still supports the mission of the Chicago school of economics with its rational choice analysis, while recognising that there is more to human existence and experience than 'rationality'. Thus, one should not underestimate the complexity of identity in

and Sen has worked at the intersection of economics and philosophy, yet their prominent status within economics is undeniable. Akerlof in 2006 and Sen in 1994 held the office of president in the American Economic Association (AEA). Despite being important in the profession, Sen has had his detractors. Pressman and Summerfield (2000: 89) mention that, when the Nobel Prize was announced for Sen in 1998, the next day's op-ed article in the *Wall Street Journal* complained that the award was given to 'an establishment leftist' with 'muddleheaded views' (Robert Pollock 'The wrong economics won'). They also mention further griping by Peter Coy in *Business Week* and Sheldon Richman in *Human Events*. It was nastily suggested that Sen did not deserve the award, but was given it as 'Noble penance' by the awarding committee since the previous year's winners Myron Scholes and Robert Merton 'were the brains behind Long-term Capital Management, a hedge fund that nearly brought down the US financial system in the Fall of 1998'.

8 Since I first provided an analysis of identity in economics in 2002 (see Kaul 2002d), evaluating Akerlof/Kranton and Sen, some other discussions have appeared (for instance, Davis 2003; Kirman and Teschl 2004). The subtitle of Davis's (2003) book mentions 'identity'. Davis undertakes to provide a theory of the individual in economics, explores the limits of methodological individualism, arguing for holistic alternatives. While providing a sophisticated account of individuality and a valid critique of computational functionalism, an interrogation of identity is not central to Davis's project in the way that it is presented here, so that his focus on individuality and its reformulation does not consider of identity and difference in relation to the power and politics of knowledge production. Kirman and Teschl (2004) distinguish themselves from Davis by saying that he 'is interested in showing how a socially embedded individual can constitute his or her own subjective, personal identity within a social space', while they 'propose to start the analysis with an individual who has a personal identity within a social space and to account for its consequences on economic behaviour and her welfare' (64). Kirman and Teschl focus on personal identity (they call it the 'who' of the economic agent, in addition to the 'what' and 'where') aiming to '*integrate the idea of a person's identity into economics*' (62, emphasis added). While I share their concern that identity matters in economics, I do not share their starting points (e.g., Stigler-Becker or Bowles-Gintis on the potential for game theory, or Bénabou and Tirole's model of the three intertemporal selves Self 0, 1 and 2), and, as my discussion in this chapter will make clear, I do not agree with Sen's approach in the way that Kirman and Teschl do. To an extent, both Davis and Kirman/Teschl see Sen's approach to identity as the way forward. Neither of them provides a detailed critique of Akerlof/Kranton. Nor do the widely recognised feminist/poststructuralist interventions in the theorising of identity play any role in their theories. This is because (a) they see economic theory as a narrow and pre-defined realm without considering how the 'economic' context comes to be constructed; (b) they do not recognise the role of power in structuring knowledge formations, neither would they recognise the 'ideological' as part of economic 'science' – according to Kirman and Teschl, 'the power of economic reasoning can be attributed to the simplicity and

relation to the economic.[9] It illustrates that the simple proliferation and accessibility of more and more identities (at least to a few people) will not necessarily mean that those identities will be adopted in a questioning manner – the chasm marked by McCloskey's remark (quoted in ibid., emphasis added), '*It's identity, stupid. Not cost and benefit.*'

5.2 Illustration one: Akerlof and Kranton on 'Economics and Identity'

5.2.1 Summary explanation

In August 2000, the *Quarterly Journal Of Economics* published an article titled 'Economics and Identity'. The paper claims to 'introduce' identity, which is defined as 'a person's sense of self', into economic analysis. The stated aim is to 'incorporate the psychology and sociology of identity into an economic model of behaviour'. Accordingly, the authors propose an amended utility function which would take into account the effect of identity on behaviour by associating identity with different social categories and how people in these categories should behave. They also construct a simple game-theoretic model showing how identity can affect individual interactions. Let me trace the main points of their argument.

(1) People have identity-related 'payoffs' from their own actions and from others' actions. Further, third parties can generate persistent changes in these payoffs, and the choice of identity is open for some but may be prescribed for others. In all these ways, since social categories are salient for human behaviour and interaction, identity can influence behaviour.
(2) Identity is based on social categories, **C**. Each person *j* has an assignment of people to these categories represented by $\mathbf{c}_j$. Each person has a conception of their own categories and that of all other people. An individual may be mapped on to

elegance of its explicative model of human behaviour' (69), whereas I have argued throughout this text that economic reasoning is not simple but simplistic, elegant in a certain self-referential sense only for the initiated, and can be seen as explicative only if one adopts a particular historical notion of explanation that elides questions of actual power or history in knowledge production; (c) their approach to 'identity' does not problematise its coming into being or question how the focus on the individual reduces the political to the juridical; (d) their approaches aim to 'expand' or 'improve' the domain of economics by 'bringing identity in', thus utilising the concept of identity additively (in contrast to the radically antidisciplinary and critical view taken in my analysis). In sum, a reading of my evaluation of Akerlof/Kranton and Sen also illustrates the limitations of Davis and Kirman/Teschl on the issue of identity in relation to the economic context.

9 Consider, for instance, two remarks by Gary Fethke, the Dean of a College of Business at the University of Iowa, to McCloskey when s/he informed him of her plans to become a woman – 'Thank God…I thought for a moment you were going to confess to converting to *socialism*!' and, jokingly mentioned that now that she's a woman, he can lower her salary! (both quoted in ibid.: 105, 112, emphasis original).

several social categories, and also, individual *j*'s mapping of another individual *k* into categories need not correspond to *k*'s own mapping. The appropriate behaviour for people in different social categories in different situations is indicated by prescriptions **P**. Prescriptions can also describe the ideal for each category in terms of physical characteristics and other attributes. Further, categories may have higher or lower social status. Identity refers both to a person's self-image and to her assigned categories.

The utility function which incorporates identity as a motivation for behaviour looks as follows:

$$\boldsymbol{U}_j = \boldsymbol{U}_j\,(\mathbf{a}_j, \mathbf{a}_{-j}, \boldsymbol{I}_j).$$

Thus, for each person *j*, utility will depend not only on the usual vectors $\mathbf{a}_j$ (for *j*'s actions) and $\mathbf{a}_{-j}$ (for others' actions), but also depend upon *j*'s identity or self-image $\boldsymbol{I}_j$. Further, a person *j*'s identity $\boldsymbol{I}_j$ itself will depend upon *j*'s assigned social categories $\mathbf{c}_j$. It will also depend upon the extent to which *j*'s own given characteristics $\in_j$ match the ideal of *j*'s assigned category, indicated by the prescriptions **P**. Last but not the least, identity will depend upon the extent to which *j*'s own or others' actions correspond to prescribed behaviour indicated by **P**. The function $\boldsymbol{I}_j\,(\cdot)$ below gives the social status of a category, and a person in a category with high social status 'may enjoy an enhanced self-image' (719).

$$\boldsymbol{I}_j = \boldsymbol{I}_j\,(\mathbf{a}_j, \mathbf{a}_{-j}; \mathbf{c}_j, \in_j, \mathbf{P}).$$

The increases or decreases in utility that derive from $\boldsymbol{I}_j$ are called '*gains or losses in identity*' (719, emphasis original).

The idea at its basic is that the individual *j* will *choose actions to maximise utility* taking all else given. In the usual tradition of argumentation in economics, the authors are of the opinion that although this 'choice' may be unconscious, the outcome remains the same. This is because, even if people are not always conscious of the motivations for their behaviour, they behave *as if* they were maximising the utility function.

(3) The reason why economists should take the utility function amended for identity seriously is because we know from psychology that a person's sense of self or the ego lies behind individual behaviour. Further, taking this into account will 'expand' economic analysis by – being able to 'explain' behaviour which might appear detrimental (the examples are: why do people self mutilate, why do people feel ambiguous about their work when being in an occupation which does not match the gender prescriptions of behaviour, why do alumni contributions reflect identity, why do people mountaineer); being able to recognise that identity underlines a new type of 'externality'[10] (the examples are: men acting to

10 An externality is said to exist when the costs or benefits of production or consumption are not completely borne by the producer or the consumer, but, for instance, by society.

affirm their masculinity against female co-workers in a 'man's job', men acting in response to an insult which if left unanswered impugns their masculinity,[11] changing group or violating prescriptions as provoking scorn and ostracism); recognising that identity reveals a new way that preferences can be changed, that is, the creation and manipulation of social categories **C** and prescriptions **P** (the examples are: advertising, professional and graduate schools, political identity[12]); the recognition that 'the choice of identity maybe the most important "economic" decision people make' (717) (the examples are: many women in the United States choosing either to be a career woman or a housewife, parents choosing schools to influence children's self-image identification and behaviour, students at college choosing where to live,[13] an immigrant choosing to become a citizen).[14]

(4) The authors then construct a 'prototype model of economic interaction in a world where identity is based on social difference' (727). Not only the tastes, but utility from actions will also depend on identity. Identity depends on two social categories – Green and Red, and how much one's own and other people's actions correspond to the behaviour prescriptions for their category. There are 'standard economic motivations for behaviour' (ibid.). Each individual in the population has a 'taste' for either of the two possible activities – Activity One and Activity Two. Engaging in the activity for which one has a taste, one earns utility V, choosing the activity not matching one's taste yields zero utility. Standard utility maximisation would imply that each person would engage in the activity corresponding to their taste.

The authors construct identity-based preferences assuming in the simplest case that all people think of themselves and others as Green. The behavioural prescription is that Greens engage in Activity One. Anyone violating this loses identity, causing a reduction in the utility of I_s (s for self). Externalities of identity mean that in a pairing of two individuals i and j, if i engages in Activity Two, it also diminishes the Green identity for j, causing j a loss in utility I_o (o for other). Now, j may choose to 'respond' and restore its identity at a cost c, causing a loss to i in amount L. This forms the basis for an interaction which is represented as a 'game tree' between Person One and Person Two.

Person One chooses Activity One > Person Two has the choice of Activity One (for V or 0) or Activity Two > (if Activity Two chosen by Person Two)

11 Akerlof and Kranton consistently cite evidence from experiments in psychology, in this case, Nisbett and Cohn (1996).

12 'Politics is often a battle over identity. Rather than take preferences as given, political leaders and activists often strive to change a population's preferences through a change in identity or prescriptions. … [s]ymbolic acts and transformed identities spur revolutions' (727).

13 'Fraternities, sororities, African-American, or other 'theme'-oriented dorms are all associated with social groups, self-images, and prescribed behaviour' (726).

14 The authors also point that this 'choice' of identity is limited in a society with racial and ethnic categories, so that while those with 'non distinguishing physical features might be able to "pass" as a member of another group … others will be constrained by their appearance, voice, or accent' (726).

Person One has the choice of Not Responding ($V - I_s$ or $V - I_o$) or Responding ($V - c$ or $V - I_s - L$).

The four possible subgame perfect equilibrium outcomes of the game are detailed – Person One deters Person Two from engaging in Activity Two when $c < I_o$ and $I_s < V < I_s + L$; Person One responds but does not deter Person Two from engaging in Activity Two when $c < I_o$ and $I_s + L < V$; Person One does not respond and Person Two engages in Activity Two when $c > I_o$ and $I_s < V$; Person Two does not engage in Activity Two regardless of Person One's response when $I_s > V$.

The three lessons to be extrapolated from this model for the authors are as follows. One, it 'establishes the connection between economic interactions and the psychology of identity, especially the implications of *identification*' (730, emphasis original). Two, it 'allows a comparative static analysis on identity related parameters' (ibid.). Three, the elementary assumptions suggest 'extensions that entail greater realism and further implications of identity for economic interaction' (ibid.).

Regarding lesson One above, the authors' point is that people internalise rules of behaviour, and experience *anxiety* when these internalised rules are violated. The authors depend on psychological literature to argue that a person's '*identity*, or *ego*, or *self*, must be constantly "defended against anxiety in order to limit disruption and maintain a sense of unity"' (728).

Regarding lesson Two above, comparative statics can be used to see how conventional economic policies may affect behaviour. They give examples of a case where one could consider how the imposition of a 'tax' T on the response to Activity Two, at certain levels, will cause behaviour to switch, and benefit Person Two. One could also consider the case of the tax being imposed on Activity Two. They also raise the possibility of policies changing prescriptions themselves, for instance, a rhetorical campaign which might make Activity Two more loathsome to Greens and cause greater conformity to the prescriptions.

Until now, I have considered the basics of how an attempt has been made to model identity in economics, which aims in part to introduce the psychological motivations for people's behaviour more explicitly into economic analysis.

Next, I will interject and critically discuss the implications of the aforesaid and evaluate the extensions to the model suggested by the authors in their paper.

5.2.2 Assessing implications

The attempt by Akerlof and Kranton to model identity in relation to economics starkly illustrates my arguments in the previous chapters.

In their attempt, identity is seen as 'a person's sense of self' and used interchangeably with ego. It represents the psychological motivations for behaviour and links directly to the social categories which people slot into. The social categories are 'different' in the sense of having different prescriptions attached to them. How well any Person (One or Two) does in terms of utility maximisation is partly dependent upon their identity, that is, the social status of their category. This social status is itself in part a function of the extent to which a person's own characteristics match the prescriptive ideal of their assigned category.

Finally, even if the abstract individual Person cannot tell the motives for their actions, the transcendental social scientist can recognise them as being oriented towards utility maximisation.

Underlying the whole endeavour is the picture of the abstract essentialist individual version of identity. Amended and embellished, this abstract essentialist individual is recognised as having psychological motivations, and inhabiting social categories. While the conventional model would have the individual as a black box not amenable to further investigation, this amendment would have the individual as tied to 'different' categories.

A couple of things should be noted. First, all the various individuals are essentially the same as far as the raw matter of subjectivity is concerned. The difference arises from the same and similar people being in different categories. However, and this is *important*, the categories by themselves are *not* systematically hierarchical. The categories are just that – categories of 'difference', partly chosen and partly not chosen markers that people find themselves in. Rationally, people would try to maximise their gains in the sum total of identity. Identity itself can metaphorically be conceptualised as *a jar*, whose contents are evaluated according to their worth, to arrive at a sum total the maximisation of which is in everyone's interest. Second, this account allows for no conceptualisation of power or oppression. When people are acting to oppress others (for instance, men discriminating against women), they are merely acting with rational empirical motivations. I shall soon come to an example of this.

The argument of the paper proceeds by alternating between the experimental world of 'subjects' in psychology, the economic world of *a priori* 'agents', and the evidential (or as the authors designate it within inverted commas, 'real-world') world of 'people'. It is not clear at all whether these different worlds in fact lend themselves to formal modelling tractability in the way that the authors proceed. I would argue that they do not, and that the paper is an attempt to whisper into the ears of mainstream economists, 'but look, our uniform economic agent can be expanded by introducing the variable of identity'.

In the sections of the paper where examples of identity related behaviour are provided, my question is this – are the authors really arguing that some but not all behaviour can be explained by introducing the variable of identity? They are, and, I would argue to the contrary. Let me explain. It is not only those who tattoo, body pierce, hair-conk (examples in the paper, 721), and so on, who behave in ways that are linked to their identity. Even those who wear dark pinstripe suits demonstrate identity related behaviour. In this regard, the authors also give the example of women who undergo female circumcision in rural Egypt or women who practise Sati in Rajasthan (721). Rather than the common imperial ideology which takes these people as being irrational, the authors try to rationalise their behaviour as stemming from the internalisation of prescriptive ideals for the different social category of women. Perhaps unaware of Spivak's (1988) article 'Can the subaltern speak? Speculations on widow sacrifice', the authors have provided us with yet another example of the way subalterns are regularly picked up as extra empirical variables who are 'spoken for' in the dominant discourse.

It is interesting to consider the way in which the authors have chosen examples of those who would overtly illustrate 'difference' to the 'norm' as people exhibiting identity-related behaviour. Identity is something possessed by the outer latitudes and longitudes of secular imperial capitalist liberal democratic polity. Or, those who affirm their identity as 'different' are not the only people who possess 'identity'. Given that this is a case in their argument, they operate firmly on the model which takes identity as the basis for difference.

Further, the authors visualise a sort of scale of prescriptive ideals attached to each social category on which different individuals score differently depending on the extent to which they conform to these ideals. One could therefore conform to sixty or forty or eighty or even a hundred per cent to the prescriptive ideals for one's social category. The more one conforms, the better it is for one's identity (sense of self). And the less one conforms, the more anxiety and loss of identity one faces.

This picture unravels if we consider how these scales of prescriptive ideals come to be attached to each social category. The authors do not really concern themselves with how the categories come to be. According to them, individuals just slot into these categories and perform better or worse in terms of conformity and internalisation of the ideals. However, *what if* the persons who fully conform and absolutely match the prescriptive ideals of their social category are *not* performing well on an externally given and internalised indicator, but actually are confirming and perpetuating the systematically hierarchical basis of society, further reinforcing their dominant position by the exercise of power? What if the process of categorisation is not a neutral cognitive mapping exercise carried out in an individualised manner with repercussions for individual people's behaviour in line with a calculation of costs and benefits, but a systematically operating oppressive hierarchy of power and dominance? The authors might say that this is not what they are engaging with; however, I am arguing that neglecting this is a severe problem. They are treating identity as a variable which can simply be added into the picture, a factor out there which exists fully formed and can simply be incorporated into the equation of utility maximisation. Identity is an outcome rather than a precedence of human interaction. In constructing their model, they completely neglect the way in which *identity is constructed out of opportunities available to people, and through discourses*. The construction of people into these categories of identity by those around them is not simply available from a transcendental perspective. Further, in their account, the politics of identification is completely absent – rather than seeing identity as a process, they treat is as a 'thing'.

Thus, the authors employ identity allegiances in ways that naturalise the discrimination or oppression that occurs due to systematic power differentials. Also, in many of their examples, the authors take as universal, particular contingent versions of (heterosexual) masculinity and femininity dominant in American society. As far as identity groupings are concerned, for the authors, the margins are simply just another grouping. There is no possibility for an ethical revolt based politics.

There is no recognition of any contingency or differentiation in the idea of the 'self'. The self is a constant, timeless, spaceless, universal continuity taking concrete forms in embodied abstract individual essentialist economic agents.

The whole scenario of modelling methodology displays the desire to get the general principles which could then be 'applied' in any specific setting. Not once is there any question of the suitability of this methodology which reduces the complexities of human behaviour to deterministic if-this-then-that kind of reactions. The social scientists, presumably, are just 'equipped' by the very nature of who they are, to make deterministic universal pronouncements on how any person's sense of self affects their behaviour in conjunction with their social category (assigned by whom? how is it perceived?). Akerlof and Kranton simply assume that everyone acts in accordance with their 'sense of self'. That this 'sense of self' is a historical and ideological construct deriving from the transcendental pretence of universalist humanism (especially of the Euro-American variety in its intellectual legacy if not geographical spread), in line with the philosophical underpinnings of enlightenment epistemology and modernist knowledge, is not recognised.

5.2.3 Evaluating extensions

In this section, I will critically evaluate the extensions to the model suggested by the authors as applications in specific 'situations'.[15] These broadly fall under three categories – identity, gender, and economics in the workplace; identity and the economics of exclusion and poverty; identity and the economics of the household. I will deal with each of these in turn.

The authors attempt to 'explain' social outcomes; explanation, as I discussed earlier, is usually in economics a process of justifying the occurrence in rational choice terms. 'Rational' and 'free' choices made by self-aware responsible essentialist individual economic agents are formalised to explain the *status quo*.

(1) The first situation relates to identity, gender, and economics in the workplace. The authors propose to expand the economic analysis of occupational segregation by the inclusion of changes in the societal notions of male and female. To begin with, all occupations are 'associated with the social categories "man" and "woman", and individual payoffs from different types of work reflect these gender associations' (732). The authors do not pay any attention to how these associations came about[16] in the first instance. By constantly using the terms man and woman to refer to gender associations, they also do not take into account the literature on the sex/gender distinction where the biological categories of man and woman do

15 According to the authors, they follow sociologists in using this concept of a situation – 'who is matched with whom and in what context' (731).

16 These associations may not simply be labels patterned after characteristics or levels of skill. See Philips and Taylor (1980) for an early argument that definitions of skill are not gender neutral.

not neatly map on to the performativity of gender, masculinity and femininity (see Butler 1990, 1993). The authors assume that jobs have gender associations. However, their ignorance of the sex/gender distinction is apparent in their not considering that the gender association of a job as masculine would disbar not only women but also 'feminine' men. Identity and embodiment resist straightforward assimilation into neat models. Treating identity as a static factor in relation to which choices (whether conscious or unconscious) are made to maximise utility by increasing the identity factor (or as they call it 'the gains in identity') is problematic because it cannot account for the way in which identity is performatively constituted, to a significant extent, by the very choices that are supposed to follow from it.

Consider the way in which the authors claim to provide 'microfoundations' for earlier models. This is because they argue for understanding the 'distaste' of men for working with women in terms of the loss that they would incur in male identity when women work in a man's job. They also argue for understanding women's assumed lower desire for labour force participation (in numerous previous economic models) in terms of the result of their identity as homemakers. The 'new' frontiers of economic analysis are 'expanded' – by formally modelling abstractions to provide justifying confirmations for previous unjustified assumptions. We are not allowed to think critically about the location of the starting point of an analysis. My adaptation of Murdoch's question,[17] 'what does it take for granted?' is a way of thinking the structurality of the structure, to ask 'how is the legitimate ground of theoretical contestation constituted?' As discussed below, instead of questioning the gender associations which are perpetuated by the exercise of hierarchical power and privilege, the theoretical invocation of these folk culture associations is neutralised as possibly being the result of women's inherent identity.

The authors seem to be somewhat aware of this, but do not see this as significant. In a footnote, they contrast their analysis with that of (a liberal feminist economist) Bergmann (1974), where 'she has argued that male employers are averse to hiring women for particular jobs, and may collude to keep women out of high-paying occupations, reserving the gains for other males' (732). 'In our theory', they argue, '*the source* of occupational segregation is *empirically motivated* – the maintenance of gender identity on the part of employees' (ibid.: emphases added).

The model, in this 'situation', has two social categories (men and women) with attached prescriptions of appropriate activities for each. A firm wishes to employ labour to perform a task which by initial prescriptions is appropriate only for men. Any woman doing this job would lose identity in amount I_s and male co-workers would lose I_o. The male co-workers may 'relieve their anxiety by taking action

17 Iris Murdoch once said that it is a legitimate question to ask of every philosopher, 'what are they afraid of?' Analogously, I would argue that it is a legitimate question to ask of every theoretical premise, 'what does it take for granted?'

against women co-workers, reducing everyone's productivity' (733). To avoid productivity losses, the firm could change gender job associations, but there is a cost involved. The authors argue that gender job associations will persist because the firm is likely to create a ' "woman's job" alongside the "man's job", rather than making the whole job gender neutral, when a new job description can piggyback on existing notions of male and female' (733). Further, they argue that there is not enough incentive for perfectly competitive firms to invest in new job categories since the job associations may be sectorwide and economywide and not firm specific. A firm would not want to rationally invest in something for which the benefits could also accrue to other firms. There is an interesting slippage here between the various worlds (experimental, economic, real) that the authors bind together. Perfectly competitive firms do not exist in reality, as the authors know. Yet, they link up the rationale of underinvestment by perfectly competitive firms with policy and attitude changes of the real-world in the examples that they give next. To illustrate their point that a shift in social attitudes and legal intervention would be necessary for changes in employment patterns, they give the example of sex discrimination law in the United States and the women's movement.[18]

Interestingly, past tense is used for describing the goals of the women's movement ('the movement goals includ*ed*', 735, emphasis added), and subsequent changes are described as if the agenda has been dealt with. It should be quite clear that the model (like most labour market models in economics) takes as its starting point the firm wishing to employ labour for a gender associated job. What if one started from the premise of a person wishing to get gainful employment in order to survive? And then, instead of assuming that the person is a rational actor out to maximise utility, and instead of wanting to get generalisable and purportedly universal (but actually provincial, located, and specific) equilibrium outcomes, one looked at contextual and concrete cases of how social provisioning can best be brought about in specific scenarios (a central argument of feminist economists; for example, Nelson 1993; see also Langley and Mellor 2002), what would we lose? We would lose, no doubt, the validity of the model, the status of the signifier science, the beauty of equilibrium possibilities, but we would gain an important achievement in recognising the ideological nature of formal methods, a meaningful body of research located in the complexity of life, and an intellectual starting premise which derives from its context rather than one which falsely universalises its specific starting premises (the idea of labour markets, formal sector jobs, notions of gender). My argument is thus, that the way in which Akerlof and Kranton have constructed the question of identity makes possible certain kinds of thinking, but rules out others while seemingly being unaware of these foreclosures.

18 While invoking the collective identity of the phrase (and a subtitle in the paper) – 'the women's movement' – it is assumed that the reader should follow that the reference is to the women's movement in the United States. A footnote informs us that '*The Feminine Mystique* was published in 1963, and the National Organisation for Women was founded in 1966' (735). Contestations within modernist knowledge, as I argued in Chapter 3, remain within their own narrow provincial ambit.

Finally, and very importantly, one would realise that history in identity matters in ways that cannot be formalised. When the authors come around to a few lines from the perspective of women's decision to participate in the labour force, they write (733, emphasis added): 'If *women's identity is enhanced by work inside the home*, they will have lower labor force attachment than men. Historically, female labor force participation rates, relative to male rates, have been both lower and more cyclically variable.' While this seems to be a factual statement in view of certain event regularities, it disguises the way in which the construction of the 'labour force' has historically excluded women and their work.

Scientific writing is not simply the writing of science, but rather a kind of writing which performs an invisiblising of its own premises. When the authors present the decision from the point of view of a woman, they never ask what reason they have to make the conditional clause, '[i]f women's identity is enhanced by work inside the home'. Further, it is presumably seen not part of the remit of the paper to question why female labour force participation has been historically lower. It is simply a decision that women have made in a certain way in the past and are now not making it in the same way. If you want to find out more, go and do history. The pigeonholed separability of modernist knowledge (the many windows in its architecture) serves the purpose of delimiting territory in a particular and always political way, yet presenting the demarcation effected in its writing as neutral taxonomy.

(2) The second situation relates to identity and the economics of exclusion and poverty. The authors take as their starting point 'identity and behaviour in poor and socially excluded communities' (737). This model is a variant of the earlier Green and Red model (see Summary in 5.2.1 earlier). They state (737, emphases added),

> Greens identify with the dominant culture, while those with Red identity reject it and the subordinate position assigned to those of their 'race', class, or ethnicity. From the point of view of those with Green identities, Reds are often *making bad economic decisions*; they might even be *described as engaging in self-destructive behaviour*. Taking drugs, joining a gang, and becoming pregnant at a young age are possible signs of Red identity.

At this point, if you think they might have termed the Red identity 'Black' – you might be right. Within a line, follow the phrases 'black ghetto poverty' and then 'significant dummy variables for "race"'. The authors are arguing that their model reflects the 'many ethnographic accounts of "oppositional" identities in poor neighbourhoods' (738).

Before going on to outline their model in this situational application, they point out the motivation for their model. This comprises of basically the citations of other work outside 'economics' on identity. Interestingly, they mention Homi Bhabha, Frantz Fanon, Mahatma Gandhi, W. E. B. DuBois, and many other people who have written in the context of African-Americans in the United States. They also mention Edward Said. However, I would argue that nothing is subsequently done in the spirit of these names. It seems that situating their motivation is rather to emphasise that many oppositional identities exist and are prevalent. And that while the lack of economic opportunity 'may also contribute to the choice of an oppositional identity', 'Red activities have negative pecuniary externalities' (739).

Their actual prototype model has two activities – One and Two, which can be 'thought of as' (740) working and not working. I will not again discuss all the conditions for the various equilibrium scenarios.[19] Rather, I am keen to point out the starting assumptions of the model. Of the two social categories Green and Red, the dominant Greens have the behavioural prescription of engaging in Activity One; that is, working – while behavioural prescriptions for category Red say that they should engage in Activity Two; that is, not working. The questions I raised regarding the origin of behavioural prescriptions in the previous section, remain pertinent.

Thus, we have (741),

> Each person *i* chooses an identity and activity, given the choices of everyone else in the community. We assume that people cannot modify their identity or activity for each individual encounter. Rather, individuals choose an identity and activity to maximise expected payoffs, given the probabilities of encounters with Greens who choose Activity One, Greens who choose Two, Reds who choose One, and Reds who choose Two.

If the model appears simplistic, consider the following possible problematisation of the 'Further Lessons from the Model' (743–747).

According to the authors, the three further lessons that one can learn from this model are based on the rationale (to oversimplify) – take people out of their neighbourhoods in order to eliminate the negative influences of interaction with those with Red identities. Therefore, residential job training programmes in the United States succeed, because poor trainees can then be taken out of their negative neighbourhoods. Also, therefore, minority kids who learn Standard English at schools which take the initiative to separate 'Green students from Red students' (744) reduce the loss in identity of Red students. And finally, 'the rhetoric and symbolism of affirmative action may affect the level of social exclusion *r*' (ibid.).

19 These are as follows (740–743). A large community, normalised to size one, of individuals. The economic return to Activity One for individual i is v_i and is uniformly distributed between zero and one. Economic return to Activity Two is normalised to zero. A Green suffers a loss in identity r which shows the extent to which someone from this community is not accepted by the dominant group in society. Red identity, which is less adaptive, does not suffer this loss. A Green (Red) loses identity from Activity Two (One) in amount I_s^G (I_s^R). "*Because Reds reject the dominant Green culture*, they are also likely to have lower economic returns to Activity One than Greens" (740, emphasis added). A Red individual i only earns $v_i - a$ from Activity One as well as suffers the loss I_s^R. There are also identity externalities when Greens and Reds meet. A Green (Red) suffers a loss I_o^G (I_o^R). All this being the case, there can be an all Green equilibrium, a mixed equilibrium, an all Red equilibrium, under various equivalencies of the parameters.

The factor of most salience in the identity of those who are socially excluded is their exclusion. Their exclusion in all cases is *from* the dominant group. The authors point out that what seems to the dominant group self-destructive behaviour does not come from individual irrationality on the part of the Reds, but derives from low economic endowments and a high degree of social exclusion. This cannot be disputed. But what the authors then extrapolate from this is open to question. Because they see identity as a commodity to be maximised, they advocate accordingly. They conclude thus (745, emphases added):

> The identity model of exclusion, then, explains why legal equality may not be enough to eliminate racial disparities. If African-Americans *choose to be Red* because of exclusion and if whites perpetuate such exclusions, even in legal ways, there can be a permanent equilibrium of racial inequality. The negative externalities and the consequences, however, *would disappear when the community is fully integrated into the dominant culture*, so that $r = a = 0$, and *everyone* in the community adopts *a Green identity*. This, of course, is the *American ideal of the melting pot*, or the new ideal of a mosaic *where difference can be maintained within the dominant culture*.

The point is this. The model is supposed to be about abstract identities Green and Red. To recall, Greens work and Reds do not. The Red identity is constructed in opposition to the Green, the *Greens come fully sprung*. We are back to the imperial model of difference – tattooing is and pinstripe suit is not an identity in the same way. Also, the reason why Reds have lower economic return from Activity One or working is attributed to *their own rejection* of the dominant Green identity. Rather like the earlier slippage, and not completely benign (liberalism is never benign, but insidious in its apparent benignity, in my view), now suddenly in the conclusion we hear about African-Americans who inhabit the 'real-world' rather than the Reds of the economic world.[20] The authors' claim that they are providing regularities is not sustainable, because their construction is not neutral, but feeds a political outcome – that of assimilation.

As a result, we start from the here and now of abstract essentialist individual view of identity, which has *no place for history or difference*. I would like to re-emphasise the points I made in my discussion of the politics of identity. Identity is not a jar to be fully filled, it is not even a score, or a function. Identity is a political living. The authors' suggestion that, in order to eliminate racial inequality, the community facing it has to be integrated into the dominant culture treats difference using a *diagnostic approach*, and the remedy prescribed involves

20 It is epistemically violent to study social exclusion (in this case that of African-Americans) in terms of abstract *r*'s and *a*'s and *i*'s. I would argue that it is completely inappropriate to carry out such analyses, even if to justify or prove that black people are not irrational in 'taking drugs, joining a gang, and becoming pregnant at a young age'. This abstraction is based on homogenising identity categories as stable and composed of essentially similar stereotypical elements.

the exercise of epistemic violence (see Bhabha 1997).[21] The challenge of difference is to be able to think difference which is not a monster that de-monstrates, verifying sameness. We remain within the imperial model of difference not just in economics (though significantly here), but in the wider modernist rendition of knowledge. Difference is not difference if it is maintained within the dominant culture. In that case it is – difference *from* the dominant culture on its terms and within its context which leaves the dominance of the dominant culture as the unquestioned centre from which difference is to be claimed as a deviation. Difference is difference when it becomes a condition for *any* identity, making *every* identity open to question.

(3) The third situation relates to identity and the economics of the household. This is a relatively short situational application of the model. The authors have in mind the asymmetric division of labour between husbands and wives. They argue that the identity model predicts this asymmetric division of labour, while the standard model based on comparative advantage does not. Let me explain.

We begin from the common observation that women do more housework than men, even if they work outside as well. This is an empirical and statistical observation. While those in disciplines which are not obsessively focused on individual choice, might have long attributed this to the existence and perpetuation of systematic patriarchy, economists would like to explain everything at the level of the individual. Theorising structural oppression affords us the opportunity of being able to talk about power and resistance. On the contrary, standard economic analysis 'explains' this asymmetry as follows. Recall again, to 'explain' means to take a social outcome, any outcome, and show how it is the result of rational behaviour on the part of individuals.

The authors summarise the comparative advantage model which generally proceeds as follows (747, emphases added):

> Husband and wife both have the same utility function, which is increasing in quantity of a household public good that derives from their joint labor.[...] Utility is decreasing in own labor inputs in outside and home production.[...] We *assume equal bargaining power*, so that each marriage partner *enjoys the*

21 No doubt, even the liberal suggestion of multiculturalism (the maintaining of difference within the dominant culture) is not immune to resistance. In her interview on neocolonialism, Spivak (1991: 226) says, '[t]his benevolent multiculturalism is one of the problems of neocolonialist knowledge-production as well.' In the context of education in humanities, '[i]t is necessary to assert even this rather pathetic kind of multiculturalism in order to put some sort of platform against the white majority racist argument that humanities education... should be devoted to a study of whatever Western culture is' (227). From Nazi Germany, Idi Amin's Uganda, and Taleban's Afghanistan to the ongoing attempts of Hindutva forces in India, history is rife with the attempts to put into action the fetishistic appeal of monocultures. As one BNP (British National Party, a far-right organisation in the United Kingdom) member, Mark Collett (incidentally, a student of economics) put it: 'the idea of a completely white society appeals to me' ('I'm drawn to a racially pure white society' 2002).

> *same level of utility.*[...] With this framework, *returns to specialization explain* the observed division of labor when a wife has the comparative advantage in home production.

That is, in order to maximise their joint utility, and *assuming* that there is equal bargaining power in the marriage, women usually do more work at home because they have comparative advantage in scrubbing the floors, washing the dishes, and staying up with an infant, to name a few components of 'home production'. This is the conventional explanation.

The trouble for the authors here is *not* – that it is pointless to talk about people's behaviour in terms of maximising utility functions, or that husbands and wives may not have the same utility function, or that the assumption of equal bargaining power is highly problematic and an unreasonable one to make, or that it is strange to start from the idea that the wife inherently (biological determinism) has comparative advantage in home production, or that all this merely confirms and provides justifications for the *status quo* – any of this, *but* the following.

Although this model *explains the lower share of housework for husbands when they do a larger share of work outside the home*, it does not explain why, even when wives do a large share of work outside the home, they still have a high share of housework. If we care to look, one explanation is structural, but then the (so-called) positive and the normative become explicitly intertwined.[22] And, as I mentioned before, 'structures' don't get good press in economics.

Therefore, the authors congratulate themselves that their model in fact *predicts* this asymmetry. This is because (747, emphasis added),

> *[a]dd to the above model* two social categories, 'men' and 'women'. Prescriptions dictate that 'men' should not do 'women's work' in the home and 'men' should earn more than their wives. [Hochschild's interviews suggest that] *many men, and some women*, hold these prescriptions. In the amended model, the *husband loses identity when he does housework* and *when his wife earns more* than half the household income. *Equality of utility is restored when the wife undertakes more housework than her husband.*

This is a rather sophisticated way of saying that 'men will be men'. The situational application ends here. The problems of where the prescriptions come from are not addressed yet again, and seemingly the asymmetric division of labour within the household, which is an oppressive and unfair system reinforced by dominant discourses of gender and sexuality, is presented as the 'natural' outcome of identity-related behaviour between two 'differently' prescriptive social categories of men and women.

22 Economists like to keep the 'positive' (what is) separate from the 'normative' (what ought to be) to do 'good science'. Once an overtly discriminatory structure is brought in as an explanation, then the explanation becomes a call for change – which the profession is not well known for.

5.2.4 Final observations

While the authors make numerous innovative claims for their attempt to incorporate or include identity into economics, these can only be upheld if one is judging from a neoclassical perspective. That identity matters is no news to others. The authors remain firmly within the ambit of the essentialist individual version of identity. Identity is introduced as a variable into economic analysis which is arguably ‘expanded’ by the inclusion of identity into the utility function. In their conclusion, the authors write, ‘Identity is *likely to affect* economic outcomes, for example, in areas of political economy, organisational behaviour, democracy, the economics of language, violence, education, consumption and savings behaviour, retirement decisions, and labor relations’ (748, emphasis added). They further raise the possibility that models incorporating ‘well-documented existing’ social categories and prescriptions could yield new results (749).

It is significant to note that this consideration of identity in no way affects our definition of what the economic is or how it should be written. It is possible to make radical claims for profoundly conservative justifications of the *status quo* instead of actually attempting to imagine radically altered knowledge in the face of the politics of identity. Identity can then be ‘brought into’ economics without being critical of any disciplinary basis.

Even when suggesting that another development of this agenda could be to examine identity across space and time (why notions of race or class vary across countries, why gender and racial integration vary across industries, and what might explain the rise and fall of ethnic tensions), the authors suggest that all these will be a ‘fruitful way of exploring the formation of identity-based preferences’ (749). And in a footnote they are at pains to point out that the formation of identity based preferences can be studied from principles of optimisation. The examples they give derive from evolutionary psychology and social cognition theory. That is, ‘hostility towards “outsiders” might be inherent to human nature as result of an evolutionary process’, and that ‘stereotypes summarise information and compensate for human beings’ limited cognitive abilities’ (ibid.). It may be difficult, however, the authors warn us, to accommodate complex social categories and prescriptions and their variety across societies and across time.[23] This last statement is telling.

23 More recently, Fang and Loury (2004) have outlined in a research paper a choice-theoretic model of ‘identity’ (conceived as reflexive perception) using a multiple-stage risk sharing game to ‘explain’ the emergence of *dysfunctional collective identities*. Their framework is motivated by *agreement* with the

> commonsense observation that – whether looking within or between countries – *economic backwardness, multi-generational poverty, and chronic underdevelopment seem to be connected in some way to the ‘culture’ of those who are disadvantaged*, and especially to what may be regarded as their ‘dysfunctional’ notions about identity. Thus, backward groups within many societies (inner-city blacks in the US, low caste people in India, or gypsies [i.e., Roma] in Europe) have been said to languish because they embrace a ‘culture of poverty’, (Banfield 1970), or because they are obsessed with their own victimhood (McWhorter 2000), or due to their adopting an ‘oppositional identity’ (Ogbu 2003). These

It should be clear, therefore, that an 'add identity and stir' approach to juxtaposing identity and economic is not what I have in mind. I hope to have illustrated the limitations and errors of such an attempt. Affirming the model of behaviour in economics as the basis for understanding the category economic is manifestly inappropriate. Further, it never moves us beyond the essentialist individual version of identity. And finally, it is ideological and *status quo*-ist in its attempts to explain and rationalise social outcomes which can better be engaged with by radically interrogating the very basis of their existence and perpetuation. As I argued in Chapter 4, it is this radical engagement with difference that the politics of identity needs to be oriented towards.

5.3 Illustration two: Sen on 'Reason before Identity'

5.3.1 Summary explanation

The 1999 piece by Amartya Sen is titled *Reason before Identity*.[24] This is an interesting text which is quite different from the one by Akerlof and Kranton. Sen's article makes a serious attempt to juxtapose identity and the basis of economic considerations, in a way that is not fatally circumscribed by 'economics'. This is in line with Sen's view that 'the issue of identity can go well beyond that of "externalities" in the way that concept is typically seen in economics' (1986: 350). However, in what follows, I will argue that it does not go far enough

> *culture-identity orientations are said to promote economically self-limiting behaviors* (regarding education, savings, or occupational choice), and to cause disadvantaged people to 'dis-identify' with success in their respective societies[...].
>
> (1–2, emphases added)

The authors contend that often such conjectures about the 'root causes of backwardness' are imprecisely stated and anecdotally supported, while their own work enables a formalisation of dysfunctional identity making 'culture' endogenous. They distinguish themselves from Akerlof and Kranton's (2000) 'utilitarian theory of identity' by stressing their 'cognitive' basis which allows them to 'assess the efficiency of people's identity choices' (3).
Fang and Loury (2004) consider collective identity only in so far as it is the same choice made by many individual people. While claiming that a person's salient experiences and narrative history lead to their choice of 'identity', they do not question the freedom and voluntarism implied in a 'choice of an inefficient dysfunctional identity'. An agent's identity is simply the 'specific method she uses to implement such acts of selective self-representation', and 'bad' identities are by definition 'dysfunctional, self-destructive, victim-based, alienated, oppositional, anti-system' (3–5). In such an account of identity, the locus of responsibility for poverty/underdevelopment lies squarely with the unprivileged. The wider social practices within which dys/functional identities operate are insufficiently investigated. Further, their account reifies 'culture' as a simplistic explanatory variable. See Bayart (2005) for a critique of the existence of fixed cultural identities, and how the very notion of 'cultural identity' stands in the way of recognising the cultural dimensions of political action and economic development. On a history of the belated deployment of the notion of culture in the American lexicon, see Evans (2005).

24 This was based on the Romanes Lecture for 1998, and also formed the basis of his later British Academy talk in November 2000.

in moving us away from the version of identity which relies upon the foundational individual. On the contrary, sometimes the author discusses identity as if it is a benign pursuit when indulged in moderation, but a scare-spectre if allowed to disrupt the Reason in the world. But, first let me explain the author's argument tracing its main points. His position begins with problematising the concept of narrow self-interested individual and cautiously claiming the influence of social identity on behaviour. He defends the liberal Rawlsian theory of justice against communitarian critiques, and conceptualises social identity as requiring both the concept of choice and that of reasoning. In sum, 'Reason must come before Identity'.

(1) In the beginning there was a passport. The author starts by narrating an incident when he was questioned by an Immigration officer at Heathrow airport in London about whether he was a close friend of the Master of Trinity College at Cambridge. 'Can one be a close friend of oneself?' he thought. His hesitation while thinking prompted the further query of whether there was some impropriety involved in his being in Britain? Identity, if one ever needs reminding, is a complicated matter.

(2) The formulation of human behaviour in the social sciences proceeds as if there is no need to take into account social identity since in deciding on what objectives to pursue and what choices to make no identification is involved other than with oneself. Especially a significant amount of economic theory is based upon the assumption of the self-interested individual which is seen as adequate in explaining human behaviour and in explaining the efficient operation of market-based economies. This is traced to Adam Smith by modern economists. However, Smith himself did not consider self-interest as the only motivation for human behaviour. He recognised as important, values such as sympathy, generosity, public-spiritedness, and other affiliative concerns.[25] While self-interest may be the explanation for why people *want* to engage in exchange, a society or an economy is further composed of distribution and production. Even exchange needs responsibility, trustworthiness, and social norms that would allow a successful market economy to prosper. The laurels of capitalism rest not merely on a triumph of unconstrained greed, but also on its moral success.

(3) Departure from narrowly defined self-interest does not necessarily mean that there is an influence of social identity on behaviour. There could instead be other influences such as the adherence to norms of acceptable behaviour, whose origin might be related to the rules of evolutionary selection of behavioural norms in which perceptions of social identity can play an instrumentally important part. Thus, ideas of identity can be important both in reflective choice and in the evolutionary selection of behavioural modes.

25 For more on Smith, refer back to Chapter 2. Also, in Chapter 6, I will argue that even when the affiliative concerns are added to the notion of the self, the underlying mode of identity is not significantly altered.

(4) Next follows a discussion of community, norms, and reasoning. While it is questionable that all departures from self-interest can be traced to social identity, there is no doubt that social identity is a significant influence on human behaviour. By social identity, the author means the influence of community and fellowship in shaping human behaviour, knowledge comprehension, ethics, and norms. Typically, economists are over-sceptical about the domain and authority of social identity, but there is also evidence of under-scepticism in some social analysis. The reference is to the ascendancy of communitarianism in contemporary social, political, and moral theorising. According to the author, there is a fundamental question relating to the manner in which our identities emerge, 'whether by choice or by passive recognition, and how much reasoning can enter into the development of identity' (6). This question is important for assessing the communitarian conceptions of rationality and the associated critique of communicable reasoning, and for assessing ethics including universalisable theories of justice.

The author finds problematic the combination of theories which make social identity the principal determinant of people's understanding, reasoning, rationality, behavioural norms and practices, personal moralities, and political commitments, along with those theories which consider the nature of rationality, knowledge, and morality as being entirely parasitic on the subjects' perceptions. Thus, criteria of rational behaviour and moral judgements can *only* be invoked *within* particular communities. In the political context, this leads to the rejection of intercultural normative judgements about behaviour and institutions, and undermines the possibility of cross-cultural exchange and understanding.

(5) Rather than making strong and morally debilitating claims for identity-based theorising, it is better used to interrogate theories of justice and rationality if they don't pay sufficient attention to the claims of community and affiliative concerns. The author discusses the Rawlsian framework of justice as fairness[26] and considers the communitarian critiques of liberal theories of justice. On the one hand, there are those who put forward rival ethical claims to that of liberal justice; for instance, the associated values of caring for other members of the same community (Bernard Williams, Stuart Hampshire). However, while these concerns can be additional to justice, according to the author they cannot disestablish the need for justice. On the other hand, a different critique comes from Michael Sandel's argument that the demands of Rawlsian justice themselves require pre-existing

26 John Rawls's (1971, 1993) liberal theories of justice are based on the notion of justice as fairness. In order to arrive at a situation where the guiding principles of social organisation paid similar attention to everyone's interests, concerns, and liberties, use is made of the device of the 'original position'. In this hypothetical state of original equality, individuals arrive at rules and guiding principles in a co-operative exercise, but they do not know who they are going to be once this social organisation is implemented, so it is in their interests to arrive at fair rules (there is an assumption of mutual disinterest). Next, particular principles of justice are identified which include the first principle of the priority of liberty, and the second principle of equity and efficiency in the distribution of opportunities (including the difference principle which is an allocational criterion that gives priority to the worst-off people in each group).

communal solidarity and social identity. The author has a threefold response to this – if the critique holds, the requirement of solidarity could be a *part* rather than a rival of the demands of justice; there is little empirical evidence in favour of the critique; and, while a sense of community is important, justice cannot solely rely on communal solidarity. This then applies between 'different economic and social groups which compete and contest; and yet they have to co-exist and co-survive. Justice *is* important, and has to go much beyond the domain of communal affection' (13, emphasis original).

(6) Social identity is therefore a matter requiring both the need for choice and for reasoning. This can be examined by considering the importance of social identity in two different ways – its *delineating* role and its *perceptual* function.

(a) The delineating role of social identity is important in diagnosing the social good, since it necessarily involves asking who is included in that aggregative exercise. But delineation still leaves room for choice and reasoning. This is because it has to be defended by reasoned support and any particular map of group partitioning can be questioned by asking whether lines can be redrawn on the same map, or whether a different map and procedure is needed. Further, '[g]iven plural delineations, alternative identities can compete for relevance, even in a given context' (15).

The author next critiques communitarian approaches since they seem to make communal identity a matter of self-realisation and not of choice. This section takes on constructing an opposition between the 'discovery' and 'choice' of identity. The author argues that on the discovery view, a person's identity is something that he or she detects rather than determines, and that while the choices of identity may be implicit and obscure, they are no less real nonetheless. Some clarifications of the choice of identity view are offered. First, choosing need not mean one-off and permanent, it can be a repeated process. Second, choice need not be unrestricted, and in fact is always limited by 'our looks, our circumstances, and our background and history' (17–18). Third, of course, the choice view does not rule out people discovering some aspect of their identity (a connection, a descent, and so on). However, even when something is discovered, the person still has to make the choice 'to decide about what importance to give to that identity compared with other competing identities – of nationality, class, political beliefs, and so on. ... Choices have to be made even when discoveries occur' (19).

Assuming that choice does not exist when it does is not only mistaken but pernicious, and such conformism typically has conservative implications. Unreasoned herd behaviour causes harm since it does not leave place for critical examination. Also, regarding the communitarian approach, 'within-group solidarity can go hand-in-hand with between-group discord' (20–21). Further, accepting one's identity without scrutiny leads to the tyrannies of newly asserted identities which may have important political roles but can also be oppressive.

(b) The perceptual role of identity is important because the 'communities or cultures' to which a person belongs can have a significant influence on reasoning, beliefs, or decisions. But while local knowledge, rational norms, particular perceptions, and values that are common in a specific community are empirically obvious, in the author's view, this does not undermine the role of choice and reasoning. The alternative is not the availability of reasoning from nowhere, but 'choices that continue to exist in any encumbered position one happens to occupy' (23). Therefore, no doubt that the way one reasons can be influenced by knowledge, presumptions, attitudinal inclinations, but this is simply influence on the nature of reasoning which cannot fully determine it. It does not follow that one 'can reason only within a particular cultural tradition, within a specific identity' (ibid.). Further, there may be considerable internal variation and difference within 'cultures' which 'an adult and competent person has the ability to question' (24). Culturalist arguments in the realm of Reason are invoked not for the West, but for non-Western cultures – 'Cairo and beyond' (writes Sen) – who are seen as 'inescapably imprisoned in the tyranny of unreasoned fundamentalism' (27). Also, in return, '[t]he constrained individuals are then seen as heroic resisters of Westernization and defenders of native tradition' (25).

(7) Finally, the author turns to the liberal theories of justice, the Rawlsian in particular, and argues that its supplemented two-stage structure of intranational and international levels in the exercise of fairness do not do justice to the conflicting demands that arise from different identities and affiliations derived through the relation between nations. An example of such identities is provided by professional identities such as those of a doctor, or 'markets and exchanges in a rapidly globalizing world economy, with its own discipline and own mores' (29).

5.3.2 Critical evaluation

Sen's argument is a nuanced one, and calls for a careful evaluation. In critically assessing it, I will draw upon the theoretical framework set up in the chapters until now.

To begin with, Sen frames his argument as partly a debate between liberal and communitarian critiques of justice. However, it is not just that. It also derives much of its force from the constructed opposition between two alternative visions of identity – one where identity is a matter of reasoned and responsible choice, and the other where identity is a culturally or community determined persona. Finally, I think it is also legitimate to read his argument as an attempt to vindicate the *universal* applicability and availability of '*universal Reason*', which, although assumed universal, is often seen as not being applicable to those from non-Western cultures. Reason, Sen seems to be saying, is *not* something that is available only to the West.

I have much sympathy with the ethical issues that he is attempting to place on the agenda here. Sen has always worked on important social issues of great relevance.[27]

27 Pressman and Summerfield (2000) provide an extensive bibliography and a survey of economic contributions of Sen which are as follows – providing a philosophical critique of traditional economic assumptions, attempting to build a more realistic economic science based on the notion of entitlements and human capabilities, and a long series of practical contributions to welfare

It is especially remarkable that he feels the need to do so, rather than simply rest his prestige as an economist on conventional economic theorising. I will argue that while Sen's endeavour can be read as challenging, it does not end up sufficiently addressing the crucial issues in relation to identity and the economic.

At the heart of the matter is the way in which identity for Sen remains within an amended but still essentially individual view. To be sure, Sen does not see human beings as abstract puppets motivated solely by greedy desires, otherwise termed 'self-interest'. However, personal identity remains something which can be claimed by individual people with mostly individual implications. Thus, although he repeatedly stresses that people are not 'merely self-concerned islands' (30) and that the world is not 'split into little islands that are not within normative reach of each other' (7), yet what he seems to be actually saying is that *possibly* people *are* islands, *possibly* the world *does* consist of little islands, *but* these people are *not exclusively self-concerned*, and the islands of the world are *within normative reach* of each other. The tone and sentiment is overarchingly humanist, in a wider cosmopolitan sense.[28] The thrust of the argument is that we all link up in many ways to mitigate the basically individual aspect of our personal identities and an example of this is collective identities.

It is worth recalling Chapter 4, where it was argued that the 'individual' limits the terrain of explanation and fixes the basic atomic structure concept that has to be mobilised in order to create meaning in social science like economics. By starting from the individuals as the basis on which one can talk about identity, one has already structured and confined what can be seen as political, and how. As Connolly (1991: 73–74) argues – it *reduces the political to the juridical*. Sen's argument maps rather well with what Connolly sees as the implications of this. First, that this condenses most issues of politics into the juridical category of rights, justice, obligation, and responsibility. And second, that the remaining issues are then seen instrumentally as contests in which individuals and aggregations compete within juridical rules to advance their 'interests' or 'principles' by rational means.

Similarly, Sen's argument places an inordinate amount of emphasis on the responsible choice of identity by individuals as relating to an important part of justice, but every time he comes to the question of contradictions between multiple identities within this box of the individual, he defers the issue to the appeal of Reason in such a case. Identity, instead of being seen as a political living, becomes, ironically (in view of Sen's aims), *a matter of responsible choice being made by the rational consumer of politics*. Politics itself takes on the shape of a hypothetical contest in the metropolitan heart of liberalism, where all the

economics that follow from the capabilities approach (poverty and inequality measurement, understanding of famine and hunger, importance of gendering economic development, difference between economic development and economic growth).

28 I will illustrate the perils of overarching cosmopolitan universal humanism in Chapter 6. I will especially consider the example of Nussbaum's work (she has also co-authored with Sen; see Nussbaum and Sen 1993). For a perspective on how even the supposedly 'universalist' modernist knowledge is grounded in provincial assumptions, see Chakrabarty (2000).

participants arrive with already constituted identities that they have chosen with a generous dose of Reason. Consequently, Sen finds himself defending that any and every participant in the arena is inherently capable of accessing a universal store of Reason (with a capital R) in a broadly similar way, although some might face greater situational constraints than others.

Sen is arguing in part against communitarian critiques, and I should make it clear that my disagreement with Sen is not my automatic endorsing of communitarianism. Discussing the specific merits of liberal or communitarian theories of justice is less my concern here, than objecting to the foundational underpinnings of some of Sen's argument. Meanwhile, it is important to mention that narrow communitarian sentiments *are* often used to legitimise oppression against those seen as not belonging to that 'community'. In my view, both liberal and communitarian perspectives in general rely upon a 'concentric' ideology of the self and the world (I discuss this concentric view in the next chapter), where there is a located 'I' at the centre of all knowledge and subjectivity. Moreover, invoking 'communities' instead of individuals does *not* mean that the centred atomic unit of the self is challenged. Often communities can themselves function as surrogate individuals on this view and carry the same implications as the idea of the individual.

To return to the present discussion, another striking point about Sen's discussion of identity is a remarkable voiding of difference. This is to be welcomed if it means a turn away from positing difference as difference from the norm. However, in the context of his aptly titled discussion ('Reason *before* Identity', emphasis added) this elision of difference is the fear of a proliferation of not simply multiple identities but the multiplicity of 'identity' in 'a world of universalised difference', which will hurt the sanity of a universal Reason.

Interestingly, Reason itself functions as an undifferentiated concept whose appeal is left ungrounded, and considered obvious. This does not address any concern which can draw from the extremely chequered fate of the exercise of Reason in world history. After all, the significant crusades of enlightenment modernity – capitalism, slavery, imperialism, colonialism, were all claimed as legitimate in the name of Reason. By invoking a timeless and universal conceptualisation of Reason as an abstract quality of all people at all times, Sen is opening himself to the charge of naively benevolent and uncritical appreciation of the excesses of 'Reason' in different times and places. Presumably, Sen will claim that, of course, excesses have in the past been carried out in the name of Reason, but that is no justification to not embrace universal Reason as an abstract good. Well enough, but if we can separate out Reason itself from projects legitimated under the name of Reason, then how do we conceptualise the abstract and timeless essence of universal Reason? In other words, wherefrom will one glance at Reason? As it is, Reason is definitely on the good side in Sen's account.

The limitations of Sen's starting premises come into view when, in his rejection of exclusively self-interested individuals, his next port of call is individuals who act in accordance with norms which might be evolutionarily selected. But, none of this critically interrogates the basis of how we came to situate the individual as the starting point of social science, what purposes does this serve, and what would be changed by a radical rethinking of it? At the very least, some crucial problems that arise by starting from the self-interested atomistic individual as the premise of society, politics, economy, are *not* addressed by just admitting that this individual is a part of society and is influenced by its surroundings. For instance, not only does starting from the individual as the basis of the social order provide a remarkable sustenance to perpetuating the logic of capitalism, it also nourishes the modernist renditions of disciplinary structurings like economics. Positing the individual as the basis of social order engenders a specific subjectivity that is individualised, objectified, desacralised, and thus fosters the logic of capitalism – a rationalisation in terms of privatised cost-benefit calculability.[29] Sure, making the point that individuals are not completely self-interested does dent the disciplinary infrastructure a bit, but this critique remains fundamentally unable to address the ruinous consequences of a tradition of applied knowledge which starts from individual premises. Any other grounding must be approached with scepticism, which may be under- or over-, but this scepticism does not apply to the basic theoretical terms of individual, Reason, choice, identity. I attach identity to this list because, even when Sen appears to question identity in a political way, he simply addresses himself to identity politics rather than a politics of identity. As I argued the contrast (between identify politics and politics of identity) in Chapter 4, thinking in terms of a politics of identity entails a politicisation of identity which gathers in its train a rethinking not just of politics but also of identity. Sen's scare-spectre of multiple identities which make solidarity impossible is based upon adopting a very particular notion of coherent individual identity as the starting point for conscious attempts to initiate solidarity. Such an account has little space for a productive rethinking of difference which does not simply obstruct, but which enables emancipatory coalitions.

In common with a lot of other analyses, Sen finds the determining particularisation of concepts such as rationality, knowledge, or morality as morally debilitating in the political context. The oft-repeated worry of 'anything goes'. I argue that this fear is often overstated. The threat of all-consuming relativism is twinned

29 Here are my theses. Taking the 'individual' as the *a priori* basic unit of analysis places the historical origins of this concept beyond scrutiny. It is no coincidence that the primacy of individual and that of capital have a mutually reinforcing trajectory. Positing the individual as the basis of social order constructs a world of people into objectified in-dividuals who form a category in a disenchanted social order. This allows an individualisation of responsibility for events and occurrences, which in turn allows a certain kind of calculability (cost-benefit type) in relation to the 'choices' of these individuals. This grid of comprehension encourages thinking in terms of a rationality based on self-interest. Further, the obliteration of specificity by designating objectifiable in-dividuals permits erosion of the boundary between people and things, a desacralisation of subjectivity that makes it possible to see the universe as a storehouse of capital. Together, these things – the objectified and thus commodifiable category in-dividual, individualisation of human responsibility, the engendering of a certain kind of cost-benefit calculability in relation to 'choices', a rationality of self-interest – structure a comprehension which has been best motivated by capitalism, especially in relation to the organisation of productive ownership in society. This has further led to competition and conflict in the process of looking for ever-newer ways of enhancing self-interest even at the expense of others. Cf. Marx.

with its polar opposite of universalism. First, it is sensible to point out the extent to which the universality of concepts such as rationality or morality is actually a universal*isation*. Second, the alternative to narrow universalisation is to admit of contextualisation. The worry that we will lose the ability to judge is based upon conceptualising judgements as only being salient if they are universally valid. Once it is accepted that judgements are themselves positional, we do give up the security of universal Reason, but we take responsibility for contextual arbitrations. Recognising the contextuality of rationality or morality does not mean that it is rendered immune to any and all responsibility. On the contrary, it means that the responsibility for justification of particular rational or moral norms is now a matter of contextual assessment.[30] The possibilities of trans-contextual dialogues are not precluded by the differences in knowledge about oppression. As Code recommends, this is the perspective of a 'mitigated relativism' which involves thinking along the lines of, '[*w*]*hose* knowledge are we talking about? Such a relativism would recognize the perspectival, locatedness of knowledge *and* its associations with subjective purposes. Yet it would develop strategies for evaluating perspectives and purposes' (1991: 320, emphasis original).

Further, as I explain below, Sen's worry that 'anything goes' could be influential in 'the defence of particular customs and traditions, on such matters as women's unequal social position, or the use of particular modes of traditional punishment' (1999: 7) is also problematic. Note that the specific examples that Sen gives of the possible dangers of this morally debilitating political context are themselves illustrative of the outer limits of an explanatory frame which combines universal Reason with particular ethics. Consider first the worry that in the political context

30 There is also another less nuanced way of refuting the fear of 'anything goes'. On this view, 'anything goes' is more the manifesto of ethical resistance than it is the credo of irresponsibility (see also Feyerabend 1987, 1988). Let me explain. Only in a world of no hierarchies or operation of power could multiple standards of different subjects based in different communities (or 'cultures') run the risk of developing into mutually unjudgeable constituencies. Thus, 'anything goes' is not a legitimate worry in *this our* world, primarily because *anything cannot and will not be allowed to go*. Everything transpires in a matrix of power and interests, and admitting the particularisation of universal concepts is not automatically to mean that their validity is established. Perforating the universality of concepts such as rationality, knowledge, or morality is less an exercise of meaningless and mutually exclusive standards of validity, and more the preconditional basis on which certain alternative understandings of rationality, knowledge, and morality can gain entry into the *museum of the legitimate competing standards*. Samuels's (1991: 522) comments in the context of economics have a wider resonance:

> It should be possible, I think, to be eclectic and agnostic with regard to the epistemological and discursive nature of economics. We should be willing to tolerate ambiguity and open-endedness, if only because, whatever our preferences, the actual process of knowledge seems 'in fact' to be one of social construction and therefore possessed of the characteristics of ambiguity and open-endedness. I appreciate that some people may consider the view presented... as due to the laxity, relativism, nihilism, indiscipline, malaise, and cynicism of our age. But epistemological and discursive pluralism is, it seems to me, what is called for by the challenges to confident knowledge, not self-deception, however subtle. This pluralism does not strictly mean that 'anything goes.' It points to the requirement that each individual does in fact have to exercise his or her own judgment. The alternative is that 'only one thing goes,' plus myopia, pretense, and false confidence.

intercultural normative judgements will be rejected. This worry seems to be innocent of the recognition that – (a) at best, there might be some limits to the validity of intercultural normative judgements about behaviour and institutions, and (b) more importantly, these intercultural normative judgements have, since the onset of modernity, *not* been intercultural but mostly unidirectional, following the imperial (and now neocolonial) gaze and in direct opposition to the path taken by benefits of capital.

Sen's examples work through an implicit tradition versus modernity characterisation. Even though he does not say it, 'the defence of *particular customs and traditions*, on such matters as women's unequal social position, or the use of *particular modes of traditional punishment*' (7, emphasis added), I would argue, has more resonance with the scare-spectres of Sati, female circumcision, Purdah, Koranic punishment, than it does with women's pay inequality, sexual harassment, or death penalty in the US prison system. I will add here that my opposition is to the author's somewhat unquestioned linking of moral debilitation with the particularity of 'custom' and 'tradition', but that I am all for women's equality in every sense. It is just that I do not see it as something which maps neatly onto the debates in question. In fact, the issue of women is involved in this debate from every angle – left, right, and centre – literally and metaphorically. But, the feminist critiques of structures of knowledge and practice (a critique which has not yet radically entrenched itself, even in feminist economics, let alone mainstream economics) that call for a radical rethinking of the very basis of knowledge are often seen as a separate issue to invoking 'women' as a legitimate cause in the service of argument. An immediate example to hand is the same text by Sen where, in his discussion of Rawlsian justice and its communitarian critiques, a feminist critique is never mentioned[31] (for an example of such externalist feminist critiques, see Pateman 1988; Okin 1989; for a recent internalist feminist critique of Rawl's theory, see Woolley 2000).

Moving on, I am not convinced that there is not more to Sen's questioning of identity. I think that his difficulties illustrate the appeal of the individual as the anchor of knowledge. While, for Sen, it is not a completely sovereign individual, yet ultimately, it is an individual '*only influenced but not determined*' as he repeatedly stresses (for instance, 1999: 23) by the particularities of the context. We get an equation like, determination minus influence is equal to some part of universal Reason (or to transpose the terms, universal Reason plus local influence is equal to determination). This is important to realise because it allows Sen to escape from thinking the structurality of the structure. And further, by maintaining that distinction between influence and determination, he is able to admit causality in the sense that ultimately the individual is the locus of responsibility and

31 In fact, Sen does not cite any woman apart from Emma Rothschild in passing. In his arguments calling for a move beyond identity which is constrained simply by the nation-state, he does not take into account the feminist literature on nations and nationalism (see Jayawardena 1986; Anthias and Yuval-Davis 1989; Tickner 1992; Walby 1996; Pettman 1996; Yuval-Davis 1997; McClintock *et al.* 1997; Enloe 2000).

determination. Then, a study of society or the world which attempts to know it, would automatically be grounded upon mediation through the individual – a one which may take many forms, but in essence knows no Other.

Let me now turn to Sen's discussion of the choice of identity. The aim is not to dispute that at a trivial level some conscious identification does happen. Rather, it is to examine the significance of choice in identity. If the point is that people must always be self-reflexively aware of their choices, and experience identity as a political living since unquestioning conformism can lead to conservatism, I would agree.[32] But the point for Sen goes beyond this. He draws upon Appiah (1996) to discuss the oppressiveness of identities, and the argument is again a warning about the perils of identity politics. While racial identities can be the basis of resistance to racism, they should not become oppressive or tyrannous (the example relates to the identity of being black or African-American). But, if racial identity is only to be invoked as an instrument to combat racism, that would leave unmarked those racial identities which are hardly ever the subject of racism. We can also look at this in the following way. In Sen's account, people choose their identity, and this choice should not be assumed away since it is a responsible decision. Of course there are constraints on choices, but 'it is not news that choices are always within certain constraints, and any choice theorist knows that *characterising the constraints faced by the chooser* is the first step in *understanding any choice that is being made*' (18, emphases added). Such a characterisation of choice, as the exercise of self-aware Reason by a responsible adult individual in the face of an assessment of constraints, belongs in the liberal arena to those who can afford to fit this picture. There are many for whom the choice of identity is not a matter of exercising responsible judgement in the face of constraints, coupled with a careful consideration, to arrive at *the* important identity in the case of multiple and conflicting identities. In order to be identified as a 'refugee' one just has to *be*, and the other identities do not compete for choice in different contexts, but are all mediated through the attributed identity in the liberal arena.[33]

Finally, the 'adult and competent person' who 'has the ability to question' (24) seems remarkably similar to the Cartesian individual. At one point, Sen writes,

32 Although, even here, questioning is not a straightforward matter – John Stuart Mill, who is approvingly mentioned by Sen as someone who published *The Subjection of Women* (1869), is also the figure who in the race debate in England was on the side that argued that they 'loved the law, not the Negroes', and *this* was why they found Governor Eyre unjustified in his brutal repression of the rebellion in Jamaica (see Chapter 3). As an aside, it is interesting to note that almost all of John Stuart Mill's work was done collaboratively with Harriet Taylor (Mill), so that it is in fact the 'Mills' who were writing when the name of the author mentioned was John Stuart (see Pujol 1992, 1995; and also Bodkin 1999).

33 The example Sen gives (see Summary in 5.3.1) is that of a professional identity such as a doctor. But I would argue that the issue is more complicated. In 1999, when attending a conference on 'women refugees' at the University of Hull in the United Kingdom, a doctor who was a black woman refugee narrated her painful case – none of her medical qualifications or practice were seen as important; she could simply not do anything and was seen only as a 'refugee'.

'I may not go so far as to argue for the slogan: "Dubito ergo sum", but that thought is not very distant either' (ibid.). Sen's strategy is to reclaim the (European) Universal as the Universal Worldwide. But the appeal of this strategy can be seen as limited for two reasons. First, it is limited for those who believe in the (European) Universal *only because* it is so, and not because it is Universal. Second, it does not allow room for exposing the narrow basis and perpetuation of the (European) Universal, something which is critical for finding alternative ways of being a valid Other.

Even the attempts by Sen (here), and by Akerlof and Kranton (for instance, in trying to use their model in the study of social exclusion to argue for the 'rationality' of behaviour on the part of those at the margins of liberal society), remain profoundly difficult for non-Nobel economists to attempt within the discipline of economics. The attempts by Sen, in particular, throughout most of his career to focus on social issues and demonstrate their neglect within conventional economics are significant. Here, his attempt to widen the umbrella of universal Reason is pertinent as a first move in considering the relations between identity and the economic. But this has limitations eventually. At some point, it is important to question the very basis of how Reason came to be associated with some and not others, and realise that extending the fabric of Reason to cover everyone will only stretch to give them thinner and more contingent coverage. Not because they are inferior, but because the particular interpretation of modernist Reason cannot be divorced from its violent exercises by those with the power to oppress. Ultimately, holes in the fabric will show, and this must be thought of as the 'event' which can disrupt the constitution of the structure.

For Sen, the many problems of identity politics point towards only one possible response – the invocation of Reason. The sanity of universal Reason then demands the elision of difference. The problematics of identity, on the other hand, can also be thought through by taking the alternative route of the politics of identity so as to politicise the picture of identity where stable identities precede difference. Difference itself can be rethought as a non-systematic ethical imperative of 'response and responsibility', a translation which *others* identity, and makes a *politics of palimpsestic configurations possible.*

To wrap up this discussion – I have critically evaluated Sen's argument for its relation between identity and the individual, its conception of politics, its treatment of difference, and its modernist ambit. A final point needs making. Isn't it curious that Sen's discussion of Reason and identity invoked the 'economic' at only two points? At the beginning, where the conception of solely self-interested individual in economic theorising was deemed inadequate. And towards the end, when he discusses the 'practical interactions across the borders [that] often involve norms and rules that are not derived through the relation between nations' (29). Consider the following (ibid., emphases added):

> This applies powerfully to the markets and exchanges in a rapidly globalizing world economy, *with its own discipline and own mores*. ... [n]ational laws are still very important ... and yet so much of global commerce

> involves direct interactions between parties – *with its own ethics, rules, and norms* – which can be supported or scrutinised or criticised in terms of inter-group relations that are not confined to relations between nations.

The economic is invoked as 'markets and exchanges' in a 'globalising world economy' comprised of the interactions of 'global commerce'. The phrases – '*with its own discipline and own mores*' and '*with its own ethics, rules, and norms*' – invoke the separate sphere of the economic where the considerations of identity take on a different ('its own') format to those detailed (which relate to culture or community).

The inadequacy of economic theorising which relies upon the self-interested individual is not linked here to peculiarities/particularities of the sphere of the economic. This is the connection between the *logic of economic theories* and *economic logic* which will only be available for scrutiny when neither identity nor the economic are available in an uncontextualised and depoliticised manner. Through the book, I have argued that this requires an interrogation of enlightenment epistemology, a dismantling of the modernist rendition of disciplinary structuring, and a postcolonial re-membering.

6 Rethinking identity translationally and reconsidering the economic

> When someone speaks of self-interest, I will be aware of how muddled this notion is. Of whose interests is he thinking? Of the self he is now? Of some future selves of his? Of the bundle of selves with whom his current self is tightly connected? I will also know that the 'selves' of that 'interest' are so dispersed that no one of them, nor of those of some other string, can ever assume to be the 'best judge'. ... Behind 'autonomy' some other self recognizing me is necessary. I now know that beyond every decision of my current self, 'some other kind of otherness' must be sought.
>
> (Pizzorno 1986: 372)

6.1 Introduction

In this chapter, I make two moves – the first is related to a rethinking of identity in terms of a translation (6.2), and the second is to analyse the separation of culture and economy as a divide between identity and the economic, by considering the relation between Value and Values (6.3).

The starting point is to argue that in the juxtaposition of identity and economic, identity needs to be rethought. The accounts of identity (except the discussion calling for a move toward the politics of identity) that I have invoked until now, are based in thinking of identity as a coherence that flows from the centred 'I' outwards – what I term a concentric architecture of identity. In contrast to this, I argue for the imperative to imagine identity as a *translation*, in a translational architecture. This will be linked to the previous discussions on the politics of identity as a politicisation of identity which is important for conceptualising knowledge and emancipation that does not rely upon the elision or the incorporation of difference.

In Section 6.2, I will dwell upon a concentric architecture of identity, pointing out that it originates in the idea of the coherent 'I' and can have 'benevolent cosmopolitan' implications when circles of affiliative concerns are added onto the 'I'. Ultimately, there are severe limitations of the benevolent cosmopolitanism that we can expect from a concentric architecture of identity. To illustrate this I will use the example of Nussbaum's cosmopolitan universalism. Following on from this I will explore the translational account of identity and its implications in terms of thinking knowledge and enabling struggles.

In Section 6.3, I will reconnect the issues of identity and the economic by arguing that the divide of identity and economic is only available to us in terms of the difference between culture and economy. It will be elaborated that this itself relies upon a crucial slippage between *the terms of* economy, economic, and economics. The edifice of the economic depends upon a singular and coherent fixing of 'Value' as that which is free of values. Questioning the identity of rational economic Value (i.e. applying the politics of identity to the question of economic Value) allows a recognition of the multiplicity of values which are erased in the distillation of Value from values. It is a translational thinking of Value in terms of values that enables us to see the significance of what is at stake in the 'rational economic fixing of values'. It is this rational economic fixing of values which manufactures the consent on the *impossibility of being irrational without also being uneconomic*. As a result, thinking economics Otherwise is not about simply bringing in the 'outside' but involves a genealogical disruption in the dominant discourse of the economic to render it visible in its performativity.

6.2 Concentric and translational architectures of identity

6.2.1 Concentric identity and cosmopolitan universalism

First, what is a concentric architecture of identity? I derive the terms 'concentric' and 'translational' from Bhabha's (1996) discussion of two texts, one by Adrienne Rich, and the other by Martha Nussbaum. However, my discussion here is not simply an explanation of Bhabha, but an appropriation.[1]

At the basis of understanding identity as concentric lies the idea of the 'I'. Let me explain. Think of a picture box with a tiny hole at its front. Nothing can be seen until the eye is put to that hole. The I in the concentric architecture of identity is the one thing which holds everything else together. Because it is so crucial in maintaining the whole picture, its integrity should, on the one hand, be always protected and defended from everything else that is not the I, and, on the other hand, never be questioned or destabilised too much.

This starting point is in itself not new, and has certainly been around as an important aspect of Enlightenment modernity and modernist rendition of knowledge. Consider Adam Smith (1759: TMS.III.I.46),

> Let us suppose that the great empire of China, with all its myriads of inhabitants, was suddenly swallowed up by an earthquake, and let us consider how a *man of humanity* in Europe, who had *no sort of connection* with that part of the world, would be affected upon receiving intelligence of this dreadful calamity. He would, I imagine, first of all, express very strongly his sorrow for the misfortune of that unhappy people, he would make many melancholy reflections upon the precariousness of human life, and the vanity of all the

1 Any references to Bhabha are explicitly acknowledged.

> labours of man, which could thus be annihilated in a moment. He would too, perhaps, if he was a man of speculation, enter into many reasonings concerning the effects which this disaster might produce upon the commerce of Europe, and the trade and business of the world in general. And when all this fine philosophy was over, when all these humane sentiments had been once fairly expressed, he would pursue his business or his pleasure, take his repose or his diversion, with the same ease and tranquillity, as if no such accident had happened. The most frivolous disaster which could befall himself would occasion a more real disturbance.

Thus redeemed, the self is free to go about its business as long as it doesn't affect Other selves. As Griswold Jr. (1999: 83, emphases added) puts it in his discussion of Smith, 'other things being equal, we have an *immediate experience of ourselves*, of our *pleasures and pains*, that we lack of others' pleasures and pains.' The benevolence of human beings comes from 'not a soft power of humanity' or 'strongest impulses of self-love', but from 'reason, principle, conscience, the inhabitant of the breast, the man within, the great judge and arbiter of our conduct' (Smith 1759: TMS.III.I.46). The 'I' functions as a designation of the boundaries of pleasure and pain, concern and detachment, a totality of response and responsibility.

As a next step, imagine numerous concentric circles radiating outwards from the I. In fact, the I is at the very centre of these circles, which, like those formed by a pebble in the pond, or a radio transmitter, extend away from it. This, I am arguing, is the dominant way in which identity is understood, imagined, and conceptualised within social science. The I of identity is the self, and its affiliative concerns radiate outwards. This is also *an identity which comes prepared in the sense of always already having a map of its situatedness and its issues*.

For Smith, as for Rousseau (recall from Chapter 3, Rousseau's statement that one cannot be affected by the calamity of Japan), the limited store of sympathy characterising the affiliative concentric circles – like water waves when the pebble is dropped into the pond or radio waves emitting from the transmitter – *die out* as the circles are enlarged. With variations on the theme of how the affiliative circles of concern are to be structured or what is their significance, the essential idea in this account of identity is the unquestionable starting point, the I of the self.

The appeal of a concentric architecture of identity can be thought of in its connectivity of affiliative concerns. Rather than have a notion of identity which is limited only by one's own community, the circles radiating outwards present the potential for imagining the self as available for cosmopolitanism.[2]

2 Yet this concentric architecture of identity is severely limited and problematic in its own way, as I discuss in Section 6.2.2 later. Meanwhile, consider some artistic usage of concentricity in kinetic sculptures to express human identity, time, movement, and violence. Gunther Uecker is a German artist whose 1992 artwork 'The Scourge Mill' for me questions what happens when geometrical geographical concerns make the world go round. The artwork consists of a small rotating central structure around which threads trailing in two opposite directions make concentric circles on the

The project of cosmopolitanism can be visualised in both liberal and radical ways (see Stevenson 2002). My illustrative example to show the eventual limitations of liberal cosmopolitanism based upon a concentric notion of identity will be Nussbaum. Nussbaum has worked on a wide range of issues from the ancient classics to the contemporary debates over women's rights and justice (for a bibliography, see Yeghiayan n.d.). The segments of Nussbaum's work of interest to me here relate to an espousal of cosmopolitan virtues based upon the liberal Rawlsian idea of an individual as a rational self and the importance of practical (moral or political) Reason. She has argued for the normative adoption of an expansive global cosmopolitan consciousness. Based upon this, her version of Sen's 'capabilities approach' is a formulation of constitutional principles and a list of central human functional capabilities (Nussbaum and Sen 1993; Nussbaum and Glover 1995; Nussbaum 2000).[3] In her conceptualisation of cosmopolitan universalism as well as in her formulation of the desirable human capabilities, she has an implicit underlying view of identity that can be described as concentric. In what follows I will attempt to unravel the notion of identity central to both Nussbaum's cosmopolitanism and her capabilities approach.

The cosmopolitan ideal is celebrated as carrying a global orientation, as opposed to a narrow and limited sense of identity. Nussbaum advocates, '[t]he world around us is inescapably international. Issues from business to agriculture, from human rights to the relief of famine call our imaginations to venture beyond narrow group loyalties and to consider the reality of distant lives' (in 'Globally Speaking' 2002). Her view is that, 'even just to show respect for people, we ought to be curious about their lives', and therefore we have to not only 'ask how the cultures of the West have influenced, have colonised, have exploited the cultures of the east', but also we 'want to know something about what those cultures have achieved in their own right' (ibid.). At first sight, this seems like an extremely

sand. Mona Hatoum is a British artist of Palestinian origin, whose artwork titled '+ and −' (1994–2004, based on her 1979 work) also deploys concentricity to question the violence of movement and affiliation. In this work, a combed and asymmetric metal rod is powered by a motor to trace concentric circles on a bed of sand, which are only semicircles as the rotation erases the marks as they are created (on view at the Museum of Modern Art (MoMA), New York). The gallery label describes how 'Hatoum mechanizes the practices of mark-making and erasure... [t]he sculpture's hypnotic and continual grooving and smoothing of sand evokes polarities of building and destroying, existence and disappearance, displacement and migration.'

3 The background for this is the distinction between growth and development, a distinction which is often only formally made and not accorded significance in economics as well as in development economics. Growth refers to the increase of national product (rising indicators such as gross domestic product or gross national product) that is an increase in the volume of goods and services produced within an economy (by a country, or by its citizens). Development, on the other hand, is an attempt to consider the quality of life; for instance, rates of infant mortality, poverty, literacy, and so on. There can be many indicators of development based upon the weightage given to each criterion. Sen's idea of 'capability' along these lines is to ask further questions, not simply related to people's satisfaction or their command over resources, 'but about what they are *actually* able to do or to be' (see also Sen 1992). Nussbaum's version of the capabilities approach also involves a list of desirable universal human capabilities.

laudable goal. The concentric identity of the cosmopolitan ideal is useful, for instance, to bring in the question of concern which is not limited by narrow self-interest. Yet this is also an identity which comes always already prepared with a map of its *own situatedness and its issues*. The liberal Western individual ought to peer on the outside as it were, since there are so many issues that are inescapably inter-national (almost all of Nussbaum's international issues, viz. famine, business, human rights, are actually those on which the West acts in the 'interests' of the distant others), and in order to be respectfully curious about other people's lives, 'we' should know something about what their achievements have been (even here, Nussbaum mentions the effect of the West upon the others and the others' own achievements, but not the effect of the others upon the West or the constitution of the West itself). As Bhabha explains (1996: 200, emphasis original), '[f]or Nussbaum, the identity of cosmopolitanism demands a *spatial* imaginary: the "self" at the centre of a series of concentric circles that move through the various cycles of familial, ethnic and communal affiliation to "the largest one, that of humanity as the whole" '.

However, difficulties arise when we want to move *beyond* this set-up which is characterised by identity *as the basis for* difference (as opposed to the other way around; see contrast earlier in Chapter 4) in the secular capitalist liberal democratic imperial polity. The cosmopolitan purposes of concentric identity, rather than questioning and politicising how identity comes into being, affirm the locus of identity as the prerequisite for any action. What if, for instance, one wants not simply to transform the self-interested identity into an affiliative one, but to politicise the having of identity itself? The difficulty with the concentric architecture of identity is that the I is affirmed as the foundational locus of identity. Anything else, in the doing, thinking, being, depends upon this pre-existing I anchored in a particular way. In this process, difference is fixed rather awkwardly. Cosmopolitanism and universalism are seen as worthy goals towards which the self must strive by acting on commonalities and fixing difference.

This cosmopolitan universalism is an important part of Nussbaum's work on women, human development, and the capabilities approach. I shall now consider two separate but commonly motivated critiques of such cosmopolitan universalism put into practice.

6.2.1.1 The fellow city dwellers

The project of cosmopolitan universalism never seriously questions the processes by which one is placed in a situation from where one can attempt universal benevolence. It is like the surge of goodwill in the hearts of a walled community that now wants to look beyond and make everyone have as good a life as 'ours'. Consider what Bhabha has to say about Nussbaum (1996: 200–201, emphasis added):

> *The task of the citizen of the world, she writes, lies in making human beings more like our 'fellow city dwellers'*, basing our deliberations on 'that interlocking commonality'. In her attempt to avoid nationalist or patriotic

> sovereignty, Nussbaum embraces a 'universalism' that is profoundly provincial. Provincial, in a specific, early imperial sense. Nussbaum too readily assumes the 'givenness' of commonalities that centres on a particular image of the 'empathetic' 'self' – as the Satrap of a belated liberal benevolence – as it generates its 'cosmopolitan' concentric circles, of equal measure and comparable worth.

The task is to make human beings more like 'our fellow city dwellers'. The whole world outside Nussbaum's fellow city dwellers has to be remade in the image of the people in Nussbaum's neighbourhood. You may think that this is too severe a critique. After all, all she really wants is to think about other people's betterment. But the point is precisely this. In the attempts to make the whole of humankind more like 'our fellow city dwellers', there is a picture implied of there being no connection between the well-being of our fellow city dwellers and destitution elsewhere. Universalism, when it is most needed, always falls short.

Linking this issue with the wider question of development, anywhere one turns, one sees 'them' being urged to 'develop' following 'our' example (for critiques, see Escobar 1995; Rahnema and Bawtree 1997; Levine 2001; Rist 2002; Bergeron 2005). Moreover, the specific approaches to development such as microcredit, while seeming to be 'self-help', can also as a gendered governmental strategy constitute forms of subjectivity to service neoliberalism.[4] Such benevolent cosmopolitan universalism underplays the links between 'our' development and 'their' destitution in history. History is seen as a chronological story of what is now 'over'. Now, we can help them to learn from our example.[5]

Following my discussion in Chapter 3, despite wanting to insert considerations of humanity or history or culture, the debates in modernist knowledge remain limited. Similarly, a cosmopolitan universalism which is based upon the concentric architecture of identity also remains securely within the unquestioned privileges of 'having' an identity which can then be encouraged elsewhere.

In other words, *the universalist and cosmopolitan contestation of the narrowly self-interested and discrete identity by inserting the concentric circles of affiliative concern remains profoundly limited by its inability to question the grounds of its own benevolent translation*. As with modernist knowledge, so with universalist social science.

4 Rankin (2001) gives the example of the construction of 'rational economic woman' in line with consolidating the neoliberal logic through a very contested transformation of political rationality in Nepal. 'When poor women are constructed as responsible clients in this way, the onus for development falls squarely on their shoulders, and their citizenship manifests not through entitlement but through the "free" exercise of individual choice' (Miller and Rose in ibid.: 29). For a review of feminist post-development thought, see Kaul (2004c). See also Spivak (2000).

5 So that continuing and exploitative neocolonial linkages are seen as rectifiable errors. If only the corporations would say 'let's see how I could protect the lives of children here, let's see how I can help to increase literacy in this country where I'm doing business, let's see how I can help to advance ecology' (Nussbaum in 'Globally Speaking' 2002).

Finally, could we ask who exactly is it that dwells in the comfortable and warm benevolent ideal of Nussbaum's 'our fellow city dwellers'? I will let Bhabha ask this question (1996: 201):

> But who are our 'fellow city dwellers' in the global sense? The 18 or 19 million refugees who lead their unhomely lives in borrowed and barricaded dwellings? The 100 million migrants, of whom over half are women fleeing poverty and forming part of an invisible, illegal workforce? The 20 million who have fled health and ecological disasters?

So that (ibid., emphases added),

> [t]hese 'extreme' conditions – or awkward questions – do not stand at the limits of the cosmopolitan ideal. It has been one of the *tensions internal* to Enlightenment and post-Enlightenment cosmopolitanism . . . – *to attempt to grasp unity of mankind without working through the relation of the part to the whole.*[. . .] In Nussbaum's argument such a tension becomes emphasised as *a certain liminality in the identity or subject of cosmopolitan process*. It is a subject peculiarly free of the complex 'affect' that makes possible social identification and affiliation.

For a moment, let us use Nussbaum as an anchor to throw back a line to my argument through the book. The epistemology of the European Enlightenment was a fabric of tensions which structured compromises in the way the purpose of theory was understood. Knowledge fashioned in this modernist rendition was never really contested since the Other functioned as a kind of limit phenomenon. Such a fixing of difference is extremely political, but this is not acknowledged within the narrow ambit of identity politics where identity precedes politics. Economics as a modernist enlightenment scientism *par excellence* is a star in this constellation to the point where its construction of the economic often goes unquestioned and, at best, attempts to extend self-interest to affiliative concerns of cosmopolitan universalism also exhibit the same inability to break out of the mirror of the Same.

Like the Victorian race debates I discussed before, the 'debate' over identity becomes – can they be made to be like 'us'[6] or should we not care since everyone has an adequate dose of universal Reason, and that we should be concerned about the moral economy for 'our society' (on moral economy, see Sayer 1999). Thinking of identity along these lines is the concentric enterprise where the centre is never questioned or politicised. That the centre – the identity that fixes difference as 'difference from': 'deviation' or 'additional interest' – needs to be questioned and politicised is ethically imperative.

6 Nussbaum's answer is a Yes. She even draws up a 'list' of human capabilities which has to be implemented everywhere. I will discuss this soon.

On a BBC (UK) radio programme ('Start the Week' 2002), the discussion about refugees and asylum-seekers took the following familiar form: too many of them come here, they are usually involved in thefts, 'good honest tax-paying' English people feel that they are being taken for a ride, how can we distinguish between the economic migrants and the political refugees, should the latter be holding a sign to say that they are political refugees, so treat them kind? The one person in the group who attempted to argue against treating people like they were just a flood of numbers was subjected to this retort from Jeremy Paxman (a well-known UK media person), 'but, they are not people, they are thousands of people, aren't they?' and the discussion moved to whether the United Kingdom was now 'full', to which the one person objecting answered, 'no, we are not full yet'.[7]

An identity which never questions the basis of its own ground, is one which can only fix difference as the Other which functions as a limit phenomenon. National identities are by definition of this form and also have the 'economic' as an important element to them. In juxtaposing identity and the economic, as I will argue later, we have the opportunity to connect value and values and question the very basis of constructing knowledge which takes the individual or the nation-state or the economy as the system existing 'out there' already performed. These are not simply 'academic' questions. Questions of knowledge are also questions of social order (cf. Shapin and Schaffer 1989), and knowledge creation is always already a form of ethics, politics, strategy, subjectivity, Reason, and being.

6.2.1.2 The final list of good things

Sen's capabilities approach is an attempt to demonstrate the limited usefulness of income as an indicator of well-being by adopting the notion of the 'capability' to designate a space within which comparisons of quality of life can be usefully made, and concerns of social inequality raised. This is a theoretical framework designed to highlight concerns about the actual level of functioning that people achieve. Sen does not further provide the list of good things which should be applied to all people always and everywhere.

This is what Nussbaum undertakes to do in her cosmopolitan universalism. She wishes to 'articulate an account of how capabilities, together with the idea of a

7 Contrast this with statistics from the period that showed refugees (and asylum-seekers) made a net contribution of approximately £2.6 billion to the UK economy, ten times more than they 'took out' (Refugee Council 2001). This figure does not take into account their contribution to society. While newspapers such as the *Daily Telegraph* (19 February 2001) talked of United Kingdom as the 'number one destination for asylum-seekers', in terms of number of refugees to total GDP in the year preceding the radio programme, UK ranked 78th in the world, and 6th in Europe (Refugee Council 2001). Further, if 'good honest tax-paying' people either cannot be bothered about democracy, or feel that they are unable to stop their governments from bombing and wrecking elsewhere every now and then – then they should recognise that everyone is a common victim of the democratic system which does not represent. Finally, this, if not anything else, should be a way of taking the blinders off nation-state ideology.

threshold level of capabilities, can provide the basis for central constitutional principles that citizens have the right to demand from their governments' (2000: 12). Menon (2002) provides a rigorous critique of this enterprise for its inability to move beyond its own origin. So that, '[w]hat is deeply puzzling is Nussbaum's calm assumption that she has arrived at the final list of good things no good person could possibly *not* want for everyone' (157, emphasis original). Nussbaum's identification of a list of central human capabilities is an attempt to achieve 'a strong universalism committed to cross cultural norms of justice' that is simultaneously 'sensitive to local particularity' (153). Sounds good.

The difficulty with this strong universalism, as Menon points out, is that it is 'just too strong', and 'local particularities' within this account can only be seen as 'tradition'. We are back to the familiar tradition versus modernity debate, in a nuanced form.[8]

The critique that Menon provides is as follows. First, in Nussbaum's account, an overwhelming role is envisaged for the state, so that human condition can be transcended by way of constitutional mechanisms. While individuals are free, the choices of children cannot be taken into account, neither can those of adults 'who do not have full moral powers' (154). The state is justified to take decisions on building codes, food, medicine, and environmental contaminants, because of 'the difficulty of making informed choices... and the burden of inquiry such choices would impose on citizens' (ibid.). The interest of the nation-state is always conflated with the interests of the 'we'. What if the nation-state itself suppresses sections of its population, and more generally does not permit the thinking of its own contingent structurality?[9]

Second, Nussbaum sees the list of capabilities as simply political goals, free of any metaphysical grounding. But this ignores that the idea of the individual as the basis for identity is itself a situated one. Consider (156, emphasis added),

> [t]his notion of individuals recognized and valued as separate persons is itself a modern conception available to the Judaeo-Christian tradition. ... The core idea of modern democracy as it evolved in the West is that *'I' am this body and that my 'self' stops at the boundaries of my skin*. Although this seems an entirely natural identification to the modern mind, it is, as we know, only about four hundred years old and has specific cultural moorings in the experience of the West. In non-Western societies this notion of the individual, separate from all other individuals, as the unit of society, is still not an uncontested one.

8 Bear in mind that *not all* local particularities get translated as tradition. Usually the characterisation goes thus – in the West, one speaks of there being a 'difference' in views; however, in the 'Orient', there is 'tradition' from within and there is 'modernity' from outside. So that there is little scope for agency on the part of the Others.

9 One should remember that more people have been killed in history by the ideology of the nation-state than by anything else ever, including religion. The *fundamentalism of the nation-state* is pernicious beyond belief, almost the unthought.

Liberal individualism, Menon rightly points out, 'never became the uncontested core of anti-imperialist struggles for democracy…and there remained always a tension between the individual and the community' (156). With reference to Nussbaum (ibid.),

> [t]he point is not that we have failed the test of meeting the standards set by Western liberal democracies. …The point is, rather, that democracy has travelled a long way and taken many shapes, often unrecognizable in terms of the criteria set by the original Western experience, and the dilemmas that arise escape easy characterization into the tradition/modernity dichotomy.

All of this links up with my argument about the politics of identity – that the individual or the state is not the uncontested starting point of politics. That it is not only some identities which have to be placed within question marks and understood as different, but *all* identities, identity itself, the having of which needs to be politicised. This will not give us a formula or a list or an equation whose 'economic' aspect can then be analysed by plugging it in. As Butler argues (2000a), these very terms of signification have to be rethought genealogically. Or even to recall Spanos (2001), we need *reconstellated genealogies* that are *not seen as a prelude* to doing something, but are in themselves a *'redoing' by rethinking of the terms of knowledge*.

The inadequacy of cosmopolitan universalist terms of concentric identity is evident from the narrowly universal*ised* elements of Nussbaum's list, which can only see one kind of state – modern secular liberal democratic capitalist constitutional[10] – 'as if it were self-evident and the only one possible' (Menon 2002: 157). This benign state is allowed to have laws of 'general applicability' which include 'mandatory military service'. Nussbaum assumes that '*the state has legitimate monopoly over coercion*', as is evident from her statements like, '[w]e want them [the soldiers] to obey a lot of time, but not all of the time' (158, emphasis original). Just like the questions I raised earlier, Menon asks Nussbaum, 'We do? Who *is* this we…?' (158).

But, all 'we's' leave their clues…

Recall my earlier example: Todorov (1985: 249) wrote, 'We want equality without its compelling to accept identity, but also difference without its degenerating into superiority/inferiority.' My addendum to this in differentiating the notion of the politics of identity is this – who poses this demand to whom?

Now, in order to finally dispel any doubts about who Nussbaum's 'we' are, consider the following (Menon 2002: 164, emphasis added): 'The universalism

10 The issue of the natures of democracy is important because, as Kaviraj (cited in Menon 2002: 156) points out, in many countries of Asia and Africa democracy entered before the notion of the individual was rooted (unlike the West, where democracy followed individualism). See Bradley (2005) for a convincing argument that non-Western (especially African) conceptions of democracy require a reappraisal of democracy itself as a form of governance.

espoused by Nussbaum includes the idea that nations which have adopted this account of human capabilities should "commend this norm strongly to other nations", *using whenever necessary "economic and other strategies to secure compliance"* '. The 'we' that can use 'economic and other strategies' is the West, like Nussbaum's 'fellow city dwellers'. In championing such cosmopolitan universalism, one need not ever remember the continual exercise of power which affords the claiming of an identity prior to its politicisation.

6.2.2 The ability to speak in translation, or, translational politics of identity

In contrast to the earlier section, I propose that we think of identity translationally. Let me explain. In Chapter 4, I had argued that by adopting the politics of identity, we can see identity as a construction within knowledge producing texts and this can give us the resources to loosen the conventional link between subjects and knowledge. So far we have seen how the identity of subjects in relation to knowledge is either based upon – the universal Cartesian subject which functions as an abstract individual and anchors universalist (and also often formalist) knowledge in its own image, where politics is the effect of shared interests – or, collective subject positions relying on commonalities of experience which have to be consciously achieved and which provide situated and perspectival knowledge, where politics is the result of shared collective subject positions. Giving up the stability of the Cartesian I and the essentialist subject positions, we need to move beyond thinking that is restricted in terms of obtaining an epistemological formula which designates a mapping between fixed and coherent subjects or subject positions and knowledge.

Identities are constructed and political, their comprehension as stable can only be at the cost of submerging their contingencies and exclusions. The constant translation between identities that enables the negotiations of difference is also an ethical project which functions to constantly *other* oneself experientially, as well as to *other* knowledge in the way that it fixes subjects. Thus, the politics of identity is a method of interrogating any coherence for the processual ways in which that coherence is manufactured in the face of difference (how identity *fixes* difference). This interrogation of texts and discourses for their power-laden constructions of identity categorisations is made possible by adopting the ethics of translation. The ethical stance of translation is what makes it possible to see what is at stake in the constructions that we then want to deconstruct. As we have seen, the concentric architecture of identity has severe limitations in its inability to question the grounds of its own situatedness. This questioning of starting points and the politicisation of identity itself becomes feasible when we give up the comforting sanity of the coherent I in any identity. Then theorisation also is not just about looking out from where we are, but a moving between multiple accounts which makes likely the recognition of the way in which categories are constructed out of difference.

So, the exhortation is to think of identity (conceptual and/or experiential) as something which is constituted in encounters, in translation. This is imperative because *identity is a political living and its continual translations should be understood as its contested experiencing.* A translation is the *experience of attempting to understand that which is different.* To begin with, let us consider 'attempting to understand'. Difference, when it is not seen as 'different from', is the always already condition of having an experience of identity. The attempt to understand should not be seen as assimilation of terms or an explanation of the unfamiliar in terms of the familiar (in line with the Enlightenment tensions of creating knowledge). Rather, it is the gesture of constituting *identity itself* through the experience of attempting to understand difference.

The principle behind modern constitutional liberal democratic individualist capitalist secular imperial polities of the nation states is thinking of identity as the basis for difference. As administrative and embedding structures of modernity, they are intimately linked to the modernist rendition of knowledge which does not allow any serious questioning of the structurality of the structure (continually attempting to exorcise its own disjointedness).

We are presented with the map of the world, and the moral economy or values are to be worked out within each basic unit of this map. Nussbaum's suggestion that each of these units adopt the list of good things which can then be administered by the state everywhere, was problematic for two main reasons. First, it was unable to give up the appeal of universalist knowledge, so that rather than emancipation being a continual and multiple 'working out' from within the contexts (which need not be limited by the nation states), it became the idea of imposing the list of good things from above in a top-down way. And second, Nussbaum, while seeming at one level to challenge an account such as that of Smith, does not move beyond the list of good things that good people can arrive at in a good city, i.e., us. Why could somebody possibly want anything else? And, even more importantly, if they did, it must be 'tradition'. Against this, I would agree with Menon, who writes, '[a]nd every "context" is by now inescapably modern – what we have to deal with is not "tradition" opposing modernity, but *alternative modernities in context*' (2002: 164, emphasis added). So that, ' "sensitivity to context" if it is to be more than a formula used to disguise universalism, must rigorously engage with context and with ideas produced within that context, even if universalism fails to survive in the process'. This rigorous engagement with context is the beginning of the process to experience identity in translation, to continually *other* oneself.

Before proceeding, I should add one important clarification. Nothing that I have argued should be construed as saying that Nussbaum 'has no right' to speak about 'that which she is not'. This, in my view, is the problematic flip side of the universalist coin – we cannot say anything about something because it is not our issue. Or, how can we say something to them (any we, any them)?

This is an easy and unethical privilege. This is also related to my characterisation of the difference between identity politics and the politics of identity – it is not about not being able to say anything, or uncritically start from what one is and build bridges with what one is not; but rather, it is about an ethical involvement in the knowledge production process which is willing to take chances, to *other* oneself through the experience of the encounter in which one is translated, and only through which one can experience identity 'translationally'. To begin with, this requires becoming a stranger to oneself. Said (1999: 295) articulates the predicament of his identity,

> I occasionally experience myself as a cluster of flowing currents. I prefer this to the idea of a solid self, the identity to which so many attach so much significance. These currents, like the themes of one's own life, flow along during the waking hours, and at their best, they require no reconciling, no harmonizing. They are 'off' and maybe out of place, but at least they are always in motion, in time, in place, in the form of all kinds of strange combinations moving about, not necessarily forward, sometimes against each other, contrapuntally yet without one central theme.

In this process of seeing identity as a contingent translation, the domain of responsibility becomes infinite.

Young asks Spivak to answer a similar concern to the one raised earlier. He asks, 'If you participate you are, as it were, an Orientalist, but of course if you don't, then you're a eurocentrist ignoring the problem.' She replies (1991: 227, emphases added unless otherwise mentioned),

> It's not just that if you participate you are an Orientalist. *If you participate in a certain kind of way* you are an Orientalist and it doesn't matter whether you are white or black. Today you don't need to have the right kind of skin colour in order to be an Orientalist.

And further,

> [l]isten, if you do it after so much homework, not just of information-gathering but learning, not just knowing – that is a difference between learning and knowing. ... If you do it in such a way that we can really talk to you, then there is no problem. But if you can just talk about doing it in this nice superficial way so that people can say you are *also interested in the Third World*, then you will get nothing. It is not *easier* [emphasis original] to do than other kinds of work. That is something that is very important because this is completely different from a chromatist argument – you have to be the right colour, a nativist argument, you have to be from the place – it just says either you do it as carefully as you do your own work or don't do it. ... *You can't just be a revolutionary tourist and be the Saviour of the world on your off days*. This is the message, as I say: you can be a new Orientalist and be one of those.

The involvement in knowledge creation is one which recognises that (to repeat) knowledge creation is always already a form of ethics, politics, strategy, subjectivity, Reason, and being.

In the case of the cosmopolitan universalism discussed earlier, Nussbaum's engagement with the context falls exceedingly short when she discusses women's rights in India. She does not engage with positions within the Indian women's movement that 'have largely moved away from seeking state initiatives for reform' (Menon 2002: 160). Similarly, Nussbaum conducts a debate with liberal individualist arguments to protect the family from state intervention, when in India these arguments would be 'communitarian, conservative and religion inspired' (ibid.: 162). The result, as Menon points out, is shadow boxing between Nussbaum and Rawls about the 'possible "tragedy" of banning dowry – the loss of "the liberty to give dowry"'. Adds Menon, '[n]obody in India defends dowry on that ground' (163).

Thus, when I wrote, a translation is the *experience of attempting to understand that which is different*: 'that which is different' – is not simply an Other which is the limit phenomenon for the self, but that which is different – is also 'one-self'. One cannot start from any unquestioned identity and then translate everything else into the language of the self. Rather, one can only experience a constantly *translated sense of identity through encounters with 'that which is different', everything.*

The position from which the subject speaks is crafted in presence of the present, but this speaking is always translational, always in memory. Bhabha quotes Rich (1996: 201), '...I'm a table set with room for the Stranger...' and '...I can't be still I'm here...'. In this *Atlas of a Difficult World* by Rich, there is a constant repetition of I'm..., I'm..., with different geopolitical locations. The idea is this. The subject here is *not* a coherent self-assured entity clearly defined by its body and its own historical narrative, which is the kind of subject that one encounters in modernist disciplinary knowledge of sociality.

For the coherent and concentric subject, the lines of identity are clearly drawn *at the I and at the eye.* Identity is the I that speaks *and appears* to speak. The I and the eye are closely interlinked. Akerlof and Kranton write (2000: 726, emphases added):

> Identity 'choice,' however is very often limited. In a society with racial and ethnic categories, for example, those with *non distinguishing physical features may be able to 'pass'* as a member of another group. But others will be constrained by their *appearance, voice, or accent.*

Similarly, Sen writes (1999: 16, emphasis added), '[t]he real options we have about our identity are *always limited by our looks, our circumstances, and our background and history.*'

Contrast this coherent and concentric subject with the translational subject of Rich.[11] Bhabha writes (1996: 202–203, emphasis added):

> The subject of 'unsatisfaction'...keeps setting new, disjunctive scenes of repetition for the recognition, perhaps misrecognition, of the speaking 'I'.

11 For more on the poetry of identity, see Harrell (2005).

> *It is both a situational form of ethical-political discourse, and a kind of identity or identification that, in its iterative field of address . . . attenuates the sovereignty of a 'representative' human or world-subject authorised in its mastery of events.*

Bear in mind that this is not the same as McCloskey's many identities ('feminist postmodern neoclassical free market economist'). Bhabha cautions that this is not a 'postmodern soufflé of identity' or 'naive and benevolent pluralism' which is equally visible from everywhere, but that this 'translation-as-transformation' is an insistence upon grasping that *the 'human' is what is always in need of translation*, rather than something which can be assumed as given under the grand and abstract sign of Humanity.

The translational architecture of identity draws attention to the continuous process of translation in the experiencing of identity. This is at work not only in the identities of those with 'non distinguishing physical features' (see Akerlof and Kranton earlier), but at work in *identity itself*. In this situational ethical-political discourse, can exist the resources for thinking the very structurality of structures and structures of knowledge. This rethinking does not take the form of a transposition of terms from discipline to discipline, self to self, state to state, but involves, a *translation arising in context*. A calling to mind, a re-calling, what I have termed elsewhere as a postcolonial re-membering.

In all of this, the I is unsatisfactory. Rather than the I grounding the is-ness of everything else, it is the is-ness of the I that remains ungrounded. As Heidegger formulated it – the I is 'a non-committal formal indicator' (in Solomon 1988: 163). Repeatedly, the generality and authority of the I have to be sieved through its re-visioning.

Further, as Bhabha points out, this space of unsatisfaction is not simply a state of denial. 'It is the need to work through the problem of memory in reconstructing a "sign" of history that *may not provide a causal or deterministic narrative*' (1996: 204, emphasis original). The *human is in translation* and the *subject is in process*, and knowledge will simply have to do in these terms. Just as 'anything goes' is less a manifesto of nihilism and more a credo of resistance (this is discussed previously in Chapter 5), similarly, the postcolonial re-membering enacted in the politics of translational identity is an attempt to translate knowledge less as a collection and more as *a transformation*.

Consider Gilbert's (2001) argument that we can employ Bhabha's conceptualisation of sociality as interstitial in order to think 'out' the concepts nation-state and the individual. The modernist characterisation of the individual and the nation-state relies upon – 'the ideal of *nationality as centralised homogeneity* and the assumption of *individuality as radically prior to all sociality*' (ibid.: 98, emphases added). Attempts to imagine translational politics of identity will need to 'break with that logic of the subject which sees it as a definitive and basic category of human experience, social or in-dividual' (99). In other words, in terms of a translational architecture, there is no 'I' of the self at the centre of identity; instead, there is a fixing of difference that takes on a complexity which is not open to easy spatio-temporal determination or assimilation. Sociality can then be conceptualised as interstitiality so that the social and the subject are 'each the limit/product of the other' (101). One might raise the question that if the subject of identity is unsatisfactory as the basis of experience as well as of sociality, and is in need of displacement, then how can we speak about agency or politics? A way of addressing this anxiety is to consider how a translational politics of identity differs from both the abstract universal subject and the collective subject positions in relation to knowledge. Rather than assume an easy clasping of the relation between subjects and knowledge which gives authority to the identity of the I in the way that it fixes difference, in translational terms, it is the subject effects that are of significance.

> [*S*]*ubject effects* are produced at the co-inciding points where discursive structures at once fail to constitute themselves as absolute totalities and are interrupted by other such structures, points of both overdetermination and underdetermination. ... Agency, subjectivity, are the interference patterns, [...] produced in this space of radical over/under-determination (ibid.: 106, emphasis original).

There is a further question of the kinds of struggles made possible by thinking of identity in translational terms, and the relation of these struggles to knowledge which is not anchored by stable coherent and satisfactory subjects. The possibility of occupying several different subject positions at the intersection of different discourses and in relation to different issues renders open the possibility of comprehending knowledge in less totalitarian and more contextual ways. As Haraway (1988: 587) writes, '[p]ositioning implies responsibility for our enabling practices', and can be the site for operationalising interstitial sociality. This requires building solidarities in the face of difference. Translation opens up the possibility of ethical struggles which are in-between, in the middle.[12] The identities in translation are not those of satisfactory individuals or communities; the identities

12 Consider the formulation of the 'middle' provided by Deleuze and Guattari (in Gilbert 2001: 106, emphases original [1988: 25]):

> The middle is by no means an average; on the contrary, it is where things pick up speed. *Between* things does not designate a localizable relation from one thing to the other and back again, but a perpendicular direction, a transversal moment that sweeps one *and* the other away, a stream without beginning or end that undermines its banks and picks up speed in the middle.

This can be compared with a formulation of the 'middle ground' offered by Code (1991: 322):

> The middle ground is located within experiences, histories, social structures, material circumstances. Its occupants are committed to examining the resources and contradictions these experiences and circumstances yield. Its openness is a source of power in which the productiveness of an ambiguity that refuses closure can be realised.

in translation are always already unsatisfactory, mobile, and perpetual. The struggle is one of ethical recognition through mediated encounters which are never simple or one's own. One way of thinking this is to deploy Katz's (2001: 1230) idea of translocal 'countertopographies that link different places analytically and thereby enhance struggles in the name of common interests'. But, as Larner (1995: 187) points out, this should lead us to asking the question not simply 'what is the epistemological basis for theory?' but rather, 'what kinds of struggle does it make possible?' The answers to this question will be determined through an ongoing and highly politicised process of engagement in which there are continuous and multiple contestations. And this is the way in which one can forge a relation between situated knowledges and a translational mode of identity. That is, simply acknowledging multiple subject positions with partial perspectives is not enough, for, as Spivak (1999: 183) cautions, 'there can be no politics founded on a continuous overdetermined multiplicity of agencies.' The politics of overdetermination is an aporia, and a translational mode of identity is required in order to contextuate the ethics of political engagements. In other words, one does not begin from an I that in a context X chooses the political commitment A, but rather that any and every I experiences its I-ness only in its translation through an undifferentiated continuum of contextual politics.

Further, it is important to note that no instrumental analysis of emancipatory engagement will be adequate. It is at the end an ethical and unquantifiable commitment which cannot be deemed a universal epistemic value for evaluation of theories. One has to do what one can as much as possible in the way that Cixous said, 'maximally . . . the feminist woman becomes part of every struggle, *in a certain way*' (in Spivak 1999: 176, emphasis original).

An example of ethics which rely upon encountering Others is available in Ahmed (2002), where she argues that feminist ethics is not simply for 'the other' or the 'not yet', but involves responding to particular others (where particularity is a mode of encounter), so that we 'face and face up to "other others"'. She imagines this as the basis for collective politics where collectivity is the collecting together *without* a common ground (as I asserted before, *in the face of difference*). Ahmed admits that such a project cannot avoid some agenda-setting, but if these agendas are set reflexively, are open-ended, and involve responsibility and commitment, then collective forms of struggles can be enabled. Discussing Spivak, she writes that, 'encounters based on a proximity that does not allow merger, benevolence or knowledge (in other words, that does not over-come distance or difference) involve work: they involve "painstaking labour"'. The politics of encountering necessitates dialogue as a way of feeling difference. The intimacy of the dialogue involves engagements which are both singular and collective (as Ahmed puts it, '*"this other" brings with her other others*'), it involves a facing of difference which allows difference to matter – which allows the encounter itself to be different because of the difference. The im/possibility of an ethics of translation (following Spivak) at once frames the encounters, and makes it inevitable that they happen. Such a rethinking of difference, knowledge, and politics has many resonances. Consider (Ahmed 2002, last emphasis original):

> Indeed, my focus on the particularity of encounters (and with it, of the relationship between the past, present and future within ethics), also suggests an intimacy between *questions of political economy* (of how the world is organised through the regulation of work, bodies and spaces) and *questions of ethics* (of ways of encountering others that are *better*).

I will explore later some of these transpositions in the context of the economic.

Heidegger writes (1968: 11): 'Memory is the gathering and convergence of thought upon what everywhere demands to be thought first of all. Memory is the gathering of recollection, thinking back.' I have argued that the concepts which are most familiar – identity, economic – require the most memory.

6.3 Identity : economic :: culture : economy[13]

6.3.1 Questioning the framing

> The content of economics is supposedly directed by the economy. ... I would not wish to deny an influence of the economy upon economics but this relationship is complex, indirect and even perverse.
>
> (Fine 1999: 407)

I do not believe that identity is something which can dress up and work around the category 'economic' without affecting it – identity, politics, and difference will need to be acknowledged. This effort will give rise to neither a formula nor a universal blueprint. Identity and economics should not be reserved for consideration only in the debates around globalisation, especially since these debates are not engaged at all in mainstream economics or in economic theory. We cannot begin from the economic as a hardcore category and consider identity as a rather frivolous add-on. In contrast to this, I am arguing for the need to juxtapose considerations of identity and the economic in a different way so that identity itself becomes politicised as the basis for knowledge. This is also a way in which the disciplinary construction and the practical application of the category of the economic is interrogated. The ultimate aim is to be able to perceive the link between the preservation of structures and structures of knowledge, and to be able to think the violence of knowledge. That is, not only are the terms of identity and economic politicised and contextualised, but the very separation and validity of these terms is questioned.

I will begin by first pointing out that the separation between identity and economic issues is only available to us because culture and economy are seen as

13 I have written this framing to designate the following – identity is to the economic as culture is to economy (A : B :: C : D).

separate and separable spheres. There is a slippage between the three terms: economy, economic, and economics. Contrary to general perception, there is *no straightforward way of linking these terms* and a memory of the difference between them is essential in order to write theories of the economic in different ways. Next, I will make a case for reconnecting the notions of 'value' and 'values'. The endeavour of economics requires the fixing of value through some assumed invariance which is usually a metaphor of nature or society. I will argue that this fixing of value is open to question by reading a nineteenth-century interrogation (by Samuel Bailey 1825) of value as fixed by political economists. This will facilitate my claim that *rationality and the economic are not separate considerations, but that there is no way of being 'irrational' without being also 'uneconomic'*. The fixing of value in translation thus actually fixes values. Finally, I will assess a recent argument for bringing together the realms of culture and economy in terms of 'moral economy'. Like Nussbaum's cosmopolitan liberalism, ultimately the notion of moral economy also needs further working out by critically linking up the operation and appeal of 'economic logic' with the 'logic of economic theories' as they exist in economics.

It seems to be a common enough belief that identity is a cultural issue, and the category of the economic influences cultural issues (via the market, for instance) but does not interact with them.[14] That the culture and economy are separate spheres occasionally (or always, depending which account one takes) traversed by the commonality of 'the market', but remain otherwise alien except along certain determinist lines. Mostly, *identity belongs to culture and the economic belongs to economy*. And since *culture and economy are separate*, there is *no reason to connect identity with the economic*. Also, any attempted linkages between these terms cannot escape the obvious fact that the *sphere of the economic has its own particular logic*. In what ensues, I am going to question everything placed in italics in this paragraph.

The separation of spheres of the 'cultural' and the 'economic' can be examined in the following ways. First, it is important to realise the extent and resilience of this separation. It pervades popular culture, academia, disciplines, and epistemology. It is not that the separation is so obvious that, at any and every level of human

14 If it was *not* believed that the economic only influences but does not interact with cultural issues, then we would find analyses not simply of 'the market', but also excavations of the theoretical basis of the market. For example, if the 'free' market is conventionally seen as the most desirable 'means of expressing consensus on economic interests' (Grampp 1951: 149), why isn't its political correlate ever recommended? Grampp puzzles that '[p]olitical anarchy has rarely suggested itself as the complement of a free market,' when the usual arguments about some people not being capable of self-restraint, their failings will be exploited by the strong, that every person has moments of errancy, would 'apply with an almost equal force to the free market also' (ibid.). He finds the reasons for this to be obscure, speculating some inherent difference in the nature and quantifiability of political and economic values. I would argue that there is not much obscurity here, for the consensus around the free market is not a call for an actual 'free market' (none such can exist), it is an illusion, a performative fiction that enables a rationale for limiting progressive or other intervention.

experience, it is bound to be recognised and enforced. Contrary to this, I would argue that it is the assumed belief in the separation of the cultural and the economic which allows popular culture, academia, disciplines, and epistemology to be distinguished from each other. In other words, the separation of the cultural and the economic (see McDowell 2000) plays an important part in structuring what counts as what kind of knowledge and how we get access to it. Thus, in addressing the separation it is crucial to consider what this separation allows in terms of knowledge and access to it. It allows the modernist rendition of knowledge to function; where the structure of knowledge has many windows, some allow access to the cultural, and others to the economic. Further, in light of my arguments in Chapter 3, it might be assumed that the windows allowing access to the economic are situated somewhere in the 'tower of science'. In actively resisting this characterisation and separation, one is questioning the modernist rendition of knowledge which does not allow the spheres of culture and economy to be seen as artificially separated, and consequently does not allow them to be identified as only contingent and in context.

Lee and LiPuma (2002) discuss how the category of culture seems to be playing catchup to the economic processes that go beyond it. They write that economics as a discipline owes its present appeal partly to the sense that it has grasped that it is dynamics of circulation that are driving globalisation – and thereby challenging traditional notions of language, culture, and nation. Thus, there is a bifurcation between *performativity* on the one hand and *circulation and exchange* on the other. While the former is seen as a quintessentially cultural phenomenon tied to the creation of meaning, the latter is seen simply as processes which transmit meanings, but are not constitutive acts in themselves. As a result, in order to develop a cultural account of economic processes, we need to rethink circulation as a cultural phenomenon (what the authors term 'cultures of circulation') with its own 'forms of abstraction, evaluation and constraint' (ibid.: 192). In this endeavour, I would argue, the importance of deconstructing economic theory is crucial. For instance, we can point out how not only is circulation seen as mere transmission without any cultural constitution, but that the economic theory (discipline of economics) which claims to provide an account of that circulation also studiously avoids areas 'where meaning is itself a socially constructed object of scrutiny' (Fine 1999: 419), which includes consumption, globalisation, and so on. In this way, the connections between the logic of economic theories and the economic logic can be traced to destabilise the separation of identity and the economic, culture and economy.

To recall the conventional view: identity belongs to culture, and the economic belongs to economy. My second point relates to a discussion bearing on this. In examining the category economic, one cannot emphasise enough the following. There is an enormous slippage that occurs between the three terms *economics – economy – economic*. This is a slippage which is unparalleled in any analogous terminology (consider, for instance, variations of the social or cultural or moral or political). There is, it almost seems, no sufficient reference to adequately designate the meanings conveyed by these three terms. This seems to me to be an important part of the matter.

Let us begin with (the) economy. The term carries connotations of careful and prudent management in the sense of avoiding excess,[15] and also the contemporary sense of a pre-existing structure out there which can be represented as the statistical summaries of indicators of production and exchange, and as in the wider sense of the bigger construct standing in for manufacturing and services and agriculture going on within national borders or international aggregates.[16]

The category economic is somewhat more metaphysical, carrying ultimate connotations of value (see Meikle 2000).[17] Value itself sits uncomfortably between and across the economic and cultural. I will shortly return to this.

15 See Macfie (1949) on the first question of economy [as in economising]: what, then, is this economizing? 'If it is something between a mere means, a technique, and an experience valuable in itself, just what is it?' (19), concluding that 'economy is more like a value experience than anything else' (33). Further thought is invited by his discussions of 'economizing' and 'being efficient', such that in real life 'our constant knowledge of the need to economize and our wish to be efficient continuously modify the systems of our desires generally' (31). Writing in an ethical vocabulary at a time when the content of these supposedly self-evident terms (economy [economising], efficiency) was still being worked out, he makes for a very interesting reading:

> Thus, economy means something unique in each of the medieval moral and political systems; something unique in free Victorian enterprise; something unique in the Orient as against the West; something unique in the public utility compared with nationalized industry or co-operative; or in a gold rush or the fine arts (33).

This subjective presentation of economy (or economising, which is the sense meant here, for example, to practise economy) as being affected by larger-value contexts is in line with Macfie's idea that generalisations cannot finally define a value. See my discussion of value and values later in this chapter.

16 Maljoo (2002) summarises Mitchell on the modern idea of the economy which is a construct of the middle third of the twentieth century. In 1920s the *Palgrave Dictionary of Political Economy* contained no separate entry for or definition of the term 'economy'. 'The economy came into being between the 1930s and the 1950s as the field of operation for novel powers of planning, regulation, statistical enumeration and representation. Through these forms of political rationality and practice it became possible to imagine the economy as a self-contained sphere, distinct from the social, the cultural, and other spheres.' See Mitchell (2002), also Scott (1999: 46–47). For a critical tracing of the links between the 'economy' and development, see Bergeron (2005).

17 As Meikle (2000) points out, the old Aristotelian distinction between the kinds of chrêmatiskê (art of acquisition) is lost in modernist thought: 'chrêmatistikê is often translated nowadays in ways that blur the very distinction Aristotle is drawing between the two arts of wealth – getting wealth as useful things and getting wealth as money' (268). He gives the examples of Rackham (1926), who translates it as 'business', and Carnes Lord (1984), who sees it as 'two forms of expertise in business'. 'Natural chrêmatiskê' (C-M-C' or exchanging commodities so that money is a means to getting useful things) is not distinguished from 'Unnatural chrêmatiskê' (M-C-M' which includes not only trade – kapêlikê – but any other activity when it is pursued for the sake of money, aims at getting money). Marx and then Keynes have famously looked at this distinction, and in Keynes's case thought that it did not matter very much, at least from the business point of view. Consider Meikle (ibid.: 257),

> Wealth is limited, as the means to any end are limited, and wealth is a set of means for the flourishing of the citizens. 'Limit' (*peras*) is an important idea in Aristotelian thought, and it is a serious matter for Aristotle that in the pursuit of wealth as money 'there is no limit to

Economics, finally, is a (Western modernist) discipline.[18] And what is more, it is a particular modernist rendition of knowledge, based on particular notions of explanation, and accommodating to changes in the general structure of knowing which were necessitated by enlightenment epistemology. When understood as political economy, it seemed to have to do with examining production, exchange, and distribution. This was somewhat connected to its earlier sense of examining the principles of the good life, and had resonance with the prudent management aspect of economy or economising. However, these considerations of the good life were always tied to the concerns of power, politics, and administration. It always involved an important role for representation, since the economy was always within the boundaries of the nation-state. How production, exchange, and distribution were understood, how these understandings were employed to organise work, reward, and leisure in practice, how would these practices be studied, collated, and perpetuated – all these are questions that make a mockery of the theory praxis divide. But, even more importantly, all of these questions were not settled as problems of knowledge but formed a crucial part of the problems of administration.

The mathematical formulation of these problems of administration as problems of pure knowledge, by adopting metaphors from physics from late nineteenth-century onwards, was an attempt *to make invisible the political and administrative function of knowledge in general* in the face of rescuing moral and epistemological legitimisation for the Western projects of imperialism proper. Since, now, it wasn't enough to discuss the problems of political economy in terms of administrative solutions to be worked out at the level of the nation-state. This enterprise would be helped if knowledge were codified, formulated, and interpreted in such a way as to obtain 'scientific principles' which could be applied in practice anywhere at any time.

The point in discussing the slippage between economy – economic – economics is this: *mostly, economics does not represent the economic, the economic does not lie in economy, economy is not the practice of economics*. Let me explain.

Economics is a Western European response to the problem of administration which rephrases it as a problem of knowledge (the conception of knowledge itself deriving from Enlightenment epistemology and its inflections). Economic is a fundamental metaphor which refers to value and can take on contextual meanings. The economy is not something studied by economics, but a construct for comprehension of administrative organisation in the society. The sense of economy as economising links up to the economic.

> the end it seeks.' True wealth consists in 'those goods . . . necessary for life and useful for the community of the city or household,' and they are limited to those needed to attain the ends of those communities.'

In the absence of such distinctions, 'market economy will always pass the test if it is judged by the accounts of human nature, human good, and wealth, offered by economics and its associated utilitarian philosophy' (258). On this, see also Roy (1992).

18 However, this does *not* mean that the non-West has not been seduced by economics.

And this might explain why attempts to define economics as science don't succeed very much.[19] Let me now return to the category economic. While it may sometimes be interpreted as that part of one's life which is involved in the economy, ultimately, the category economic carries within it the connotations of value and worth. It may seem obvious, but it is important to point out that the category economic is not parasitic upon economics. In fact, in its connotations of value, *the economic cuts across culture and economy*.

That is why the economic can be placed in conversation with identity, and unshackled from its narrow conceptualisations in economics. Therefore, I'm arguing that we need new ways of writing the economic which examine its construction and comprehension as an intrinsic part of the social,[20] rather than as a narrow logic of cost and benefit which derives from a particular historical and temporal interpretation of casting it as the outcome of translating problems of administration into problems of pure knowledge.

This immediately means two things. First, it means a constant endeavour to write the economic in different ways, linking it up with the politics of identity. And second, it is equally important to continue to point out the disjunction between economic and economics. This task is important since it will challenge the exclusive claim of economists upon the category of the narrow and universalised economic which itself is based upon claims to science, a model of individual choice, and a particular version of identity.

6.3.2 An example of value and values

Let me illustrate my arguments aforesaid with an example relating to the question of value and values. There is no general agreement on the basis of value amongst

19 Marshall defined economics as 'a study of mankind in the ordinary business of life'. Robbins defined economics as 'a science which studies human behaviour as a relationship between ends and scarce means that have alternative uses.' Viner is said to have defined it as 'economics is what economists do'. For a brief overview and cites, see Larkin (1996).

20 To take an example, Skinner (1999) considers the links between eighteenth-century sensibility and the economic. The traditionally supposed discursive or disciplinary separation between the kinds of stories that novels tell and the ones that are told by political economy does not bear up to analysis. In fact, the stories not only transgress, but often the sphere of sentimentalism is deeply involved in constructing the economic values and processes which are deemed apposite to it. Her analysis of several works over the last six decades of the century reveals how sentimental fiction can offer an *active critique of economic and political issues*. The twin discourses of sensibility and femininity in that period (but also generally) promoted 'economy' as a moral virtue as against the dangerous possibilities of 'excess'. Thus, while economy had to do with 'household management' (a woman running a home), it was also to do with frugality, discretion, and parsimony of desire. A woman could be 'economical' in many senses, especially as household Oeconomy was still her preserve which she had to manage in an economic manner, while political economy was essentially a masculine space. *Once we open the floodgates to the various meanings of the economy and the various ways in which they can be read and interpreted, then discourses of humanism and economics can no longer be disentangled with ease.* The utmost importance then owes to the context in which the utterance is made and interpreted. Similar border crossing could be useful for analyses of class and race in an economic context.

the various schools of economics. The standard of invariance to designate value is based in metaphors of nature and society. In contrast, by admitting the inherently subjective nature of value it becomes aligned to admit valuation and values. However, this would not allow universal social science since it would mean a coming together of culture and economy in determining the economic. The story proceeds in the following stages:

6.3.2.1 Mirowski and the theories of value in economics

Mirowski (1989: 395–400) categorises the different theories of value in rival schools in economics. I shall reiterate his four classes of theories.

- A *substance* theory of value: basis for classical political economy, neo-Ricardian theory, and Marxian economics. This draws upon the substance conceptions of motion.
- A *field* theory of value: basis for neoclassical economics. This draws upon mid-nineteenth-century energetics (physics) and field formalism.
- The *social* theory of value: basis for locating the invariant in institution of accounting conventions or in the legal definition of property rights or money itself.
- The full-scale denial of value: Samuel Bailey (see 6.3.2.2).

Regarding the last, Mirowski writes,

> This position argues that no economic phenomenon is conserved through time, and therefore scientific analysis is impossible. Whatever one might think of the truth of this option, it should be clear that the nihilism inherent in the programme assures that in this instance there can be no legitimate research programme called economics.

The point is that in order to posit the existence of value, something has to be grounded as the invariant or conservation principle. These conservation principles have usually derived from natural or scientific metaphors, but can also be derived from social invariances. Recall the one stable point that Archimedes wanted to be able to move the world, or the cogito of Descartes.

6.3.2.2 Bailey and his dissertation on value

The 1825 *Critical Dissertation On The Nature, Measures, And Causes Of Value*, which Mirowski uncharacteristically dismisses as a denial of value, was an attempt to consider the nature of value in political economy, especially that of David Ricardo and James Mill. In fact, Bailey's charge against political economists was not that 'they deny the impossibility of an invariable measure, but that they maintain, almost without exception, *invariableness to be necessary to constitute a measure of value*, while *I contend that invariableness has nothing to do with it*' (1826: 15, empases added).[21]

Value, claimed Bailey, cannot but be relational. He took strong exception to the claims of designating value by, for instance, 'resolving the effects of time into the expenditure of labour' (1825: 219). An example given in Mill's *Elements Of Political Economy* was taken to illustrate the point – Mill had argued, if wine put in the cellar increases in value by one-tenth by being kept for one year, one-tenth more of labour may be correctly considered as having been expended on it. Bailey argued, '[d]octrines of this kind, which attempt to reduce all phenomena to a uniform expression, ought to be rigidly scrutinized' (ibid.: 220). For him, the only accumulation having occurred in this case was *an arithmetical, not an actual* one. And he was keen on maintaining the difference.

Why am I discussing Bailey? Because, in Bailey's difficulties with the political economists' conception of value, one can find a basic and continuing difficulty in representations of the economic.

> On a review of the subject it appears, that *economists attempt too much*. They wish to *resolve all* the causes of value *into one*, and thus reduce the science to a simplicity of which it will not admit. *They overlook the variety of considerations operating on the mind in the interchange of commodities*. These considerations are the causes of value, and the attempt to proportion the quantities in which commodities are exchanged for each other to the degree in which one of these considerations exists, must be vain and ineffectual (1825: 231, emphases added)

And further,

> A false simplification in matters of fact can be of no service, and can only tend to perplex the mind of the inquirer by those perversions of language, those distortions of expression, and those circuitous expedients of logical ingenuity, which it unavoidably engenders (ibid.: 232).

Bailey's point can be read as a call against fixing the economic too narrowly in political economy. Recall: *They overlook the variety of considerations operating on the mind in the interchange of commodities*. He's arguing against political economists picking up the term value and flattening out all its dimensions into the one. The economic for him has an unavoidably subjective characterisation, something which can vary. Value, for him, does not need an invariance.

In my reading, this sense of value is amenable to admitting the processual considerations of valu-*ation*, and need not necessarily be something that applies

21 This remark is dated 1826 because it is contained in Samuel Bailey's response *Letter To A Political Economist* which was published in 1826, after a political economist's review of Bailey's 1825 *Critical Dissertation*.

only to commodities.[22] Value can be aligned to Values – worthy of espousing – and, since the subjective dimension of value and values is acknowledged, it allows for admitting the politicised nature of the contest for values.

If Mirowski finds in Bailey a full-scale denial of value, on the contrary, I find in him an affirmation of value. But this is because Mirowski's discussion of value is based upon a discussion of research programmes that have an agenda to appear scientific, and thus value is based upon some metaphorical invariance. On the other hand, my aim discussing the concept of value is to acknowledge the insufficient and unidimensional grasp of it in the concept of economic shackled to economics. Rather, I would like to conceptualise of the link between value and values as an example of the link between identity and the economic.

Now, I shall complete the story for you.

6.3.2.3 Review by the political economist

Very few in economics would know Bailey today. A review of his dissertation which appeared in *The Westminster Review* in 1826, and is sometimes attributed to James Mill, was scathing. The work is sophistry, metaphysics (and, '[t]his is not metaphysics; it is jargon,' ibid.: 162),[23] a continuous snarl, blundering, lack of knowledge and abundance of conceit, much ado about nothing. The reviewer's opinion is along the lines of: We can tell whether the reference to a 'dog' is to an animal or to a star. Similarly, we can tell when value refers to its technical or ordinary sense. Hobbes was profound when he said 'there is nothing relative but terms'.

In referring to Bailey's discussion about 'feelings or states of mind' in relation to the causes of value, the reviewer further finds that 'our language-master has puzzled himself through several pages' (168) when the answer is

22 In a different way, Goux, following Marx, also argues for perceiving the link between value and values in the centrality of time (i.e., over time the invariant standard of value such as the universal equivalent of money comes to seem timeless). As he writes, 'only a genesis of values, a genesis of the value form, can deconstruct the artifice of their hypostasis' (in Sorensen 1999: 88). And further,

> At the universal equivalent's origin is the basic equation in which one commodity is valued in terms of another commodity, and that commodity comes over time to be regarded as money, the universal equivalent, through social custom and habit. Though the source of the universal equivalent's value is customary practice through time, its identity as a standard deceptively announces a timeless, placeless value (93).

A continuing artistic comedy of values around the bank note as the measure of money is enacted in the work of J. S. G. Boggs, whose art resembles currency notes (it is one-sided on art paper and has the words 'I promise to promise to promise') but challenges the entire concept of money since he frequently offers it in settlement of an obligation, getting in return 'real' legal currency (see Weschler 1999).

23 To wit: 'Metaphysical terms are edge tools, and should not be meddled with by those who are not used to the handling of them' (Reviewer, 1826: 162).

simple – Demand is the cause of value. There is no puzzle about that; … To call it the Cause, is a metaphysical blunder… One number is a measure of another, and one is said to measure another exactly when it is the same… value is value (168–170).

Although,

> It is curious enough, that the grand cause of the puzzle in regard to value, and of the difficulties in expounding will, motion, space, and time, should be the same: viz. the want of distinct names for the *relatio*, and the *fundamentum relationis* (171).

And finally,

> in every department of literature, that ['much ado about nothing'] is a *spirit which ought to be repressed*; but because *in Political Economy is peculiarly noxious*. While the knowledge of the science is still confined to a comparatively small number, it has two powerful classes of enemies, the interested, and the ignorant; who, we daily see, assume to themselves a merit in decrying it (172, emphases added).

Unfortunately, a fundamental critique of economics (political economy) would possibly meet the same fate at the hands of the mainstream today, as it did in 1826.

6.3.2.4 Valuing culture and economy

I will now link these ideas back to the earlier discussion on separation of the realms of culture and economy. Sayer (1999) will be an illustration for this. Sayer calls for putting values back into both culture and economy. I agree with his concerns, but I would argue that they can be expanded on three counts. First, he argues for bringing culture and economy closer, rather than emphasising on scrutinising the process by which we have come to see them as separate. Second, he argues for a moral economy, and I will aim to illustrate that his notion of the moral economy does not radically contest the conventional economy. Third, he does not engage with economics (which he presumably sees as a science) but only laments the limited concerns of political economy. However, his move is nonetheless a crucial one to make. In the light of what I have been arguing in this section, I think that a stronger case can be made for the linking up of identity and economic, and for challenging economics.

Sayer starts by making the point that we live in a highly economised culture which has considerably accommodated to division of labour, class, commodification, and instrumental rationality. While early political economy was bound up with moral and political philosophy, increasingly with the development of capitalism people have lost control over their economic lives, and the competitive laws of global economy have tended to reduce the purchase of normative standpoints on political economy. In many societies, old moral principles are declining, and '[t]hese developments also reflect the rise of the (cultural) politics of recognition relative to the (economic) politics of distribution' (54).

In common with many social theorists, Sayer does not discuss economics very much. This is problematic because in taking the 'competitive laws of global economy' as insurmountable, so much has already been given away. As I have repeatedly emphasised, the heart of the so-called economic logic is not inaccessible to criticism. Further, the important need is precisely to link the cultural politics of recognition with the economic politics of distribution. The economic is, as it were, handed over to economics, no questions asked. As an example, consider '[n]ow an economic view of culture is bound to be an instrumental one . . .' (60).

Now consider Sayer's conceptualisation of a moral economy as a way of understanding both culture and economy and the relation between them. 'The moral economy embodies norms regarding the responsibilities and rights of individuals and institutions with respect to others and regarding the nature and qualities of goods, services and environment' (68).

He further writes (69, emphasis added),

> For *our society* the fundamental questions of moral economy might include the following.
>
> - Whose keeper are we? Who is our keeper? – What are our responsibilities towards children, the elderly, the disabled and infirm, to distant others and future generations, and to the environment?
> - What standards of care and provision should we expect to receive, give and fund? – what goods should be provided?
> - How should we discharge our responsibilities to others? – through paying taxes to fund transfer payments? through direct unpaid labour? By paying others to do the work?
> - How should these responsibilities be allocated between men and women, between parents and non-parents, between different age groups, between people of different incomes and wealth?
> - What standard of living should people expect? Should there be limits on pay and income from capital?
> - To what extent should people be reliant on wages/salaries for their income? (How far should income be subject to the 'stark utopia' of the 'self-adjusting' market (Polanyi, 1957)?)
> - What things should not be commodified?

It is clear that we need more people to be asking these questions, and that the concept of a moral economy is a valuable one. Yet, my argument is that Sayer has not gone far enough. In defining the very basis of moral economy in the 'responsibilities and rights of individuals and institutions', he has converted the political into the juridical and embraced an individual view of identity. This links with his perception of the divide between the cultural politics of recognition and the economic politics of distribution.

But, an even more important point is to indicate the limit of his moral economy – 'our society'. The formulation of the moral economy maps quite well on to the formulation of Western post-industrial secular capitalist liberal democracies. This becomes limiting when it *confines moral economy as a social contract to be worked out at the level of each nation state*. This is problematic because the very working out of the moral economy as a social contract in the nation state of 'our society' could be linked directly to oppression, exploitation, or injustice elsewhere. An example is the political voice in one nation-state which argues for more active exportation of arms and weapons to places under the threat of war, *because it would create jobs and livelihoods at home, and benefit 'our' economy*. At no point does Sayer's notion of the moral economy pose any challenge to the representative legitimacy of the nation-state, or even to the basic capitalist economic order (with the add-on of social democracy). His notion of the moral economy is like a liberal social contract which has to be worked out on an island – which it probably is. If one cannot expect a critical social theorist to challenge the grounding legitimacy of the nation-state, the constitution of the we, and the our society, the appeal of the nation-state must be strong indeed.

Further, in thus limiting the terms of his discussion of moral economy, I would argue that he's not being humble or speaking only for what he knows, but rather exercising his claim to *a privilege only available to some*. This is the privilege of being able to shut our doors and windows, sit down together, and decide what would be good for us. It is not available to those who have no roof or structure to commune in this way – fragile nation-states at the mercy of the powers from history that be. In our neocolonial world, there are many out in the cold usually because their structures were torn down, or because they can never realistically hope to have enough to start building. For example, the power asymmetries necessarily mean that a United States or a United Kingdom can agree upon the good and ethical moral economies of their societies (not that they do, but they could), and by the same stroke inflict interminable misery on national economies dependent on the export of primary produce to the United States or the United Kingdom.

But, leave all this aside. Even on the terms of his own moral economy, Sayer does not link the preservation of structures with the preservation of structures of knowledge. To wit, he follows up his humane list of questions thus (69, emphases added),

> Of course, in a sense *many of these are academic questions*, for in practice the arrangements to which they refer *depend heavily on the working of the economic system* and on convention and power (in the lifeworld as well as systems) rather than being decided normatively in any considered manner. However, from a normative point of view – and any critical social science presupposes such a standpoint – they are crucial to the *any assessment of economy in the broad sense*.

By saying that these crucial questions are academic, Sayer seems to be saying that – basically the *status quo* relies upon the 'working of the economic system' among other things, and as critical social theorists we can't really say much about that.

My illustration is complete, unless value is linked with values, economic is linked with identity, the slippage between economics/economy/economic is realised, and economics is challenged for its representation of the 'economic system'; even well-meaning attempts to bring together considerations of culture and of economy will remain fundamentally circumscribed.

6.4 Conclusion

Interrogating the economic logic based upon one-dimensional value requires challenging more thoroughly the construction of the category economic by economics. Towards this end, in this book, I have compromised the epistemological bases of economics as a science, I have discussed the limitations of modernist knowledge in the face of the Other, and argued for juxtaposing identity with the economic.

To sum up, I present a long (because) profound quote from Butler (2000a: 277–278, emphases added), who is less intimidated by the economic than Sayer,

> My sense is that our work *is commonly motivated by a desire for a more radically restructured world*, one which would have *economic equality and political enfranchisement* imagined in much more radical ways than they currently are. The question, though, that remains to be posed for us, I believe, *is how we will make the translations* between the philosophical commentary on the field of politics and the reimagining of political life. This is surely the kind of question which will render productive and dynamic the *opposition between formalism and historicism, between the ostensibly a priori and the a posteriori*. One might reply that any notion of economic equality will rely on a more generalised understanding of equality, and that that is part of what is interrogated by this kind of work. Or one might reply that any notion of a future of radically transformed economic relations will rely on the notion of futurity, and futurity is part of what is being attended to here. *But such responses go only part of the distance in answering the question that is posed. For what happens to the notion of equality when it becomes economic equality? And what happens to the notion of the future when it becomes an economic future? We ought not simply to 'plug in' the economic as the particular field whose conditions of possibility can be thought out on a priori level.* It may also be that the very *sphere of the economic needs to be rethought genealogically*. Its separation from the cultural, for instance, by structuralist legacies within anthropology might need to be rethought against those who claim that the very separation of those spheres is a consequence of capital itself.

In rethinking genealogically the sphere of the economic, we have to also loosen its subsumption under the official discourse of economics. This will mean a demonstration of economic theories not as reflections of an autonomous economy, but as textual productive enterprises fixing values under the supposed invariance of value, something that inhibits the translation of the self into Otherness and confines the basis of knowledge to a narrow relation between theory and critique. The politicisation of the having of identity is simultaneously a questioning of theory's claims to explaining the economic, a recognition of difference as the basis for identity, and a call for attending to knowledge production in Other ways.

Part 5

In conclusion

7 Writing economic theory an*Other* way

> The *classical concept of competence* supposes that one can rigorously dissociate knowledge (in its act or in its positing) from the event that one is dealing with, and especially from the ambiguity of written or oral marks – let's call them gramophonies. Competence implies that a meta-discourse is possible, neutral and univocal with regard to a field of objectivity, whether or not it possesses the structure of a text. *Performances ruled by this competence must in principle lend themselves to a transition with nothing left over on the subject of the corpus that is itself translatable.* Above all, they should not essentially be of narrative type. *In principle one doesn't tell stories in a university; one does history, one recounts in order to know and to explain*; one speaks about narrations or epic poems, but events and stories must not be produced in the name of institutionalizable knowledge.
>
> (Manjali 2001: 118, emphases added)

7.1 A recap

In this final part, I wish to move forward in light of the concerns that I have raised throughout the book. Let me recall the thread of these concerns. To begin with, there was the question of how what we think counts as knowledge in a social science is not simply a matter of how can we best be scientific about the social realm, but rather a question of excavating how the very basis of what it means to be scientific is itself intimately tied to the larger tensions in the picture of enlightenment epistemology. In the context of what it means to know, an important part is played by the ability to explain, so that, it seems as if explanation remains an unchanging anchor of a social science like economics. However, the changing nature of what we mean by an explanation as demonstrated in the first part of the book, has itself been an important trajectory in economics. Further, the mutations of enlightenment epistemology in the nineteenth century which coincided with the turn to neoclassical economics, also marked the moralisation of objectivity, the mechanisation of science, and the aspiration in social sciences like economics to achieve a form of representation which was 'pure' because it supposedly did not involve any interpretation, for instance the mathematisation of the economic discourse.

One could remain within the ambit of discussing how theories negotiate between the received understandings of scientific knowledge and the particularities of the social realm. But this would not draw any attention to how what counts as knowledge in social science is not simply a problem of knowledge, or science, but also a movement in history, in time and in place. Therefore, it is important to highlight that economics as a social science could have aspired to universal ideals of knowing only within a modernist comprehension of knowledge as characterised by Cartesian subjectivity and taxonomised separability. These terms of supposedly universal knowing are keenly dependent on maintaining a split between science and politics, on managing the 'Other' as a limit phenomenon, and on a certain appreciating and positive correlation between the status of science and the West. This being the case, modernist knowing and being as the foundation of enlightenment epistemological theorising, does not simply meet its Other in history and time, but actively needs, seeks, and creates at its edges the Other as an irrational and seemingly irrelevant possibility which is actually important for its own self coherence. What seem as contestations in this modernist epistemological worldview are often actually a play of the 'Same Self'. In order to challenge this provincialism of supposedly universal knowing, simply taking up a social science like economics and critiquing its evolution will not do. What is needed instead is to undermine the very separations it relies upon profoundly in order to marshal claims to knowledge. I have termed this a particular way of re-membering in presence of the present, a postcolonial moment. In order to disrupt the modernist disciplinary logic that relies upon creating knowledge based on manufacturing conceptual abstractions and universalising their essence, we need to place difference at the heart of self and identity. I have chosen to mount this critique by arguing for a juxtaposition of questions of identity with questions of the economic.

This leads to a discussion of the essentialist abstract individual model of identity in the discourse of economics. A reflection on this view of identity, especially as it obtains within economics, provides an entry point into critiquing the model of knowledge which relies upon a universal subject. One response has been that of standpoint theory, and its political correlate of identity politics. However, even this endeavour has its limitations which can be addressed if we move to thinking of not simply identity politics, but the politics of identity. Further, where identity is discussed in economics, this bringing together is shown to be unsatisfactory. Specific examples illustrate the point. As a result, we need to rethink both individual and collective ways of considering identity because they remain within what I characterise as a concentric mode of identity. The pitfalls of this view are illustrated. In contrast to this, the case is made for the thinking of identity in a translational mode.

Finally, this need to juxtapose identity and the economic requires not only rethinking of identity, but also of the economic. This is important because there is a slippage between the notions of economy, economic, and economics which has significant implications for the way in which culture and economy are understood as separate spheres, with the economy as having a universal logic of its own. This is open to question as we realise that the translations between value and values are only fixed by maintaining as constant and invariant a universal metaphor as the standard which designates value. However, any such fixing of value (in metaphorical invariance of substance, the formalism, social conventions, and so on) is only achieved by isolating the economic logic from values which are seen to belong to the cultural sphere. Calls to integrate culture and economy in terms such as 'the moral economy' remain inadequate. What is needed is to deconstruct the economic itself as an *a priori* possibility. The economic is not something that draws upon a separate understanding of rationality. It is important to realise that within the dominant framework, there is no way of being irrational without also being uneconomic. This ability to compare and calculate in commensurate terms, identify invariances, and arrive at the economically rational decision which is overdetermined by universal Reason, is what allows a particular kind of theorising to be seen as social scientific designation of the pre-existing economic, when it is actually a particular fixing of values in value.

In this concluding part I will proceed as follows. The rethinking of the economic in relation to identity will allow us to write economic theory an*Other* way, and this will also be a rewriting of the conditions of theory itself. Rather than being seen as emanating from a fixed and centred self's perception of the world as inevitably determined by history, time, and place, theory will be a way of *othering* (making Other) knowledge. 'Travelling' in its many senses will be not something that threatens theoretical certainties, but is an inextricable part of the understanding of theorising and knowledge. The tensions between the general and particular, part and the whole, and the self and the Other, only achieved legitimacy in the light of the aspirations to universal knowing. If the politics of intellectual authority are reoriented to contextuality, we will have newer ways of thinking about knowledge and its dissemination.

7.2 Writing economic theory an*Other* way

The very first significance of beginning to think about writing economic theory an*Other* way is to finally get over the belief that 'I know the wheel is crooked, but economics is still the best game in town' (Solow paraphrased in Reder 1999: 362). The deparochialising of economics is also by the same token an interrogation of the modernist rendition of knowledge. The way one would *write* such *theory* will be radically different and strange – for it would involve a questioning of the theorist, the writing process, the method, as well as an attempt to generate meaning from what is perceived to be at hand. The discourse of economics is a particularly powerful metanarrative (even more so in this late capitalist neocolonial unipolar world saturated with an often unexamined but accepted economic logic). By writing an*Other* way we can dig into the ways and means by which the foundations of a discipline are laid – and then expose these bases as contingent and particular. This is also an exercise in establishing the difference between an *impossible* universal and general economic knowledge (aesthetically aspired for by most practitioners) *and* an actual process of universal*isation* and general*isation* of a particular form of knowledge based on a particularised model of human subjectivity – and the havoc this causes in terms of dissonance to those who are not adequately imbricated in the belief systems underlying this universalised model of knowledge and subjectivity.

Within the context of economics, the questioning of mainstream methods or selection of the 'economic' domain is at the same time a questioning of its knowledge claims and the possibility of their justification. This would place more stress on examining the *mechanisms* which allow such knowledge claims to be uttered as legitimate; laying bare the *expectations* that are associated with the possibility of having made such claims; and unpacking the *historical investment* implicit in such endeavours of knowledge creation and justification.

It is not just that economic theory can be written another way but that we *need* to write economic theory an*Other* way. The 'economic' is not everywhere the same – its construction, motivations, contexts, trajectories, encounters, meanings, may be different, contradictory, ambiguous – in time and in place. The same is true for economies as complicated contested spaces of interaction. Value needs to be unshackled from its modernist capitalist annexation. Economics does not have a meaningful theory of value, and as I pointed out in the previous chapter, the economic logic of the dominant neoliberal kind cannot accommodate an ethical concern for the Other. It is incapable of meaningfully conceptualising the social, or being transformed through an ethicality for the Other which is not-me and never-me – an alterity.[1] The economic logic is not hospitable to such ideas, to postcolonial memory.

Let me trace some of the contours of writing economic theory in unfamiliar ways. An important concern that I have in this regard is that the economic should not be too easily available as a category split from the social or the political, and at the same time the dominant representations of the category economic which are afforded to us by the so-called descriptions or explanations of the economy in economics (conventional 'economic theory' as I pointed out in Chapter 1) need to be challenged. What is the aim of all this? My motivation for undertaking this is to stress that – the economic logic as we find it in our neoliberal age is *not* impossible to perforate, and that this is a task in which we need to rethink the purpose and status of theory, its relation to critique, and the relation of knowledge in general to emancipation. How does this translate in relation to economics, its practitioners and practice? I argue that an appreciation of the emphases as

1 It is not surprising that economic logic is incapable of admitting alterity, it may even be a function of logic itself. Just as the truisms of dominant and unchallenged self-interest are secured by the scientistic axiomatics of 'economic theory', similarly logic itself has a heritage in authority. Nye (1990: 182) describes this as follows: 'the atomized statements that logic reconnects in syllogisms or propositional calculi are themselves spoken, but it is by a certain kind of speaker, a speaker who is alienated from himself, who speaks from no coherent interpersonal experience, from no stable communal reality. It is no accident that logic flourished when the human community had failed.' Alterity, in contrast, requires a thinking *beyond the self*, especially in the Levinasian sense, it 'demands further thought, demands that thought go further – than it has ever gone or *can* go' (Cohen in Levinas 1987: 26).

outlined earlier require us to start from jettisoning the conventional one-way relation between 'theory' and the 'world' in economics, where theories can only follow from an external mind-independent world 'out there'. Once the focus turns to seeing economic theories as *productive* enterprises, we can understand theories as producing or naming their own real. This opens up several radical possibilities – to visualise a radically different role of critique, to consider economy/economics as a text, to link the logic of economic theories with an all-pervasive economic logic, to think through the theory/praxis problematique which underscores enlightenment epistemology, to appreciate the importance of identity re-imagined as translational, and to examine the relation between epistemology and emancipation. These possibilities underline the centrality of the Other in the writing of more radical theories of the economic and encourage changes in pedagogy. These changes entail a contextualised approach to social political economy and a critical questioning of dominant ways of teaching, reading and writing economy/economic/economics in the academy.

7.2.1 Theories as textual productions

> Theory itself has no *con*-sequence. It is autosequential rather than automatic. Theory is the production of theory, lost in its setting to work. It is always withdrawn from that open end as it is from that which it wants to theorize.
>
> (Spivak 1999: 194, emphasis original)

Generally, theory is seen as 'anything which is, or can be, articulated in the form of a statement or set of statements which purport to offer, or which can be taken as offering, an explanation of something' (Gaukroger, in Ekegren 1999: 5). Moreover, as Ahmed (2000: 98) points out, within particular disciplines, 'theory' as a form of naming can do a lot of work – it can suggest more difficult, more advanced, and so on. In the first two chapters, I examined the competing ways in which theory has historically been characterised in economics, it has at different times meant wordy expositions of the classical political economists, and the almost wordless and symbol-dominated axiomatics of modern economics.

Further, theories are seen as serving the purpose of defining, explaining, or predicting an economic reality 'out there'. As Klein (1998: 193–194, emphasis added) puts it:

> A 'real-world economic system' – the mediate referent of a theory, an international, national, regional economy; a market; and economic agent, to mention a few – is usually a highly complex structure in itself. This complexity is augmented by the fact that economic systems are merely relatively autonomous subsystems of larger, encompassing, 'real-world systems'. *It is the task of the economic theorist intellectually to extricate the economic subsystem from the conceptual whole it is interwoven with, to reconstruct it with the necessary details, and to draw a blueprint describing the channels which connect the former and the latter.*

In contrast, thinking of theories as textual productions is an important move for imagining the writing of economic theory in other ways. I will first critically discuss the various ways in which this endeavour has materialised within economics, and then argue for further developments.

Recognising the textual nature of economy/economic/economics implies being alive to processes by which 'economy' is distilled out of 'society' and exploring the boundaries of the economic, and its definitional politics. In the identification of what gets counted as being the 'economic', controversy is underplayed. This delineation/demarcation of the 'economic' itself is an intensely political act, for often privileges accrue to what gets defined as being so. What gets counted as economic is what is amenable to the neoclassical economic method (see Nelson 1993; Strassmann 1993a, b), and so the 'established order tends to produce . . . the *naturalisation of its own arbitrariness*' (Bourdieu 1977: 164). We can deconstruct the conventional ideas of economy/ics (as objective universal knowledge about an externally existing economy/reality), by engaging considerations about the role of the author, the text, intentionality, language and the effects of power. Such a reading of economic knowledge as textual production can enable us to see such knowledge claims as contingent, as exclusionary stories complicit with power.

Often economists attempting to question the factual truth status of economic theories formulate their arguments by resisting the fact/value distinction adhered to in positive economics, and by claiming that economic theories are not simply representations of a reality out there, but are stories about the economic realm. This characterisation of economics as storytelling is also run together with claims for the 'textuality' of economic theories. As I will go on to argue, my aim of looking at theories as textual productions is not limited to or necessarily mapped by this way of considering textuality of theories in economics. For instance, Ward (1972: 179–190) characterised economics as storytelling, defined as 'an attempt to give an account of an interrelated set of phenomena in which fact, theory and value are all mixed together in the telling'. He argued that the standard stories of economics paint a picture not explicitly stated but conveyed across by the 'selection of topics and emphases' (183), such as those fitting a capitalist economy.

The most famous proponent of the rhetoric approach in economics is McCloskey (1986) who argues that economics as a field of enquiry emphasises facts and logic at the expense of metaphor and story. While economists may like to think that they are practising science, they need to realise that in their actual workaday practices they constantly confront disagreements over values, and practise the rhetorical skills of persuasion to advance their cause. The biggest problem that I find with McCloskey's rhetoric approach is the way in which attention to textual detail is invoked as an additional tool that economists can employ in their reasoning. Evidence the following argument made by McCloskey and Klamer (1995: 195, emphases added) which is based on the idea that since 'knowledge is information *plus* judgement' economists should pay attention to their rhetoric

> If the economy depends on the faculty of speech, then the economy will require verbal interpretation . . . Economic institutions will look to some

> degree like religious ceremonies or social gatherings. They will need to be read in terms of human intentions and beliefs. *An economy that depends on speech is one that can be listened to and read, like a text*... But the economist who can adjust will have *an additional set of scientific tools, those of interpretation*. One cannot ignore a quarter of national income, the human as against the mechanical part of knowledge. *The conclusion is not that the present tools are worthless and should be discarded. They are worth a lot and should be kept*, for their present uses and for bringing measurement into an interpretive economics. *But if the economy needs sometimes to be drilled rather than hammered, or planed rather than sawn, the economist had better have a drill and a plane*.

This kind of attention to textuality combines arguments for literary analysis of logic with a surprising inability to see that 'reading the economy as a text' is not simply a matter of using another tool, but of recognising that economic theories are textual ideological products which function in interested ways.

Thus, rhetoric is seen as another new method in the armoury of a 'new' but still mainstream economics. In suggesting a prescriptive viewing of economics as a contest of persuasion and rhetoric, McCloskey also implicitly holds a 'marketplace of ideas' view wherein the approach that is dominant is ostensibly that which could convince the most (see Stettler 1995). This is a depoliticised addendum rather than a radical envisioning of economics, especially when viewed in its failure to address those who want to situate economic theories as interested productions of a modernist imperial discipline which crucially relies upon its exclusions in order to sustain its claim to knowledge. In my view, it is a stylistic, rather than an ethical critique, postmodern though it may be.

This means that the call for reading theories as textual productions is not simply asking us to read the 'texts' of economics, but to read economics as a text. Let me give two more examples. Lavoie (1991: 2) argues that hermeneutics would apply to economics on two different levels, 'our understanding of the texts of economics; and our understanding of "texts" of the economy – that is, the price movements, or monetary institutions, or industrial organisation of economies, each of which is the meaningful product of human minds'. Again, Brown (1994b) uses the term 'reading the economy as a text' while drawing upon Barthes and Bakhtin, and, of course, McCloskey (see also Henderson 1995). She outlines the ways in which we can 'read' the economy: mechanisms that compile, sift, and sort the fragmented text of the economy (such as statistical data and econometric techniques) or, the ways in which notions are interpreted in different theoretical approaches (for instance, the account of competition in Walrasian, Hayekian, and Schumpeterian approaches). Her critique comes across somewhat as empirical addendum, that we can 'read' things in these other ways. The political implications of her call for exploring the text of the economy as being 'fragmented and multivoiced' are enacted as being simply an addition to the methods, rather than any recognition or possibility of the politics of such a move.

Not all the attention to textuality in economics has been stylistic in this way. The concerns of power are related to those of textuality in the work of Strassmann (1993a, b, 1994; Strassmann and Polanyi 1995), who highlights the ways in which disciplinary authority can mean that the conversation of economics is laden with power imbalances. Her conception of economics as storytelling and economists as storytellers crucially draws attention to the masculinist nature of the mainstream narratives. When we see knowledge about the economy as the result of textual production, several observations are forthcoming. In a story about stories, it is interesting to ask, what do the stories we tell, tell about us? It is instructive to note what is the outside of mainstream stories about the economy: women, non-marketable ideas/objects, environment, history, emotions, non-reductive, non-formalisable, non-measurable elements of comprehension. The agent (*homo economicus*) is patterned after an individual with the sorts of privileges in society which traditionally accrue to privileged men (England 1993; Grapard 1995, 1996; Hewitson 1999). Similarly, the notion of free choice does not take into account people who do not have free choice: those who are forced owing to need, or, those who do not feel at ease with the neoclassical capitalist ideology. There is no space for people who, socially and representationally (for instance through minority stereotyping), find themselves at the sites where choices aren't just individual or free but governed by others' perception of oneself (see Cudd 1997). This story appeals to audiences who see their own image in its interstices. For the few who see themselves in it, it is a powerful story. For those who do not recognise themselves in the text, there is the role of holding up the institutionalised story as its outside.

Against this background, one can further argue not simply for questioning the stories that economists tell as their value-laden creations but for reading the very construction of entities such as economy, or the category economic, or the discipline economics as textual productions. The imperative is to see a text not just in terms of a general interpretation of a 'text' which can be 'read', but a *textual productive enterprise.*[2] The practitioners and practices are part of the performance of an enterprise of knowledge creation which produces its own Real (the economy) and then claims privileged access to it *as if* it existed already performed. The entity 'economy' or category 'economic' is itself the production of the very theories that are supposed to reflect it. And this view of economics as a text (of which economists are themselves a part) helps us to appreciate the very *particular locatedness* of this text. Economics, as a *contingent episteme*, is an ideological product embodying Western enlightenment imperial colonial modernity (see Kanth 1997a, b). By thinking of economics and creating knowledge about the economy as a text, we can examine the ways in which economic

2 What is a text? Consider Bennington's (in Royle 2000: 7) remarks:

> '"Text" is not quite an extension of a familiar concept, but a displacement or reinscription of it. Text in general is any system of marks, traces, referrals (don't say reference, have a little more sense than that). Perception is a text. ...There is no essential difference between language and the world, the one as subject, the other as object. There are traces'.

knowledge is contingent. Following Shapiro's (1989b: 13) discussion of a critical political perspective, one could analogously ask: how does reading the economy as a text necessarily involve a questioning of the privileged forms of representation whose dominance has led to the unproblematic acceptance of subjects, objects, acts, and themes through which the economic world is constituted.

This questioning of the demarcation of legitimate economic knowledge is a questioning both of the arbitrary boundaries of the economic, as well as of the epistemological foundations of what counts as knowledge and how can it be accessed. Theories which conventionally explain, predict, or describe a reality can now be seen as interested productions of reality. Rather than re-presenting a pre-given reality, theory *produces* the very reality it seeks to explain (cf. MacKenzie 2002). This performative role of theories enables us to appreciate better the intertwined discursive/material in social theory. For instance, economic theories hinging on self-interest become a paean for an ontology of hedonistic egoism, creating what they name. Also, then we can attend to the manifest 'violence' of economic theories. As I have argued, this violence is exemplified by the way in which economic theory withholds recognition as economic agents from those who do not fit its standard story. Further, it is important to trace the link between this epistemic 'writing out' and the historical and cultural conditions of its performance. As a response to the political, social, cultural events, economics alternates between being the handmaiden of governance, historical facilitator and legitimiser of colonialism and neocolonialism, and mathematical representation of 'the economy'. Yet this should alert us to the parallels between those epistemically written out of the economic theories and those at the receiving end of the cruelties of economic logic.

The way one would write an*Other* economic theories will be radically different. Let me point out a contrast between this view of theory as a textual production with the conventional one as a collection of causal explanatory variables.

Theory has become, partly as a consequence of enlightenment epistemology and the modernist rendition of disciplinary knowledge, the expectation of something which can provide answers. These answers, as theorists especially in economics would very well know, are hoped-for answers not just to the 'problems of knowledge' (which are themselves constructed in tune with the structures of knowledge), but answers to the administration of structures. The trouble with this construal of theory in social science as providing answers to the governance of society is that it leaves completely unquestioned and unthought the very basic concepts which spring fully formed and appear to relate to praxis instead.

Now, against this view of theory which is quite deeply linked to a particular way of thinking about causality, contrast theory as *an exploration of discontinuous trends that determine so that you can't translate easily*. This is the view afforded to us by Spivak's (1991: 246) understanding of determinant as determination (*Bestimmung*),

> In fact if you put the three adjectives together, politico, economico or, technologico, what you would get is overdetermination. . . . Overdetermination

> in the sense of *anders determiniert* rather than just *vielfach determiniert*,[3] not just an arithmetical collection of determinants, but determination – to translate Freud's phrase, otherwise. In other words discontinuous trends that determine so that you can't translate easily.

So that we challenge the straightforward simplicities of knowledge as the application of theories, theorising as the attribution of causality and the addition of determinants. Rather, the boundaries of the knowledge creation process become porous, theorising becomes about encountering the discontinuities in an overdetermined world and letting them affect the process of theorising itself. Theory is not the collection of determinants, but the exploration of (over) determination in the face of multiplicity. As Scott (1988: 33) writes, '[w]e need theory that will let us think in terms of pluralities and diversities rather than of unities and universals.' This does not give us easy answers, but lets difference make a difference to theorising.

While the conventional view of theory will see critique as a matter of pointing out errors, and accordingly knowledge as an accumulation on the road to progress, the latter sees critique and theory as inseparably intertwined and often indistinguishable.

7.2.2 *The altered role of critique*

> It is simply no good moaning unless you can offer something that can be used as a springboard for others.
>
> (Dasgupta 1998: 24)

Seeing theorising as a textual productive enterprise radically alters the way we perceive the role of critique. It is important to recall that 'theory and critique' are often characterised, both in the mainstream and even in most critical approaches in economics, in a stable way where the purpose of the latter is the advancement of the former. This is the better critique leading to better theory, an 'eventually we will get there' view. Within this, critique is seen as largely atheoretical and not an end in itself. The narrow economics vision of critique as criticism never allows much to be questioned (and further critique must provide immediate alternatives – something challenged rightly by Strassmann and Polanyi 1995).

Within the modernist versions of knowledge, the purpose of critique is the unified advancement of theory by pointing out its errors or omissions, but this leaves no space for challenging the way in which the theoretical terrain is fundamentally constituted. In challenging the completeness of theoretical space, critique needs also to replay that space differently, to rescue its contours and shake away its certainties. Like Lady Macbeth's 'damned spot' that would not rub off, history sticks to a postcolonial theory of the economic (and of economics – as

3 Roughly equivalent to: 'Different' rather than just a 'Multiple' sense of determination.

a contingent episteme whose coming of age seamlessly ties in with the post-enlightenment esteem of modernism).

It is interesting to note that critique can lend itself to different characterisations once we think theory Otherwise. Walsh (2000: 7) writes that a theory is not only black with fact and white with convention but also red with values. The threads of a theory are even more tangled – with the many colours of implicatedness, involvement, and an always already insinuation, an engagement that is not prior to a factual world but woven into what it seeks to represent. And on this view, critique can be seen as a way of disturbing the *status quo* with particular end/s in mind (Butler, 2000b); as the basis for an emancipatory politics achieved by proceeding to theorise differently; or, it can *be* theory at any given instance in time.

By this last point I mean the following. If we see economics as a particular text rather than an objectivist scientistic enterprise, then we can overcome the nostalgia for critique as subservient to unified theoretical advancement. Critique functions differently in a textual reading and in a purportedly objectivist scientific enterprise. The idea of critical questioning and change in science is strongly tied to the notion of *accumulation and verification* of knowledge. This notion of critique has carried over into economics. There is, however, no determinate fixing of meaning in a textual reading. It is not an attempt to build a solid mass of ever-fixed knowledge, but rather constant reinterpretations and renegotiations. In reading economic knowledge as a text, we recognise *critique as theory* at a situated point in time. The shifting, slipping, sandly meanings of the economic can be recognised as irremediably mediated and contextual. Thus, we can untangle critique from its slavish role at the feet of unified theoretical advancement and see it as consisting of multiply erupting strands of theory.

This might seem strange at first, to consider critique as theory, especially since a lot of potent contemporary critique is in some way or the other a rebellion against 'theory'. It should be remembered that 'theory' in its grand, unified, solid (neoclassical) sense is the 'theoretical' value which critique has traditionally been deemed to lack. So, one is arguing both for an unprivileging of the theoretical status and also for the recognition of critique as having theoretical value which is not dependent on better theories being developed.

If there is anything common to the many ways in which we can conceive of critique, it is a desire for change, for betterment sometimes (though often admitting a contested notion of 'betterment'), for including consideration of the 'outside'. This discussion on the nature of critique is relevant because often economists can tend to think of critique as mere criticism. I am making the point that there is a difference between the two, that critique is fundamentally an ethical epistemological position. This is because it is the recognition of plurality of voices, a liberation from the standard narrative, a quest for avoiding theoretical foreclosure. As Lyotard argues, a resisting of totality is important – 'we have paid a high enough price for the nostalgia of the whole and the one' (1984), and we now need to understand the burden imposed by 'the mortgage of critique and theory', where 'critique remains within the field of the criticised thing and within the paranoiac, dogmatic relation of knowledge' (in Larrain 1994: 106–107 [1974]).

Considering the emancipatory possibilities of critique leads one to interrogate the relationship between knowledge and freedom. Conventionally, emancipation is deemed to be a matter of 'the truth shall set you free', a relation where knowledge is redeeming, enabling, enlightening, and seemingly the more access to a universal store of knowledge one has, the greater are one's chances for freeing oneself from oppression.[4] However, if we look in greater detail at this story (enlightenment epistemology), we can see why it is problematic. Knowledge is not a disinterested factual store of truth, which provides ready-made solutions for combating oppression, but is rather best seen as a successive questioning of previous knowledge claims. Flax (1992) argues that knowledge is not innocent, but a *belief* in the innocence of knowledge serves many purposes. It allows theorists to overcome the conflicts between knowledge and power by inserting the wedge of Reason. It further cements the legitimacy of the theorist in gaining privileged access to some Real. It views the Reason-led exercise of 'proper' knowledge (acquired by scientific means) as benevolent and emancipatory. And finally, it absolves the seekers of such transcendent knowledge (in its many forms of God, Science, Truth) from accepting responsibility for the ways in which such knowledge can be exclusionary, interested, specific, and non-freeing. Universal emancipation if only we had enough knowledge is a false promise of Western enlightenment modernity. It is also dangerous for it obscures the processual ways in which discourses actually function in creating legitimacy.

The temptation to view knowledge as a disinterested factual store of truth which provides ready-made solutions for combating oppressions is re-visited throughout the many endeavours of critical social theory. Typically, the ability to meaningfully conceptualise emancipation in such critical social theory requires the anterior presence of a transcendental subject who acts as the marker of knowledge. In order to further utilise such theoretical apparatus, this model of subjectivity is then illegitimately universalised. Its illegitimacy is in contrast to a contextualist notion of emancipation which is meaningful only within the frame of specific locational questions and particular struggles.

As Ahmed (2000: 102) points out, critique is about recognising that categories are used which 'may be exclusionary, or even violent, when they are not recognised as categories'. All '[c]losures are nervous' to an extent, and '[c]ritique in the strong sense, is never done. One cannot say it has been achieved' (Spivak 1991: 249). An ethical and emancipatory critical political practice would challenge not only the relation between theory and critique but also continually enact incursions to explode the theory/praxis problematique – the enlightenment epistemological belief in the separation of theory and praxis.

4 An interesting example of a link between ontology, explanation, and emancipation is provided by the critical realist accounts, where it is argued that 'explanation is emancipation'. See Collier (1994: 169–204).

7.2.3 Theory/praxis problematique

> [The] nice notion of the relationship between theory and practice has caused and is causing a good deal of suffering in the world . . . the field of work is a broken and an uneven place. The conventional highway of a politically correct single issue is merely the shortest distance between two signposted exits.
>
> (Spivak 1999: 197)

This theory/praxis (gap) problematique – where theory and praxis are understood in a distinct relation – posits theory as promise and the praxis as performance. Such (typical) attributions postulate a necessary wedge between the *sophisticated theoretical understanding* of events and *atheoretical material brute* struggles which can be undertaken following on from such theoretical understandings. It relies upon the notion of theory as providing an unmediated access to a transcendent (underlying) material reality, and the further possibility of such theory to be harnessed for universal good in practice. This is an artificial divide which is useful to preserve the notion of 'innocent knowledge' which in practice leads to uninterrogable power.

On the other hand, the discursive construction of this divide and its resilience draws attention to the difficulty of imagining knowledge which is not (as I argued before) a prelude to effective intervention in the world, but is itself always-already a form of ethics, politics, strategy, subjectivity, Reason, and being. Attention to theory should not be construed as the giving up of praxis, neither should a focus on praxis be seen as anti-theoretical. As Hall (1988: 69–70) puts it:

> If you ask me what is the object of my work, the object of the work is to always reproduce the concrete in thought – not to generate another good theory, but to give better-theorized account of concrete historical reality. This is not an anti-theoretical stance. I need theory in order to do this. But the goal is to understand the situation you started out with better than before.

One should not underestimate, nor deny the complexity of the theory-praxis problematique within the politics of identity. Discussing the relation between deconstruction and activist politics, Spivak (1991: 233–234) has the following to say:

> Grassroots activists (as opposed to urban radicals) in Third World must use what is at hand, they cannot sit around and decide which individual rights are native. They have to use models that they know, on the field, they have to use models that are capitalist in order to fight the multinationals. In the tribal movement the activists know that the tribals who were considered animals in the fifties and sixties must be encouraged to establish accounts in the banks. Of course this is inserting them into capitalism. They must be supported when they try to claim citizen's rights and they know that the constitution is not something that fell into tribal law and culture. It doesn't belong to tribal law and culture, the Indian constitution.

Spivak's remarks raise a more nuanced issue in the theory/praxis problematique, namely that we have to be able to 'talk across worlds'. Nagar (2002) discusses this difficulty of combining the languages of theory and praxis. She argues that it is imperative for the theory in Western academy to talk across worlds – 'worlds that are separated not just socially, geopolitically and materially, but also in their understandings of what constitutes relevant theory and politics' (182). This is not the same as the claim that people who 'do' theory are not engaged in political work, or that political activists are not engaged in theory, but that it is critical that the languages of knowledge are 'accessible and relevant to multiple audiences *here* and *there*' (184, emphasis in original). I need to clarify this point a little further. By saying that the languages of knowledge should be accessible to multiple audiences, one does not mean that the printed marks on paper, the terms and concepts used, should not push the boundaries of thought further, neither does one mean that audiences over 'there' do not want theory or are not interested in theorising. Against this, what has been asserted here is that the process of theorising should be committed to an ethical politics which is foundational upon the encountering of difference, of Others, and of 'other Others'. To take an example, the fact that this book draws upon interdisciplinary vocabularies does not mean that it is rendered automatically inaccessible to certain audiences. To think so would be to foreclose the possibility of certain engagements with certain audiences. In contrast, talking across the worlds implies that the language of knowledge (different from the common understanding of language) is one which cannot afford to elide difference. For instance, consider the way in which the discourse of economics assumes the 'legitimate' terrain of knowledge and of its application. This involves focusing on certain privileged actors who (with access to capital and freedom of choice) interact in a certain setting arbitrarily defined as the economy in ways that are limited to a capitalist setting – but this discourse is universalised as the theory of economics worldwide. It does not have any space for different audiences who are then inserted at odd-points in its fabric. In this case, the language of knowledge is not accessible to multiple audiences, the politics of knowledge creation are not ethical. Neither is the situation any different when Sayer's moral economy discussions exercise the privileged rights to confine the terrain of such theorising to that of the 'West'. Any project of knowledge creation must constantly foreground its own positioning in relation to the way in which it has fixed difference. On this account, theory and praxis are not straightforwardly separable, they reside in the continuum of the encounters through which they are differentiated. Singular theorists do not create objective and universalisable knowledge about their subjects of study. To recall Ahmed (see Chapter 6), ethical projects of various collectivities involving the painstaking labour of work are generated through encounters (if it is not to be simply merger, benevolence, or knowledge).[5]

5 It is also important to clarify that the encounters referred to here are not 'fieldwork'. To quote from Ahmed (2002: 16),

> This work is differentiated from anthropological knowledge: it is not fieldwork. Rather, as a form of encounter, it involves getting closer to others in order to occupy or inhabit the

A recognition of the constitutive linkages between theory and praxis allows us to further explore the relations between epistemology and emancipation in the writing of theory Otherwise.

7.2.4 Emancipation and epistemology

> I do not need epistemology to justify my desire, my life, my love. I need politics; I need to build a world that does not require such justifications.
>
> (Phelan 1994: 55)

Most economic understanding would have us believe in a model of the world where human beings are the centre[6] of the universe and nature[7] is at their disposal to produce and consume (though in schizoid states) according to their beliefs (preferences) in order to maximise their utility under conditions of endless want. Questioning this is to bring about the realisation that it is not as if we produce and consume in a silent empty docile world with only identical me-selves, but that we, our beliefs, and our very identities – we ourselves are produced by an external world of Others.

Analysing events solely at the level of the individuals is mistaken not only because it leaves out the diverse social factors operating at supra-individual levels, but also because it allows individual subjects to be seen as if they pre-exist discourses about subjectivity. Starting from the proposition of the pre-formed, knowing, and discriminating individual who then proceeds to voluntarily undertake transactions or exchanges obscures the fact that this is a very *particular* model of individual subjectivity – which needs to be historically, geographically, and temporally *situated* to be seen as meaningful. But, taken as the very *basis* of all other economic understanding, it serves to 'write out' the myriad methods of knowledge creation that *actually make* humans into such individual 'subjects'.

The destabilisation of an essentialist identity does not inaugurate a free-for-all where there are no constraints and no choices; rather, thinking emancipation in terms of collective identities which are based in the first instance on an ethical primacy of difference, places responsibility at the heart of knowing/being.

distance between us. Such encounters must supplement collective activism precisely because they prevent 'us' from assuming we can gain 'access' to the difference of those others who are positioned differently by the networks and flows of global capitalism.

6 Of course, there are many ways in which this idea of the central human being plays out, for it is never just a central human being but a central man, and a central white man – his other attributes may be middle-class, able-bodied, anglo-saxon, protestant, heterosexual, and procreatively inclined.

7 The ever-present 'nurturing feminine' outside which is to be 'controlled'. For a discussion of ecological and feminist issues in relation to economics, see O'Hara; Perkins; Pietila; Brennan; Jochimsen and Knobloch; McMahon; Mellor, all in *Ecological Economics* (1997). A contrast can be found in Tacconi (1998).

The processual nature of achieving while maintaining identities as *an outcome* (rather than an antecedent) of political practice is an invitation to *continually Other* oneself, thus analysing power at the site of knowledge. It emphasises that 'the constituted character of the subject is the very precondition of its agency... [it is a] loss of epistemological certainty, but this loss of certainty does not necessarily entail political nihilism as its result' (Butler 1992: 12, 17). Translational architectures of identity radically change the way we think about knowledge and about the self by foregrounding the Other as constitutive to identity.

The ensuing relation between emancipation and epistemology is by no means uncomplicated. The narratives of emancipatory claims are painfully contingent and contested, even amongst what would seem to be the most innocuously apparent identity groupings of race, class, gender. This question of the *anxious identities that we inhabit* is particularly important for the status of epistemology in emancipatory projects. The comforting certainty of the transcendent subject is replaced with the ever more unstable, fleeting subject positions that we come into as both the creators of knowledge about the way we behave and (in a typical circular and cumulative causation case) ourselves being created in the image of that knowledge.

The way forward will involve an overcoming of the conventional project of epistemology itself. In the words of Code (1991: 314), '[a]s long as "epistemology" bears the stamp of the postpositivist, empiricist project of determining necessary and sufficient conditions for knowledge and devising strategies to refute skepticism, there can be no feminist epistemology.' She argues that it is the pivotal ideals of the conventional epistemological project – objectivity, impartiality, universality – which will need reconstruction in order to move towards transformative emancipatory projects. As discussed earlier, these emancipatory projects cannot be based simply on essentially similarised collective standpoints of the oppressed. Instead, thinking must proceed in terms of 'a complex configuration of specificities, *positionality*' (ibid.: 317, emphasis original). Responsible critical inquiry will involve the painstaking labour of encountering through ethical collectivities in the interests of emancipation. This emancipation is not available simply by adding women to the existing framework of knowledge, but requires a rethinking of those frameworks. 'They must transform the terms of the discourse, challenge the structures of the epistemological project' (324). In what follows, I will explore one of the ways in which theorising as the anchor of knowledge creation can be *othered* by linking theory to travel.

7.2.5 ***Making theory hospitable to travel***

> The key to 'where you are' is an amalgam of the emphases conveyed by travel, otherness, and being.
>
> (Spivak 1999: 193)

Writing theories of the economic should be a self-aware exercise of power and of memory. The worlded world is multiple and recognising this does not mean an unconcern for whether the subaltern eats (cf. Sylvester 1999). The divide between theory and praxis is agonistic, futile and dangerous for it restricts the terms of critique. A 'writing' of 'economic theory' needs to proceed from completely unimaginable (and yet much imagined) premises. The very conceptualisation of 'knowledge' and what it means to know is to be altered. The individual subject transcendental referent that holds together the uber-theory, the urtext of the economic, the original map of economics will hang questioned. There is no economic self in market economy that economics can divine by models, but is constituted by utterances, differently and never alike. It needs to be written in its various presences, in locations and in memory (temporal, spatial, geographical, historical, ideological, to name some). Liberal humanism, global cosmopolitanism, integrative expansive ideas of universal emancipation, the general nature of human economic behaviour sharply distinguished from social, political, moral, and cultural – will never move beyond the transcendental universal modernist referent individual. We are not all part of one big market where we can either enthusiastically embrace modernist, capitalist, utilitarian ideas *or* be labelled primitive, uncivilised, backward, time-warped savages who cannot understand commerce or science or maths. Representations of progress have always relied on such imaginaries, in economics and elsewhere.

Writing is difficult. The mark privileges and the unsaid is not the same as the unwritten – it is political and poetic for it constitutes the legitimacy of voice, the transfer and translation of value. Writing economic theory an*Other* way is to question that which we think we know – the 'economic' – To admit the possibility that we cannot always think out the *a priori* 'economic'; that we cannot imagine its negotiations for every Other always – And so the whole set of ideas that are consonant with this particular way of delineating the economic, cannot be universal either – Its basis in individualism, in self-interest, in the calculus of comprehension, in value, in ownership, in consumption, in production, in extraction, and in deprivation. How was it that this concept became universal and disciplined so that to defy the 'economic logic' you had to be a child, a lunatic, or a 'primitive' non-European?[8]

It is not enough to exhaust the ethics of criticality at the door of the present as we find it. Questioning the hegemonic conceptualisation of the economic and the disciplinary motivations for the science of economics in the present is not enough. Rather, criticality demands making contingent the very basis of the present as an originary moment. Thus, when we juxtapose the considerations of identity with the economic and question the desire for universal knowledge, it is not simply a call to write theories of the economic an*Other* way, but significantly,

8 Or perhaps a libertine! Note the on-screen persona of John Wilmot, the second Earl of Rochester, a dissolute poet: When he witnesses a nobleman chastising his servant (Alcock) for filching two shillings, he decides to employ the rogue. Alcock is bewildered until his new master (the Earl of Rochester) explains that his previous six shilling pay was actual thievery on the part of the nobleman. But why employ such a character? 'The moral of the incident', answers Rochester, 'is that any experiment of interest in life will be carried out at your own expense. Mark it well' (The Libertine).

it is a call for re-imagining the writing of theory itself. To borrow Spivak's formulation, it is first and foremost important in the context of the expectations of theorising to enact the 'persistent critique of what one cannot not want' (1991: 248). In other words, to question our desire for the adequacy of a theory which can be written without Othering oneself. A sense of theory which originates from the foundation of its homing concepts – self, discipline, subject, world.

To take this idea further, I would briefly like to suggest an exploration of 'theory' and 'travel'. Within enlightenment epistemology and modernism, theory has functioned as a home on the road to knowledge. The writing of theory grounds the certainties of experiencing in stable ways. In this formulation, one must always be careful in guarding knowledge against the contamination of the strange, the unknown, the inhospitable, the foreign, the Other. The encounter with the Other is always structured in the expectation of cohering the self. One is at home in the familiarity of stable foundations. In contrast to this, I am arguing for exploring the linkage of theory to travel.

To begin with, this will involve getting over the Humean caution against 'travellers' tales'. When Hume warned against 'travellers' tales' (see Coleman 1995: 67), he was immunising knowledge against difference. Travel could lead to 'strange' notions, experiences, and convictions, because it makes the familiar unfamiliar. Now, to disrupt the universalising certainties of modernist knowledge we need the reverse. In the words of a poet (MacNiece 1935), there is an urgent need to realise that 'the world is incorrigibly plural'. But instead of distrusting the unfamiliar, this should inaugurate a re-imagining of theorising as a travel to Otherness. Theories themselves travel and much travel is theory.

Clifford (1986, 1989, 1997) considers the link between travel and theory where he writes that theory (from Greek *theorein*: a practice of travel and observation, a man sent by the *polis* to another city to witness a religious ceremony) is a product of displacement, comparison, a certain distance. *To theorise, one leaves home*. Consider the following (1989, emphases added),

> *Travel*: a figure for different modes of dwelling and displacements, for *trajectories and identities, for storytelling and theorizing in a postcolonial world* of global contacts. *Travel*: a range of *practices for situating the self* in a space or spaces grown too large, a form both of *exploration and discipline*. … *Theory*, a product long associated with Western discursive spaces – a status that permitted it to speak confidently of 'human' history, culture, psyche etc. – now is marked by specific historical centers and horizons. … Theory is no longer naturally 'at home' in the West – *a powerful place of Knowledge, History, or Science, a place to collect, sift, translate, and generalize*. Or, more cautiously, this privileged place is now increasingly contested, cut across, by other locations, claims, trajectories of knowledge articulating racial, gender, and cultural differences.

The postcolonial has involved marking 'the West' as a contested site of power: its legitimacy to speak under the sign of the human is questioned and its own constitution unravelled. While theory at home (in and with the promise of its adequacy) in enlightenment epistemology pretended to be the product of an exercise of knowledge in surveying the 'assumed topography of an already worlded world' (ibid.), we must now learn to recognise theorising as worlding the world in and through its travels.

But if we can see theory as travel, there is also the disciplinary dimension of seeing theories as 'travelling' through representation, resistance, and institutionalisation. This is Said's (1983: 226–247) notion of 'traveling theory', where theory travels from its originating context to new ones where it is critically appropriated and reinterpreted. Said identifies four stages of this travel that theories undertake as follows: one, the departure from the point of origin; two, passage through different contexts; three, transplantation into a new context with its own conditions of acceptance; and, four, re-emergence of the initial idea transformed by its displacement and new uses (ibid.: 226–227).[9] As a basic idea, this approach to theorising as involving transcontextuality is crucial.

Thus, many productive vistas can be afforded by thinking travel with theory.[10] Theory is not simply the rooted preserve of the powerful, it travels along routes. The concept of 'routes' (the emphasis in identity on the migratory routes of its inhabiting rather than its fixed 'roots', see Clifford 1997) along which theoretical ideas travel to new contexts is a meaningful terrain – a migrant intertextual inbetween hybrid space. A powerful resisting non-assimilative space that questions the dominant alignment of ideas as natural or normal. A catachrestic and detourning[11] space. A space for imagining theoretical endeavours that challenges the practice of theory itself – its ability to be adequate. Theory not as interpreting or explaining but *understanding its own conditions of performance and its particular arrangements of mediation in making and accessing the world.* The relation of theorising to travel invites the thinking of location not as a fixed point but as a site for struggle, ' "where" we are is a matter of dispute' (Ahmed 2000: 98). Further, in order to appreciate the different contexts arising from encounters with others, we can imagine a continual translation of oneself, a translation which can be conceptualised as a travelling, for instance as in Lugones's (1987) concept of world-travelling.

9 The example Said gives of a theory which has voyaged thus is Lukács's theory of reification. In 1994, Said revisited his earlier work, writing 'Travelling theory reconsidered'. For a recent engagement of both these versions of travelling theory in relation to postcolonial approaches to exoticism, see Forsdick (2002).

10 Seller (1994) provides an interesting example of self-reflexive critical thinking of theorising through the encounters of travel to unfamiliarity. The answer to her provocatively titled 'Should a feminist philosopher stay at home?' (about encountering women's studies at an Indian University) is ultimately, 'I think it is not so much a question of whether to stay at home, as of *learning how to travel*' (247, emphasis added).

11 Detournment is a situationist term which can be understood as '...to arrange disparate elements of the dominant culture together to form a new work, esp. in a way that reveals the true meaning and function of the original elements. Detournment as revolutionary activity reverses the systematic fragmentation of specialists...' ('Some Terms' n.d.).

Adopting the idea of 'travel' as the basis for theorising, interaction, the trajectory of theories, and the politics of identity – we can begin to think 'writing' itself as a performance whose conditions of possibility in knowledge creation become inextricably ethical. An engaged writing that cannot but be political. *For writing is a deeply divided and dividing act, subject as it is to the politics of elision and ellipsis*. The excess of meaning that hides behind the silhouette of the alphabet and plays in the silent spaces between – animates them with absence. What writing allows and what it does not let happen. Language, the maker-doer 'can only indefinitely tend towards justice by acknowledging and practising the violence within it' (Derrida quoted in Baker 1993:16). Like concurrent prison sentences, histories run concurrently (though not in parallel), and the history one remembers and writes depends on the routes one has travelled.

7.3 Pedagogy re-visited: contextual social political economic*es* (econo-mixes)

> And what is critical consciousness at bottom if not an unstoppable predilection for alternatives.
>
> (Said 1983: 247)

Writing theories of the economic an*Other* way is about exploring the alternatives that Said has in mind. But this involves moving beyond the disciplinary enforcements of separable social, political, and economic to a contextual social political economy as the basis for theoretical praxis. What stands in the way? Appropriating Spivak from another context (1991: 242),

> Why do people not talk about it? Well, that has to do with the teaching machine, that has to do with the institution. I mean the nature of disciplines, the nature of the institution, the nature of the teaching machine is basically reactionary, it seems to me. It is placed within individualism and competition, it is placed within the fierce desire for allocation and grants, it is placed within the desire to be validated within that story and the inertia of the tradition of already-produced knowledge which gives you the job satisfaction of being a specialist, the job satisfaction of reproducing yourself among your students. This stuff is reactionary so how do you expect such institutions and such machines to produce recognition?

I have now come full circle. From metaphor to metaphor: from the work done by the 'system as machine' idea of enlightenment epistemology to the work done by the 'teaching machine'. The point remains relevant. It is important to critically think the relation between the preservation of structures and the preservation of structures of knowledge, taking this also as an invitation to think the violence of knowledge.

We cannot continue to write economic theory as it is written by the mainstream. Indeed, we cannot write theory, or even consider knowledge, as based upon the epistemic certainties derived from a submerging of difference. The teaching machine may be one way of practising the insurrectional politics of reading and writing economy/economic/economics in Other ways. There are some promising signs. Many students and scholars the world over are declaring the crisis in economics with the onset of the Post-Autistic Economics (PAE) movement, supported by the 'Cambridge 27 call for opening up economics' and the 'Kansas City proposal: an international open letter to all economics departments' (see http://www.paecon.net). In the spirit of pluralism, ethical responsibility, and critical thought, the call is for rethinking teaching, practice, and ethics in economics (see Fullbrook 2003, 2004).

In this critical vein, together with poststructuralist feminist and postcolonial themes, we can begin to think of contextual social political economic praxis, a non-universalist way of creating specific and interested economic knowledges.[12] As universally valid theoretical frameworks become problematic, a recognition of difference is brought about. Often attempts to consider difference see it as 'diversion or division from sameness', as variations on the theme, but they don't let difference make a difference. Within a contextual praxis, difference is fundamental Otherness and involves considering specific history and context as the starting point of the theoretical life-cycle, rather than its culminatory application. By moving consciously in the direction of a multidisciplinary praxis we invite the authoring of contextualised theories in a framework of methodological pluralism, and this can insurrect certain relevant notions in our economic consideration of the world. An attention to contexts and praxis of a wider social political economy can also help to accommodate diverse insights. What (events, phenomena, behaviour) is currently a paradox or anomaly if viewed in economic terms might become more comprehensible when viewed in a theoretical constellation of varied motivations including the social or the political. Equally, new and locationally relevant issues might come into consideration. This will connect the political and the economic; economic knowledge will not be universally valid, and what is considered (defined) 'economic' will be understood differently across different contexts. Racial and cultural elements can be introduced into the analysis and localised struggles for meaning can arbitrate between competing accounts. Such a praxis will still be capable of admitting a contested notion of emancipation. Recognising the 'contingent foundations'[13] of all knowledge about

12 This is in contrast to the standard appeal to generalisable solutions, for example the general 'country-assistance strategy' for every poorer/impoverished nation followed by the World Bank with the same four-step programme of privatisation, followed by capital market liberalisation, then marketbased pricing, and 'free trade' (see Palast 2002; Stiglitz 2002; Chossudovsky 2003; for a linking of neoclassical economics and neoliberalism in relation to development economics that does not spare Sen and Stiglitz, see Herrera 2006).

13 Butler (1992: 3–21) advocates avoiding gestures of conceptual mastery. This is not the advent of nihilistic relativism but the very precondition of a politically engaged critique. 'The task is to interrogate what the theoretical move that establishes foundations authorises, and what precisely it excludes or forecloses;' not do away with the category of universality but to 'relieve the category of its foundationalist weight in order to render it as a site of permanent political contest' (7–8).

the economy, the way ahead can perhaps be negotiated by admitting 'strategic essentialism',[14] by deploying strategically essentialist categories for explicitly (contested) emancipatory politics.

The aesthetic aspirations of conventional economic theorising especially regarding the need for universally valid, objective knowledge lead to a 'violent' (epistemically) and 'oppressive' (materially) exercise where sets of people and ideas get 'written out' of the economy. Mapping of human interactions is not akin to postulating the ideal gas law, not the least because power is the constant twin to knowledge. It continuously mutates and transforms, it censors and creates. A *focus on power as operative in localised settings with a historicised present* is essential to attempt critical theorising. Examples of such endeavours might include examining the complicity between neoliberalism and neocolonialism in specific developmental rhetoric such as microcredit, foreign investment, and aid; interrogating the role of corporatised media in representing and constructing the 'economic' aspect/rationale in 'social political' issues; bringing into relief the disjuncture between economic theory and governmental practice on the overdetermined issue of the movement of human beings (the 'labour' that travels); and constructing sociologies and philosophies of economics as a profession, in both the West and non-West, and excavating its links to policy making and its status in governmental discourse.

Once the legitimacy of standard theories and theorising is questioned in this manner, the economy isn't a single, simple, universal entity that is omnipresent and lends itself to total comprehension. The economy itself is recognised as a creative metaphor which needs to be filled with particular meanings at particular situations. It need not be that kind of theorising which excludes gender, race, class, culture, ecology. The perforated boundaries of the economy can then be explored with contextual comprehensions. Theorising 'economic*es*' (economixes) or *multiple contextual social political scenarios of the economic* is a way of admitting possibilities and can also be extremely useful in testing the limits of overdetermination (events and processes as the site and result of multitude of determinations) in critical theoretical practice.

7.4 Conclusion: penpoints on mirrors[15]

> It was done from a desire to live, to make life possible, and to rethink the possible as such . . . although this insight does not in itself constitute a political revolution, no political revolution is possible without a radical shift in one's notion of the possible and the real.
>
> (Butler 1999: xx–xxiii)

14 Adopting and adapting deconstruction specifically for the postcolonial field, Spivak advocated strategic essentialism, 'a strategic use of positivist essentialism in a scrupulously visible political interest' (Landry and MacLean 1996: 214). The goal of such essentialist critique is not the exposure of error, but the interrogation of the essentialist terms. In relation to deconstructive critical practices, she argues that essentialising is unavoidable, '[s]o then strategically you can look at essentialism, not as descriptions of the way things are, but as something that one must adopt to produce a critique of everything' (Spivak 1990: 51).

15 I have coined the phrase 'penpoints on mirrors' to capture the idea of a writing that reflects its own contidtions of performance. The term 'penpoints' draws from the title of Ngugi Wa Thiong' O's

> ... this is what I hold and what in turn holds me in its grip, the aleatory strategy of someone who admits that [s]he does not know where [s]he is going ...
>
> (Derrida 1983: 35)

Writing theories of the economic in Other ways thus entails new self-reflexive ways of theorising, critiquing, practising, reading, and writing the economy/economic/economics which are informed by a deconstruction of enlightenment epistemology and modernist renditions of knowledge. Identity and economic, culture and economy, value and values, are not separations explained by history: rather, history requires their explanation in the modernist politics of knowledge. Here are the words of Thomas Babington Macaulay in defence of the East India Company in the same year the British parliament voted to end slavery in the British West Indies (in Sharpe 1993: 7, emphases added), '[i]t is scarcely possible to calculate the benefits which we might derive from the diffusion of European civilisation among the vast population of the East. ... *To trade with civilised men is infinitely more profitable than to govern savages.*'

It is a meaningless reverie to see critique as indulging in endless disputes on solely the scientific nature of economics. There never was or will be an 'economic' *per se* – except in the logic of economic theory. And it is for this reason that postcolonial memory has travelled to interrogate economic theory. This, I might add, is not a luxurious dalliance but crucial. 'Something else' leads down a conditioned mental cul-de-sac. We ask: what? – the story has to be told in familiarities. And yet the meeting of ideas can be an*Other* way of writing theory, as contextual social political economic praxes. A self-reflexive critical praxis (see Spivak 1993) that seeks to generate meaningful totalities at contingent theoretical moments, to enable one to talk (strategically) unambiguously of oppression as well as resistance to it. A contextual totality which draws from the intersectionality of social political and economic fabric – but not an attempt at master formula or overall answers. When one 'brings different things together to realise a third, which may have some features of all those other elements but is certainly not identical to any one of them: it becomes a third particularity' (Wa Thiong'O 1998: 11–12). No doubt, such engagements upset conventional ways of telling accepted stories in economics, let alone face the question, what is economics about? Like the anxieties of the regime in Bertolt Brecht's poem,[16] power, even as disciplinary power, seeks to censure the unfamiliar.

(1998) book *Penpoints, Gunpoints and Dreams* in which he explores the confrontation between art (penpoints) and the state (gunpoints) both of which are rooted in words and hold the society together.

16 Some lines from Brecht's 'Anxieties of the Regime' (in Wa Thiong'O 1998: 9–10)

> Given the immense powers of the regime
> Its camps and torture cellars
> Its well-fed policemen
> Its intimidated or corrupt judges
> Its card indexes and lists of suspended persons
> Which fill whole buildings to the roof
> One would think they wouldn't have to
> Fear an open word from a simple [wo]man ...

Carry on regardless. The 'wild anthropologists' (as Spivak calls postcolonial peoples) have much work to do in making visible the disavowed emancipatory problematics that provide the foundations for post-enlightenment imperial modernism. Economics, in whose *bildungsroman* one can read chapters on capitalism and imperialism, is a modernist project *par excellence*, locked into its airy metaphors of exchange, choice, and agency – yet all in a world of no Other, no alterity. Writing economic theory an*Other* way is an important step in refiguring the altered possibilities of knowledge in/of economics. In this difficult engagement, 'let a hundred flowers bloom and we don't mind even the weeds' (Guha in Shohat and Stam 1994: 203). Penpoints on mirrors. Shall we?

Bibliography

Addleson, Mark (1995) *Equilibrium versus Understanding: Towards the Restoration of Economics as Social Theory*, London: Routledge.

Ahmed, Sara (2000) 'Whose Counting', *Feminist Theory* 1, 1: 97–103.

Ahmed, Sara (2002) 'This Other and Other Others', Paper from author.

Ahmed, Sara, Kilby, Jane, Lury, Celia, McNeil, Maureen and Skeggs, Beverley (2000) *Transformations: Thinking Through Feminism*, London: Routledge.

Akerlof, George A. and Kranton, Rachel E. (2000) 'Economics and Identity', *The Quarterly Journal of Economics* CXV, 3: 715–753.

Alexander, M. Jacqui and Mohanty, Chandra Talpade (eds) (1997) *Feminist Genealogies, Colonial Legacies, Democratic Future*, London: Routledge.

Allen, Beth (2000) 'The Future of Microeconomic Theory', *Journal of Economic Perspectives* 14, 1: 143–150.

Alsop, Rachel, Fitzsimons, Annette and Lennon, Kathleen (2002) *Theorizing Gender*, Cambridge: Polity Press.

Amariglio, Jack (1988) 'The Body, Economic Discourse, and Power: An Economist's Introduction to Foucault', *History of Political Economy* 20, 4: 583–613.

Amariglio, Jack and Ruccio, David (2002) 'Modern Economics: The Case of the Disappearing Body?', *Cambridge Journal of Economics* 26, 1: 81–103.

Amariglio, Jack A., Callari, Antonio, Resnick, Stephen, Ruccio, David and Wolff, Richard (1996) 'Non Determinist Marxism: The Birth of a Postmodern Tradition in Economics', in Fred E. Foldvary (ed.) *Beyond Neoclassical Economics: Heterodox Approaches to Economic Theory*, Aldershot: Edward Elgar Publishing, 134–147.

Amis, Martin (2002) 'The Voice of the Lonely Crowd', *The Guardian*, 1 June. Online. Available http://books.guardian.co.uk/review/story/0,12084,725608,00.html (Accessed 10 December 2002).

Anand, Dibyesh (2007) *Geopolitical Exotica: Tibet in Western Imagination*, Minneapolis: University of Minnesota Press.

Anderson, Chas (2002) 'Re: HES: QUERY – History of AD-AS Graph', *HES*. Online posting. Available email: hes@eh.net (19 June 2002).

Anthias, Floya and Yuval-Davis, Nira (eds) (1989) *Women-Nation-State*, London: Macmillan Press.

Arrow, Kenneth J. (1994) 'Methodological Individualism and Social Knowledge', *The American Economic Review* 84, 2: 1–9.

Arrow, Kenneth (1995/1972) 'Some Mathematical Models of Race Discrimination in the Labor Market', in William Darity Jr (ed.) *Economics and Discrimination*, Aldershot: Edward Elgar Publishing, 298–314.

Arrow, Kenneth J. (1998) 'What has Economics to say about Racial Discrimination?', *Journal of Economic Perspectives* 12, 2: 91–100.

Arrow, Kenneth and Debreu, Gerard (1954) 'Existence of an Equilibrium for a Competitive Economy', *Econometrica* 22, 3: 265–290.

'A S. African Native's Homecoming' (2002) *Los Angeles Times*, 4 May.

Bachelard, Gaston (1969) *The Poetics of Space*, Catherine Porter (trans.), Boston: Beacon Press.

Backhouse, Roger E. (1992) 'Should We Ignore Methodology?', *The Royal Economic Society Newsletter* 78, July.

Backhouse, Roger E. (ed.) (1994) *New Directions in Economic Methodology*, London: Routledge.

Backhouse, Roger E. (1998) 'If Mathematics Is Informal, Then Perhaps We Should Accept That Economics Must Be Informal Too', *The Economic Journal* 108, 451: 1848–1858.

Baert, Patrick (1996) 'Realist Philosophy of the Social Sciences and Economics: A Critique', *Cambridge Journal of Economics* 20, 5: 513–522.

Bailey, Samuel (1967/1825) *A Critical Dissertation On The Nature, Measures, And Causes Of Value; Chiefly in Reference to the Writing of Mr. Ricardo and His Followers; and, A letter To a Political Economist; Occasioned by an Article in the Westminster Review on the Subject of Value*, London: Frank Cass [R. Hunter].

Baillie, Caroline, Dunn, Elizabeth and Zheng, Yi (eds) (2004) *Travelling Facts: The Social Construction, Distribution, and Accumulation of Knowledge*, Frankfurt: Campus Verlag.

Baker, Robert (1993) 'Crossings of Levinas, Derrida, and Adorno: Horizons of Nonviolence', *diacritics* 23, 4: 12–41.

Balak, Benjamin (2000) 'McCloskey: Ethically Deconstructing Economic Thought', paper presented at the Tenth World Congress of Social Economics, Cambridge University, UK.

Barker, Drucilla K. (1995) 'Economists, Social Reformers and Prophets: A Feminist Critique of Economic Efficiency', *Feminist Economics* 1, 3: 26–39.

Barker, Drucilla and Kuiper, Edith (eds) (2003) *Toward a Feminist Philosophy of Economics*, London: Routledge.

Barnett, Stuart (ed.) (1998) *Hegel After Derrida*, London: Routledge.

Bayart, Jean-Francois (2005) *The Illusion of Cultural Identity*, Steven Rendall, Janet Roitman and Cynthia Schoch (trans.), London: University of Chicago Press.

Becker, Carl L. (1932) *The Heavenly City of the Eighteenth-Century Philosophers*, London: Yale University Press.

Beckert, Jens (2002) *Beyond the Market: The Social Foundations of Economic Efficiency*, Barbara Harshav (trans.), Princeton: Princeton University Press.

Beed, Clive (1991) 'Philosophy of Science and Contemporary Economics: an Overview', *Journal of Post Keynesian Economics* 13, 4: 459–494.

Beed, Clive and Beed, Cara (2000) 'The Status of Economics as a Naturalistic Social Science', *Cambridge Journal of Economics* 24, 4: 417–435.

Belsey, Catherine (2002) 'Making Space: Perspective, Vision and the Lacanian Real', *Textual Practice* 16, 1: 31–55.

Bendle, Mervyn F. (2002) 'The Crisis of "Identity" in High Modernity', *British Journal of Sociology* 53, 1: 1–18.

Bergeron, Suzanne (2000) ' "The Challenge of Inclusion" and the Representation of Narrative Agents in World Bank Literature', Paper from author.

Bergeron, Suzanne (2002) 'Disciplining Gender: Culture, Institutions, and Interdisciplinary Knowledge in *Engendering Development*', Paper presented at the International Association for Feminist Economics Meetings, Los Angeles, USA.

Bergeron, Suzanne (2005) *Fragments of Development: Nation, Gender, and the Space of Modernity*, Ann Arbor: University of Michigan Press.

Bergmann, Barbara (2002) 'Conversation with Barbara Bergmann', in Paulette I. Olson and Zohreh Emami (eds) *Engendering Economics: Conversations with Women Economists in the United States*, London: Routledge, 53–72.

Berlin, Isaiah (1956) *The Age of Enlightenment*, New York: Mentor Books.

Bernasconi, Robert (1998) 'Hegel at the Court of the Ashanti', in Stuart Barnett (ed.) *Hegel After Derrida*, London: Routledge, 41–63.

Bertrand, Marianne and Mullainathan, Sendhil (2004) 'Are Emily and Greg More Employable than Lakisha and Jamal? A Field Experiment on Labor Market Discrimination', *American Economic Review* 94, 4: 991–1013.

Best, Beverley (1999) 'Postcolonial and the Deconstructive Scenario: Representing Gayatri Spivak', *Environment and Planning D: Society and Space* 17, 475–94.

Beverley, John (1999) *Subalternity and Representation: Arguments in Cultural Theory*, London: Duke University Press.

Bhabha, Homi K. (1994) *The Location of Culture*, London: Routledge.

Bhabha, Homi K. (1996) 'Unpacking My Library... Again', in Iain Chambers and Lidia Curti (eds) *The Post-Colonial Question: Common Skies, Divided Horizons*, London: Routledge, 199–211.

Bhabha, Homi K. (1997) 'Liberalism's Sacred Cow', *Boston Review*, Online. Available http://bostonreview.mit.edu/BR22.5/bhabha.html (10 December 2002).

Bhagwati, Jagdish (2001) 'After Seattle: Free Trade and the WTO', *International Affairs* 77, 1: 15–29.

Bicchieri, Cristina (1988) 'Should a Scientist Abstain from Metaphor?' in Arjo Klamer, Robert Solow and Donald McCloskey (eds) *The Consequences of Economic Rhetoric*, Cambridge: Cambridge University Press, 100–116.

Bishop, Alan J. (1995) 'Western Mathematics: The Secret Weapon of Cultural Imperialism', in Bill Ashcroft, Gareth Griffiths and Helen Tiffin (eds) *The Post-Colonial Studies Reader*, New York: Routledge, 71–76.

Black, Max (1962) *Models and Metaphors: Studies in Language and Philosophy*, Ithaca: Cornell University Press.

Blaug, Mark (1980a) 'Economic Methodology in One Easy Lesson', *British Review of Economic Issues* 2, 6: 1–16.

Blaug, Mark (1980b) *The Methodology of Economics: Or How Economists Explain*, Cambridge: Cambridge University Press.

Blaug, Mark (1988) 'Economics Through a Looking Glass: The Distorted Perspective of The New Palgrave Dictionary of Economics', *Institute of Economic Affairs (IEA) Occasional Paper* 78, June.

Blaug, Mark (2001) 'No History of Ideas, Please, We're Economists', *Journal of Economic Perspectives* 15, 1: 145–164.

Bleicher, Josef (1980) *Contemporary Hermeneutics: Hermeneutics as Method, Philosophy and Critique*, London: Routledge.

Blendon, Robert J., Benson, John M., Brodie, Mollyann, Morin, Richard, Altman, Drew E., Gitterman, Daniel, Brossard, Mario and James, Matt (1999) 'Bridging The Gap between the Public's and the Economists' Views of the Economy', in Robert Garnett (ed.) *What do Economists Know? New Economics of Knowledge*, London: Routledge, 86–100.

Bodkin, Ronald G. (1999) 'Women's Agency in Classical Economic Thought: Adam Smith, Harriet Taylor Mill and J. S. Mill', *Feminist Economics* 5, 1: 45–60.

Boland, Lawrence (1992) *The Principles of Economics: Some Lies My Teacher Told Me*, London: Routledge.

Boland, Lawrence (1997) *Critical Economic Methodology: A Personal Odyssey*, London: Routledge.

Boundas, Constantin V. (2001) 'Gift, Theft, Apology', *Angelaki: Journal of the Theoretical Humanities* 6, 2: 1–5.

Bourdieu, Pierre (1977) *Outline of a Theory of Practice*, Richard Nice (trans.), Cambridge: Cambridge University Press.

Boylan, Thomas A. and O'Gorman, Paschal F. (1995) *Beyond Rhetoric and Realism in Economics: Towards a Reformulation of Economic Methodology*, London: Routledge.

Bradley, Matthew Todd (2005) '"The Other": Precursory African Conceptions of Democracy', *International Studies Review* 7, 3: 407–431.

Bramen, Carrie Tirado (2002) 'Why the Academic Left Hates Identity Politics', *Textual Practice* 16, 1: 1–11.

Brennan, Teresa (1997) 'Economy for the Earth: the Labour Theory of Value without the Subject/Object Distinction', *Ecological Economics* 20, 2: 175–185.

Brown, Robert H. (1993) 'Modern Science: Institutionalisation of Knowledge and Rationalization of Power', *The Sociological Quarterly* 34, 1: 153–168.

Brown, Stuart, Fauvel, John and Finnegan, Ruth (eds) (1981) *Conceptions of Inquiry: A Reader*, London: Methuen & Co.

Brown, Vivienne (1994a) *Adam Smith's Discourse: Canonicity, Commerce and Conscience*, London: Routledge.

Brown, Vivienne (1994b) 'The Economy as Text', in Roger E. Backhouse (ed.) *New Directions in Economic Methodology*, London: Routledge, 368–382.

Browne, M. Neil and Quinn, J. Kevin (1999) 'Dominant Economic Metaphors and the Postmodern Subversion of the Subject', in Martha Woodmansee and Mark Osteen (eds) *The New Economic Criticism: Studies at the Intersection of Literature and Economics*, London: Routledge, 131–149.

Bruni, Luigino (2002) 'Re: HES: QUERY – Inequality', *HES*. Online posting. Available email: hes@eh.net (25 June 2002).

Bulgakov, Sergei (2000/1912) *Philosophy of Economy: The World as Household*, Catherine Evtuhov (trans.), New Haven: Yale University Press.

Butler, Judith (1990) *Gender Trouble: Feminism and the Subversion of Identity*, London: Routledge.

Butler, Judith (1992) 'Contingent Foundations: Feminism and the Question of "Postmodernism"', in Judith Butler and Joan W. Scott (eds) *Feminists Theorize the Political*, London: Routledge, 3–21.

Butler, Judith (1993) *Bodies that Matter: On the Discursive Limits of 'Sex'*, London: Routledge.

Butler, Judith (1999) *Gender Trouble: Feminism and the Subversion of Identity*, Rev. Ed., London: Routledge.

Butler, Judith (2000a) 'Dynamic Conclusions', in Judith Butler, Ernesto Laclau and Slavoj Žižek (eds) *Contingency, Hegemony, Universality: Contemporary Dialogues on the Left*. London: Verso, 263–280.

Butler, Judith (2000b) 'The Value of Being Disturbed', *Theory and Event* 4, 1. Online. Available http://muse.jhu.edu/journals/theory_&_event/v004/4.1butler.htm (Accessed 12 August 2000).

Byron, George Gordon (1824) *Don Juan* Online. Available http://www.literaturecollection.com/a/lord-byron/don-juan/1/ (Accessed 10 February 2007).

Caldwell, Bruce J. (1982) *Beyond Positivism: Economic Methodology in the Twentieth Century*, London: George Allen & Unwin Ltd.

Caldwell, Bruce (ed.) (1993) *The Philosophy and Methodology of Economics Vol I–III*, Aldershot: Edward Elgar Publishing.

Caldwell, Bruce J. (2002) 'Re: HES: QUERY – History of AD–AS graph', *HES*. Online posting. Available email: hes@eh.net (18 June 2002).

Caplan, Bryan (2002) 'Systematically Biased Beliefs about Economics: Robust Evidence of Judgemental Anomalies from the Survey of Americans and Economists on the Economy', *The Economic Journal* 112, 479: 433–458.

Caraça, João (2001) 'Ceremonial Inadequacy: In Search of a New Enlightenment', *European Journal of Social Theory* 4, 3: 287–290.

Caute, David (1973) *The Fellow – Travellers: A Postscript to the Enlightenment*, London: Weidenfeld and Nicolson Limited.

Chakrabarty, Dipesh (2000) *Provincializing Europe: Postcolonial Thought and Historical Difference*, Princeton: Princeton University Press.

Chambers, Iain and Curti, Lidia (eds) (1996) *The Post-Colonial Question: Common Skies, Divided Horizons*, London: Routledge.

Charusheela, S. (2000) 'On History, Love, and Politics', *Rethinking Marxism* 12, 4: 45–61.

Chick, Victoria (1998) 'On Knowing One's Place: The Role of Formalism in Economics', *The Economic Journal* 108, 1859–1869.

Chodorow, Nancy (1978) *The Reproduction of Mothering*, London: University of California Press.

Chossudovsky, Michel (2003) *The Globalization of Poverty and the New World Order*, Quebec: Global Research.

Chow, Rey (1994) 'Where Have All the Natives Gone?, in Padmini Mongia (ed.) *Contemporary Postcolonial Theory*, New York: Arnold.

Christensen, Kimberley (2001) ' "Thank God... I Thought for a Moment You Were Going to Confess to Converting to Socialism!": Gender and Identity in Deirdre McCloskey's Crossing', *Feminist Economics* 7, 2: 105–120.

Clark, Henry C. (1993) 'Women and Humanity in Scottish Enlightenment Social Thought: the Case of Adam Smith', *Historical Reflections* 19, 3: 335–361.

Clark, John J. (1997) *Oriental Enlightenment: The Encounter Between Asian and Western Thought*, London: Routledge.

Clifford, James (1986) *The Predicament of Culture: Twentieth Century Ethnography, Literature, and Art*, Cambridge, MA.: Harvard University Press.

Clifford, James (1989) 'Notes on Travel and Theory', *Inscriptions* 5. Online. Available http://humwww.ucsc.edu/CultStudies/PUBS/Inscriptions/vol_5/clifford.html (Accessed 17 November 2001).

Clifford, James (1997) *Routes: Travel and Translation in the Late Twentieth Century*, Cambridge, MA.: Harvard University Press.

Coate, Stephen and Loury, Glenn C. (1993) 'Will Affirmative-Action Policies Eliminate Negative Stereotypes?', *The American Economic Review* 83, 5: 1220–1240.

Code, Lorraine (1991) *What Can She Know? Feminist Theory and the Construction of Knowledge*, Ithaca: Cornell University Press.

Colander, David (2000) 'New Millennium Economics: How Did It Get This Way, and What Way Is It?', *Journal of Economic Perspectives* 14, 1: 121–132.

Colander, David (2003) 'The Aging of an Economist', *Journal of the History of Economic Thought* 25, 2: 157–176.

Colander, David and Klamer, Arjo (1987) 'The Making of an Economist', *Journal of Economic Perspectives* 1, 2: 95–111.

Coleman, William O. (1995) *Rationalism and Anti-Rationalism in the Origins of Economics: The Philosophical Roots of 18th Century Economic Thought*, Aldershot: Edward Elgar Publishing.

Collier, Andrew (1994) *Critical Realism: An Introduction to Roy Bhaskar's Philosophy*, London: Verso.

Collins, Patricia Hill (1997) 'Comment on Hekman's "Truth and Method: Feminist Standpoint Theory Revisited": Where's the Power?' *Signs: Journal of Women in Culture and Society* 22, 2: 375–381.

Connolly, William E. (1991) *Identity/Difference: Democratic Negotiations of Political Paradox*, Ithaca: Cornell University Press.

Connor, Steven (2002) 'Ghosts in the Machine', *The Guardian*, 2 March. Online. Available http://books.guardian.co.uk/Print/0,3858,4365670,00.html (Accessed 9 December 2002).

Cooper, Brian (2001) 'Social Statistics and Questions of "Difference" in Economics', paper presented at the Allied Social Sciences Association Meetings, New Orleans, USA.

Cooper, Brian P. (2003) 'Social Classifications, Social Statistics, and the "Facts" of "Difference" in Economics', in Drucilla K. Barker and Edith Kuiper (eds) *Toward a Feminist Philosophy of Economics*, London: Routledge, 161–179.

Corbey, Raymond and Leerssen, Joep (eds) (1991) *Alterity, Identity, Image: Selves and Others in Society and Scholarship*, Amsterdam: Rodopi.

Crespo, Ricardo F. (1998) 'Controversy: Is Economics a Moral Science?', *The Journal of Markets and Morality* 1, 2: 201–211.

Csicsery-Ronay, Istvan (1997) *Notes on Mutopia*. Online. Available http://jefferson.village.virginia.edu/pmc/text-only/issue.997/csicsery.997 (Accessed 2 December 1998).

Cudd, Ann (1997) 'On Social Groups', Paper from author.

Cudd, Ann E. (2000) 'Multiculturalism as a Cognitive Virtue of Scientific Practice', Paper from author.

Cullenberg, Stephen, Amariglio, Jack and Ruccio, David (2001) 'Introduction', in Stephen Cullenberg, Jack Amariglio and David Ruccio (eds) *Postmodernism, Economics and Knowledge*, London: Routledge.

Custers, Peter (1997) *Capital Accumulation and Women's Labour in Asian Economies*, London: Zed Books.

D'haen, Theo and Bertens, Hans (eds) (1994) *Liminal Postmodernisms: The Postmodern, the (Post-)Colonial, and the (Post-)Feminist*, Amsterdam: Rodopi.

Damisch, Hubert (1994/1987) *The Origin of Perspective*, John Goodman (trans.), Cambridge, MA: MIT Press.

Darity Jr., William (1995) *Economics and Discrimination*, 2 vols, Aldershot: Edward Elgar Publishing.

Dasgupta, Partha (1998) 'Modern Economics and its Critics, 1'. Online. Available http://www.econ.cam.ac.uk/faculty/dasgupta/modecon.pdf (Accessed 2 August 2000).

Daston, Lorraine and Galison, Peter (1992) 'The Image of Objectivity', *Representations* 40, fall: 81–128.

Davis, John B. (1999) 'Postmodernism and Identity Conditions for Discourses', in Robert F. Garnett Jr (ed.) *What do Economists Know?*, London: Routledge, 155–168.

Davis, John (2003) *Theory of the Individual in Economics: Identity and Value*, London: Routledge.

Davis, John B., Wade Hands, D. and Maki, Uskali (eds) (1998) *The Handbook of Economic Methodology*, Aldershot: Edward Elgar Publishing.

De Sousa Santos, Boaventura (2001a) 'Toward an Epistemology of Blindness: Why the New Forms of "Ceremonial Adequacy" neither Regulate nor Emancipate', *European Journal of Social Theory* 4, 3: 251–279.

De Sousa Santos, Boaventura (2001b) 'In Search of the Negation of the Negation', *European Journal of Social Theory* 4, 3: 291–294.

De Vroey, Michel (1999) 'The Marshallian Market and the Walrasian Economy. Two Incompatible Bedfellows', *Scottish Journal of Political Economy* 46, 3: 319–338.

Debreu, Gerard (1959) *Theory of Value: An Axiomatic Analysis of Economic Equilibrium*, New York: Wiley.

Debreu, Gerard (1984) 'Economic Theory in the Mathematical Mode', *The American Economic Review* 74, 3: 267–278.

Delanty, Gerard (2000) *Modernity and Postmodernity: Knowledge, Power and the Self*, London: Sage Publications.

Delany, Paul (1999) 'Who Paid for Modernism?', in Martha Woodmansee and Mark Osteen (eds) *The New Economic Criticism: Studies at the Intersection of Literature and Economics*, London: Routledge, 335–351.

Deleuze, Gilles and Guattari, Felix (1983) *Anti-Oedipus: Capitalism and Schizophrenia*, Minneapolis: University of Minnesota Press.

Derrida, Jacques (1983) 'The Time of a Thesis: Punctuations', in Alan Montefiore (ed.) *Philosophy in France Today*, Cambridge: Cambridge University Press, 34–50.

Derrida, Jacques (1987) *Positions*, Alan Bass (trans.), London: The Athlone Press.

Derrida, Jacques (1989) 'Some Statements and Truisms about Neologisms, Newisms, Postisms, Parasitisms, and Other Small Seismisms', in David Carroll (ed.) *States of 'Theory': History, Art, Critical Discourse*, New York: Columbia University Press, 63–94.

Derrida, Jacques (1994) 'From Spectres of Marx'. Online. Available http://www.angelfire.com/on/pisd/archive/FromSpectresofMarx.htm (Accessed 28 August 2000).

Descartes, Rene (1641) *Meditation II: Of the Nature of the Human Mind; And That It Is More Easily Known Than the Body*, Online. Available http://www.msu.org/intro/content_intro/texts/descartes/descartes2.html#med2 (Accessed 9 December 2002).

Dillon, Michael (2000) 'Poststructuralism, Complexity and Poetics', *Theory, Culture & Society* 17, 5: 1–26.

Dimand, Robert W. (2001) 'Economists and "The Other" Before 1914', paper presented at the Union for Radical Political Economics session, Allied Social Science Association meetings, New Orleans, USA.

Douglas-Fairhurst, Robert (2002) 'The Victorians and the Visual Imagination', *Notes and Queries* 49, 1: 153–157.

Dow, Sheila (1995) 'The Appeal of Neoclassical Methodology: Some Insights from Keynes' Epistemology', *Cambridge Journal of Economics* 19, 6: 715–733.

Dow, Sheila (1998) 'Controversy: Formalism In Economics', *The Economic Journal* 108, 451: 1826–1828.

Dowd, Douglas (2000) *Capitalism and its Economics: A Critical History*, London: Pluto Press.

Du Gay, Paul, Evans, Jessica and Redman, Peter (eds) (2000) *Identity: A Reader*, London: Sage Publications.

Dunthorne, Hugh (1991) *The Enlightenment*, London: Historical Association.

During, Simon (1995) 'Rousseau's Patrimony: Primitivism, Romance and Becoming Other', in Francis Barker, Peter Hulme and Margaret Iversen (eds) *Colonial Discourse / Postcolonial Theory*, Manchester: St Martin's Press.

Easterly, William (2001) *The Elusive Quest for Growth: Economists' Adventures and Misadventures in the Tropics*, Massachusetts: MIT Press.

Ebert, Teresa L. (1996) *Ludic Feminism and After: Postmodernism, Desire & Labour in Late Capitalism*, Michigan: University of Michigan Press.

Ekegren, Peter (1999) *The Reading of Theoretical Texts: A Critique of Criticism in the Social Sciences*, London: Routledge.

Elam, Diane (1994) *Feminism and Deconstruction*, London: Routledge.

Ellerman, David P. (1991) 'Myth and Metaphor In Orthodox Economics', *Journal of Post Keynesian Economics* 13, 4: 545–564.

Elster, Jon (ed.) (1986) *The Multiple Self*, Cambridge: Cambridge University Press.

Elster, Jon (1998) 'Emotions and Economic Theory', *Journal of Economic Literature* 36, 1: 47–74.

Engelstad, Ericka and Gerrard, Siri (eds) (2005) *Challenging Situatedness: Gender, Culture and the Production of Knowledges*, Delft: Eburon Publishers.

England, Paula (1993) 'The Separative Self: Androcentric Bias in Neoclassical Assumptions', in Marianne A. Ferber and Julie A. Nelson (eds) *Beyond Economic Man: Feminist Theory and Economics*, London: University of Chicago Press, 37–53.

England, Paula (1995) 'A Feminist Critique of Rational-Choice Theories: Implications for Sociology', in Jane Humphries (ed.) *Gender and Economics*, Aldershot: Edward Elgar Publishing, 42–56

England, Richard W. (ed.) (1994) *Evolutionary Concepts in Contemporary Economics*, Ann Arbor: University of Michigan Press.

Enloe, Cynthia (2000) *Bananas, Beaches and Bases: Making Feminist Sense of International Politics*, Rev. Ed., London: University of California Press.

Ermarth, Elizabeth (2000) 'What Counts as Feminist Theory?', *Feminist Theory* 1, 1: 113–118.

Escobar, Arturo (1995) *Encountering Development: The Making and Unmaking of The Third World*, Princeton: Princeton University Press.

Ethnomathematics Digital Library (EDL) (n.d.) *A Program of Pacific Resources for Education and Learning*. Online. Available http://www.ethnomath.org/ (Accessed 20 November 2006).

Evans, Brad (2005) *Before Cultures: The Ethnographic Imagination in American Literature 1865–1920*, London: University of Chicago Press.

Eze, Emmanuel Chukwudi (1997) *Postcolonial African Philosophy: A Critical Reader*, Oxford: Blackwell Publishers.

Fabian, Johannes (1983) *Time and the Other: How Anthropology Makes its Object*, New York: Columbia University Press.

Fang, Hanming and Loury, Glenn C. (2004) *Toward an Economic Theory of Dysfunctional Identity*, Yale University: Cowles Foundation Discussion Paper No. 1483, Online. Available http://cowles.econ.yale.edu/P/cd/d14b/d1483.pdf (Accessed 10 February 2007).

Featherstone, Mike, Lash, Scott and Robertson, Ronald (eds) (1995) *Global Modernities*, London: Sage Publications.

Feiner, Susan F. (1999) 'A Portrait of *Homo Economicus* as a Young Man', in Martha Woodmansee and Mark Osteen (eds) *The New Economic Criticism: Studies at the Intersection of Literature and Economics*, London: Routledge, 193–209.

Feiner, Susan and Roberts, Bruce (1990) 'Hidden by the Invisible Hand: Neoclassical Economic Theory and the Textbook Treatment of Race and Gender', *Gender and Society* 4, 2: 159–181.

Feiner, Susan and Roberts, Bruce (1995) 'Using Alternative Paradigms to Teach About Race and Gender: a Critical Thinking Approach to Introductory Economics', *The American Economic Review* 85, 2: 367–371.

Ferber, Marianne (2002) 'Conversation with Marianne Ferber', in Paulette I. Olson and Zohreh Emami (eds) *Engendering Economics: Conversations with Women Economists in the United States*, London: Routledge, 31–52.

Ferber, Marianne A. and Nelson, Julie A. (eds) (1993) *Beyond Economic Man: Feminist Theory and Economics*, London: University of Chicago Press.

Ferber, Marianne A. and Nelson, Julie A. (eds) (2003) *Feminist Economics Today: Beyond Economic Man*, London: University of Chicago Press.

Ferreira, M. Jamie (1994) 'Hume and Imagination: Sympathy and 'the Other', *International Philosophical Quarterly* XXXIV, 1, 133: 39–57.

Feyerabend, Paul (1987) *Farewell to Reason*, London: Verso.

Feyerabend, Paul (1988) *Against Method*, Rev. Ed., London: Verso.

Fine, Ben (1999) 'A Question of Economics: Is It Colonizing the Social Sciences?', *Economy and Society* 28, 3: 403–425.

Flax, Jane (1990) *Thinking Fragments: Psychoanalysis, Feminism, and Postmodernism in the Contemporary West*, London: University of California Press.

Flax, Jane (1992) 'The End of Innocence', in Judith Butler and Joan Scott (eds) *Feminists Theorize the Political*, London: Routledge, 445–463.

Fleetwood, Steve (ed.) (1999) *Critical Realism in Economics: Development and Debate*, London: Routledge.

Folbre, Nancy (1994) *Who Pays for the Kids? Gender and the Structures of Constraint*, London: Routledge.

Folbre, Nancy (n.d.) 'The Distribution of the Costs of Children'. Online. Available http://www-unix.oit.umass.edu/~folbre/folbre/pdf/peopleoverheads.pdf (Accessed 10 November 2002).

Folbre, Nancy and Hartmann, Heidi (1988) 'The Rhetoric of Self-Interest: Ideology and Gender in Economic Theory', in Arjo Klamer, Robert Solow and Donald McCloskey (eds) *The Consequences of Economic Rhetoric*, Cambridge: Cambridge University Press, 184–206.

Foldvary, Fred E. (ed.) (1996) *Beyond Neoclassical Economics: Heterodox Approaches to Economic Theory*, Aldershot: Edward Elgar Publishing.

Forsdick, Charles (2002) 'Travelling Concepts: Postcolonial Approaches to Exoticism', *Paragraph: A Journal of Modern Critical Theory* 24, 3: 12–29.

Foucault, Michel (1980) *Power/knowledge: Selected Interviews and Other Writings 1972–1977*, Colin Gordon (ed.), London: Harvester Wheatsheaf.

Foucault, Michel (1984) 'What is Enlightenment?', in Paul Rabinow (ed.) *The Foucault Reader*, London: Pantheon, 32–50.

Franco, Jean (1988) 'Beyond Ethnocentrism: Gender, Power, and the Third-World Intelligentsia', in Cary Nelson and Lawrence Grossberg (eds) *Marxism and the Interpretation of Culture*, Urbana: University of Illinois Press, 503–515.

Freedman, Robert (ed.) (1961) *Marx on Economics*, London: Penguin Books.

Friedman, Milton (1953) *Essays in Positive Economics*, London: University of Chicago Press.

Fukuyama, Francis (1992) *The End of History and the Last Man*, New York: Free Press.

Fulbrook, Edward (ed.) (2002) *Intersubjectivity in Economics*, London: Routledge.

Fullbrook, Edward (ed.) (2003) *The Crisis in Economics*, London: Routledge.

Fullbrook, Edward (ed.) (2004) *A Guide to What's Wrong with Economics*, London: Anthem Press.

Fuss, Diana (1994) 'Interior Colonies: Frantz Fanon and the Politics of Identification', *diacritics* 24, 3: 20–42.

Gagnier, Regenia (2000) *The Insatiability of Human Wants: Economics and Aesthetics in Market Society*, London: University of Chicago Press.
Galbraith, James K. (2000) 'How the Economists Got it Wrong', *The American Prospect* 11, 7.
Galbraith, John Kenneth (1970) 'Economics in the Industrial State: Science and Sedative: Economics as a System of Belief', *American Economic Review* 60, 2: 469–478.
Gandhi, Leela (1998) *Postcolonial Theory: A Critical Introduction*, Edinburgh: Edinburgh University Press.
Gare, Arran (2002) 'Human Ecology and Public Policy: Overcoming the Hegemony of Economics', *Democracy and Nature* 8, 1: 131–141.
Garfinkel, Alan (1981) *Forms of Explanation: Rethinking the Questions in Social Theory*, New Haven: Yale University Press.
Garnett, Robert F. Jr (ed.) (1999) *What do Economists Know? New Economics of Knowledge*, London: Routledge.
Gedalof, Irene (1999) *Against Purity: Rethinking Identity with Indian and Western Feminisms*, London: Routledge.
Gibson-Graham, J. K. (1996) *The End of Capitalism (As we knew it): A Feminist Critique of Political Economy*, Oxford: Blackwell Publishers.
Gilbert, Jeremy (2001) 'Against the Empire: Thinking the Social and (Dis)Locating Agency "Before, Across and Beyond Any National Determination"', *Parallax* 7, 3: 96–113.
Gilman, Charlotte Perkins (1898) *Women and Economics: A Study of the Economic Relation between Men and Women as a Factor in Social Evolution*, Boston: Small, Maynard & Co.
Gintis, Herbert (1972) 'Consumer Behavior and the Concept of Sovereignty: Explanations of Social Decay', *American Economic Review* 62, 1–2: 267–278.
'Globally Speaking' (2002) *Program 6: Global Citizenship, Extended Interview: Professor Martha Nussbaum*. Online. Available http://abc.net.au/global/radio/nassbaum.htm (Accessed 10 December 2002).
Goux, Jean-Joseph (1999) 'Cash, Check, or Charge?', John R. Barberet (trans.), in Martha Woodmansee and Mark Osteen (eds) *The New Economic Criticism: Studies at the Intersection of Literature and Economics*, London: Routledge, 114–127.
Graham, Julie and Amariglio, Jack (1995) 'What Difference Does Difference Make? Gender, Sexuality and Economic Theory', Paper from author.
Grampp, William D. (1951) 'The Moral Hero and the Economic Man', *Ethics* 61, 2: 136–150.
Grapard, Ulla (1995) 'Robinson Crusoe: The Quintessential Economic Man?', *Feminist Economics* 1, 1: 33–52.
Grapard, Ulla (1996) 'How to See the Invisible Hand, or, from the Benevolence of the Butcher's wife', Paper from author.
Grapard, Ulla (2000) 'Trading Bodies, Trade in Bodies: The 1878 Paris World Exhibition as Economic Discourse', Paper from author.
Grapard, Ulla and Hewitson, Gillian (eds) (2007) *Robinson Crusoe's Economic Man: A Construction and Deconstruction*, London: Routledge.
Griswold Jr., Charles L. (1999) *Adam Smith and the Virtues of Enlightenment*, Cambridge: Cambridge University Press.
Grootenboer, Hanneke (2005) *The Rhetoric of Perspective: Realism and Illusionism in Seventeenth-Century Dutch Still-Life Painting*, London: University of Chicago Press.
Grossberg, Lawrence (1996) 'The Space of Culture, The Power of Space', *The Post-Colonial Question: Common Skies, Divided Horizons*, New York: Routledge.
Gunning, Patrick (2002) 'Re: HES: QUERY – Inequality,' *HES*. Online posting. Available email: hes@eh.net (25 June 2002).

Hacking, Ian (ed.) (1981) *Scientific Revolution*, Oxford: Oxford University Press.

Hahn, Frank (1990) 'John Hicks the Theorist', *The Economic Journal* 100, 401: 539–549.

Hahn, Frank (1992a) 'Reflections', *Royal Economic Society Newsletter* 77, April.

Hahn, Frank (1992b) 'Answer to Backhouse: Yes', *Royal Economic Society Newsletter* 78, July.

Hahn, Frank and Hollis, Martin (eds) (1979) *Philosophy and Economic Theory*, Oxford: Oxford University Press.

Hall, Catherine (2002) 'The Egalitarian Instinct', *The Guardian Saturday Review*, 20 April. Excerpt from *Civilising Subjects: Metropole and the Colony in English Imagination 1830 to 1867*, Cambridge: Polity Press.

Hall, Stuart (1988) 'The Toad in the Garden: Thatcherism among the Theorists', in Cary Nelson and Lawrence Grossberg (eds) *Marxism and the Interpretation of Culture*, Urbana: University of Illinois Press, 35–57.

Hall, Stuart (1992) 'The West and the Rest: Discourse and Power', in Stuart Hall and Bram Gieben (eds) *Formations of Modernity*, Cambridge: Polity Press, 275–320.

Hall, Stuart (1997) 'The Spectacle of the "Other"', in Stuart Hall (ed.) *Representation: Cultural Representations and Signifying Practices*, London: Sage Publications Ltd, 223–290.

Hall, Stuart (2000) 'Who Needs "Identity"?', in Paul du Gay, Jessica Evans and Peter Redman (eds) *Identity: A Reader*, London: Sage Publications, 15–30.

Hall, Stuart and du Gay, Paul (eds) (1996) *Questions of Cultural Identity*, London: Sage Publications.

Hampshire, Stuart (1956) *The Age of Reason*, New York: Mentor Books.

Hampson, Norman (1968) *The Enlightenment*, Middlesex: Penguin Books.

Hankins, Thomas L. (1985) *Science and the Enlightenment*, Cambridge: Cambridge University Press.

Haraway, Donna (1985) 'A Manifesto for Cyborgs: Science, Technology, and Socialist Feminism in the 1980s', *Socialist Review*, 80: 65–108.

Haraway, Donna (1988) 'Situated Knowledges: The Science Question in Feminism and the Privilege of Partial Perspective', *Feminist Studies* 14, 3: 575–601.

Harding, Sandra (1986) *The Science Question in Feminism*, Ithaca: Cornell University Press.

Harding, Sandra (ed.) (1987) *Feminism and Methodology: Social Science Issues*, Milton Keynes: Open University Press.

Harding, Sandra (1997) 'Comment on Hekman's "Truth and Method: Feminist Standpoint Theory Revisited": Whose Standpoint Needs the Regimes of Truth and Reality?', *Signs: Journal of Women in Culture and Society* 22, 2: 382–391.

Harding, Sandra (1998) *Is Science Multicultural?: Postcolonialisms, Feminisms, and Epistemologies*, Bloomington: Indiana University Press.

Harding, Sandra (1999) 'The Case for Strategic Realism: a Response to Lawson', *Feminist Economics* 5, 3: 127–133.

Hardy, Thomas (1895) *Jude the Obscure*. Online. Available http://www.mastertexts.com/Hardy_Thomas/Jude_the_Obscure/Chapter06002.htm (Accessed 9 December 2002).

Harrell, D. Fox (2005) 'Algebra of Identity: Skin of Wind, Skin of Streams, Skin of Shadows, Skin of Vapor', *CTHEORY*, Online. Available http://www.ctheory.net/printer.aspx?id=489 (Accessed 20 November 2006).

Harris, Henry (ed.) (1995) *Identity: Essays Based on Herbert Spencer Lectures Given in the University of Oxford*, Oxford: Clarendon Press.

Hartsock, Nancy (1983) 'The Feminist Standpoint: Developing the Ground for a Specifically Historical Materialism', in Sandra Harding and Merrill Hintikka (eds) *Discovering Reality: Feminist Perspectives on Epistemology, Metaphysics, Methodology and Philosophy of Science*, Dordrecht: Reidel/Kluwer, 283–310.

Hartsock, Nancy (1997) 'Comment on Hekman's "Truth and Method: Feminist Standpoint Theory Revisited": Truth or Justice?', *Signs: Journal of Women in Culture and Society* 22, 2: 367–374.

Hausman, Daniel (1989) 'Explanatory Progress in Economics', *Social Research* 56, 2: 361–381.

Hausman, Daniel M. (1992) *Essays on Philosophy and Economic Methodology*, Cambridge: Cambridge University Press.

Heath, Eugene (1995) 'The Commerce Of Sympathy: Adam Smith On The Emergence Of Morals', *Journal of the History of Philosophy* XXXIII, 3: 447–466.

Heidegger, Martin (1968) *What is Called Thinking?*, J. Glenn Gray (trans.), London: Harper & Row.

Heilbroner, Robert (1990) 'Economics as Ideology', in Warren J. Samuels (ed.) *Economics as Discourse*, Dordrecht: Kluwer Academic Publishers, 101–116.

Hekman, Susan J. (1997a) 'Reply to Hartsock, Collins, Harding, and Smith', *Signs: Journal of Women in Culture and Society* 22, 2: 399–402.

Hekman, Susan J. (1997b) 'Truth and Method: Feminist Standpoint Theory Revisited', *Signs: Journal of Women in Culture and Society* 22, 2: 341–365.

Hekman, Susan J. (1999a) 'Identity Crises: Identity, Identity Politics, and Beyond', in Susan J. Hekman (ed.) *Feminism, Identity and Difference*, London: Frank Cass Publishers, 3–26.

Hekman, Susan J. (1999b) *The Future of Differences: Truth and Method in Feminist Theory*, Oxford: Polity Press.

Hekman, Susan (2000) 'Beyond Identity: Feminism, Identity and Identity Politics', *Feminist Theory* 1, 3: 289–308.

Heller, Agnes (1999) *A Theory of Modernity*, Oxford: Blackwell Publishers.

Hempel, Carl Gustav (1965) *Aspects of Scientific Explanation, and Other Essays in the Philosophy of Science*, New York: Free Press.

Henderson, James P. (2000) 'Political Economy Is a Mere Skeleton Unless…': What Can Social Economists Learn from Charles Dickens?', *Review of Social Economy* 58, 2: 141–151.

Henderson, Willie (1995) *Economics as Literature*, London: Routledge.

Henderson, Willie, Dudley-Evans, Tony and Backhouse, Roger (eds) (1993) *Economics and Language*, London: Routledge.

Henry, John F. (1990) *The Making of Neoclassical Economics*, London: Unwin Hyman Publishers.

Herrera, Rémy (2006) 'The Neoliberal "Rebirth" of Development Economics', *Monthly Review* 58, 1. Online. Available http://www.monthlyreview.org/0506herrera.htm (Accessed 30 November 2006).

Hewitson, Gillian J. (1999) *Feminist Economics: Interrogating the Masculinity of Rational Economic Man*, Aldershot: Edward Elgar Publishing.

Hibben, John Grier (1910) *The Philosophy of the Enlightenment*, London: Longmans Green & Co.

Hicks, John R. (1979) *Causality In Economics*, Oxford: Blackwell Publishers.

Hirshleifer, Jack (1985) 'The Expanding Domain of Economics', *American Economic Review* 75, 6: 53–68.

Hollis, Martin and Nell, Edward J. (1975) *Rational Economic Man: A Philosophical Critique of Neo-Classical Economics*, Cambridge: Cambridge University Press.

Huxley, Aldous (1994/1956) *The Doors of Perception and Heaven and Hell*, London: Flamingo.

'I Am Drawn to a Racially Pure White Society' (2002). *The Guardian* 1 May. Online. Available http://society.guardian.co.uk/localgovelections/story/0,8150,707923,00.html (Accessed 1 May 2002).

Ingham, Geoffrey (1996) 'Some Recent Changes in the Relationship between Economics and Sociology', *Cambridge Journal of Economics* 20, 2: 243–275.

Israel, Jonathan I. (2001) *Radical Enlightenment: Philosophy and the Making of Modernity 1650–1750*, Oxford: Oxford University Press.

James, Henry (1999/1881) *The Portrait of a Lady*, Oxford: Oxford University Press.

Jameson, Frederic (1991) *Postmodernism, or The Cultural Logic of Late Capitalism*, London: Verso.

'Japan Women Called Child Machines' (2007) *BBC News*. Online. Available http://news.bbc.co.uk/2/hi/asia-pacific/6306685.stm (Accessed 27 January 2007).

Jaschik, Scott (2006) 'The Dismal and Unwelcome Science?', *Inside Higher Ed* 13 December. Online. Available http://www.insidehighered.com/news/2006/12/13/econ (Accessed 12 August 2007).

Jayawardena, Kumari (ed.) (1986) *Feminism and Nationalism in the Third World*, London: Zed Books.

Jochimsen, Maren and Knobloch, Ulrike (1997) 'Making The Hidden Visible: The Importance of Caring Activities and Their Principles for Any Economy', *Ecological Economics* 20, 2: 107–112.

Joseph, George Gheverghese (2000) *The Crest of the Peacock: The Non-European Roots of Mathematics*, Princeton: Princeton University Press.

Joseph, George Gheverghese, Reddy, Vasu and Searle-Chatterjee, Mary (1990) 'Eurocentrism in the Social Sciences', *Race & Class* 31, 4: 1–25.

Juan Jr., E. San (1999) *Beyond Postcolonial Theory*, New York: St. Martin's Press.

Kamuf, Peggy (ed.) (1991) *A Derrida Reader*, New York: Columbia University Press.

Kant, Immanuel (1784/1996) 'An Answer to the Question: What is Enlightenment?', Reprinted in David Wootton (ed.) *Modern Political Thought: Readings from Machiavelli and Nietzsche*, Indianapolis: Hackett, 573–577.

Kanth, Rajani Kannepalli (1997a) *Against Economics: Rethinking Political Economy*, Aldershot: Ashgate Publishing.

Kanth, Rajani Kannepalli (1997b) *Breaking with the Enlightenment: The Twilight of History and the Rediscovery of Utopia*, Amherst: Humanity Books.

Kanth, Rajani Kannepalli (2005) *Against Eurocentrism: A Transcendent Critique of Modernist Science, Society and Morals*, Basingstoke: Palgrave Macmillan.

Katz, Cindi (2001) 'On the Grounds of Globalization: A Topography for Feminist Political Engagement', *Signs: Journal of Women in Culture and Society* 26, 4: 1213–1234.

Kaul, Nitasha (2001a) 'Experimental Economics', in Jonathan Mitchie (ed.) *Reader's Guide to the Social Sciences*, London: Fitzroy Dearborn, 542–543.

Kaul, Nitasha (2001b) 'Feminism in Economics: Theoria and Aporia', in Carolyn Brina, Carolyn Britton and Alison Assiter (eds) *Millenial Visions: Feminism into the 21st Century*, Cardiff: Cardiff University Press, 27–38.

Kaul, Nitasha (2002a) 'Review of Engendering Development', *Journal of Development Studies* 38, 6: 170–172.

Kaul, Nitasha (2002b) 'A Critical "Post" to Critical Realism', *Cambridge Journal of Economics* 26, 6: 707–726.

Kaul, Nitasha (2002c) 'Friday and His Master's Voice: Re/De-Scribing the Margins', paper presented at the International Association of Feminist Economics Meetings, Los Angeles, USA.

Kaul, Nitasha (2002d) 'Interrogating the Subject-World of Economic Epistemology: Re-imagining Theory and Difference', Unpublished thesis, University of Hull.

Kaul, Nitasha (2002e) 'Review of Feminism, Identity and Difference', *Feminist Economics* 8, 2: 127–131.

Kaul, Nitasha (2003a) 'The Anxious Identities We Inhabit: Post'isms and Economic Understandings', in Drucilla K. Barker and Edith Kuiper (eds) *Toward a Feminist Philosophy of Economics*, London: Routledge, 194–210.

Kaul, Nitasha (2003b) 'Review of Engendering Economics', *The Economic Journal* 113, 485: 203–206.

Kaul, Nitasha (2004a) 'Writing Economic Theory anOther Way', in Eiman Zein-Elabdin and S. Charusheela (eds) *Postcolonialism Meets Economics*, London: Routledge, 183–200.

Kaul, Nitasha (2004b) 'Identity and the Marketplace: Symbolic Geography of Janpath Bazaar', paper presented at the Stanford Humanities Center, Stanford University and at the Social Science History Association Meetings, Chicago, USA.

Kaul, Nitasha (2004c) 'Review of Feminist Post-Development Thought', *International Feminist Journal of Politics* 6, 2: 353–355.

Kawash, Samira (1999) 'Fugitive Properties', in Martha Woodmansee and Mark Osteen (eds) *The New Economic Criticism: Studies at the Intersection of Literature and Economics*, London: Routledge, 277–289.

Keen, Steve (2001) *Debunking Economics: The Naked Emperor of the Social Sciences*, London: Pluto Press.

Keller, Evelyn Fox and Longino, Helen E. (eds) (1996) *Feminism and Science*, Oxford: Oxford University Press.

Keohane, Robert O. (1988) 'The Rhetoric of Economics as Viewed by a Student of Politics', in Arjo Klamer, Robert Solow and Donald McCloskey (eds) *The Consequences of Economic Rhetoric*, Cambridge: Cambridge University Press, 240–246.

Keynes, John Neville (1891) *The Scope and Method of Political Economy*, London: Macmillan & Co.

Kimmerle, Heinz (1998) 'On Derrida's Hegel Interpretation', in Stuart Barnett (ed.) *Hegel After Derrida*, London: Routledge, 227–238.

King, John E. (1988) *Economic Exiles*, London: Macmillan Press.

Kirman, Alan P. (1992) 'Whom or What Does the Representative Individual Represent?', *Journal of Economic Perspectives* 6, 2: 117–136.

Kirman, Alan and Teschl, Miriam (2004) 'On the Emergence of Economic Identity', *Revue De Philosophie Économique* 9, June: 59–86.

Klamer, Arjo (1990) 'The Textbook Presentation of Economic Discourse', in Warren J. Samuels (ed.) *Economics as Discourse: An Analysis of the Language of Economists*, Dordrecht: Kluwer Academic Publishers, 129–154.

Klamer, Arjo and Leonard, Thomas (1994) 'So What's an Economic Metaphor?', in Philip Mirowski (ed.) *Natural Images in Economic Thought: Markets Read in Tooth and Claw*, Cambridge: Cambridge University Press, 20–51.

Klamer, Arjo, McCloskey, Donald N. and Solow, Robert M. (1988) *The Consequences of Economic Rhetoric*, Cambridge: Cambridge University Press.

Klein, Erwin (1998) *Economic Theories and their Relational Structures: A Model-Theoretic Characterisation*, Basingstoke: Macmillan Press.

Klein, Philip A. (ed.) (1994) *The Role of Economic Theory*, Dordrecht: Kluwer Academic Publishers.

Koritz, Amy and Koritz, Douglas (1999) 'Symbolic Economics: Adventures in the Metaphorical Marketplace', in Martha Woodmansee and Mark Osteen (eds) *The New Economic Criticism: Studies at the Intersection of Literature and Economics*, London: Routledge, 408–419.

Kornai, Janos (1971) *Anti-Equilibrium: On Economic Systems Theory and the Tasks of Research*, Amsterdam: North Holland Publishing Company.

Kramnick, Issac (ed.) (1995) *The Portable Enlightenment Reader*, Middlesex: Penguin Books.

Krugman, Paul (1998) 'Two Cheers From Formalism', *The Economic Journal* 108, 451: 1829–1836.

Kuhn, Thomas (1962) *The Structure of Scientific Revolutions*, London: University of Chicago Press.

Kuiper, Edith and Barker, Drucilla (eds) (2006) *Feminist Economics and the World Bank: History, Theory and Policy*, London: Routledge.

Kuiper, Edith and Sap, Jolande (with Feiner, Susan, Notburga, Ott and Tzannatos, Zafiris) (eds) (1995) *Out of the Margins: Feminist Perspectives on Economics*, London: Routledge.

Kurien, C. T. (1996) *Rethinking Economics: Reflections Based on a Study of the Indian Economy*, New Delhi: Sage Publications.

Lagueux, Maurice (1999) 'Do Metaphors Affect Economic Theory?', *Economics and Philosophy*, 15, 1: 1–22.

Landry, Donna and MacLean, Gerald (eds) (1996) *The Spivak Reader: Selected Works of Gayatri Chakravorty Spivak*, London: Routledge.

Langley, Paul and Mellor, Mary (2002) ' "Economy", Sustainability and Sites of Transformative Space', *New Political Economy* 7, 1: 49–65.

Larkin, Andrew (1996) 'RE: Definition of Economics', *HES*. Online posting. Available email: hes@eh.net (9 September 1996).

Larner, Wendy (1995) 'Theorising Difference in Aotearoa/New Zealand', *Gender, Place and Culture* 2, 2: 177–190.

Larrain, Jorge (1994) *Ideology and Cultural Identity: Modernity and the Third World Presence*, Cambridge: Polity Press.

Lash, Scott and Friedman, Jonathan (eds) (1992) *Modernity and Identity*, Oxford: Blackwell Publishers.

Lash, Scott and Urry, John (1994) *Economies of Signs and Space*, London: Sage Publications.

Latour, Bruno (1993) *We Have Never Been Modern*, London: Harvester Wheatsheaf.

Lavoie, Don (ed.) (1991) *Economics and Hermeneutics*, London: Routledge.

Lawson, Tony (1997) *Economics and Reality*, London: Routledge.

Lawson, Tony (1999a) 'Economics and Explanation', Paper from author.

Lawson, Tony (1999b) 'Feminism, Realism and Universalism', *Feminist Economics* 5, 2: 25–59.

Lawson, Tony (2003) *Reorienting Economics*, London: Routledge.

Lawson, Tony (2006) 'The Nature of Heterodox Economics', *Cambridge Journal of Economics* 30, 4: 483–505.

Lee, Benjamin and LiPuma, Edward (2002) 'Cultures of Circulation: The Imaginations of Modernity', *Public Culture* 14, 1: 191–213.

Lee, Frederic S. (2002) *Challenging the Mainstream: Essays on the history of Heterodox Economics in the 20th Century*, Unpublished manuscript from author.

Lennon, Kathleen (1999) 'Epistemology and Feminism', Paper from author.

Lennon, Kathleen and Whitford Margaret (eds) (1994) *Knowing the Difference: Feminist Perspectives in Epistemology*, London: Routledge.

Lerner, Abba (1972) 'The Economics and Politics of Consumer Sovereignty', *The American Economic Review* 62, 1–2: 258–266.

Levinas, Emmanuel (1987) *Time and the Other*, Richard A. Cohen (trans.), Pittsburgh: Duquesne University Press.

Levine, David P. (2001) 'Political Economy and the Idea of Development', *Review of Political Economy* 13, 4: 523–536.

Lewis, Martin W. and Wigen, Karen E. (1997) *The Myth of Continents: A Critique of Metageography*, Berkeley: University of California Press.

Linder, Marc (1977) *Anti-Samuelson*, 2 vols, New York: Urizen Books.

Litt, Theodore (1957) 'Reason, Tradition and Freedom', in Jogindar Singh and Desh Raj Goel (eds) *Spirit of Our Time: An Anthology of Essays, Articles and Discussions on Contemporary Problems of Art, Literature, Politics, Economics, Education, Science and Sociology*, Delhi: Jiwan Prakashan, Delhi, 139–146.

Little, Daniel (ed.) (1995) *On the Reliability of Economic Models*, Dordrecht: Kluwer Academic Publishers.

Llewelyn, John (1985) *Beyond Metaphysics?: The Hermeneutic Circle in Contemporary Continental Philosophy*, London: Macmillan Press.

Llewelyn, John (1986) *Derrida on the Threshold of Sense*, London: Macmillan Press.

Lloyd, Genevieve (1993) *The Man of Reason: 'Male' and 'Female' in Western Philosophy*, Minneapolis: University of Minnesota Press.

Longino, Helen E. (1988) 'Science, Objectivity, and Feminist Values', *Feminist Studies* 14, 3: 561–574.

Longino, Helen E. (1990) *Science as Social Knowledge: Values and Objectivity in Scientific Inquiry*, Princeton: Princeton University Press.

Longino, Helen E. (1992) 'Subjects, Power, Knowledge: Description and Prescription in Feminist Philosophies of Science', in Linda Alcoff and Elizabeth Potter (eds) *Feminist Epistemologies*, London: Routledge.

'Love Rats Point To Female Sex Drug' (2002) *BBC News*. Online. Available http://news.bbc.co.uk/hi/english/health/newsid_1993000/1993988.stm (Accessed 20 May 2002).

Lucas Jr., Robert E. (2000) 'Some Macroeconomics for the 21st Century', *Journal of Economic Perspectives* 14, 1: 159–168.

Lugones, Maria (1987) 'Playfulness, "World"-Travelling, and Loving Perception', *Hypatia* 2, 2: 3–19.

Lydall, Harold (1998) *A Critique of Orthodox Economics: An Alternative Model*, London: Macmillan Press.

Lyotard, Jean-Francois (1984) *The Postmodern Condition: A Report on Knowledge*, Geoff Bennington and Brian Massumi (trans.), Manchester: Manchester University Press.

McClelland, Peter (1975) *Causal Explanation and Model Building in History, Economics, and the New Economic History*, Ithaca: Cornell University Press.

McClintock, Anne (1994) 'The Angel of Progress: Pitfalls of the Term "Postcolonialism"', in Francis Barker, Peter Hulme and Margaret Iversen (eds) *Colonial Discourse/Postcolonial Theory*, Manchester: Manchester University Press, 253–266.

McClintock, Anne (1995) *Imperial Leather: Race, Gender and Sexuality in the Colonial Contest*, London: Routledge.

McClintock, Anne, Mufti, Aamir and Shohat, Ella (eds) (1997) *Dangerous Liaisons: Gender, Nation and Postcolonial Perspectives*, Minneapolis: University of Minnesota Press.

McCloskey, Deirdre (1994) *Knowledge and Persuasion in Economics*, Cambridge: Cambridge University Press.

McCloskey, Deirdre (2000) 'Postmodern Market Feminism: A Conversation with Gayatri Chakravorty Spivak', *Rethinking Marxism* 12, 4: 27–37.

McCloskey, Donald N. (1986) *The Rhetoric of Economics*, Sussex: Harvester Press.

McCloskey, Donald and Klamer, Arjo (1995) 'One Quarter of GDP is Persuasion', *AEA Papers And Proceedings* 85, 2: 191–195.

McDowell, Linda (2000) 'Acts of Memory and Millennial Hopes and Anxieties: the Awkward Relationship between the Economic and the Cultural', *Social and Cultural Geography* 1, 1: 15–24.

McEwan, Ian (2002) *Atonement*, 2001, London: Quality Paperbacks Direct.

Macfie, A. L. (1949) 'What Kind of Experience is Economizing?', *Ethics* 60, 1: 19–34.

Machan, Tibor (1998) 'The Normative Basis of Economic Science', *Economic Affairs* 18, 2: 43–7.

MacKenzie, Donald (2002) 'The Imagined Market', *London Review of Books*, 24, 21: 22–24.

Mackenzie, Iain (2001) 'Unravelling The Knots: Post-Structuralism and Other "Post-Isms" ', *Journal of Political Ideologies* 6, 3: 331–345.

McLachlan, Hugh and Swales, J. Kim (1978) *Friedman, Explanation and the Nature of Economic Theory*, Strathclyde: University of Strathclyde Department of Economics discussion paper.

McLennan, Gregor (2000) 'Sociology's Eurocentrism and the "Rise of the West" Revisited', *European Journal of Social Theory* 3, 3: 275–291.

McMahon, Martha (1997) 'From the Ground up: Ecofeminism and Ecological Economics', *Ecological Economics* 20, 163–173.

McNay, Lois (2000) *Gender and Agency: Reconfiguring the Subject in Feminist and Social Theory*, Cambridge: Polity Press.

MacNiece, Louis (1935) *Snow* (a poem). Online. Available http://www.artofeurope.com/mac niece/mac5.htm (10 December 2002).

Maljoo, Mohammad (2002) 'HES: QUERY – Economy as Process', *HES*. Online posting. Available email: hes@eh.net (Accessed 21 April 2002).

Malkki, Lisa (1992) 'Citizens of Humanity: Internationalism and the Imagined Community of Nations', *Diaspora* 3, 1: 41–68.

Manjali, Franson (2001) *Literature and Infinity*, Shimla: Indian Institute of Advanced Study.

Marcos, Subcomandante Insurgente (2001) *Our Word is Our Weapon*, Juana Ponce de Leon (ed.), London: Serpent's Tail.

Martin, Michael and McIntyre, Lee C. (eds) (1994) *Readings in the Philosophy of Social Science*, London: MIT Press.

Meek, Ronald (1976) *Social Science and the Ignoble Savage*, Cambridge: Cambridge University Press.

Mehta, J. K. (1962) *A Philosophical Interpretation of Economics*, London: Allen & Unwin Ltd.

Meikle, Scott (2000) 'Quality and Quantity in Economics: The Metaphysical Construction of the Economic Realm', *New Literary History* 31, 2: 247–268.

Mellor, Mary (1997) 'Women, Nature and the Social Construction of "Economic Man" ', *Ecological Economics* 20, 129–140.

Menon, Nivedita (2002) 'Universalism Without Foundations?', *Economy and Society* 31, 1: 152–169.

Milberg, William (1993) 'Natural Order and Postmodernism in Economic Thought', *Social Research* 60, 2: 255–277.

Miller, David W. (2002) 'Women Economists Have not Advanced as Readily as Male Peers, Scholar Says', *IAFFE-L*. Online posting. Available email: iaffe-l@lists.carleton.ca (14 February 2002).

Minh-ha, Trinh T. (1996) 'The Undone Interval', Conversation with Annamaria Morelli in Iain Chambers and Lidia Curti (eds) *The Post-Colonial Question: Common Skies, Divided Horizons*, London: Routledge, 3–16.

Mirowski, Philip (1989) *More Heat Than Light: Economics as Social Physics, Physics as Nature's Economics*, Cambridge: Cambridge University Press.

Mirowski, Philip (1991a) 'The When, the How, and the Why of Mathematical Expression in the History of Economic Analysis', *Journal of Economic Perspectives* 5, 1: 145–157.

Mirowski, Philip (1991b) 'Postmodernism and the Social Theory of Value', *Journal of Post Keynesian Economics* 13, 4: 565–582.

Mirowski, Philip (1994a) *Natural Images in Economic Thought: Markets Read in Tooth and Claw*, Cambridge: Cambridge University Press.

Mirowski, Philip (1994b) 'What are the Questions?', in Roger E. Backhouse (ed.) *New Directions in Economic Methodology*, London: Routledge, 50–74.

Mirowski, Philip (2002) *Machine Dreams: Economics Becomes a Cyborg Science*, Cambridge: Cambridge University Press.

Mirowski, Philip and Cook, Pamela (1990) 'Walras' "Economics and Mechanics": Translation, Commentary, Context', in Warren J. Samuels (ed.) *Economics as Discourse*, Dordrecht: Kluwer Academic Publishers, 189–215.

Mitchell, Timothy (2002) *Rule of Experts: Egypt, Techno-Politics, Modernity*, London: University of California Press.

Mizuta, Hiroshi and Sugiyama, Chuhei (eds) (1993) *Adam Smith: International Perspectives*, Basingstoke: Macmillan Press.

Mohanty, Chandra Talpade (1988) 'Under Western Eyes: Feminist Scholarship and Colonial Discourses', *Feminist Review* 30, Autumn: 61–88.

Mohanty, Chandra Talpade, Russo, Ann and Torres, Lourdes (eds) (1991) *Third World Women and the Politics of Feminism*, Indianapolis: Indiana University Press.

Mohanty, Satya P. (1997) *Literary Theory and the Claims of History: Postmodernism, Objectivity, Multicultural Politics*, Ithaca: Cornell University Press.

Moore-Gilbert, Bart (1997) *Postcolonial Theory: Contexts, Practices, Politics*, London: Verso.

Morgan, Mary S. and Morrison, Margaret (1999) *Models as Mediators: Perspectives on Natural and Social Science*, Cambridge: Cambridge University Press.

Mortley, Raoul (1991) *French Philosophers in Conversation*, London: Routledge.

Moya, Paula M. L. (2002) *Learning from Experience: Minority Identities, Multicultural Struggles*, London: University of California Press.

Moya, Paula M. L. and Hames-Garcia, Michael R. (eds) (2000) *Reclaiming Identity: Realist Theory and the Predicament of Postmodernism*, London: University of California Press.

Mudimbe, V. Y. (1988) *The Invention of Africa: Gnosis, Philosophy, and the Order of Knowledge*, Indianapolis: Indiana University Press.

Myers, Milton L. (1983) *The Soul of Modern Economic Man*, London: University of Chicago Press.

Nagar, Richa (2002) 'Footloose Researchers, "Traveling" Theories, and the Politics of Transnational Feminist Praxis', *Gender, Place and Culture* 9, 2: 179–186.

Nandy, Ashis (1983) *The Intimate Enemy: Loss and Recovery of Self Under Colonialism*, Oxford: Oxford University Press.

Narayan, Uma (1997) *Dislocating Cultures: Identities, Traditions, and Third-World Feminism*, London: Routledge.

Nash, John (2000) 'Deconstruction and its Audiences: "A New Enlightenment for the Century to Come"?', *Paragraph* 23, 2: 119–134.

Nelson, Julie A. (1993) 'The Study of Choice or the Study of Provisioning? Gender and the Definition of Economics', in Marianne A. Ferber and Julie A. Nelson (eds) *Beyond Economic Man: Feminist Theory and Economics*, London: University of Chicago Press, 23–36.

Nelson, Julie A. (1995) 'Feminism and Economics', *Journal of Economic Perspectives* 9, 2: 131–148.

Nelson, Julie A. (1996) *Feminism, Objectivity and Economics*, London: Routledge.

Nelson, Julie A. (2000) 'Confronting the Science/Value split: Notes on Feminist Economics, Institutionalism, Pragmatism and Process Thought', Paper from author.

Nelson, Robert H. (1991) *Reaching For Heaven On Earth: The Theological Meaning of Economics*, Maryland: Rowman and Littlefield Publishers Inc.

Nicholson, Linda J. (ed.) (1990) *Feminism/Postmodernism*, London: Routledge.

Nietzsche, Frederick (1873) *On Truth and Lie in an Extra-Moral Sense*. Online. Available http://www.geocities.com/thenietzschechannel/tls.htm (Accessed 9 December 2002).

Norris, Christopher (1997) *Against Relativism: Philosophy of Science, Deconstruction and Critical Theory*, Oxford: Blackwell Publishers.

Nussbaum, Martha (2000) *Women and Human Development: The Capabilities Approach*, Cambridge: Cambridge University Press.

Nussbaum, Martha and Glover, Jonathan (eds) (1995) *Women, Culture, and Development: A Study of Human Capabilities*, Oxford: Clarendon Press.

Nussbaum, Martha and Sen, Amartya (1993) *The Quality of Life*, Oxford: Clarendon Press.

Nye, Andreas (1990) *Words of Power: A Feminist Reading of the History of Logic*, London: Routledge.

O'Hara, Sabine U. (1997) 'Towards A Sustaining Production Theory', *Ecological Economics* 20, 2: 141–154.

O'Neill, John (2001) 'The Time(s) of the Gift', *Angelaki: journal of the theoretical humanities* 6, 2: 41–48.

Okin, Susan (1989) *Justice, Gender, and the Family*, New York: Basic Books.

Olafson, Frederick A. (2001) *Naturalism and the Human Condition: Against Scientism*, London: Routledge.

Olson, Paulette I. and Emami, Zohreh (2002) *Engendering Economics: Conversations with Women Economists in the United States*, London: Routledge.

Ormerod, Paul (1994) *The Death of Economics*, London: Faber and Faber Ltd.

Outhwaite, William (1987) *New Philosophies of Social Science: Realism, Hermeneutics and Critical Theory*, London: Macmillan Press.

Outram, Dorinda (1995) *The Enlightenment*, Cambridge: Cambridge University Press.

Pack, Spencer J. (2002) 'Re: HES: QUERY – History of AD–AS graph', *HES*. Online posting. Available email: hes@eh.net (23 June 2002).

Palast, Gregory (2002) *The Best Democracy Money Can Buy: An Investigative Reporter Exposes the Truth About Globalization, Corporate Cons, and High Finance Fraudsters*, London: Pluto Press.

Pateman, Carol (1988) *The Sexual Contract*, Cambridge: Polity Press.

Perelman, Michael (1996) *The End of Economics*, London: Routledge.

Perkins, Ellie (1997) 'Women, Ecology and Economics: New Models and Theories', *Ecological Economics* 20, 2: 105–106.

Perlman, Mark (1996) *The Character of Economic Thought, Economic Characters, and Economic Institutions: Selected Essays by Mark Perlman*, Ann Arbor: The University of Michigan Press.

Persky, Joseph (2000) 'The Neoclassical Advent: American Economics at the Dawn of the 20th Century', *Journal of Economic Perspectives* 14, 1: 95–108.

Pettman, Jan Jindy (1996) *Worlding Women: A Feminist International Politics*, London: Routledge.

Pfaff, William (2001) 'Culture Does Count – And in Africa Today it Counts for a Lot', *International Herald Tribune*. Online. Available http://www.iht.com/cgi-bin/generic.cgi?template=articleprint.tmplh&ArticleID=10906 (Accessed 18 February 2001).

Pheby, John (1988) *Methodology and Economics: A Critical Introduction*, London: Macmillan Press.

Phelan, Shane (1994) *Getting Specific: Postmodern Lesbian Politics*, Minneapolis: University of Minnesota Press.

Phelan, Shane (1999) 'Bodies, Passions, and Citizenship', in Susan J. Hekman (ed.) *Feminism, Identity and Difference*, London: Frank Cass Publishers, 56–79.

Phillips, Anne and Taylor, Barbara (1980) 'Sex and Skill: Notes Towards a Feminist Economics', *Feminist Review* 6: 79–88.

Pieterse, Jan Nederveen (2001) 'Emancipation and Regulation: Twin Pillars of Modernity?', *European Journal of Social Theory* 4, 3: 281–284.

Pieterse, Jan Nederveen and Parekh, Bhikhu (eds) (1995) *The Decolonization of Imagination: Culture, Knowledge and Power*, London: Zed Books.

Pietila, Hilkka (1997) 'The Triangle of Human Economy: Household-Cultivation-Industrial Production, an Attempt at Making Visible the Human Economy In Toto', *Ecological Economics* 20, 2: 113–127.

Piirto, Jane (2000) 'Why Are There So Few? (Creative Women: Visual Artists, Mathematicians, Scientists, Musicians)'. Online. Available http://www.ashland.edu/~jpiirto/why_are_there_so_few.htm (Accessed 19 October 2000).

Pizzorno, Alessandro (1986) 'Some Other Kinds of Otherness: A Critique of "Rational Choice" Theories', in Alejandro Foxley, Michael S. McPherson and Guillermo O'Donnell (eds) *Development, Democracy, and the Art of Trespassing: Essays in Honor of Albert O. Hirschman*, Notre Dame: University of Notre Dame Press, 355–373.

Polanyi, Livia and Strassmann, Diana (1996) 'Storytellers and Gatekeepers in Economics', in Victoria L. Bergvall, Janet M. Bing and Alice F. Freed (eds) *Rethinking Language and Gender Research: Theory and Practice*, New York: Addison Wesley Longman Limited, 126–151.

Poovey, Mary (1988) 'Feminism and Deconstruction', *Feminist Studies* 14, 1: 51–67.

Poovey, Mary (1998) *A History of the Modern Fact: Problems of Knowledge in the Sciences of Wealth and Society*, London: University of Chicago Press.

Pope, Alexander (1733/1734) *An Essay on Man*. Online. Available http://www.library.utoronto.ca/utel/rp/poems/pope11.html (Accessed 9 December 2002).

Porter, Roy (1990) *The Enlightenment*, London: Macmillan Press.

Porter, Theodore M. (1994) 'Rigor and Practicality: Rival Ideals of Quantification in Nineteenth-Century Economics', in Philip Mirowski (ed.) *Natural Images in Economic Thought: Markets Read in Tooth and Claw*, Cambridge: Cambridge University Press, 128–170.

Prakash, Gyan (1994) 'Subaltern Studies as Postcolonial Criticism', *The American Historical Review* 99, 5: 1475–1490.

Pressman, Steven and Summerfield, Gale (2000) 'The Economic Contributions of Amartya Sen', *Review of Political Economy* 12, 1: 89–113.

Pujol, Michele (1992) *Feminism and Anti-Feminism in Early Economic Thought*, Aldershot: Edward Elgar Publishing.

Pujol, Michele (1995) 'Into the Margin!', in Edith Kuiper and Jolande Sap (with Susan Feiner, Ott Notburga and Zafiris Tzannatos) (eds) *Out of the Margins: Feminist Perspectives on Economics*, London: Routledge, 17–34.

Putnam, Hilary (1981) *Reason, Truth and History*, Cambridge: Cambridge University Press.

Racevskis, Karlis (1993) *Postmodernism and the Search for Enlightenment*, London: University Press of Virginia.

Radnitzky, Gerald and Bernholz, Peter (eds) (1987) *Economic Imperialism: The Economic Approach Applied Outside the Field of Economics*, New York: Paragon House Publishers.

Rahnema, Majid and Bawtree, Victoria (eds) (1997) *The Post-Development Reader*, London: Zed Books.

Rainger, Ronald (1978) 'Race, Politics, and Science: The Anthropological Society of London in the 1860s', *Victorian Studies* 22, Autumn: 51–70.

Rankin, Katharine N. (2001) 'Governing Development: Neoliberalism, Microcredit, and Rational Economic Women', *Economy and Society* 30, 1: 18–37.

Rattansi, Ali (1997) 'Postcolonialism and its Discontents', *Economy and Society* 26, 4: 480–500.

Rawls, John (1971) *A Theory of Justice*, Cambridge, MA.: Harvard University Press.

Rawls, John (1993) *Political Liberalism*, New York: Columbia University Press.

Reder, Melvin W. (1999) *Economics: The Culture of a Controversial Science*, London: University of Chicago Press.

Refugee Council (2001) 'Press Release', 29 November. Online. Available http://www.refugeecouncil.org.uk/news/november2001/relea037.htm (Accessed 10 November 2002).

Resnick, Stephen A. and Wolff, Richard D. (1982) 'Marxist Epistemology: The Critique of Economic Determinism', *Social Text*, 6, Fall: 31–72.

Ricoeur, Paul (1974) *The Conflict of Interpretations: Essays in Hermeneutics*, Evanstan: Northwestern University Press.

'Right and Left Blaze Thatcherite Trail' (2002). *BBC News*. Online. Available http://news.bbc.co.uk/2/hi/uk_news/politics/2035914.stm (10 June 2002).

Rist, Gilbert (2002) *The History of Development: From Western Origins to Global Faith*, London: Zed Books.

Robbins, Lionel (1932) *An Essay on the Nature and Significance of Economic Science*, London: Macmillan Press.

Robertson, Pat (1992) 'Feminism encourages . . . ', Remarks at US Republican Party Convention, London: Silver Moon Bookshop Postcard.

Robinson, Joan (1977) 'What are the Questions?', *Journal of Economic Literature* 15, 4: 1318–1339.

Rosenau, P. M. (1992) *Post-modernism and the Social Sciences: Insights, Inroads, and Intrusions*, Princeton: Princeton University Press.

Rosenberg, Alexander (1992) *Economics: Mathematical Politics or Science of Diminishing Returns?*, London: University of Chicago Press.

Roth, Marty (2001) 'Gilman's Arabesque Wallpaper', *Mosaic* 34, 4: 145–162.

Rothschild, Emma (2001) *Economic Sentiments: Adam Smith, Condorcet and the Enlightenment*, London: Harvard University Press.

Rousseau, Jean Jacques (1755) *A Discourse on Political Economy*. Online. Available http://www.constitution.org/jjr/polecon.htm (Accessed 9 December 2002).

Roy, Ramashray (1992) 'Modern Economics and the Good Life: A Critique', *Alternatives* 17, 3: 371–403.

Royle, Nicholas (2000) 'What is Deconstruction?', in Nicholas Royle (ed.) *Deconstructions: A User's Guide*, Basingstoke: Palgrave.

Ruben, David-Hillel (1990) *Explaining Explanation*, London: Routledge.

Ruben, David-Hillel (ed.) (1993) *Explanation*, Oxford: Oxford University Press.

Ruccio, David F. (1991) 'Postmodernism and Economics', *Journal of Post Keynesian Economics* 13, 4: 495–510.

Ruccio, David and Amariglio, Jack (2003) *Postmodern Moments in Modern Economics*, Princeton: Princeton University Press.

Sahgal, Nayantara (1985) *Rich Like Us*, New Delhi: Harper Collins.

Said, Edward (1978) *Orientalism*, London: Penguin Books.

Said, Edward (1983) *The World, the Text, and the Critic*, Cambridge, MA.: Harvard University Press.

Said, Edward (1994) 'Traveling Theory Reconsidered', in Robert M. Polhemus and Roger B. Henkle (eds) *Critical Reconstructions*, Stanford: Stanford University Press.

Said, Edward (1999) *Out of Place: A Memoir*, London: Granta Books.

Salanti, Andrea and Screpanti, Ernesto (eds) (1997) *Pluralism In Economics: New Perspectives in History and Methodology*, Aldershot: Edward Elgar Publishing.

Samson, Melanie (1995) 'Towards a "Friday" Model of International Trade: A Feminist Deconstruction of Race and Gender Bias in the Robinson Crusoe Trade Allegory', *Canadian Journal of Economics* 28, 1: 143–158.

Samuels, Warren J. (ed.) (1990) *Economics as Discourse: An Analysis of the Language of Economists*, Dordrecht: Kluwer Academic Publishers.

Samuels, Warren J. (1991) ' "Truth" And "Discourse" in the Social Construction of Economic Reality: An Essay on the Relation of Knowledge to Socioeconomic Policy', *Journal of Post Keynesian Economics* 13, 4: 511–524.

Samuelson, Paul (1952) 'Economic Theory and Mathematics: An Appraisal', *The American Economic Review* 42, 2: 56–66.

Samuelson, Paul A. (1972) 'Maximum Principles in Analytical Economics', *The American Economic Review* 62, 3: 249–262.

Sardar, Ziauddin (1992) 'When Dracula Meets the "Other": Europe, Columbus, and the Columbian Legacy', *Alternatives* 17, 4: 493–517.

Sardar, Ziauddin (1999) *Orientalism*, Buckingham: Open University Press.

Sassower, Raphael (1985) *Philosophy of Economics: A Critique of Demarcation*, London: University Press of America.

Sayer, Andrew (1999) 'Valuing Culture and Economy', in Larry Ray and Andrew Sayer (eds) *Culture and Economy After the Cultural Turn*, London: Sage Publications, 53–75.

Sayer, Andrew (2000) *Realism and Social Science*, London: Sage Publications.

Schabas, Margaret (2005) *The Natural Origins of Economics*, London: University of Chicago Press.

Schoemaker, Paul J. H. (1991) 'The Quest for Optimality: A Positive Heuristic of Science?', *Behavioural and Brain Sciences* 14, 2: 205–245.

Schouls, Peter A. (1989) *Descartes and the Enlightenment*, Edinburgh: Edinburgh University Press.

Schuerewegen, Franc (1994) 'A Telephone Conversation: Fragments', *diacritics* 24, 4: 30–40.

Schwarzenegger, Arnold (2004) 'Remarks at Republican National Convention'. Online. Available http://www.usatoday.com/news/politicselections/nation/president/2004-08-31-schwarzeneggerfulltext_x.htm (Accessed 22 February 2007).

Scott, David (1999) *Refashioning Futures: Criticism after Postcoloniality*, Princeton: Princeton University Press.

Scott, Joan W. (1988) 'Deconstructing Equality Versus Difference: or, the Uses of Poststructuralist Theory for Feminism', *Feminist Studies* 14, 1: 33–50.

Seligman, Ben B. (1962) *Main Currents in Modern Economics: Economic Thought since 1870*, New York: Free Press of Glencoe.

Seller, Anne (1994) 'Should a Feminist Philosopher Stay at Home?', in Kathleen Lennon and Margaret Whitford (eds) *Knowing the Difference: Feminist Perspectives in Epistemology*, London: Routledge, 230–248.

Sen, Amartya K. (1977) 'Rational Fools: A Critique of the Behavioural Foundations of Economic Theory', *Philosophy and Public Affairs* 6, 4: 317–344.

Sen, Amartya (1986) 'Rationality, Interest, Identity', in Alejandro Foxley, Michael S. McPherson and Guillermo O'Donnell (eds) *Development, Democracy, and the Art of Trespassing: Essays in Honor of Albert O. Hirschman*, Notre Dame: University of Notre Dame Press, 343–353.

Sen, Amartya (1992) *Inequality Reexamined*, Cambridge, MA.: Harvard University Press.

Sen, Amartya (1995) 'Rationality and Social Choice', *The American Economic Review* 85, 1: 1–24.

Sen, Amartya (1999) *Reason before Identity*, Oxford: Oxford University Press.

Shackle, G. L. S. (1972) *Epistemics and Economics: A Critique of Economic Doctrines*, Cambridge: Cambridge University Press.

Shapin, Steven and Schaffer, Simon (1989) *Leviathan and the Air-Pump: Hobbes, Boyle and the Experimental Life*, Princeton: Princeton University Press.

Shapiro, Michael J. (1989a) 'Representing World Politics: The Sports/War Intertext', in James Der Derian and Michael J. Shapiro (eds) *International/Intertextual Relations: Postmodern Readings of World Politics*, Lexington: D. C. Heath Press, 69–96.

Shapiro, Michael J. (1989b) 'Textualizing Global Politics', in James Der Derian and Michael J. Shapiro (eds) *International/Intertextual Relations: Postmodern Readings of World Politics*, Lexington: D. C. Heath Press, 11–22.

Shapiro, Michael J. (1993) *Reading 'Adam Smith': Desire, History and Value*, London: Sage Publications.

Sharpe, Jenny (1993) *Allegories of Empire: The Figure of Woman in the Colonial Text*, Minneapolis: University of Minnesota Press.

Shershow, Scott Cutler (2005) *The Work and the Gift*, London: University of Chicago Press.

Shohat, Ella and Stam, Robert (eds) (1994) *Unthinking Eurocentrism: Multiculturalism and the Media*, London: Routledge.

Shotter, John and Gergen, Kenneth (eds) (1989) *Texts of Identity*, London: Sage Publications.

Skinner, Gillian (1999) *Sensibility and Economics in the Novel, 1740–1800: The Price of a Tear*, Basingstoke: Macmillan Press.

Smith, Adam (1759) *Theory of Moral Sentiments III.I.46*. Online. Available http://www.econlib.org/library/Smith/smMS3.html (Accessed 9 December 2002).

Smith, Dan (2001) 'The Problem of Essentialism', in Inger Skjelsbæk and Dan Smith (eds) *Gender, Peace and Conflict*, London: Sage Publications, 32–46.

Smith, Dorothy E. (1974) 'Women's Perspective as a Radical Critique of Sociology', *Sociological Inquiry* 44, 1: 7–14.

Smith, Dorothy E. (1997) 'Comment on Hekman's "Truth and Method: Feminist Standpoint Theory Revisited"', *Signs: Journal of Women in Culture and Society* 22, 2: 392–398.

Solomon, Robert C. (1988) *Continental Philosophy since 1750: The Rise and Fall of the Self*, Oxford: Oxford University Press.

Solow, Robert M. (2000) 'Towards a Macroeconomics of the Medium Run', *Journal of Economic Perspectives* 14, 1: 151–158.

'Some Terms' (n.d.) *Against Sleep and Nightmare.* Online. Available http://www.againstsleepandnightmare.com/ASAN/ASAN5/defs5.html (Accessed 10 February 2007).

Soper, Kate (2001) 'Feminism and Enlightenment', in Carolyn Brina, Carolyn Britton and Alison Assiter (eds) *Millenial Visions: Feminism into the 21st Century*, Cardiff: Cardiff University Press, 9–26.

Sorensen, Janet (1999) ' "I Talk to Everybody in Their Own Way": Defoe's Economies of Identity', in Martha Woodmansee and Mark Osteen (eds) *The New Economic Criticism: Studies at the Intersection of Literature and Economics*, London: Routledge, 75–94.

Souhami, Diana (2002) *Selkirk's Island*, London: Phoenix.

Southard, John (1997) 'Colonial Education'. Online. Available http://www.english.emory.edu/Bahri/Education.html (Accessed 10 February 2007).

Spanos, William (2001) 'The Specter of History: Rethinking Thinking in the Post-Cold War Age', *Mosaic* 34, 4: 21–46.

Spivak, Gayatri Chakravorty (1988) 'Can the Subaltern Speak?', in Cary Nelson and Lawrence Grossberg (eds) *Marxism and the Interpretation of Culture*, Urbana: University of Illinois Press, 271–313.

Spivak, Gayatri Chakravorty (1990) *The Post-Colonial Critic: Interviews, Strategies, Dialogues*, Sarah Harasym (ed.), London: Routledge.

Spivak, Gayatri Chakravorty (1991) 'Neocolonialism and the Secret Agent of Knowledge', Interviewed by Robert Young, *Oxford Literary Review* 13, 1–2: 220–251.

Spivak, Gayatri Chakravorty (1993) *Outside in the Teaching Machine*, London: Routledge.

Spivak, Gayatri Chakravorty (1994) 'Poststructuralism. Marginality, Postcoloniality and Value', in Padmini Mongia (ed.) *Contemporary Postcolonial Theory*, New York: Arnold, 198–222.

Spivak, Gayatri Chakravorty (1999) *A Critique of Postcolonial Reason: Towards a History of the Vanishing Present*, Cambridge, MA.: Harvard University Press.

Spivak, Gayatri Chakravorty (2000) 'Other Things are Never Equal: A Speech', *Rethinking Marxism* 12, 4: 37–45.

Spivak, Gayatri Chakravorty (2002) 'Class and Culture in Diaspora', Keynote Lecture at the Translating Class, Altering Hospitality Conference, CongressCATH, 22 June, Leeds, UK.

'Start The Week' (2002) *BBC Radio 4 FM*, 17 June.

Stettler, Michael (1995) 'The Rhetoric of McCloskey's Rhetoric of Economics', *Cambridge Journal of Economics* 19, 3: 391–403.

Stevenson, Nick (2002) 'Cosmopolitanism and the Future of Democracy: Politics, Culture and the Self', *New Political Economy* 7, 2: 251–267.

Stigler, George (1984) 'Economics – the Imperial Science', *Scandinavian Journal of Economics* 86, 3: 301–313.

Stiglitz, Joseph (2002) *Globalization and its Discontents*, London: Penguin Books.

Strassmann, Diana (1993a) 'The Stories of Economics and the Power of the Storyteller', *History of Political Economy* 25, 1: 147–165.

Strassmann, Diana (1993b) 'Not a Free Market: The Rhetoric of Disciplinary Authority in Economics', in Marianne A. Ferber and Julie A. Nelson (eds) *Beyond Economic Man: Feminist Theory and Economics*, London: University of Chicago Press, 54–68.

Strassmann, Diana (1994) 'Feminist Thought and Economics; Or, What Do the Visigoths Know?', *AEA Papers and Proceedings* 84, 2: 153–158.

Strassmann, Diana and Polanyi, Livia (1995) 'Shifting the Paradigm: Value in Feminist Critiques of Economics', *Forum for Social Economics* 25, 1: 3–19.

Stretton, Hugh (2000) *Economics: A New Introduction*, London: Pluto Press.

Strugnell, Anthony (1996) *Postmodernism versus Enlightenment and the Problem of the Other in Raynal's Histoire Des Deux Indes*, Studies on Voltaire and the Eighteenth-Century, No. 341, Voltaire Foundation.

Sudan, Rajani (1999) 'Feminising Race', in Susan J. Hekman (ed.) *Feminism, Identity and Difference*, London: Frank Cass Publishers.

Swedberg, Richard (1990) *Economics and Sociology: On Redefining Their Boundaries*, Princeton: Princeton University Press.

Sylvester, Christine (1999) 'Development Studies and Postcolonial Studies: Disparate Tales of the "Third World" ', *Third World Quarterly* 20, 4: 703–721.

Szabados, Bela (1997) 'Wittgenstein's Women: The Philosophical Significance of Wittgenstein's Misogyny', *Journal of Philosophical Research* 22: 483–508.

Szostak, Rick (1999) *Econ-Art: Divorcing Art from Science in Modern Economics*, London: Pluto Press.

Tacconi, Luca (1998) 'Scientific Methodology for Ecological Economics', *Ecological Economics* 27, 1: 91–105.

Taiwo, Olufemi (1998) 'Exorcising Hegel's Ghost: Africa's Challenge to Philosophy', *African Studies Quarterly: The Online Journal for African Studies* 1, 4. Online. Available http://www.africa.ufl.edu/asq/v1/4/2.htm (Accessed 10 February 2007).

Taylor, Charles (1989) *Sources of the Self: The Making of the Modern Identity*, Cambridge, MA.: Harvard University Press.

Te Heesen, Anke (2002) *The World in a Box: The Story of an Eighteenth-Century Picture Encyclopedia*, London: University of Chicago Press.

The Chambers Dictionary (1999) Edinburgh: Chambers Harrap Publishers.

The Libertine (Movie) (2005) Directed by Laurence Dunmore, UK.

The World Bank (2001) *Engendering Development: Through Gender Equality in Rights, Resources, and Voices*, Oxford: Oxford University Press.

Thompson, Grahame (1997) 'Where Goes Economics and Economies', *Economy and Society* 26, 4: 599–610.

Thompson, Grahame (1999) 'How Far Should We Be Afraid of Conventional Economics? A Response to Ben Fine', *Economy and Society* 28, 3: 426–433.

Thomson, William (1999) 'The Young Person's Guide to Writing Economic Theory', *Journal of Economic Literature* XXXVII, March: 157–183.

Tickner, Ann J. (1992) *Gender in International Relations: Feminist Perspectives on Achieving Global Security*, New York: Columbia University Press.

Todorov, Tzvetan (1984) *The Conquest of America: The Question of the Other*, Richard Howard (trans.), New York: Harper and Row.

Tribe, Keith (1999) 'Adam Smith: Critical Theorist?', *Journal of Economic Literature* XXXVII, June: 609–632.

Turgenev, Ivan (1861) *Fathers and Sons*. Online. Available http://www.ibiblio.org/eldritch/ist/fas.htm (Accessed 10 February 2007).

Turner, Bryan S. (2001) 'Cosmopolitan Virtue: On Religion in a Global Age', *European Journal of Social Theory* 4, 2: 131–152.

Ullmann-Margalit, Edna (1978) 'Invisible-Hand Explanations', *Synthese: An International Journal for Epistemology, Methodology and Philosophy of Science* 39, 2: 263–291.

Van Staveren, Irene (2001) *The Values of Economics: An Aristotelian Perspective*, London: Routledge.

Venn, Couze (1999) 'Narrating the Postcolonial', in Mike Featherstone and Scott Lash (eds) *Space of Culture: City, Nation, World*, London: Sage.

Venn, Couze (2000) *Occidentalism: Modernity and Subjectivity*, London: Sage Publications.

Voltaire, François Marie Arouet de (1759) *Candide*. Online. Available http://www.library.csi.cuny.edu/dept/history/lavender/candide.html (Accessed 9 December 2002).

Von Wright, Georg Henrik (1971) *Explanation and Understanding*, London: Routledge & Kegan Paul.

Wa Thiong'O, Ngugi (1998) *Penpoints, Gunpoints, and Dreams: Towards a Critical Theory of the Arts and the State in Africa*, Oxford: Clarendon Press.

Wade Hands, David (2001) *Reflection without Rules: Economic Methodology and Contemporary Science Theory*, Cambridge: Cambridge University Press.

Wagner, Peter (2001) 'Epistemology and Critique', *European Journal of Social Theory* 4, 3: 284–287.

Walby, Sylvia (1990) *Theorizing Patriarchy*, Oxford: Blackwell Publishers.

Walby, Sylvia (1996) 'Woman and Nation', in Gopal Balakrishnan (ed.) *Mapping the Nation*, New York: Verso.

Walsh, Vivian (2000) 'Smith after Sen', *Review of Political Economy* 12, 1: 5–25.

Walters, William (1999) 'Decentring the Economy', *Economy and Society* 28, 2: 312–323.

Ward, Benjamin (1972) *What's Wrong with Economics?*, London: Basic Books.

Warren, Peter N. (1994) 'Delta Force: Conservatism's Best Young Economists', *Policy Review* 70, Fall: 72–80.

Weintraub, E. Roy (1998) 'Controversy: Axiomatisches Miβverstandnis', *The Economic Journal* 108, 451: 1837–1847.

Wennerlind, Carl (2000) 'The Historical Specificity of Scarcity', Paper from author.

Weschler, Lawrence (1999) *Boggs: A Comedy of Values*, London: University of Chicago Press.

West, David (1996) *An Introduction to Continental Philosophy*, Cambridge: Polity Press.

Weston, Samuel C. (1994) 'Towards a Better Understanding of the Positive/Normative Distinction in Economics', *Economics and Philosophy* 10, 1: 1–17.

Whitehead, Alfred North (1933) *Adventures of Ideas*, Cambridge: Cambridge University Press.

Whitford, Margaret (1991) *The Irigaray Reader*, David Macey (trans.), Oxford: Blackwell Publishers.

Whitman, Walt (1990) 'Song of Myself', *Leaves of Grass*, Oxford: Oxford University Press.

Wichterich, Christa (2000) *The Globalized Woman: Reports from a Future of Inequality*, Patrick Camiller (trans.), London: Zed Books.

Williams, Rhonda M. (1993) 'Race, Deconstruction, and the Emergent Agenda of Feminist Economic Theory', in Marianne A. Ferber and Julie A. Nelson (eds) *Beyond Economic Man: Feminist Theory and Economics*, London: University of Chicago Press, 144–152.

Wilmore, Larry (2002) 'RE: HES QUERY – Hayek', *HES*. Online posting. Available email: hes@eh.net (10 January 2002).

Wilson, Rodney (1997) 'Morality in Economics', *Humanomics* 13, 3/4: 3–32.

Winter, Bronwyn (2000) 'Who Counts (or Doesn't Count) What as Feminist Theory?', *Feminist Theory* 1, 1: 105–111.

Witt, Charlotte (1996) 'How Feminism is Re-writing the Philosophical Canon', *Society for Women in Philosophy (SWIP) Web*. Online. Available http://www.uh.edu/~cfreelan/SWIP/Witt.html (Accessed 24 September 1999).

Wolff, Richard and Resnick, Stephen (1987) *Economics: Marxian versus Neoclassical*, Baltimore: Johns Hopkins University Press.

Woodmansee, Martha and Osteen, Mark (eds) (1999) *The New Economic Criticism: Studies at the Intersection of Literature and Economics*, London: Routledge.

Woodward, Kathryn (ed.) (1997) *Identity and Difference*, London: Sage Publications.

Woolley, Frances (2000) 'Degrees of Correction: A Critique of Rawl's Theory of Mutual Disinterest', *Feminist Economics* 6, 2: 1–21.

Wootton, Barbara (1938) *Lament for Economics*, London: George Allen & Unwin Ltd.

Yeghiayan, Eddie (n.d.) *Martha Craven Nussbaum: A Selected Bibliography*. Online. Available http://sun3.lib.uci.edu/~eyeghiay/Philosophy/Colloquia/nussbaum.html (Accessed 10 December 2002).

Yeo, Eileen Janes (1996) *The Contest for Social Science: Relations and Representations of Gender and Class*, London: Rivers Oram Press.

Yolton, John W., Porter, Roy, Rogers, Pat and Stafford, Barbara Maria (eds) (1995) *The Blackwell Companion to the Enlightenment*, Oxford: Blackwell Publishers.

Young, Robert J. (1995) 'Colonialism and the Desiring Machine', in *Colonial Desire: Hybridity in Theory, Culture and Race*, London: Routledge, 159–182.

Young, Robert (2002) 'Postpositivist Realism and the Return of the Same: The Rational Subject and Post(post)modern Liberalism', *Cultural Logic: An Electronic Journal of Marxist Theory and Practice* 5. Online. Available http://www.clogic.eserver.org/2002/young.html (Accessed 20 November 2006).

Yuval-Davis, Nira (1997) *Gender and Nation*, London: Sage Publications.

Zeeman, Christopher (2002) 'Mathematics and the Discovery of Perspective in the Renaissance', *Venn Lecture*, 13 March, University of Hull, UK.

Zein-Elabdin, Eiman and Charusheela, S. (eds) (2004) *Postcolonialism Meets Economics*, London: Routledge.

Žižek, Slavoj (2002) 'Revolution must strike twice', *London Review of Books* 24, 14: 13–15.

Index